McGraw-Hill Ryerson

Pre-Calculus 12

Student Workbook

AUTHORS

Scott Carlson
B.Ed., B.Sc.
Golden Hills School Division No. 75
Alberta

Barbara Gajdos
B.Ed.
Calgary Catholic School District
Alberta

Andrea Hook
B.Sc., B.Ed.
Ottawa-Carleton District School Board
Ontario

Emily Kalwarowsky
B.Ed., B.Sc.
Northland School Division
Alberta

Antonietta Lenjosek
B.Sc., B.Ed.
Ottawa Catholic School Board
Ontario

McGraw-Hill
Ryerson

Toronto   Montréal   Boston   Burr Ridge, IL   Dubuque, IA   Madison, WI   New York
San Francisco   St. Louis   Bangkok   Bogotá   Caracas   Kuala Lumpur   Lisbon   London
Madrid   Mexico City   Milan   New Delhi   Santiago   Seoul   Singapore   Sydney   Taipei

COPIES OF THIS BOOK
MAY BE OBTAINED BY
CONTACTING:

McGraw-Hill Ryerson Ltd.

WEB SITE:
http://www.mcgrawhill.ca

E-MAIL:
orders@mcgrawhill.ca

TOLL-FREE FAX:
1-800-463-5885

TOLL-FREE CALL:
1-800-565-5758

**OR BY MAILING YOUR
ORDER TO:**
McGraw-Hill Ryerson
Order Department
300 Water Street
Whitby, ON L1N 9B6

Please quote the ISBN and
title when placing your order.

The **McGraw·Hill** Companies

**McGraw-Hill
Ryerson**

**McGraw-Hill Ryerson
Pre-Calculus 12 Student Workbook**

ISBN-978-0-07-073891-1
ISBN-0-07-073891-2

http://www.mcgrawhill.ca

1 2 3 4 5 6 7 8 9 10 MP 10 9 8 7 6 5 4 3 2 1

Printed and bound in Canada

Care has been taken to trace ownership of copyright material contained in this text.
The publishers will gladly accept any information that will enable them to rectify
any reference or credit in subsequent printings.

TI-84™ and TI-Nspire™ are registered trademarks of Texas Instruments.

PUBLISHER: Jean Ford
PROJECT MANAGER: Janice Dyer
DEVELOPMENTAL EDITORS: Kelly Cochrane, Jackie Lacoursiere, Susan Lishman,
  Paul McNulty
MANAGER, EDITORIAL SERVICES: Crystal Shortt
SUPERVISING EDITOR: Jaime Smith
COPY EDITOR: Linda Jenkins, Red Pen Services
ANSWER CHECKER: Daniela Spiroska
EDITORIAL ASSISTANT: Erin Hartley
MANAGER, PRODUCTION SERVICES: Yolanda Pigden
PRODUCTION COORDINATOR: Scott Morrison
COVER DESIGN: Michelle Losier
ELECTRONIC PAGE MAKE-UP: APTARA
COVER IMAGE: © Bill Frymire/Masterfile

Acknowledgements

The publishers, authors, and editors of *McGraw-Hill Ryerson Pre-Calculus 12 Student Workbook* wish to extend their sincere thanks to the reviewers who contributed their time, energy, and expertise to the creation of this workbook. We are grateful for their thoughtful comments and suggestions.

John Agnew
University of Victoria
British Columbia

Karen Bedard
School District No. 22 (Vernon)
British Columbia

Lindsay Collins
South East Cornerstone School
Division No. 209
Saskatchewan

Julie Cordova
St. James-Assiniboia School
Division
Manitoba

Steven Daniel
Department of Education,
Culture and Employment
Northwest Territories

Ashley Dupont
St. Maurice School (Independent)
Manitoba

Janet Fedorvich
Alexis Nakota Sioux Nation
School (Independent)
Alberta

Carol Funk
School District No. 68 (Nanaimo/
Ladysmith)
British Columbia

Jessika Girard
Conseil Scolaire Francophone
No. 93
British Columbia

Marge Hallonquist
Elk Island Catholic Schools
Alberta

Jeni Halowski
Lethbridge School District No. 51
Alberta

Jason Harbor
North East School Division
No. 200
Saskatchewan

Contents

Chapter 1 Function Transformations...................1

1.1 Horizontal and Vertical Translations..........1

1.2 Reflections and Stretches............................9

1.3 Combining Transformations 18

1.4 Inverse of a Relation 26

Chapter 1 Review.....................................35

Chapter 1 Skills Organizer 38

Chapter 2 Radical Functions............................39

2.1 Radical Functions and Transformations.....39

2.2 Square Root of a Function......................47

2.3 Solving Radical Equations Graphically.....55

Chapter 2 Review.....................................63

Chapter 2 Skills Organizer 65

Chapter 3 Polynomial Functions 66

3.1 Characteristics of Polynomial Functions....66

3.2 The Remainder Theorem........................78

3.3 The Factor Theorem 84

3.4 Equations and Graphs of Polynomial
Functions 91

Chapter 3 Review.....................................103

Chapter 3 Skills Organizer 108

Chapter 4 Trigonometry and the Unit Circle 109

4.1 Angles and Angle Measure.....................109

4.2 The Unit Circle 120

4.3 Trigonometric Ratios............................129

4.4 Introduction to Trigonometric Equations.. 138

Chapter 4 Review.....................................145

Chapter 4 Skills Organizer 148

**Chapter 5 Trigonometric Functions
and Graphs 149**

5.1 Graphing Sine and Cosine Functions......149

5.2 Transformations of Sinusoidal
Functions 158

5.3 The Tangent Function 167

5.4 Equations and Graphs of Trigonometric
Functions 175

Chapter 5 Review.....................................183

Chapter 5 Skills Organizer 187

Chapter 6 Trigonometric Identities 188

6.1 Reciprocal, Quotient, and Pythagorean
Identities..188

6.2 Sum, Difference, and Double-Angle
Identities..197

6.3 Proving Identities 205

6.4 Solving Trigonometric Equations
Using Identities 215

Chapter 6 Review.....................................224

Chapter 6 Skills Organizer 228

Chapter 7 Exponential Functions. 229

7.1 Characteristics of Exponential
Functions 229

7.2 Transformations of Exponential
Functions 238

7.3 Solving Exponential Equations 249

Chapter 7 Review.....................................256

Chapter 7 Skills Organizer 259

Chapter 8 Logarithmic Functions....................260

8.1 Understanding Logarithms 260

8.2 Transformations of Logarithmic
Functions 267

8.3 Laws of Logarithms 275

8.4 Logarithmic and Exponential
Equations 282

Chapter 8 Review.....................................292

Chapter 8 Skills Organizer 296

Chapter 9 Rational Functions 297

9.1 Exploring Rational Functions Using
Transformations. 297

9.2 Analysing Rational Functions 305

9.3 Connecting Graphs and Rational
Equations 314

Chapter 9 Review.....................................321

Chapter 9 Skills Organizer 324

Chapter 10 Function Operations 325

10.1 Sums and Differences of Functions.......325

10.2 Products and Quotients of
Functions 335

10.3 Composite Functions 345

Chapter 10 Review.....................................356

Chapter 10 Skills Organizer 363

**Chapter 11 Permutations, Combinations,
and the Binomial Theorem 364**

11.1 Permutations 364

11.2 Combinations.....................................374

11.3 The Binomial Theorem.........................383

Chapter 11 Review.....................................390

Chapter 11 Skills Organizer 393

Answers...394

Overview

This McGraw-Hill Ryerson Pre-Calculus 12 Student Workbook is designed to complement the student resource.

Student Workbook Features for Students
- Each section begins with Key Ideas that summarize the concepts needed to complete the exercises.
- The sections continue with working examples that guide you through the skills needed to complete the exercises.
- The working examples often include references to the *Pre-Calculus 12* student resource. These references suggest that you compare the methods used to solve the examples, or review similar examples to help consolidate your understanding of the concepts.
- Exercises are organized into three sections: Practise, Apply, and Connect.
- A selection of questions in the exercise sections include references to similar questions in the *Pre-Calculus 12* student resource.
- A review of all sections is included at the end of each chapter.
- Each chapter includes a Skills Organizer that assists you in summarizing the important information in that chapter.
- Answers to all questions are provided at the back of the book.
- To access Study Checks for each chapter, which will help you identify what skills and concepts you need to reinforce, go to www.mhrprecalc12.ca and follow the links to the Student Workbook.

Student Workbook Features for Teachers
- For SMART Board™ lessons related to each topic, go to www.mhrprecalc12.ca and follow the links to the Student Workbook.

Chapter 1 Function Transformations

1.1 Horizontal and Vertical Translations

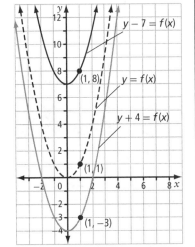

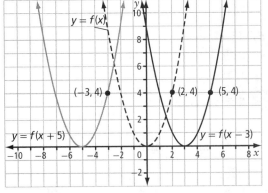

> ## KEY IDEAS

- A translation can move the graph of a function up or down (vertical translation) and right or left (horizontal translation). A translation moves each point on the graph by the same fixed amount so that the location of the graph changes but its shape and orientation remain the same.

- A vertical translation of function $y = f(x)$ by k units is written $y - k = f(x)$. Each point (x, y) on the graph of the base function is mapped to $(x, y + k)$ on the transformed function. Note that the sign of k is opposite to the sign in the equation of the function.

  – If k is *positive*, the graph of the function moves *up*.
    Example: In $y - 7 = f(x)$, $k = 7$. Each point (x, y) on the graph of $y = f(x)$ is mapped to $(x, y + 7)$. If $f(x) = x^2$, as illustrated, $(1, 1)$ maps to $(1, 8)$.

  – If k is *negative*, the graph of the function moves *down*.
    Example: In $y + 4 = f(x)$, $k = -4$. Each point (x, y) on the graph of $y = f(x)$ is mapped to $(x, y - 4)$. If $f(x) = x^2$, $(1, 1)$ maps to $(1, -3)$.

- A horizontal translation of function $y = f(x)$ by h units is written $y = f(x - h)$. Each point (x, y) on the graph of the base function is mapped to $(x + h, y)$ on the transformed function. Note that the sign of h is opposite to the sign in the equation of the function.

  – If h is *positive*, the graph of the function shifts to the *right*.
    Example: In $y = f(x - 3)$, $h = 3$. Each point (x, y) on the graph of $y = f(x)$ is mapped to $(x + 3, y)$. If $f(x) = x^2$, $(2, 4)$ maps to $(5, 4)$.

  – If h is *negative*, the graph of the function shifts to the *left*.
    Example: In $y = f(x + 5)$, $h = -5$. Each point (x, y) on the graph of $y = f(x)$ is mapped to $(x - 5, y)$. If $f(x) = x^2$, $(2, 4)$ maps to $(-3, 4)$.

- Vertical and horizontal translations may be combined. The graph of $y - k = f(x - h)$ maps each point (x, y) in the base function to $(x + h, y + k)$ in the transformed function.

Working Example 1: Graph Translations of the Form $y - k = f(x - h)$

a) For $f(x) = |x|$, graph $y + 6 = f(x - 4)$ and give the equation of the transformed function.

b) For $f(x)$ as shown, graph $y + 5 = f(x + 2)$.

Solution

a) For $f(x) = |x|$, the transformed function $y + 6 = f(x - 4)$ is represented by $y + 6 = |x - 4|$.

$h = $ _____ means a horizontal translation _____ units to

the _____.
   (*left* or *right*)

$k = $ _____ means a vertical translation _____ units _____.
                                          (*up* or *down*)

> The parameters h and k have the opposite signs to what appear in the equation.

Key points: (x, y) maps to $(x + h, y + k)$

(x, y)	$\rightarrow$	$(x + h, y + k)$
$(-5, 5)$	$\rightarrow$	
$(0, 0)$	$\rightarrow$	
$(5, 5)$	$\rightarrow$	

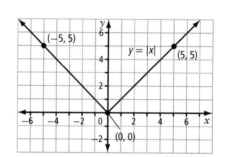

Add these points to your graph and draw in the lines. Be sure to continue the lines to the edge of the graph.

b) The function $y = f(x)$ shown in the graph below will be transformed as follows:
$y + 5 = f(x + 2)$.

> The translated function should be congruent to the base function.

$h = $ _____ means a horizontal translation _____ units to the _____.
                                                     (*left* or *right*)

$k = $ _____ means a vertical translation _____ units _____.
                                          (*up* or *down*)

Choose key points from the graph (e.g., maximum and minimum values, endpoints) and map them to new coordinates under the transformation. Then, graph the new function.

(x, y)	$\rightarrow$	$(x + h, y + k)$
$(-3, 0)$	$\rightarrow$	

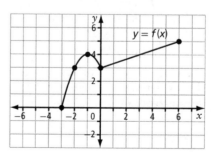

Working Example 2: Determine the Equation of a Translated Function

Determine an equation of the form $y - k = f(x - h)$ given the following graphs of $f(x)$ and of the transformed function.

a)

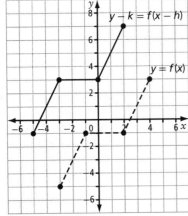

b)

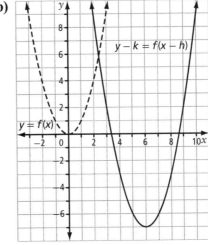

Solution

a) Verify that the shapes are congruent by comparing slopes and lengths of line segments.

Identify key points in the base function and where they are mapped to in the translation.

Work backward from the graph to determine the parameters h and k.

$(x, y) \rightarrow$ _____

$h =$ _____ $k =$ _____

This function is not easily described with an equation, so continue to call the base function $y = f(x)$. The equation describing the transformed function is:

b) Verify that the shapes are congruent by looking at the step pattern, starting at the vertex.

Identify key points (e.g., maximum and minimum values, intercepts).

$(x, y) \rightarrow$ _____

$h =$ _____ $k =$ _____

What is the equation of the base function? (Hint: What kind of function is it?)

What is the equation of the transformed function?

> Adding k to both sides of the equation $y - k = (x - h)^2$ will give the equation of a parabola in vertex form. Verify that this works.

📖 Also see Example 3 on pages 10 and 11 of *Pre-Calculus 12*.

Check Your Understanding

Practise

1. Identify the values of the parameters h and k for each of the following functions.

   a) $y = f(x - 10)$ $h =$ _____ $k =$ _____

   b) $y - 3 = f(x + 2)$ $h =$ _____ $k =$ _____

   c) $y = f(x - 17) + 13$ $h =$ _____ $k =$ _____

   > You may need to rearrange the equation before answering.

   d) $y + 7 = (x + 1)^2$ $h =$ _____ $k =$ _____

   e) $y - 4 = |x|$ $h =$ _____ $k =$ _____

2. Given $h = 2$ and $k = -5$, write an equation for each transformed function $y - k = f(x - h)$.

   a) $f(x) = x^2$

   b) $f(x) = |x|$

   c) $f(x) = \frac{1}{x}$

3. Describe, using mapping notation, how the graphs of the following functions can be obtained from the graph of $y = f(x)$. Then, describe each transformation in words.

   a) $y = f(x - 25)$ $(x, y) \rightarrow$ _____

   This represents a _____ translation _____ by _____ units.
                 (*horizontal* or *vertical*)   (*right/left/up/down*)

   b) $y + 50 = f(x)$ $(x, y) \rightarrow$ _____

   This represents a _____ translation _____ by _____ units.
                 (*horizontal* or *vertical*)   (*right/left/up/down*)

   c) $y - 10 = f(x + 20)$ $(x, y) \rightarrow$ _____

   This represents a _____.

   📖 See also #8 on page 13 of *Pre-Calculus 12*.

4. Given the graph of $y = f(x)$, graph the transformed function on the same set of axes. Write the transformation using mapping notation.

a) Graph $y + 7 = f(x + 2)$.

$h =$ _____ means a horizontal translation _____ units to the _____.
(left or *right)*

$k =$ _____ means a vertical translation _____ units _____.
(up or *down)*

Key points: (x, y) maps to $(x + h, y + k)$

(x, y)	$\rightarrow$	$(x + h, y + k)$
$(0, 4)$	$\rightarrow$	

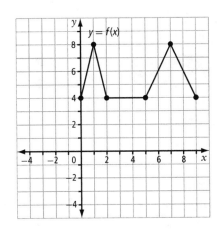

Verify that your mapping is correct by checking that the translated function is congruent to the base.

b) Graph $y + 2 = f(x - 5)$.

Key points:

(x, y)	$\rightarrow$	$(x + h, y + k)$

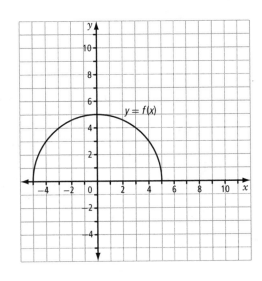

Apply

5. The graph of the function $f(x) = x^2$ is translated 6 units to the right and 4 units down to form the transformed function $y = g(x)$.

   a) Identify the values of the parameters h and k. $h =$ _____ $k =$ _____

   b) Write the transformation $f(x) \rightarrow g(x)$ using mapping notation.

   _____

   c) Determine the equation of the function $y = g(x)$. _____

   d) Graph $f(x)$ and $g(x)$ on the same set of axes.

   Key points:

(x, y)	$\rightarrow$	$(x + h, y + k)$

   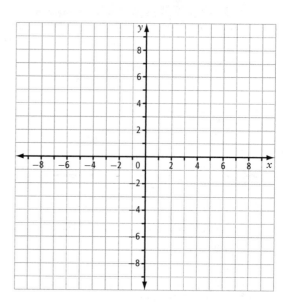

   e) Compare the vertex of $f(x)$ to that of $g(x)$. What do you notice?

   Vertex of $f(x)$:   Vertex of $g(x)$:

   f) Compare the domain and range of $f(x)$ to those of $g(x)$. What do you notice?

   Domain of $f(x)$:   Domain of $g(x)$:

   Range of $f(x)$:   Range of $g(x)$:

6. The graph of the function $f(x) = \frac{1}{x}$ is translated 5 units to the left and 2 units up to form the transformed function $y = g(x)$.

   a) Identify the values of the parameters h and k. $h =$ _____ $k =$ _____

   b) Write the transformation $f(x) \rightarrow g(x)$ using mapping notation.

      _____

   c) Determine the equation of the function $y = g(x)$. _____

   d) Graph $f(x)$ and $g(x)$ on the same set of axes.

      Key points:

(x, y)	$\longrightarrow$	$(x + h, y + k)$

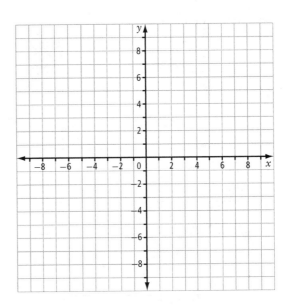

   e) Compare the domain, range, and asymptotes of $f(x)$ to those of $g(x)$. What do you notice?

      Domain of $f(x)$:   Domain of $g(x)$:

      Range of $f(x)$:   Range of $g(x)$:

      Horizontal asymptote of $f(x)$:   Horizontal asymptote of $g(x)$:

      Vertical asymptote of $f(x)$:   Vertical asymptote of $g(x)$:

Connect

7. Complete the table using equations, mapping notation, and diagrams. Be sure to include information on the location of key features (such as vertex and asymptotes) where applicable.

Function	Horizontal Translation		Vertical Translation	
	to the right 1 unit	to the left 3 units	up 2 units	down 4 units
Quadratic $y = x^2$				
Absolute value $y = |x|$				
Reciprocal $y = \frac{1}{x}$				
Any function $y = f(x)$				

> ### KEY IDEAS

- A reflection creates a mirror image of the graph of a function across a line of reflection. Any points where the function crosses the line of reflection do not move (invariant points). A reflection may change the orientation of the function but its shape remains the same.

Vertical reflection:
- $y = -f(x)$
- $(x, y) \rightarrow (x, -y)$
- line of reflection: x-axis
- also known as a reflection in the x-axis

Horizontal reflection:
- $y = f(-x)$
- $(x, y) \rightarrow (-x, y)$
- line of reflection: y-axis
- also known as a reflection in the y-axis

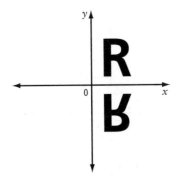
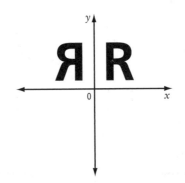

- A stretch changes the shape of a graph but not its orientation. A vertical stretch makes a function shorter (compression) or taller (expansion) because the stretch multiplies or divides each y-coordinate by a constant factor while leaving the x-coordinate unchanged. A horizontal stretch makes a function narrower (compression) or wider (expansion) because the stretch multiplies or divides each x-coordinate by a constant factor while leaving the y-coordinate unchanged.

Vertical stretch by a factor of $|a|$:
- $y = a\,f(x)$ or $\frac{1}{a}y = f(x)$
- $(x, y) \rightarrow (x, ay)$
- shorter: $0 < |a| < 1$
- taller: $|a| > 1$

Horizontal stretch by a factor of $\frac{1}{|b|}$:
- $y = f(bx)$
- $(x, y) \rightarrow \left(\frac{1}{b}x, y\right)$
- wider: $0 < |b| < 1$
- narrower: $|b| > 1$

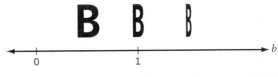

Working Example 1: Graph Reflections of a Function $y = f(x)$

Given $y = f(x)$, graph the indicated transformation on the same set of axes. Give the mapping notation representing the transformation. Identify any invariant points.

a) $y = f(-x)$ **b)** $y = -f(x)$

Solution

a) $y = f(-x)$ represents a _____ reflection of the function in the _____ -axis.
                                      (horizontal or vertical)   *(x or y)*

Key points:

(x, y)	$\rightarrow$	
$(-6, 6)$	$\rightarrow$	
$(-2, -2)$	$\rightarrow$	
$(0, -2)$	$\rightarrow$	
$(3, 1)$	$\rightarrow$	
$(5, 0)$	$\rightarrow$	

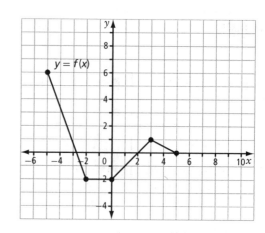

Invariant point(s): _____

b) $y = -f(x)$ represents a _____ reflection of the function in the _____-axis.
                                      (horizontal or vertical)   *(x or y)*

Key points:

(x, y)	$\rightarrow$	
$(-6, 6)$	$\rightarrow$	
$(-2, -2)$	$\rightarrow$	
$(0, -2)$	$\rightarrow$	
$(3, 1)$	$\rightarrow$	
$(5, 0)$	$\rightarrow$	

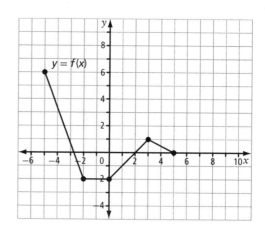

Invariant point(s): _____

Working Example 2: Graph Vertical and Horizontal Stretches of a Function $y = f(x)$

Given $y = f(x)$, graph $y = 5f(3x)$ on the same set of axes. Give the mapping notation representing the transformation.

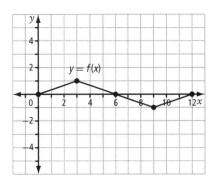

Solution

For $y = 5f(3x)$,

$a =$ _____ represents a vertical stretch by a factor of _____.
Will the new graph be shorter or taller than the graph of the base function?

$b =$ _____ represents a horizontal stretch by a factor of _____.
Will the new graph be wider or narrower than the graph of the base function?

Apply the transformations in two stages: vertical stretch first, followed by the horizontal stretch. Graph using key points at the end of each stage. Use a different colour for each stage.

> Does the order matter?

Vertical stretch by a factor of 5, followed by a horizontal stretch by a factor of $\frac{1}{3}$:

(x, y)	$\rightarrow$		$\rightarrow$	
$(0, 0)$				
$(3, 1)$				

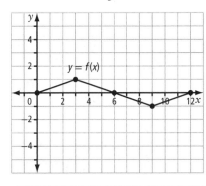

Compare the domain and range of the base function to those of the image. How many patterns (width-wise) could fit in the width of the base function?

Working Example 3: Write the Equation of a Transformed Function

The graph of the function $y = f(x)$ has been transformed by a series of stretches and/or reflections. Write the equation of the transformed function $g(x)$.

a)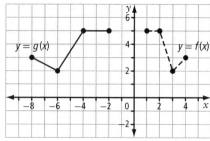

b)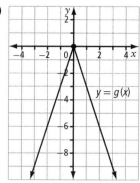

Solution

a) Key points:

$f(x)$	$\rightarrow$	$g(x)$
(1, 5)	$\rightarrow$	(−2, 5)
(2, 5)	$\rightarrow$	
(3, 2)	$\rightarrow$	
(4, 3)	$\rightarrow$	
(x, y)	$\rightarrow$	

Has the orientation changed (reflection)?

In which direction?

Has the shape changed (stretch)?

In which direction?

By how much?

Equation: _____

b) The base function $f(x)$ is not shown. What must it be? Add it to the graph.

Key points:

$f(x)$	$\rightarrow$	$g(x)$
(−3, 3)	$\rightarrow$	
(0, 0)	$\rightarrow$	
(3, 3)	$\rightarrow$	
(x, y)	$\rightarrow$	

Has the orientation changed (reflection)?

In which direction?

Has the shape changed (stretch)?

In which direction?

By how much?

Equation: _____

> How can you tell whether $g(x)$ is narrower or taller than $f(x)$? Does it matter? What other common function has this property?

Check Your Understanding

Practise

1. Graph the horizontal reflection (reflection in the *y*-axis) of each function. State the equation of the reflected function in simplified form. Note any features of the function that change and any that stay the same.

a)

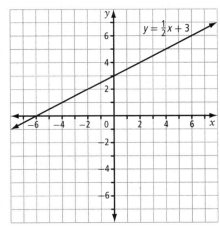

Equation of function: $y = \frac{1}{2}x + 3$

Equation of reflected function:

_____

Notes:

b)

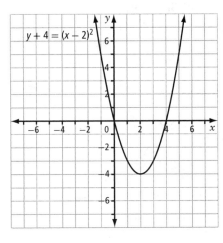

Equation of function: $y + 4 = (x - 2)^2$

Equation of reflected function:

_____

Notes:

c)

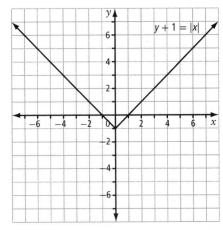

Equation of function: $y + 1 = |x|$

Equation of reflected function:

_____

Notes:

2. Graph the vertical reflection (reflection in the x-axis) of each function. State the equation of the reflected function in simplified form. Note any features of the function that change and any that stay the same.

a)

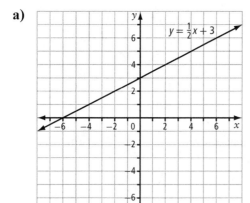

Equation of function: $y = \frac{1}{2}x + 3$

Equation of reflected function:

_____

Notes:

b)

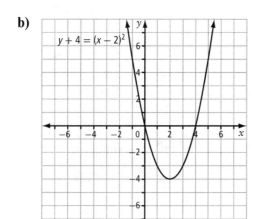

Equation of function: $y + 4 = (x - 2)^2$

Equation of reflected function:

_____

Notes:

c)

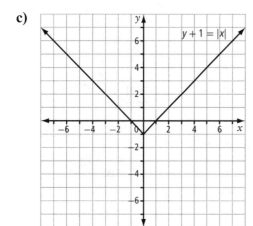

Equation of function: $y + 1 = |x|$

Equation of reflected function:

_____

Notes:

3. Given $f(x) = x^2$, graph the following transformations. Give the equation and mapping notation for each transformation.

   a) vertical stretch by a factor of $\frac{1}{4}$

   Key points: (x, y) maps to (x, ay)

(x, y)	$\rightarrow$	
$(0, 0)$	$\rightarrow$	
$(\pm 1, 1)$	$\rightarrow$	
$(\pm 2, 4)$	$\rightarrow$	
$(\pm 3, 9)$	$\rightarrow$	
$(\pm 4, 16)$	$\rightarrow$	

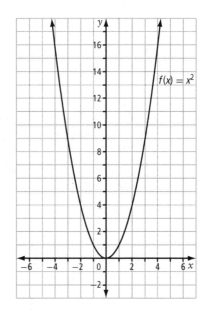

   Equation: _____

   b) horizontal stretch by a factor of 2 (b = reciprocal of the stretch factor)

   Key points: (x, y) maps to $\left(\frac{1}{b}x, y\right)$

(x, y)	$\rightarrow$	
$(0, 0)$	$\rightarrow$	
$(\pm 1, 1)$	$\rightarrow$	
$(\pm 2, 4)$	$\rightarrow$	
$(\pm 3, 9)$	$\rightarrow$	
$(\pm 4, 16)$	$\rightarrow$	

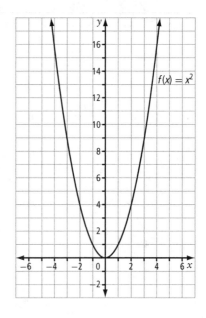

   Equation: _____

4. Compare your answers in parts a) and b) of #3.

   a) Show algebraically why both transformations result in the same transformed function.

   b) Give another example of a pair of horizontal and vertical stretches that would result in the same transformed function.

Apply

5. Write an equation representing each of the following transformations of $y = f(x)$. Then, graph each transformation.

   a) vertical stretch by a factor of 2

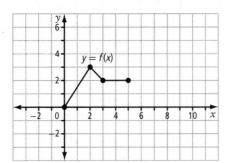

   Equation of transformed function:

   b) reflection in the x-axis and horizontal stretch by a factor of 2

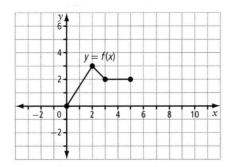

   Equation of transformed function:

   c) reflection in the y-axis and horizontal stretch by a factor of $\frac{1}{2}$

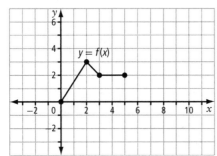

   Equation of transformed function:

   > Recall that $y = f(bx)$ results in a horizontal stretch of $\frac{1}{|b|}$.

Connect

6. Use sketches, graphs, equations, mapping notation, and words to describe how to achieve the following transformations to the graph of $y = x^2$.

Shorter	Taller

Narrower	Wider

KEY IDEAS

- Types of transformations include stretches, reflections, and translations.

- Multiple transformations can be applied to the same function. The same order of operations followed when you work with numbers (sometimes called BEDMAS) applies to transformations: first multiplication and division (stretches, reflections), and then addition/subtraction (translations).

  $$y - k = af(b(x - h))$$

- The following three-step process will help you to keep organized.

  Step 1: horizontal stretch by a factor of $\frac{1}{|b|}$ followed by reflection in the y-axis if $b < 0$

  Step 2: vertical stretch by a factor of $|a|$ followed by reflection in the x-axis if $a < 0$

  Step 3: horizontal and/or vertical translations (h and k)

  $$(x, y) \rightarrow \left(\frac{1}{b}x, y\right) \rightarrow \left(\frac{1}{b}x, ay\right) \rightarrow \left(\frac{1}{b}x + h, ay + k\right)$$

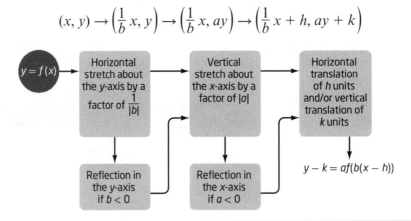

Working Example 1: Combinations of Transformations

Graph each of the following transformed functions. Show each stage of the transformation in a different colour and label each stage.

a) $y + 2 = -\left|\frac{1}{3}x - \frac{4}{3}\right|$

b) $y - 5 = \frac{1}{2}f(-x)$

Solution

a) The transformations applied to $y = |x|$ to obtain $y + 2 = -\left|\frac{1}{3}x - \frac{4}{3}\right|$ are, in order,

i) _____

ii) reflection in the x-axis

iii) _____

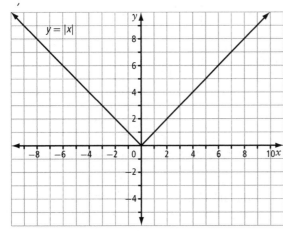

Be sure to factor the input of the function so that it is in the form $f[b(x - h)]$.

b) The transformations applied to $y = f(x)$ to obtain $y - 5 = \frac{1}{2}f(-x)$ are, in order,

i) reflection in the y-axis

ii) vertical stretch by a factor of _____

iii) _____

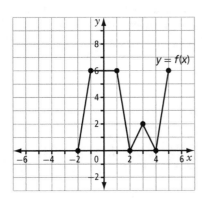

Working Example 2: Determine the Equation of a Translated Function

Determine an equation for $g(x)$ of the form $y - k = af(b(x - h))$ given the graphs of $y = f(x)$ and of the transformed function $y = g(x)$.

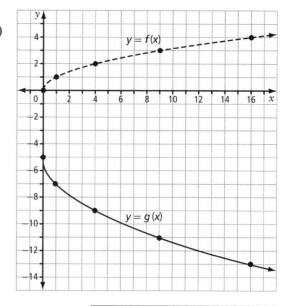

Solution

Work backward through the three stages of transformations.

Horizontal and vertical translations:
Any points $(x, 0)$ on the graph of $f(x)$ are unaffected by vertical stretches and reflections.

Any points $(0, y)$ on the graph of $f(x)$ are unaffected by horizontal stretches and reflections.

So, the key point $(0, 0)$ on the graph of $f(x)$ can be used to determine the horizontal and vertical translations.

In the equation for $g(x)$, $h =$ _____ and $k =$ _____.

> Before proceeding, add a sketch to the graph above that shows $g(x)$ without translations.

Vertical stretches and reflections:
• Is the transformed function reflected across the x-axis? (Y/N)
• Is the transformed function the same shape as the base function? (Y/N)

If the answer to the second question is no, measure the vertical distance between the x-axis and key points on $f(x)$. Then, measure the vertical distance between the x-axis and the image points on $g(x)$ and subtract the value of k. Compare the vertical distances.

In $g(x)$, $a =$ _____.

Horizontal stretches and reflections:
• Is the transformed function reflected in the y-axis? (Y/N)
• Is the transformed function the same shape as the base function? (Y/N)

If the answer to the second question is no, measure the horizontal distance between the y-axis and key points on $f(x)$. Then, measure the horizontal distance between the y-axis and the image points on $g(x)$ and subtract the value of h. Compare the horizontal distances.

In $g(x)$, $b =$ _____.

Now, put the transformations together.

Equation representing $g(x)$: _____

📖 Also see Example 3 on pages 37 and 38 of *Pre-Calculus 12*.

Check Your Understanding

Practise

1. Describe, in order, the transformations represented by each equation.

> You may need to factor the equation before answering.

a) $y + 5 = 4f(-x) - 5$

i) VSF = 4

ii) HR in y-axis

iii) VT 5 down

b) $y = -f(2x + 14)$

i)

ii)

iii)

c) $y = 1.75 f[0.25(x - 1.5)]$

i)

ii)

iii)

d) $y - 3 = -\frac{1}{2}f(-3x - 3) + 3$
$-3(x+1)$

i) VR in x-axis, VSF of $\frac{1}{2}$

ii) HSF of $\frac{1}{3}$ HR in y-axis

iii) HT = -1 VT = 3

2. Determine the equation of each transformed function.

a) $y = f(x)$ is stretched horizontally by a factor of 6, reflected in the x-axis, and translated 7 units down. $x -7$

b) $y = |x|$ is reflected in the y-axis, stretched vertically by a factor of $\frac{1}{2}$, and translated 3 units to the right.

c) $y = x^2$ is reflected in the x-axis, stretched horizontally by a factor of 3, and translated so that the vertex is at $(10, -4)$. $y = -(\frac{1}{3}(x-10))^2 - 4$
$\quad$ h $\quad$ k

3. The key point $(1, 10)$ is on the graph of $y = f(x)$. Determine the coordinates of its image point under each transformation.

a) $y + 4 = f(x - 5) \, -4$

$(x, y) \to (\frac{x}{6} + h, a y + k)$

$(1, 10) \to (\frac{1}{1} + 5, 1(10) - 4)$
$\to (6, 6)$

b) $y = -f(x + 12)$

$(x, y) \to$

$(1, 10) \to$

c) $y = 3f(-0.5x + 10)$

$(x, y) \to$

$(1, 10) \to$

📖 This is similar to #6 on page 39 of *Pre-Calculus 12*.

4. If the key point $(-2, -8)$ is on the graph of $y = f(x)$, determine the coordinates of its image point under each of the transformations in #3.

Apply

5. The graph of the function $y = g(x)$ is given. Graph each of the following transformations of the function. Show each stage of the transformation in a different colour.

   a) $y + 2 = -g(2x)$

   i)

   ii)

   iii)

   b) $y = g(-4x + 12)$

   i)

   ii)

   iii)

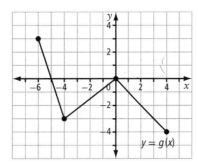

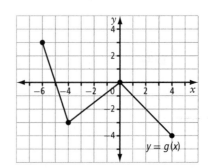

6. The graph of the function $f(x) = |x|$ is stretched vertically by a factor of 2, reflected in the x-axis, and translated 6 units to the left and 3 units down to form the transformed function $y = g(x)$.

   a) Determine the equation of the function $y = g(x)$.

   b) Graph $y = g(x)$.

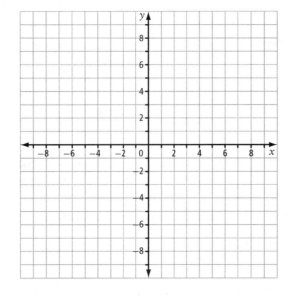

Start by graphing the base function $y = f(x)$.

7. The graph of the function $f(x) = \frac{1}{x}$ is stretched horizontally by a factor of 4, reflected in the x-axis, and translated 4 units to the right and 1 unit down to form the transformed function $y = g(x)$.

a) Determine the equation of the function $y = g(x)$.

b) Graph $y = g(x)$.

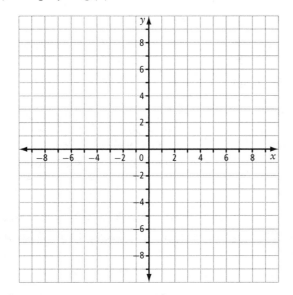

8. Determine an equation for $g(x)$ of the form $y - k = af(b(x - h))$ given the graphs of $y = f(x)$ and the transformed function $y = g(x)$.

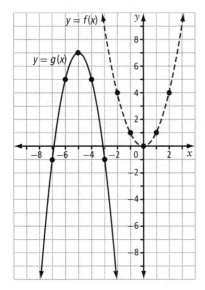

Equation:

9. Determine an equation for $g(x)$ of the form $y - k = af(b(x - h))$ given the graphs of $y = f(x)$ and the transformed function $y = g(x)$.

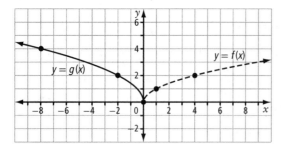

Equation:

10. Determine an equation of the form $y - k = af(b(x - h))$ given the following graphs of $y = f(x)$ and of the transformed function $y = g(x)$.

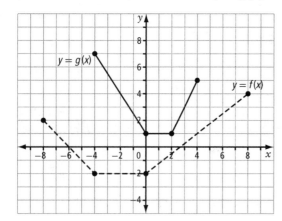

Consider each of the possible types of transformations in reverse order: translations, vertical stretches and reflections, and horizontal stretches and reflections.

For additional similar questions, see #10 on page 40 of *Pre-Calculus 12*.

Connect

11. Choose your transformations:

   a) horizontal stretch by a factor of _____ (a = _____); horizontal reflection? (Y/N)

   b) vertical stretch by a factor of _____ (b = _____); vertical reflection?(Y/N)

   c) translations by _____

Write equations representing the transformed function after each stage of the transformation. Simplify each equation if necessary.

Function	Horizontal Stretch and/or Reflection	Vertical Stretch and/or Reflection	Translations
$y = f(x)$			
$y = x$			
$y = \|x\|$			
$y = x^2$			
$y = \frac{1}{x}$			

<< **KEY IDEAS** >>

- The inverse of a function $y = f(x)$ is denoted $y = f^{-1}(x)$ if the inverse is a function. The -1 is not an exponent because f represents a function, not a variable. You have already seen this notation with trigonometric functions. Example: $\sin^{-1}(\theta)$, where $f(\theta) = \sin(\theta)$ and the variable is θ.

- The inverse of a function reverses the processes represented by that function. For example, the process of squaring a number is reversed by taking the square root. The process of taking the reciprocal of a number is reversed by taking the reciprocal again.

- To determine the inverse of a function, interchange the x- and y-coordinates.

$$(x, y) \rightarrow (y, x)$$

or

$$y = f(x) \rightarrow x = f(y)$$

or

reflect in the line $y = x$

- When working with an equation of a function $y = f(x)$, interchange x for y. Then, solve for y to get an equation for the inverse. If the inverse is a function, then $y = f^{-1}(x)$.

- If the inverse of a function is not a function (recall the vertical line test), restrict the domain of the base function so that the inverse becomes a function. You will see this frequently with quadratic functions. For example, the inverse of $f(x) = x^2$, $x \geq 0$, is $f^{-1}(x) = \sqrt{x}$. The inverse will be a function only if the domain of the base function is restricted.

- Restricting the domain is necessary for any function that changes direction (increasing to decreasing, or vice versa) at some point in the domain of the function.

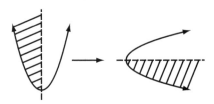

Working Example 1: Determine the Inverse of a Relation

Determine the inverse of the given relation when it is described as

a) an equation **b)** a table of values **c)** a graph

Solution

a) $f(x) = -\frac{2}{3}x + 5$

Steps:

1. Substitute y for $f(x)$. $y = -\frac{2}{3}x + 5$

2. Interchange x and y.   ———— $= -\frac{2}{3}$ ———— $+ 5$

3. Solve for y.

4. If the inverse is a function, substitute $f^{-1}(x)$ for y.

b) Key points: x- and y-coordinates are interchanged

(x, y)	$\rightarrow$	(y, x)
$(-3, 7)$	$\rightarrow$	
$(0, 5)$	$\rightarrow$	
$(3, 3)$	$\rightarrow$	
$(6, 1)$	$\rightarrow$	

c) The inverse of $f(x)$ is the reflection in the line $y = x$. Choose key points and interchange the x- and y-coordinates.

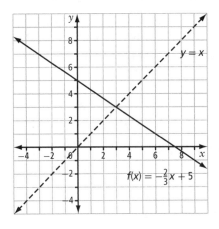

Identify any invariant point(s): _____

Note that the equation, table of values, and graph all represent the same function. It is a good idea when working with inverses to verify your algebra using a graph.

> What happens to the y-intercept?
> What happens to the x-intercept?

> Is the inverse of a linear function always a function?

Working Example 2: Determine the Equation of the Inverse of a Quadratic Function

Determine algebraically the equation of the inverse of the function $f(x) = (x + 3)^2 - 1$. Verify graphically that the relations are inverses of each other.

Solution

Let $y = f(x)$. To determine the inverse, interchange x and y (everywhere it says x, write y, and vice versa).

Solve for y.

> When taking the square root of both sides, be sure to take the square root of the whole expression on each side.

Next, create the graph of $f(x) = (x + 3)^2 - 1$ and its inverse. Compare the graph to your solution above to verify that your algebra is correct (compare, for example, coordinates of the vertex and direction of opening).

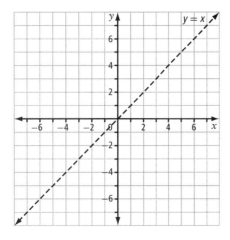

> To graph the inverse, choose some key points from the base function and interchange the x- and y-coordinates.

Is the inverse a function? (Y/N)

Divide the inverse into two branches ($+$ and $-$) at the vertex. Do the same for the base function.

In the base function, the equation of the axis of symmetry is

$x = $ _____

Restrict the domain to $\{x \mid x \geq$ _____, $x \in \mathbb{R}\}$.

Restricting the domain of $f(x)$ to the positive branch of the original parabola ($x \geq -3$) gives only the positive root from the equation of the inverse relation $y = \pm\sqrt{x + 1} - 3$.

Therefore, for the function $f(x) = (x + 3)^2 - 1$, $x \geq -3$, the inverse is

$f^{-1}(x) = $ _____.

Alternatively, you could choose the negative branch and write that the inverse of the function:

$f(x) = (x + 3)^2 - 1$, $x \leq -3$, is $f^{-1}(x) = $ _____.

Practise

1. Graph the inverse relation of each function below. Determine whether the inverse is a function. Identify any invariant points.

a)

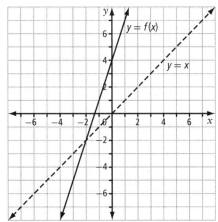

The inverse of $f(x)$ _____ a function.
(*is* or *is not*)

b)

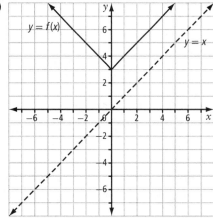

The inverse of $f(x)$ _____ a function.
(*is* or *is not*)

c)

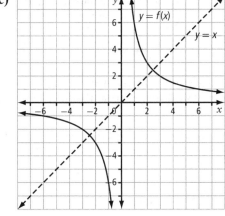

The inverse of $f(x)$ _____ a function.
(*is* or *is not*)

d)

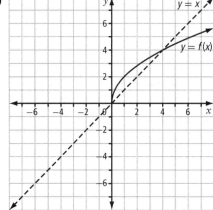

The inverse of $f(x)$ _____ a function.
(*is* or *is not*)

e)

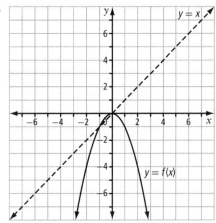

The inverse of $f(x)$ _____ a function.

(*is* or *is not*)

f)

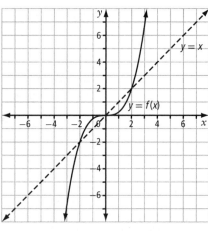

The inverse of $f(x)$ _____ a function.

(*is* or *is not*)

2. Determine algebraically the inverse of each function. Verify by sketching the graph of the function and its inverse.

a) $f(x) = x - 4$

Steps:

1. Substitute y for $f(x)$.

2. Interchange x and y.

3. Solve for y.

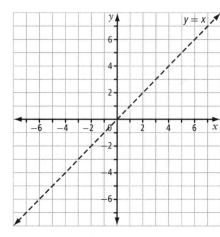

4. Restrict the domain if necessary. Then, substitute $f^{-1}(x)$ for y.

The inverse of $f(x) = x - 4$ is $f^{-1}(x) = $ _____.

b) $f(x) = -6x - 2$

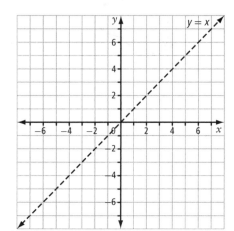

The inverse of $f(x) = -6x - 2$ is

$f^{-1}(x) = $ _____.

c) $f(x) = \frac{3}{5}x - 3$

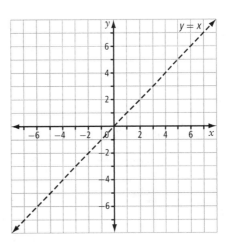

The inverse of $f(x) = \frac{3}{5}x - 3$ is

$f^{-1}(x) = $ _____.

d) $f(x) = \frac{1}{2}(x + 6)$

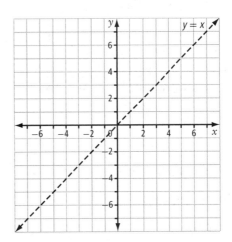

The inverse of $f(x) = \frac{1}{2}(x + 6)$ is

$f^{-1}(x) = $ _____.

3. For each graph, identify a restricted domain for which the function has an inverse that is also a function.

a)

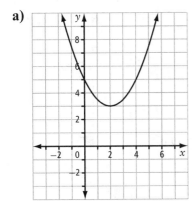

Axis of symmetry: _____

Domain: _____

b)

Axis of symmetry: _____

Domain: _____

4. Determine algebraically the inverse of each function. Restrict the domain of the base function so that the inverse is a function. Verify by sketching the graph of the function and its inverse.

a) $f(x) = -x^2 + 6$

Steps:

1. Substitute y for $f(x)$.

2. Interchange x and y.

3. Solve for y.

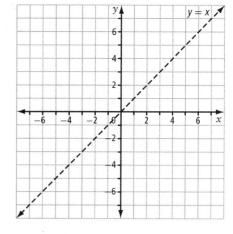

4. Restrict the domain if necessary. Then, substitute $f^{-1}(x)$ for y.

The inverse of $f(x) = -x^2 + 6$, _____, is $f^{-1}(x) =$ _____.

b) $f(x) = \frac{1}{2}x^2 + 4$

Steps:

1. Substitute y for $f(x)$.

2. Interchange x and y.

3. Solve for y.

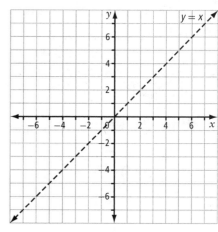

4. Restrict the domain if necessary. Then, substitute $f^{-1}(x)$ for y.

The inverse of $f(x) = \frac{1}{2}x^2 + 4$, _____, is $f^{-1}(x) =$ _____.

📖 For more practice with quadratics, try #12 on page 54 of *Pre-Calculus 12*.

Apply

5. Determine the equation of the inverse of $f(x) = x^2 + 6x + 7$. Verify by sketching the graph of the function and its inverse.

Hint: Complete the square.

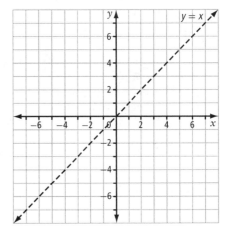

📖 See also #10 on page 53 of *Pre-Calculus 12*.

6. One of the factors that doctors use to determine the age of a fetus is the crown-to-rump length (CRL) measured during an ultrasound. A recent study determined that the average CRL, in millimetres, of a fetus with gestational age x days could be represented by the function $f(x) = 0.016\ 34(x - 26.643)^2$. This formula applies between 6 and 15 weeks of gestation.

   a) What are the restrictions on the domain of this function?

   b) Determine an equation that would allow a doctor to determine gestational age, in days, if the CRL, in millimetres, is known.

   c) If the CRL of a fetus is 7.4 cm, predict the gestational age in weeks.

Connect

7. Complete the table using words, equations, and diagrams. A few prompts are included to help you get started.

$f(x)$ is ...	Key Features of $f(x)$	$f^{-1}(x)$ is ...	Key Features of $f^{-1}(x)$
Linear (slope > 0) 	slope: y-intercept: x-intercept:		slope: y-intercept: x-intercept:
Linear (slope < 0) 			
Quadratic ($a > 0$) 	vertex:		vertex:
Quadratic ($a < 0$) 			

Chapter 1 Review

1.1 Horizontal and Vertical Translations, pages 1–8

1. Write an equation to represent each translation of the function $y = |x|$.

a)

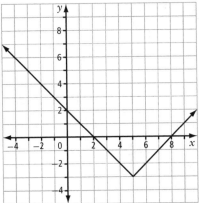

b)

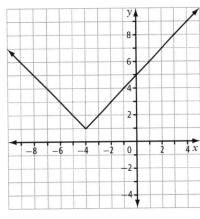

Equation: _____   Equation: _____

2. For $y = f(x)$ as shown, graph the following.

a) $y - 2 = f(x - 3)$

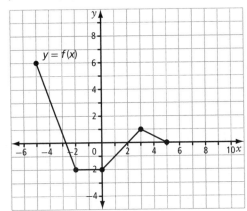

b) $y + 2 = f(x + 1)$

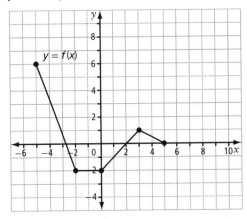

1.2 Reflections and Stretches, pages 9–17

3. The key point $(12, -5)$ is on the graph of $y = f(x)$. Determine the coordinates of its image point under each transformation.

a) $y = -f(x)$

$(x, y) \rightarrow$

$(12, -5) \rightarrow$

b) $y = f(-4x)$

$(x, y) \rightarrow$

$(12, -5) \rightarrow$

c) $y = 2f\left(\dfrac{1}{3}x\right)$

$(x, y) \rightarrow$

$(12, -5) \rightarrow$

4. Describe the following transformations of $y = f(x)$ and sketch a graph of each transformation.

a) $y = -f(-x)$

   Description:

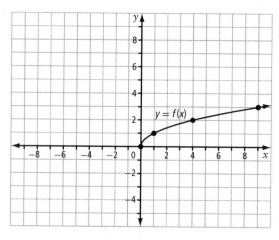

b) $y = 3f(2x)$

   Description:

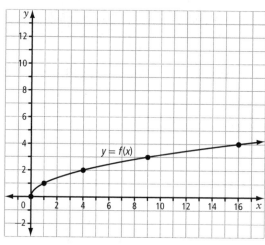

1.3 Combining Transformations, pages 18–25

5. The graph of the function $y = f(x)$ is given. Graph each of the following transformations of the function. Show each stage of the transformation in a different colour.

a) $y - 5 = \frac{1}{2}f\left(\frac{2}{3}(x - 6)\right)$

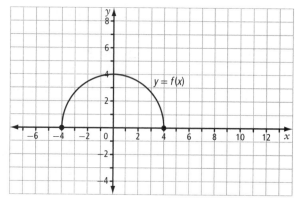

b) $y = -f(4x + 12)$

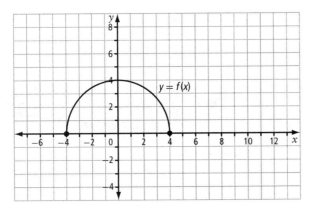

1.4 Inverse of a Relation, pages 26–34

6. Determine algebraically the inverse of each function. If necessary, restrict the domain so that the inverse of $f(x)$ is also a function. Verify by sketching the graph of the function and its inverse.

a) $f(x) = -\frac{1}{2}x + 5$

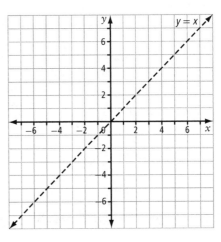

b) $f(x) = 2(x - 1)^2$

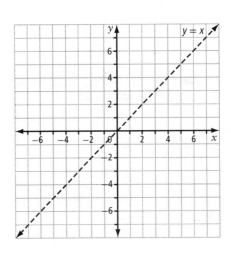

Chapter 1 Skills Organizer

Complete the tables to review the key concepts you have learned in this chapter about transformations and functions.

Transformation of Functions

Transformation	Parameter	Effect on Graph of $y = f(x)$		
		Location	Shape	Orientation
Vertical translation	_____ > 0			
	_____ < 0			
Horizontal translation	_____ > 0			
	_____ < 0			
Reflection: $y = -f(x)$	_____ < 0			
Reflection: $y = f(-x)$	_____ < 0			
Vertical stretch	factor of $|\!\_\_\_\_\!|$			
Horizontal stretch	factor of $\dfrac{1}{|\!\_\_\_\_\!|}$			
Order of transformations: _____ _____ _____				

Inverse of a Relation

Function	Inverse
$y = f(x)$	_____
Domain: A	Domain: _____
Range: B	Range: _____
The inverse, f^{-1}, of the function f maps y to x if and only if _____ .	

Chapter 2 Radical Functions

2.1 Radical Functions and Transformations

> ### KEY IDEAS

Base Radical Function
- The base radical function $y = \sqrt{x}$ has the following graph and properties:
    - x-intercept of 0
    - y-intercept of 0
    - domain: $\{x \mid x \geq 0, x \in \mathbf{R}\}$
    - range: $\{y \mid y \geq 0, y \in \mathbf{R}\}$
    - The intercepts and domain and range suggest an endpoint at $(0, 0)$, and no right endpoint.

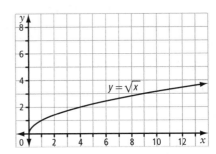

- The graph is shaped like half of a parabola. The domain and range indicate that the half parabola is in the first quadrant.

Transforming Radical Functions
The base radical function $y = \sqrt{x}$ is transformed by changing the values of the parameters a, b, h, and k in the equation $y = a\sqrt{b(x - h)} + k$. The parameters have the following effects on the base function:

a	• vertical stretch by a factor of $\lvert a \rvert$ • if a is $a < 0$, the graph of $y = \sqrt{x}$ is reflected in the x-axis
b	• horizontal stretch by a factor of $\dfrac{1}{\lvert b \rvert}$ • if b is $b < 0$, the graph of $y = \sqrt{x}$ is reflected in the y-axis
h	• horizontal translation • $(x - h)$ means the graph of $y = \sqrt{x}$ moves h units right. For example, $y = \sqrt{x - 1}$ means that the graph of $y = \sqrt{x}$ moves 1 unit right. • $(x + h)$ means the graph of $y = \sqrt{x}$ moves h units left. For example, $y = \sqrt{x + 5}$ means that the graph of $y = \sqrt{x}$ moves 5 units left. This translation has the opposite effect than many people think. It is a common error to think that the $+$ sign moves the graph to the right and the $-$ sign moves the graph to the left. This is not the case.
k	• vertical translation • $+ k$ means the graph of $y = \sqrt{x}$ moves k units up • $- k$ means the graph of $y = \sqrt{x}$ moves k units down

Working Example 1: Explain How to Recognize Transformations

Explain how to transform the graph of $y = \sqrt{x}$ to obtain $y = -2\sqrt{4(x-3)} + 1$. Sketch the graph of each function. Then, identify the domain and range of each function.

Solution

Begin by identifying the parameters and the effect each has on the base function.

- Parameter $a =$ ___-2___, resulting in a ___vertical reflection VSF___ by a factor of ___2___.

  Since a is negative, the graph is reflected in the ___y-axis___.

- Parameter $b =$ ___4___, resulting in a ___HSF___

  by a factor of ___¼___.

  > Why is the graph not reflected in the y-axis?

- Parameter $h =$ ___3___, so the graph is translated ___right___ by ___3___ units.

- Parameter $k =$ ___1___, so the graph is translated ___up___ by ___1___ units.

Apply the transformations to sketch the graph of transformed function.

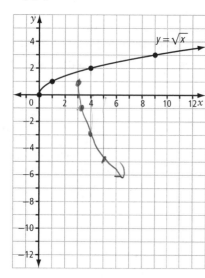

> Create a table of values and describe how the transformations are reflected in the values.

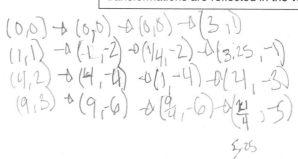

$(0,0) \rightarrow (0,0) \rightarrow (0,0) \rightarrow (3,1)$

$(1,1) \rightarrow (1,-2) \rightarrow (\frac{1}{4},-2) \rightarrow (3.25,-1)$

$(4,2) \rightarrow (4,-4) \rightarrow (1,-4) \rightarrow (4,-3)$

$(9,3) \rightarrow (9,-6) \rightarrow (\frac{9}{4},-6) \rightarrow (\frac{21}{4},-5)$

5.25

The domain of the base function is $\{x \mid x \geq 0, x \in R\}$ and its range is $\{y \mid y \geq 0, y \in R\}$. The domain and range of the transformed function are

domain: $\{x \mid x \geq 3, x \in R\}$

range: $\{y \mid y \leq 1, y \in R\}$

Working Example 2: Use Transformations to Sketch a Graph

Use transformations to sketch the graph of $y = 4\sqrt{-2(x + 3)} - 5$.

Solution

The function $y = 4\sqrt{-2(x + 3)} - 5$ is expressed in the form $y = a\sqrt{b(x - h)} + k$. Identify each parameter and how it will transform the graph of $y = \sqrt{x}$.

- $a =$ __4__ results in a __vertical__ stretch by a factor of __4__.
- $b =$ __-2__ results in a __horizontal__ stretch by a factor of __½__, and a reflection

  in the __x__-axis.
- $h =$ __-3__ results in a __vertical__ translation of __3__ units __left__.

  (left or *right)*
- $k =$ __-5__ results in a __horizontal__ translation __5__ units __down__.

  (up or *down)*

Sketch the graph of $y = \sqrt{x}$ and plot four identifiable points.

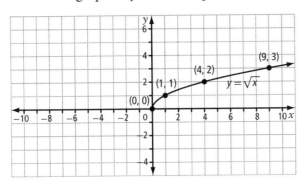

Using the four points on the graph of the base function, $y = \sqrt{x}$, complete the table to determine the resulting coordinates on the graph of $y = 4\sqrt{-2(x + 3)} - 5$. One of the points has been done for you.

Point on $y = \sqrt{x}$	(0, 0)	(1, 1)	(4, 2)	(9, 3)	
Vertical stretch	(0,0)	(1,4)	(4, 8)	(9,12)	4.5
Horizontal stretch	(0,0)	(-½,4)	(2, 8)	(9½,12)	
Reflection in the __x__-axis	(0,0)	(-½, 4)	(−2, 8)	(-9/2,12)	
Horizontal translation	(0,-5)	(-3.5,4)	(−5, 8)	(-½,12)	
Vertical translation	(-3,-5)	(-3.5,-1)	(−5, 3)	(-½,9)	
Point on $y = 4\sqrt{-2(x + 3)} - 5$	(-3,-5)	(-3.5,-1)	(−5, 3)	(-½,9)	

Plot the four points from the bottom row of the table to help you sketch the graph of $y = 4\sqrt{-2(x + 3)} - 5$ on the grid above.

> What other method can you use for transforming the graph? Which method do you prefer?

📖 To see a similar question, refer to Example 2 on pages 65–67 in *Pre-Calculus 12*.

Working Example 3: Determine a Radical Function From a Graph

Use the graph below to write the equation of the corresponding radical function in the form $y = a\sqrt{b(x - h)} + k$.

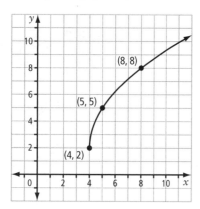

How could you compare this graph to the graph of $y = \sqrt{x}$ to determine the equation of the transformed function?

Solution

You can use the endpoint and the coordinates of another point on the graph of the transformed function to determine the equation.

Identify the endpoint of the transformed function: _____.

The endpoint represents the parameters (h, k).

Why are you able to determine h and k from the endpoint of the translated graph?

There is no reflection in the x-axis or y-axis, so the a or b parameters are _____.
(*negative* or *positive*)

The graph is stretched. This stretch can be viewed as being either a horizontal or vertical

stretch. To determine the factor by which the graph has been stretched, begin by identifying

one other point that the graph passes through: _____.

View as a Vertical Stretch	View as a Horizontal Stretch
Substitute h, k, x, and y into $y = a\sqrt{x - h} + k$ and solve for parameter _____.	Substitute h, k, x, and y into $y = \sqrt{b(x - h)} + k$ and solve for parameter _____.
Equation of the function: _____	Equation of the function: _____

To see a similar question, refer to Example 3 on pages 68–69 in *Pre-Calculus 12*.

Check Your Understanding

Practise

1. Explain how to transform the graph of $y = \sqrt{x}$ to obtain the graph of each function. State the domain and range in each case.

   a) $y = 3\sqrt{-(x + 4)} - 2$

   b) $y = -2\sqrt{4(x - 3)} + 5$

   c) $y = 4\sqrt{5(x + 1)} - 4$

   d) $y = -\sqrt{-3(x + 2)}$

2. Write the radical function that results from applying each set of transformations to the graph of $y = \sqrt{x}$.

   a) vertical stretch by a factor of 3, reflection in the x-axis, a translation of 4 units right and 2 units down

   $$y = -3\sqrt{-(x-4)} - 2$$

   b) horizontal stretch by a factor of $\frac{1}{4}$, reflection in the y-axis, a translation of 5 units left and 3 units up

   $$y = -\sqrt{-4(x+5)} + 3$$

   c) vertical stretch by a factor of 2, horizontal stretch by a factor of 3, translation of 4 units left and 1 unit up

   $$y = 2\sqrt{1/3(x+5)} + 1$$

   d) vertical stretch by a factor of 3, horizontal stretch by a factor of $\frac{1}{2}$, reflection in the x-axis and y-axis, and translation of 6 units left

   $$y = -3\sqrt{-2(x+6)}$$

3. Match each function with its graph.

a) $y = 2\sqrt{2(x-2)} + 2$

b) $y = -2\sqrt{2(x-2)} + 2$

c) $y = 2\sqrt{-2(x-2)} + 2$

d) $y = -2\sqrt{-2(x-2)} + 2$

A *a* *d*

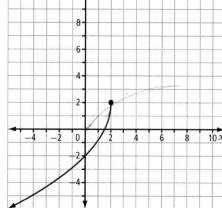

B *a*

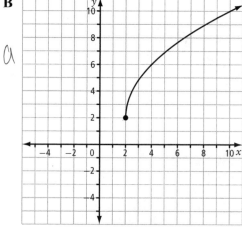

C *D*

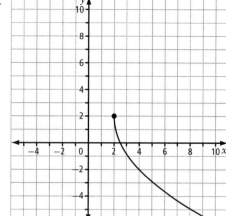

D *C*

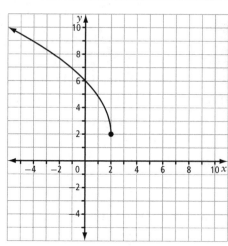

4. Sketch the graph of each function using transformations.

a) $y = 3\sqrt{x-1} + 4$ sp (1,4)

$a = \underline{3}, b = \underline{1}, h = \underline{1}, k = \underline{4}$

b) $y = -4\sqrt{x+3} - 2$

$-4\sqrt{1+3} - 2 \quad -10$

$-4(2) - 2$

g

$3\sqrt{5-1} + 4$

$3\sqrt{4} + 4$

$3(2) + 4$

10

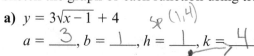

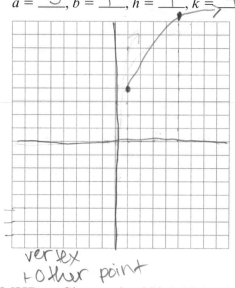

vertex
+ other point

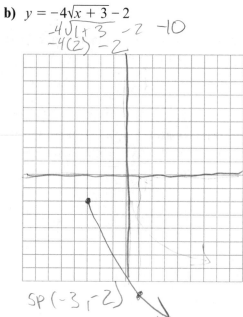

sp (-3, -2)

c) $y = 2\sqrt{4(x-1)} + 3$

d) $y = -3\sqrt{-2(x+1)} - 4$

Apply

5. For each graph, write the equation of a radical function of the form $y = a\sqrt{b(x-h)} + k$.

a)

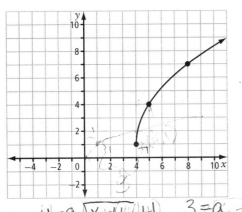

b)

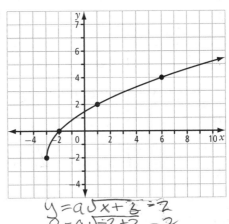

replace the point →

$y = a\sqrt{x-4} + 1$

$4 = a\sqrt{5-4} + 1$

$4 = a\sqrt{1} + 1$

$3 = a$

$y = 3\sqrt{x-4} + 1$

$y = a\sqrt{x+2} = 2$

$0 = a\sqrt{-2+2} - 2$

$2 = a\sqrt{0}$

$2 = a$

$y = 2\sqrt{x+3} - 2$

$\sqrt{x} \quad \sqrt{x}$

$\sqrt{x} - \sqrt{x}$

c)

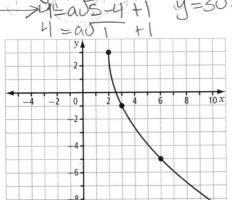

d)

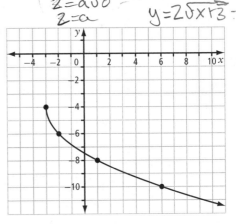

6. Consider the function $y = \frac{1}{2}\sqrt{6x}$.

   a) Describe the transformations that were applied to $y = \sqrt{x}$ to obtain this function.

   b) Write a function equivalent to $y = \frac{1}{2}\sqrt{6x}$ in the form $y = a\sqrt{x}$. Describe the transformation applied to $y = \sqrt{x}$ to obtain this new function.

   c) Write a function equivalent to $y = \frac{1}{2}\sqrt{6x}$ in the form $y = \sqrt{bx}$. Describe the transformation applied to $y = \sqrt{x}$ to obtain this new function.

Connect

7. Joanne claims that when writing the equation of a radical function given its graph, you only need to find three parameters: a, h, and k, or b, h, and k. Do you agree? Explain using examples.

KEY IDEAS

Graphing $y = f(x)$ and $y = \sqrt{f(x)}$

- To graph $y = \sqrt{f(x)}$, you can set up a table of values for the graph of $y = f(x)$. Then, take the square root of the elements in the range, while keeping the elements in the domain the same.

- When graphing $y = \sqrt{f(x)}$, pay special attention to the invariant points, which are points that are the same for $y = f(x)$ as they are for $y = \sqrt{f(x)}$. The invariant points are $(x, 0)$ and $(x, 1)$ because when $f(x) = 0$, $\sqrt{f(x)} = 0$, and when $f(x) = 1$, $\sqrt{f(x)} = 1$.

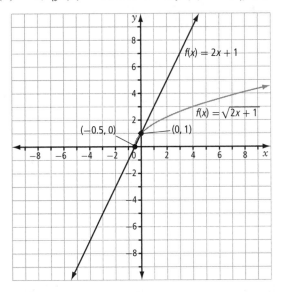

Domain and Range of $y = \sqrt{f(x)}$

- You cannot take the square root of a negative number, so the domain of $y = \sqrt{f(x)}$ is any value for which $f(x) \geq 0$.

- The range is the square root of any value in $y = f(x)$ for which $y = \sqrt{f(x)}$ is defined.

The Graph of $y = \sqrt{f(x)}$

$f(x) < 0$	$f(x) = 0$	$0 < f(x) < 1$	$f(x) = 1$	$f(x) > 1$
$y = \sqrt{f(x)}$ is **undefined** because you cannot take the square root of a negative number.	The graphs of $y = \sqrt{f(x)}$ and $y = f(x)$ **intersect** at $x = 0$.	The graph of $y = \sqrt{f(x)}$ is **above** the graph of $y = f(x)$.	The graphs of $y = \sqrt{f(x)}$ and $y = f(x)$ **intersect** at $x = 1$.	The graph of $y = \sqrt{f(x)}$ is **below** the graph of $y = f(x)$.

Working Example 1: Compare Graphs of a Linear Function and the Square Root of the Function

a) Given $f(x) = 4x - 3$, graph the functions $y = f(x)$ and $y = \sqrt{f(x)}$.

b) Compare the graphs.

Solution

a) Determine the y-value in the second column of the table. Then, complete the third column by taking the square root of the second column. Use the table of values to sketch the graphs of $y = f(x)$ and $y = \sqrt{f(x)}$. (Hint: You could graph $y = f(x)$ on your graphing calculator and then use the table function to complete the second column of the table.)

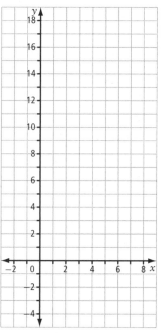

x	$y = 4x - 3$	$y = \sqrt{4x - 3}$
0	-3	$\sqrt{-3}$ (undefined)
0.75		
0.8		
1		
2		
3		
5		

b) From your table of values, determine the points of intersection:

(_____, 0); (_____, 1)

How is the x-intercept of the graph of $y = 4x - 3$ related to the graph of the function $y = \sqrt{4x - 3}$?

Why are these points of intersection referred to as *invariant points*?

For which values of x is the graph of $y = \sqrt{4x - 3}$ above the graph of $y = 4x - 3$? How are these values related to the invariant points?

For which values of x is the graph of $y = \sqrt{4x - 3}$ below the graph of $y = 4x - 3$?

📖 To see a similar question, refer to Example 1 on pages 80–81 in *Pre-Calculus 12*.

Working Example 2: Explore the Domains and Ranges of Functions and Their Square Roots

Find the domain and range for $y = x^2 + x - 5$ and $y = \sqrt{x^2 + x - 5}$.

Solution

To find the domain and range of the quadratic function $y = x^2 + x - 5$, graph the function using graphing technology and identify the minimum value.

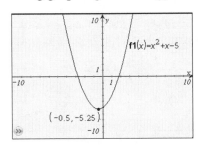

The graph shows that the function extends to the left and right infinitely. So, the domain of the function is

_____.

The function opens upward and has a minimum value of

_____, so the range of this function is _____.

When considering the domain and range of $y = \sqrt{x^2 + x - 5}$, remember that you cannot take

the square root of a _____ number. So, you can only find the square root of this
        (negative or *positive)*

function when $x^2 + x - 5$ _____ 0.
                    (≤ or ≥)

To find the values for which $y = x^2 + x - 5$ are positive, determine the values of the zeros of the function or the x-intercepts of the graph.

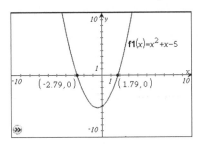

The x-intercepts are approximately _____ and

_____. Therefore, the domain of $y = \sqrt{x^2 + x - 5}$ is

_____. The range is _____.

Check the domain and range of $y = \sqrt{x^2 + x - 5}$ by graphing the equation on a graphing calculator and examining the graph. How does this graphing screen confirm the domain and range you determined?

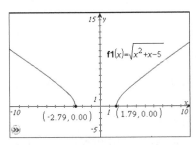

To see a similar question, refer to Example 2 on pages 82–83 in *Pre-Calculus 12*.

Working Example 3: Graph the Square Root for a Function From the Graph of the Function

Given the graph of $y = f(x)$, sketch the graph of $y = \sqrt{f(x)}$.

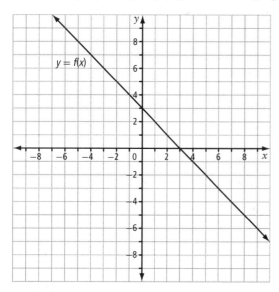

When graphing the square root of a function, what is the significance of the points where $f(x) = 0$ and $f(x) = 1$?

Solution

Create a table of values using the graph of the function.

- First consider the invariant points on $y = f(x)$. Add these to the table.
- Locate any key points on $f(x)$ that are greater than $y = 1$. Add these values to your table.
- Complete the third column of the table by taking the square root of the y-values.

x	y	$\sqrt{y}$

On the same grid as the graph of $y = f(x)$ above,

- plot the invariant points of $y = f(x)$
- draw a smooth curve between the invariant points, and above the graph of $f(x)$
- plot $\sqrt{y}$ for the key points you identified in your table of values, and draw a smooth curve between these points

To see a similar question, refer to Example 3 on pages 84–85 in *Pre-Calculus 12*.

Check Your Understanding

Practise

1. For each point on the graph of $y = f(x)$, determine the corresponding point on the graph $y = \sqrt{f(x)}$. Round answers to the nearest tenth, if necessary.

a) (3, 0) ~~Put in for f(x)~~

$y = \sqrt{0}$
$y = 0$

b) (−5, 25)

$y = \sqrt{25}$
$y = 5$ (−5, 5)

c) (9, 15)

$y = \sqrt{15}$
$y =$

d) (4, −16)

2. Graph $y = f(x)$ and $y = \sqrt{f(x)}$ for the given function.

a) $f(x) = 3 - 2x$

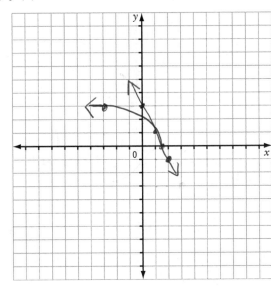

$f(x) = \sqrt{3 - 2x}$

y int.   slope −2

x-int.

$3 - 2x = 0$
$-2x = -3$
$x = 3/2$

$y = 3 - 2(1)$
$y = 1$
(1, 1)

$y = \sqrt{3 - 2(-3)}$
$y = \sqrt{9}$
$y = 3$
(−3, 3)

b) $f(x) = x^2 - 5$

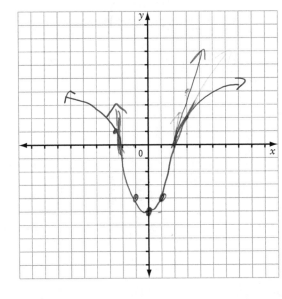

$f(x) = x^2 - 5$
parabola that opens up at (0, 5)

$y = 1^2 - 5$
$y = -4$
(1, −4)

$y = \sqrt{x^2 - 5}$
$y =$

3. Match each graph of $y = f(x)$ with the corresponding graph, $y = \sqrt{f(x)}$.

a)

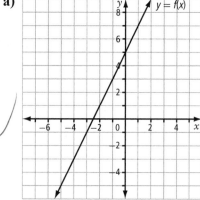

b)

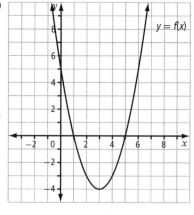

c)

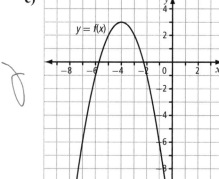

d)

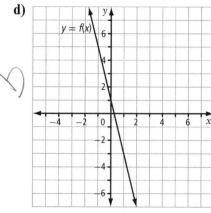

A

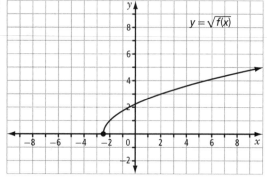

B

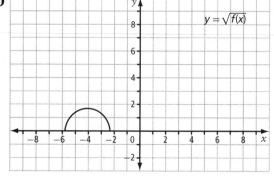

C

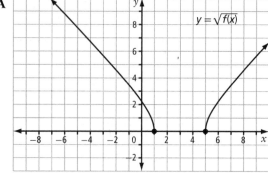

D

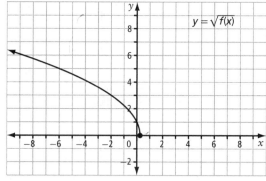

any straight line = XER, YER

$\frac{x^2 + 2 \geq 0}{x^2 \geq -2}$ (crossed out)

4. State the domain and range of $y = f(x)$ and $y = \sqrt{f(x)}$.

a) $f(x) = 2x - 4$

D: $\{x \mid x \in R\}$

R: $\{y \mid y \in R\}$

$y = \sqrt{2x-4}$

$2x - 4 \geq 0$

$2x \geq 4$

$x \geq 2$

$x \mid x \geq 2$

$y \mid y \geq 0$

b) $f(x) = x^2 + 2$

D: $\{x \mid x \in R\}$

R: $\{y \mid y \geq 2\}$

$y = \sqrt{x^2 + 2}$

D: $\{x \mid x \in R\}$ (with crossed out text)

R: $\{y \mid y \geq \sqrt{2}\}$

c) $f(x) = x^2 - 4$

D: $\{x \mid x \in R\}$

R: $\{y \mid y \geq -4\}$

d) $f(x) = -x^2 + 3$ *opens down*

V. $x \in R$

$y \leq 3$

Apply

5. Given the graph of $y = f(x)$, sketch the graph of $y = \sqrt{f(x)}$ on the same grid.

a)

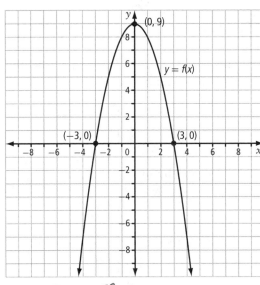

$SP(0,9)$ $y = x^2 + 9$

$(3,0)$ $0 = (3)^2 + 9$

$(3,0)$ $-9 = 9a$

$(3,0)$ $-1 = a$

$y = -x^2 + 9$

$y = \sqrt{-x^2 + 9}$

b)

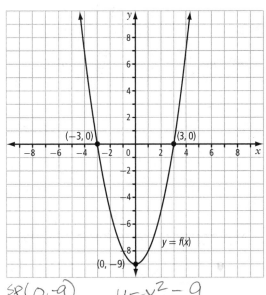

$SP(0,-9)$ $y = x^2 - 9$

$0 = (3)^2 - 9$

$9 = 9a$

$1 = a$

$y = x^2 - 9$

$y = \sqrt{x^2 - 9}$ ← *put in original points for new points*

Connect

6. Explain why the points where $f(x) = 0$ and $f(x) = 1$ are always invariant points when graphing the square root of a function.

7. Conal uses his graphing calculator to graph the functions $f(x) = 3x + 2$ and $f(x) = \sqrt{3x + 2}$. He produces the graph shown here.

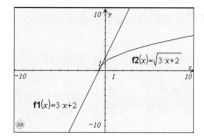

From his graph, Conal claims that $3x + 2 \geq \sqrt{3x + 2}$.

a) Using your knowledge of radical functions, explain why Conal is mistaken.

b) Describe two graphing strategies that Conal could use to redraw the functions so that it is clear that $3x + 2$ is not greater than $\sqrt{3x + 2}$ for all x-values.

c) Using one of your strategies described in part b), graph the functions so that the x-values for which $3x + 2$ is not greater than $\sqrt{3x + 2}$ are clear. Sketch the graphs below.

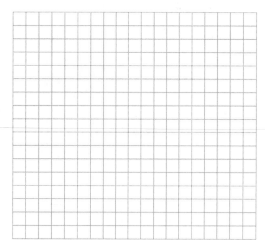

KEY IDEAS

Strategy for Solving Algebraically

Step 1: List any restrictions for the variable. You cannot take the square root of a negative number, so the value of the variable must be such that any operations under the radical sign result in a positive value.

Step 2: Isolate the radical and square both sides of the equation to eliminate the radical. Then, solve for x.

Step 3: Find the roots of the equation (that is, the value(s) of x that make the equation have a value of zero).

Step 4: Check the solution, ensuring that it does not contain *extraneous roots* (solutions that do not satisfy the original equation or restrictions when substituted in the original equation).

Example:

$7 = \sqrt{12 - x} + 4,\ x \le 12$	Identify restrictions.
$3 = \sqrt{12 - x}$	Isolate the radical.
$3^2 = (\sqrt{12 - x})^2$	Square both sides.
$9 = 12 - x$	Solve for x.
$3 = x$	

Check:
Solution meets the restrictions.

$7 = \sqrt{12 - 3} + 4$
$7 = \sqrt{9} + 4$
$7 = 7$

Strategies for Solving Graphically

- **Method 1: Graph a Single Equation**

  Graph the corresponding function and find the zero(s) of the function.

  Example:

  $$2 + \sqrt{x + 4} = x + 6$$
  $$\sqrt{x + 4} - x - 4 = 0$$

  Graph $y = \sqrt{x + 4} - x - 4$.

  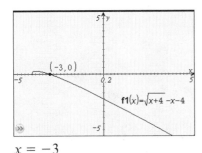

  $x = -3$

- **Method 2: Graph Two Equations**

  Graph each side of the equation on the same grid, and find the point(s) of intersection.

  Example:
  $$2 + \sqrt{x + 4} = x + 6$$

  Graph $y = 2 + \sqrt{x + 4}$ and $y = x + 6$.

  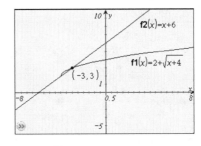

  $x = -3$

Working Example 1: Relate Roots and *x*-Intercepts

Consider $2\sqrt{x-4} - 3 = 0$.

a) Determine the roots algebraically.

b) Graph the corresponding function and determine the *x*-intercepts.

c) Compare the roots of the equation to the *x*-intercepts of the graph of the corresponding function.

Solution

a) Begin by stating the restrictions for the variable.

You cannot take the square root of a negative number, so in the equation $2\sqrt{x-4} - 3 = 0$,

(_____) ≥ 0. Therefore, $x \geq$ _____.

$$2\sqrt{x-4} - 3 = 0$$

$2\sqrt{x-4} - 3 +$ _____ = _____

$2\sqrt{x-4} =$ _____   Isolate the radical.

$4($_____$) = 3^2$ Square both sides.

_____ − _____ $= 9$

$4x = 9 +$ _____   Solve.

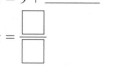

The solution is $x =$ _____.

> How can you check your solution?

b) Rewrite the equation as $y = 2\sqrt{x-4} - 3$.

Then, enter the equation into your graphing calculator.

Graph the function and determine the root, or _____.

The function has a single *x*-intercept at $x =$ _____.

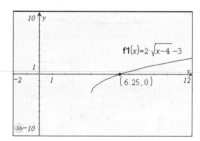

c) The root that was determined algebraically is equal to the _____ of the graph of the function $y = 2\sqrt{x-4} - 3$.

📖 To see a similar question, refer to Example 1 on page 91 in *Pre-Calculus 12*.

Working Example 2: Explore a Radical Equation Involving an Extraneous Root

Solve the equation $3 + \sqrt{x - 1} = x$ algebraically.

Solution

a) State the restrictions for the variable: _____.

> What restriction have you identified? Why are there only restrictions for the variable under the radical?

$$3 + \sqrt{x - 1} = x$$

$3 - \underline{\hspace{1.5cm}} + \sqrt{x - 1} = x - \underline{\hspace{1.5cm}}$ Isolate the radical.

$\sqrt{x - 1} = \underline{\hspace{2.5cm}}$

$(\sqrt{x - 1})^2 = (x - \underline{\hspace{1cm}})^2$ Square both sides.

$x - 1 = (x - \underline{\hspace{1cm}})(x - \underline{\hspace{1cm}})$

$0 = x^2 - \underline{\hspace{1.5cm}} x + \underline{\hspace{1.5cm}} - x + 1$ Equate to 0.

$0 = x^2 - \underline{\hspace{1.5cm}} x + \underline{\hspace{1cm}}$ Combine like terms.

$0 = (x - \underline{\hspace{1cm}})(x - \underline{\hspace{1cm}})$ Factor and solve.

$(x - \underline{\hspace{1.5cm}}) = 0$ or $(x - \underline{\hspace{1.5cm}}) = 0$

$x = \underline{\hspace{1cm}}$ $x = \underline{\hspace{1cm}}$

Check against the restriction and by substituting the value(s) in the original equation.

For $x = $ _____

Left Side	Right Side

For $x = $ _____

Left Side	Right Side

Left Side _____ Right Side
(= or ≠)

Left Side _____ Right Side
(= or ≠)

The root $x = $ _____ does not satisfy the original equation, so it is

an _____ root.

📖 To see a similar question, refer to Example 2 on pages 92 in *Pre-Calculus 12*.

Working Example 3: Approximate Solutions to Radical Equations

a) Solve $4 + \sqrt{x + 4} = x - 4$ graphically.

b) Verify the solution algebraically.

Solution

a) There are two methods to solving a radical equation graphically.

Method 1: Use a Single Function and Find the x-Intercept(s)

Begin by stating the restrictions: $x \geq$ _____.
Then, equate the function to 0.

$$4 + \sqrt{x + 4} = x - 4$$

$$\text{_____} - \text{_____} + 4 + \sqrt{x + 4} = x - 4 + \text{_____} - \text{_____}$$

$$\text{_____} - \text{_____} + \sqrt{x + 4} = 0$$

Enter the left-hand side of the equation into a graphing

calculator. Then determine the _____.

Sketch the resulting graph on the grid.

The solution to the equation $4 + \sqrt{x + 4} = x - 4$ is _____.

Method 2: Use a System of Two Functions and Find the Point of Intersection

Enter the left-hand side of the equation, $4 + \sqrt{x + 4}$, into your graphing calculator. Then, enter the right-hand side of the equation, $x - 4$. Graph the equations on the same

axes and determine the _____. Sketch your graph on the grid.

The x-value of the _____ is $x =$ _____.

b) Check the solution algebraically by substituting it into the original equation:

$$4 + \sqrt{\text{_____} + 4} = \text{_____} - 4$$

$$4 + \sqrt{\text{_____}} = \text{_____}$$

$$4 + \text{_____} = \text{_____}$$

The solution, $x =$ _____, is correct.

📖 To see a similar question, refer to Example 3 on pages 93–94 in *Pre-Calculus 12*.

Check Your Understanding

Practise

plug in y = 0

1. Determine the root(s) of each equation algebraically.

   a) $y = \sqrt{x + 3} - 5$

   $0 = \sqrt{x+3} - 5$
   $(5)^2 = (\sqrt{x+3})^2$
   $25 = x + 3$
   $x = 22$

   b) $y = -\sqrt{x + 6} + 7$

   $0 = -\sqrt{x+6} + 7$
   $(-7)^2 = (-\sqrt{x+6})^2$
   $49 = x + 6$
   $x = 43$

   c) $2\sqrt{x - 4} - 1 = 7$

   d) $\sqrt{x + 1} + 3 = 5$

2. Find the *x*-intercepts of each equation graphically. Include a sketch for each.

   a) $y = \sqrt{x - 2} - 1$

   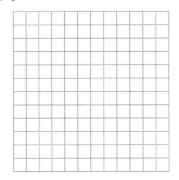

   b) $y = -\sqrt{x + 3} + 2$

   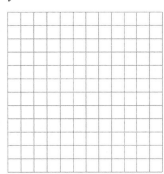

   c) $y = \sqrt{x + 5} - 2$

   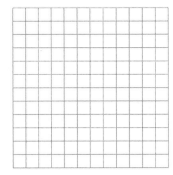

   d) $y = -\sqrt{x + 2} - 2$

   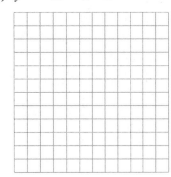

3. Identify any restrictions on the variables. Then, use technology to solve each equation graphically. Sketch the graph on the grid.

a) $\sqrt{x + 2} - 4 = -2$

$y_1 \qquad y_2$

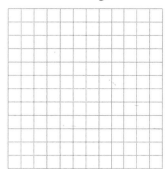

b) $\sqrt{x - 5} = 3$

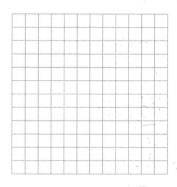

c) $3\sqrt{1 - x} = 12$

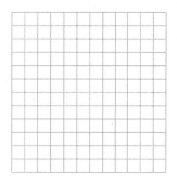

d) $-2\sqrt{1 - 4x} = -6$

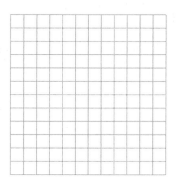

$(x - 2)(x - 2)$
$x^2 - 2x \quad 2x + 4$

4. Identify any restrictions on the variables. Then, solve each equation algebraically.

a) $x = \sqrt{x + 10} + 2$

$x \geq 10$

$(x - 2)^2 = (\sqrt{x + 10})^2$

$x^2 - 4x + 4 = x + 10$

$x^2 - 5x - 6 = 0$

$(x + 1)(x - 6) = 0$

$x \neq 1 \qquad x = 6$

b) $x + 2 = \sqrt{-6x - 12}$

c) $x - 4 = \sqrt{-x + 4}$

d) $x = \sqrt{-5x + 26} + 4$

Apply

5. The equation $\sqrt{2x-5} + 4 = 1$ has no solution.

a) Verify algebraically.

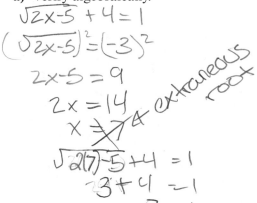

$$\sqrt{2x-5} + 4 = 1$$
$$(\sqrt{2x-5})^2 = (-3)^2$$
$$2x-5 = 9$$
$$2x = 14$$
$$x = 7 \quad \text{extraneous root}$$

$$\sqrt{2(7)-5} + 4 = 1$$
$$-3 + 4 = 1$$
$$1 = 1 ✗$$

b) Verify graphically.

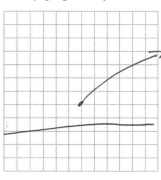

6. Use what you know about the graph of the base function $f(x) = \sqrt{x}$ and transformations. For each of the following, use a graphical method to solve the equation $f(x) = 0$.

a) $f(x) = \sqrt{x-4}$

$$0 = \sqrt{x-4}$$
$$0 = x-4$$
$$x = 4$$
$$(4, 0)$$
translated 4 right

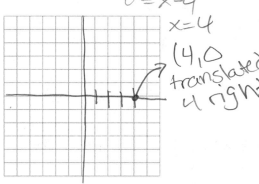

b) $f(x) = \sqrt{x} - 3$

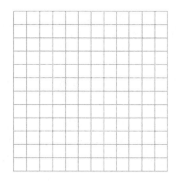

c) $f(x) = -\sqrt{x} + 1$

d) $f(x) = \sqrt{-x} - 3$

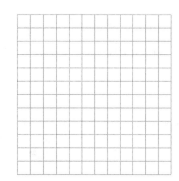

Connect

7. Create a radical function of the form $y = \sqrt{bx} + k$ with a zero of $x = 8$ that passes through $(2, -2)$.

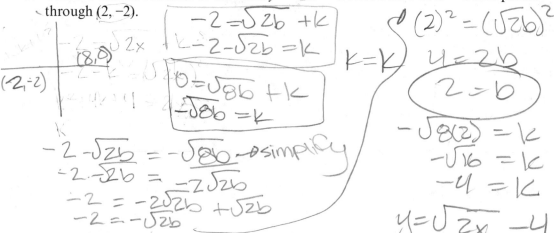

$$-2 = \sqrt{2b} + k$$
$$k = -2 - \sqrt{2b} = k$$

$$0 = \sqrt{8b} + k$$
$$-\sqrt{8b} = k$$

$$-2 - \sqrt{2b} = -\sqrt{8b} \rightarrow simplify$$
$$-2 - \sqrt{2b} = \frac{-\sqrt{8b}}{-2\sqrt{2b}}$$
$$-2 = -2\sqrt{2b} + \sqrt{2b}$$
$$-2 = -\sqrt{2b}$$

$$(2)^2 = (\sqrt{2b})^2$$
$$k = k \quad 4 = 2b$$
$$\boxed{2 = b}$$

$$-\sqrt{8(2)} = k$$
$$-\sqrt{16} = k$$
$$-4 = k$$

$$y = \sqrt{2x} - 4$$

8. Amber solved the equation $\sqrt{3x - 1} - 4 = 1$ as follows:

$$\sqrt{3x - 1} - 4 = 1$$
$$(\sqrt{3x - 1})^2 - (4)^2 = (1)^2$$
$$3x - 1 - 16 = 1$$
$$3x - 17 = 1$$
$$3x = 18$$
$$x = 6$$

Identify and correct her error.

9. The equation $3 + \sqrt{2x + 7} = 1$ has no solution.

   a) Explain why it has no solution.

   b) Create another equation with no solution.

Chapter 2 Review

2.1 Radical Functions and Transformations, pages 39–46

1. Explain how to transform the graph of $y = \sqrt{x}$ to obtain the graph of each transformed function. Then, draw a sketch of the new function.

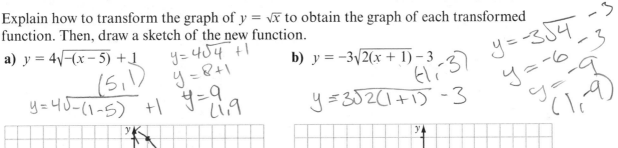

   a) $y = 4\sqrt{-(x-5)} + 1$

   b) $y = -3\sqrt{2(x+1)} - 3$

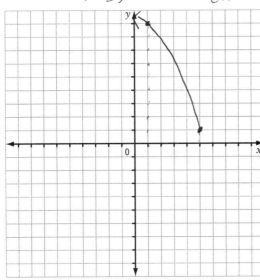

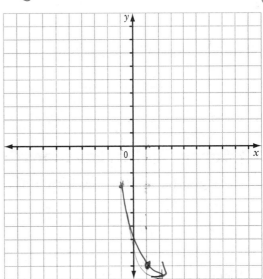

2. For each graph, write the equation of a radical function in the form $y = a\sqrt{b(x-h)} + k$. State the domain and range.

   a)

   b)

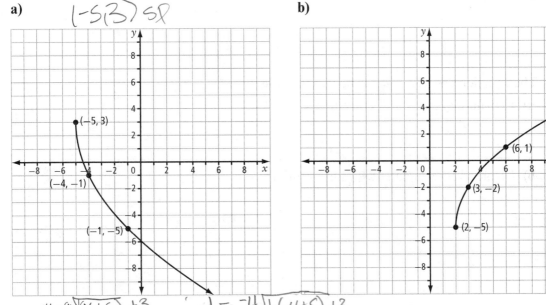

2.2 Square Root of a Function, pages 47–54

3. Use technology to graph $y = \sqrt{f(x)}$ given the following functions. Sketch the graph on the grid. State the domain and range.

a) $f(x) = 4x - 1$

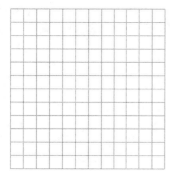

b) $f(x) = x^2 - 9$

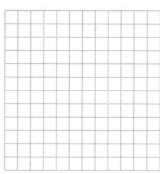

2.3 Solving Radical Equations Graphically, pages 55–62

4. Determine the root(s) of each radical equation algebraically.

a) $0 = \sqrt{x - 2} - 3$

b) $x = \sqrt{x - 2} + 4$

5. Identify any restrictions on the variables. Then, solve each radical equation graphically.

a) $\sqrt{x - 1} - 5 = -2$

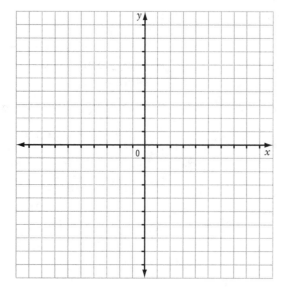

b) $\sqrt{x + 3} = -1$

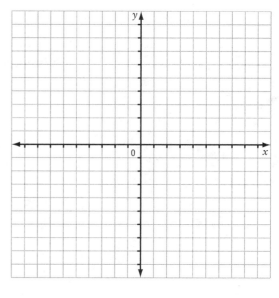

Chapter 2 Skills Organizer

Complete the graphic organizer for the concepts learned in Chapter 2. Fill in each box with notes and examples.

Definition	Example	Base Function: Graph and Characteristics

How to Solve Algebraically	How to Solve Graphically

Extraneous Roots	Restrictions	Graphing Using Transformations

Chapter 3 Polynomial Functions

3.1 Characteristics of Polynomial Functions

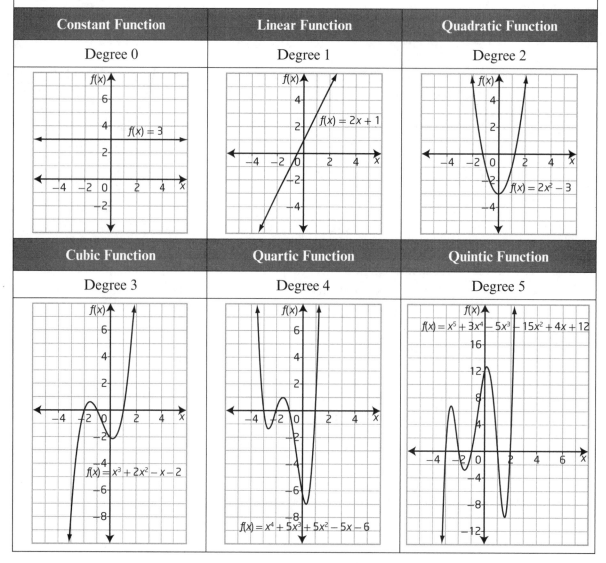

> ### KEY IDEAS
>
> **What Is a Polynomial Function?**
> A polynomial function has the form $f(x) = a_n x^n + a_{n-1}x^{n-1} + a_{n-2}x^{n-2} + \cdots + a_2 x^2 + a_1 x + a_0$
> where
> - n is a whole number
> - x is a variable
> - the coefficients a_n to a_0 are real numbers
> - the degree of the polynomial function is n, the exponent of the greatest power of x
> - the leading coefficient is a_n, the coefficient of the greatest power of x
> - the constant term is a_0

Types of Polynomial Functions

Constant Function	Linear Function	Quadratic Function
Degree 0	Degree 1	Degree 2
$f(x) = 3$	$f(x) = 2x + 1$	$f(x) = 2x^2 - 3$

Cubic Function	Quartic Function	Quintic Function
Degree 3	Degree 4	Degree 5
$f(x) = x^3 + 2x^2 - x - 2$	$f(x) = x^4 + 5x^3 + 5x^2 - 5x - 6$	$f(x) = x^5 + 3x^4 - 5x^3 - 15x^2 + 4x + 12$

Characteristics of Polynomial Functions

Graphs of Odd-Degree Polynomial Functions

- extend from quadrant III to quadrant I when the leading coefficient is positive, similar to the graph of $y = x$

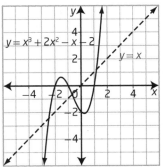

- extend from quadrant II to IV when the leading coefficient is negative, similar to the graph of $y = -x$

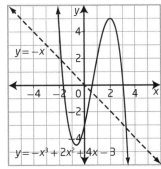

- have at least one x-intercept to a maximum of n x-intercepts, where n is the degree of the function
- have y-intercept a_0, the constant term of the function
- have domain $\{x \mid x \in R\}$ and range $\{y \mid y \in R\}$
- have no maximum or minimum values

Graphs of Even-Degree Polynomial Functions

- open upward and extend from quadrant II to quadrant I when the leading coefficient is positive, similar to the graph of $y = x^2$

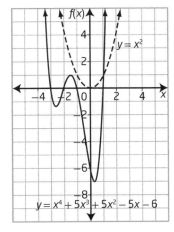

- open downward and extend from quadrant III to IV when the leading coefficient is negative, similar to the graph of $y = -x^2$

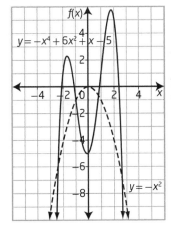

- have from 0 to a maximum of n x-intercepts, where n is the degree of the function
- have y-intercept a_0, the constant term of the function
- have domain $\{x \mid x \in R\}$; the range depends on the maximum or minimum value of the function
- have a maximum or minimum value

Working Example 1: Identify Polynomial Functions

Which of these functions are polynomials? Justify your answer. State the degree, the leading coefficient, and the constant term of each polynomial function.

a) $g(x) = 4^x$

b) $h(x) = 6 - 5x^3$

c) $y = x^{-2} + 1$

d) $y = \sqrt[3]{x} - 2$

Solution

a) $g(x) = 4^x$

The function $g(x) = 4^x$ _____ a polynomial function.
                           (is or is not)

It is an _____ function.

The base of 4^x is a _____ and the exponent is a _____, so it is not of the form x^n.

b) $h(x) = 6 - 5x^3$

The function $h(x) = 6 - 5x^3$ _____ a polynomial function.
                               (is or is not)

The leading coefficient is _____, the degree is _____, and the constant term is _____.

c) $y = x^{-2} + 1$

The function $y = x^{-2} + 1$ _____ a polynomial function.
                              (is or is not)

x^{-2} is the same as _____, because the exponent is negative.

The function $y = x^{-2} + 1$ is a _____ function.

d) $y = \sqrt[3]{x} - 2$

The function $y = \sqrt[3]{x} - 2$ _____ a polynomial function.
                                   (is or is not)

$\sqrt[3]{x}$ can be rewritten as _____, which has a _____ exponent.

The function $y = \sqrt[3]{x} - 2$ is a _____ function.

Working Example 2: Match a Polynomial Function With Its Graph

For each polynomial function, identify the following characteristics:
- the type of function and whether it is of even or odd degree
- the end behaviour of the graph of the function
- the number of possible x-intercepts
- whether the graph has a maximum or minimum value
- the y-intercept

Then, match each function to its corresponding graph.

a) $f(x) = 2x^3 - 4x^2 + x + 2$

b) $g(x) = -x^4 + 10x^2 + 5x - 6$

c) $h(x) = -2x^5 + 5x^3 - x + 1$

d) $p(x) = x^4 - 5x^3 + 16$

A
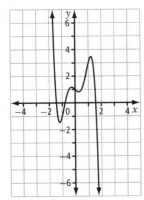

B
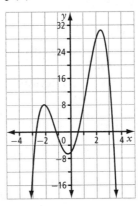

C
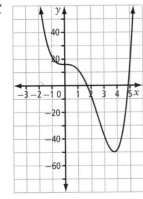

D
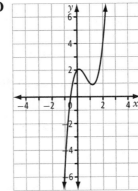

Solution

a) $f(x) = 2x^3 - 4x^2 + x + 2$ has degree _____, so it is an _____ function.
                                                                  (*even* or *odd*)

This is a _____ polynomial function.
(*constant* or *linear* or *quadratic* or *cubic* or *quartic* or *quintic*)

Its graph has at least _____ x-intercept(s) and at most _____ x-intercepts.

The leading coefficient is _____, so the graph of the function extends from
                              (*positive* or *negative*)

quadrant _____ into quadrant _____.

Since the degree is _____, this function _____ a maximum or minimum value.
     (*even* or *odd*)   (*has* or *does not have*)

The graph has a y-intercept of _____.

This function corresponds to graph _____.
           (*A* or *B* or *C* or *D*)

b) $g(x) = -x^4 + 10x^2 + 5x - 6$ has degree _____, so it is an _____ function.
                   (*even* or *odd*)

This is a _____ polynomial function.

Its graph has at least _____ x-intercept(s) and at most _____ x-intercepts.

Since the leading coefficient is _____, the graph of the function opens _____
       (*positive* or *negative*)   (*upward* or *downward*)

and has a _____ value.
  (*maximum* or *minimum*)

The graph has a y-intercept of _____.

This function corresponds to graph _____.

c) $h(x) = -2x^5 + 5x^3 - x + 1$ has degree _____, so it is an _____ function.
                  (*even* or *odd*)

This is a _____ polynomial function.

Its graph has at least _____ x-intercept(s) and at most _____ x-intercepts.

The leading coefficient is _____, so the graph of the function extends from
       (*positive* or *negative*)

quadrant _____ into quadrant _____.

Since the degree is _____, this function _____ a maximum or minimum value.
     (*even* or *odd*)   (*has* or *does not have*)

The graph has a y-intercept of _____.

This function corresponds to graph _____.

d) $p(x) = x^4 - 5x^3 + 16$ has degree _____, so it is an _____ function.
              (*even* or *odd*)

This is a _____ polynomial function.

Its graph has at least _____ x-intercept(s) and at most _____ x-intercepts.

The leading coefficient is _____, so the graph of the function opens _____
       (*positive* or *negative*)   (*upward* or *downward*)

and has a _____ value.
  (*maximum* or *minimum*)

The graph has a y-intercept of _____.

This function corresponds to graph _____.

Working Example 3: Application of a Polynomial Function

An antibacterial spray is tested on a bacterial culture. The population, P, of bacteria t minutes after the spray is applied is modelled by the function $P(t) = -2t^3 - 2t^2 + 3t + 800$.

a) What is the population of the bacteria 3 min after the spray is applied?

b) How many bacteria were in the culture before the spray was applied?

c) What is the population of the bacteria 8 min after the spray is applied? Why is this not realistic for this situation? Explain.

Solution

a) Substitute $t =$ _____ into the function and evaluate the result.

$$P(\underline{\hspace{1cm}}) = -2(\underline{\hspace{1cm}})^3 - 2(\underline{\hspace{1cm}})^2 + 3(\underline{\hspace{1cm}}) + 800$$

$$= \underline{\hspace{1cm}}$$

After 3 min there are _____ bacteria in the culture.

See page 112 of *Pre-Calculus 12* for a different method of solving this question.

b) The number of bacteria before the spray was applied occurs when $t =$ _____.

This is the _____-intercept of the graph.

It is the _____ term of the function.
　　　　(*constant* or *variable*)

There were _____ bacteria before the spray was applied.

c) Substitute $t =$ _____ into the function and evaluate the result.

$$P(\underline{\hspace{1cm}}) = -2(\underline{\hspace{1cm}})^3 - 2(\underline{\hspace{1cm}})^2 + 3(\underline{\hspace{1cm}}) + 800$$

$$= \underline{\hspace{1cm}}$$

After 8 min there are _____ bacteria in the culture.

It is not realistic for the number of bacteria to be _____.
　　　　　　　　　　　　　　　　　　　(*positive* or *negative*)

This means that the spray has worked and there are _____ bacteria remaining.

Check Your Understanding

Practise

1. Determine whether each function is a polynomial function. Justify your answers.

   a) $f(x) = 2x^4 - 3x + 2$

   The degree is _____, which is an _____ number.

   $f(x)$ _____ a polynomial function.
      (*is* or *is not*)

   b) $y = 3^x + 5$

   The term 3^x means this is an _____ function.

   This function _____ a polynomial function.
          (*is* or *is not*)

   c) $g(x) = 9$

   $g(x)$ has degree _____.

   This function _____ a polynomial function.
          (*is* or *is not*)

   d) $y = x^{-2} + 7x^3 + 1$

2. Complete the table for each polynomial function.

Polynomial Function	Degree	Type	Leading Coefficient	Constant Term
a) $f(x) = 6x^3 - 5x^2 + 2x - 8$	3			
b) $y = -2x^5 + 5x^3 + x^2 + 1$		Quintic		
c) $g(x) = x^3 - 7x^4$				0
d) $p(x) = 10x - 9$				
e) $y = -0.5x^2 + 4x + 3$				
f) $h(x) = 3x^4 - 8x^3 + x^2 + 2$			3	
g) $y = -5$		Constant		

3. For each graph of a polynomial function,
   • determine whether the function has odd or even degree
   • determine whether the leading coefficient is positive or negative
   • state the number of x-intercepts
   • state the domain and range

   a) $f(x) = -x^3 - x^2 + 5x - 3$

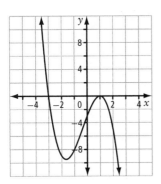

   The graph extends from quadrant _____ to quadrant _____.

   The function has _____ degree.

   The leading coefficient is _____.

   There are _____ x-intercepts.

   Domain: _____

   Range: _____

   b)

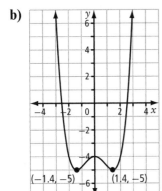

   c)

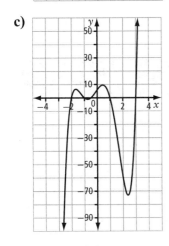

4. For each function, use the degree and the sign of the leading coefficient to describe the end behaviour of its graph. State the possible number of x-intercepts and the value of the y-intercept.

a) $g(x) = 4x^5 - x^3 + 3x^2 - 6x + 2$

The degree is _____ with a _____ leading coefficient.

The graph extends from quadrant _____ to quadrant _____.

There are a maximum of _____ x-intercepts. The y-intercept is _____.

b) $y = -x^4 - 2x^5 + x^3 - 3x^2 + x$

c) $h(x) = x - 7x^3 - 6$

d) $y = 3x^5 - 2x^4 + 5x^3 - x^2 + x + 3$

e) $p(x) = 5x^4 - 6x - 1$

Apply

5. Sonja claims that all graphs of polynomial functions of the form $y = ax^n + x + b$, where a, n, and b are odd integers, extend from quadrant II to quadrant IV. Do you agree? Use examples to explain your answer.

6. A skateboard manufacturer determines that its profit, P, in dollars, can be modelled by the function $P(x) = 1000x + 1.25x^4 - 3200$, where x represents the number, in hundreds, of skateboards sold.

a) What is the degree of the function $P(x)$?

b) What are the leading coefficient and the constant of this function? What does the constant represent in this context?

c) Describe the end behaviour of the graph of this function.

d) What are the restrictions on the domain of this function? Explain how you determined those restrictions.

e) What do the x-intercept(s) of the graph represent in this context?

f) What is the profit from the sale of 1200 skateboards?

7. Ali moves forward and backward along a straight path. Ali's distance, D, in metres, from a tree is modelled by the function $D(t) = t^3 - 12t^2 + 36t + 5$, where t represents the time, in seconds.

a) What is the degree of function $D(t)$?

b) What are the leading coefficient and the constant of this function? What does the constant represent in this situation?

c) Describe the end behaviour of the graph of this function.

d) What are the restrictions on the domain of this function? Explain how you determined the restrictions.

e) How far is Ali from the tree after 7 s?

f) Sketch the function. Then, graph the function using technology. How does the graph compare to your sketch?

8. By analysing the effect of growing economic conditions, the predicted population, P, of a town in t years from now can be modelled by the function $P(t) = 6t^4 - 6t^3 + 200t + 12\ 000$. Assume this model can be used for the next 15 years.

a) What are the key features of the graph of this function?

b) What is the current population of this town?

c) What will the population be 10 years from now?

d) When will the population of the town be approximately 175 000?

Connect

9. On each set of axes, sketch a polynomial function with the given characteristics.

a) A polynomial function with degree 3, a positive leading coefficient, and 2 *x*-intercepts.

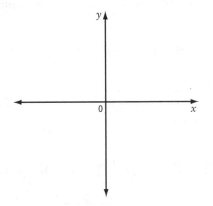

b) A polynomial function with degree 4, a negative leading coefficient, and 4 *x*-intercepts.

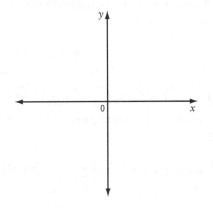

c) A polynomial function with degree 5, a negative leading coefficient, and 3 *x*-intercepts.

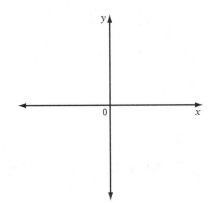

d) A polynomial function with degree 4, a positive leading coefficient, and 2 *x*-intercepts.

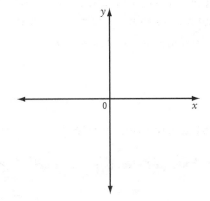

> ## KEY IDEAS
>
> **Long Division**
> You can use long division to divide a polynomial by a binomial: $\dfrac{P(x)}{x-a} = Q(x) + \dfrac{R}{x-a}$
>
> The components of long division are
> - the dividend, $P(x)$, which is the polynomial that is being divided
> - the divisor, $x - a$, which is the binomial that the polynomial is divided by
> - the quotient, $Q(x)$, which is the expression that results from the division
> - the remainder, R, which is the value or expression that is left over after dividing
>
> To check the division of a polynomial, verify the statement $P(x) = (x - a)Q(x) + R$.
>
> **Synthetic Division**
> - a short form of division that uses only the coefficients of the terms
> - it involves fewer calculations
>
> **Remainder Theorem**
> - When a polynomial $P(x)$ is divided by a binomial $x - a$, the remainder is $P(a)$.
> - If the remainder is 0, then the binomial $x - a$ is a factor of $P(x)$.
> - If the remainder is *not* 0, then the binomial $x - a$ is *not* a factor of $P(x)$.

Working Example 1: Divide a Polynomial by a Binomial of the Form $x - a$

a) Divide $P(x) = 9x + 4x^3 - 12$ by $x + 2$. Express the result in the form $\dfrac{P(x)}{x-a} = Q(x) + \dfrac{R}{x-a}$.

b) Identify any restrictions on the variable.

c) Write the corresponding statement that can be used to check the division.

Solution

a) $x + 2\overline{)4x^3 + 0x^2 + 9x - 12}$

> Why is the order of the terms different?
> Why is it necessary to include the term $0x^2$?

> 📖 See Example 1 on page 120 of *Pre-Calculus 12* for help with long division.

$$\frac{4x^3 + 9x - 12}{x + 2} = \underline{\hspace{5cm}}$$

b) Since division by _____ is not defined, the divisor cannot be _____:

$x + 2 \neq$ _____ or $x \neq$ _____.

c) The corresponding statement that can be used to check the division is

_____ = _____.

Working Example 2: Apply Polynomial Division to Solve a Problem

The volume, V, in cubic centimetres, of gift boxes is given by $V(x) = 2x^3 + x^2 - 27x - 36$. The height, h, in centimetres, is $x + 3$. What are the possible dimensions of the boxes in terms of x?

Solution

Divide the volume of the box by the height to obtain an expression for the area of the base of the box.

$x + 3 \overline{)2x^3 + x^2 - 27x - 36}$

$\boxed{\dfrac{V(x)}{h} = lw, \text{ where } lw \text{ is the area of the base}}$

Since the remainder is _____, express the volume $2x^3 + x^2 - 27x - 36$ as (_____)

(_____).

The quotient _____ represents the area of the base.

This expression can be factored as _____.

The factors represent the possible _____ and _____ of the base.

Expressions for the dimensions, in centimetres, are _____, _____, and _____.

Working Example 3: Divide a Polynomial Using Synthetic Division

a) Use synthetic division to divide $5x^2 - x + 2x^3 - 6$ by $x + 2$.

b) Check your results using long division.

Solution

a) Write the terms of the dividend in order of _____ powers.
            (*ascending* or *descending*)

_____

Fill in the missing values and perform the division.

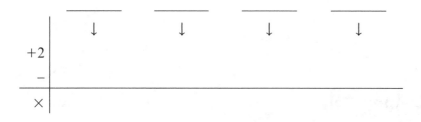

📖 See Example 3 on page 122 of *Pre-Calculus 12* for help with synthetic division.

$(2x^3 + 5x^2 - x - 6) \div (x + 2) =$ _____; Restriction: _____

b) $x + 2\overline{)2x^3 + 5x^2 - x - 6}$

The result obtained from long division is _____ that using

                                   (*the same as* or *different from*)

_____ division.

Working Example 4: Apply the Remainder Theorem

a) Use the remainder theorem to determine the remainder when $P(x) = 3x^4 - x^3 - 5$ is divided by $x - 3$.

b) Verify your answer using synthetic division.

Solution

a) Since the binomial is $x - 3$, determine the remainder by evaluating $P(x)$ at $x =$ _____,

or $P($_____$)$.

$P($_____$) = 3($_____$)^4 - ($_____$)^3 - 5$

     $=$ _____

> Why is it necessary to write the polynomial this way?

The remainder when $3x^4 - x^3 - 5$ is divided by $x - 3$ is _____.

b) To use synthetic division, first rewrite $P(x)$ as $P(x) =$ _____.

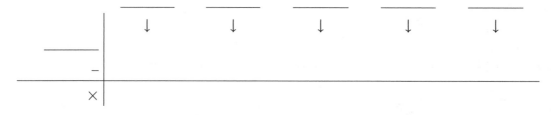

The remainder when using synthetic division is _____.

Check Your Understanding

Practise

1. **a)** Use long division to divide $x^3 + 3x^2 - 2x + 5$ by $x + 1$. Express the result in the form
$\dfrac{P(x)}{x-a} = Q(x) + \dfrac{R}{x-a}$.

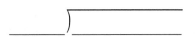

b) Identify any restrictions on the variable.

c) Write the corresponding statement that can be used to check the division. Then, verify your answer.

2. Divide using long division. Then, verify your answer using synthetic division.

   a) $(2x^2 - x + 5) \div (x + 3)$ **b)** $(x^3 - x - 10) \div (x + 4)$

c) $(3x^4 + 2x^3 - 6x + 1) \div x$ **d)** $(-4x^4 + 11x - 7) \div (x - 3)$

3. Express each result in #2 above in the form $\dfrac{P(x)}{x-a} = Q(x) + \dfrac{R}{x-a}$.

Identify any restrictions on the variable.

a) $\dfrac{2x^2 - x + 5}{x + 3}$ **b)**

c)   **d)**

4. Determine the remainder when each polynomial function is divided by $x - 2$. Use the remainder theorem.

a) $P(x) = 2x^3 + 3x^2 - 17x - 30$ **b)** $P(x) = x^3 + x^2 - 4x + 4$

5. Determine each remainder.

a) $(6x^2 - x + 15) \div (x + 1)$ **b)** $(x^3 - x^2 - 2x - 1) \div (x + 2)$

c) $(2x^3 - 5x^2 - 13x + 2) \div (x - 4)$ **d)** $(x^4 - 3x^2 - 5x + 2) \div (x - 2)$

Apply

6. For each dividend, determine the value of k if the remainder is -2.

   a) $(2x^3 - 5x^2 - 4x + k) \div (x + 1)$

   b) $(x^3 - 4x^2 + kx + 10) \div (x - 3)$

   c) $(3x^3 + kx^2 - 13x + 4) \div (x + 2)$

   d) $(kx^3 - 4x^2 - 5x + 8) \div (x - 2)$

7. For what value of m will the polynomial $P(x) = x^3 + 6x^2 + mx - 4$ have the same remainder when it is divided by $x - 1$ and $x + 2$?

   Since the remainder is the same, determine the value of m by solving $P(1) = P(\underline{\hspace{1cm}})$.

8. You can model the volume, in cubic centimetres, of a rectangular box by the polynomial function $V(x) = 3x^3 + x^2 - 12x - 4$. Determine expressions for the other dimensions of the box if the height is $x + 2$.

Connect

9. When the polynomial $bx^3 + cx^2 + dx + e$ is divided by $x - a$, the remainder is zero.

   a) What can you conclude from this result?

   b) Write an expression for the remainder in terms of a, b, c, d, and e.

KEY IDEAS

Factor Theorem
The factor theorem states that $x - a$ is a factor of a polynomial $P(x)$ if and only if $P(a) = 0$.
If and only if means that the result works both ways. That is,
- if $x - a$ is a factor then, $P(a) = 0$
- if $P(a) = 0$, then $x - a$ is a factor of a polynomial $P(x)$

Integral Zero Theorem
- The integral zero theorem describes the relationship between the factors and the constant term of a polynomial. The theorem states that if $x - a$ is a factor of a polynomial $P(x)$ with integral coefficients, then a is a factor of the constant term of $P(x)$ and $x = a$ is an integral zero of $P(x)$.

Factor by Grouping
- If a polynomial $P(x)$ has an even number of terms, it may be possible to group two terms at a time and remove a common factor. If the binomial that results from common factoring is the same for each pair of terms, then $P(x)$ may be factored by grouping.

Steps for Factoring Polynomial Functions
To factor polynomial functions using the factor theorem and the integral zero theorem,
- use the integral zero theorem to list possible integer values for the zeros
- next, apply the factor theorem to determine one factor
- then, use division to determine the remaining factor
- repeat the above steps until all factors are found

Working Example 1: Use the Factor Theorem to Test for Factors of a Polynomial

Which binomials are factors of the polynomial $P(x) = x^3 + 4x^2 + x - 6$? Justify your answers.

a) $x - 1$ **b)** $x - 2$ **c)** $x + 2$ **d)** $x + 3$

Solution

Use the factor theorem to evaluate $P(a)$ given $x - a$.

a) For $x - 1$, substitute $x = $ _____ into the polynomial expression.

$P(\underline{\hspace{1cm}}) = $

Since the remainder is _____, $x - 1$ _____ a factor of $P(x)$.

(is or *is not)*

b) For $x - 2$, substitute $x = $ _____ into the polynomial expression.

$P($ _____ $) = $

Since the remainder is _____, $x - 2$ _____ a factor of $P(x)$.
                                                    (*is* or *is not*)

c) For $x + 2$, substitute $x = $ _____ into the polynomial expression.

$P($ _____ $) = $

Since the remainder is _____, $x + 2$ _____ a factor of $P(x)$.
                                                    (*is* or *is not*)

d) For $x + 3$, substitute $x = $ _____ into the polynomial expression.

$P($ _____ $) = $

Since the remainder is _____, $x + 3$ _____ a factor of $P(x)$.
                                                    (*is* or *is not*)

Working Example 2: Factor Using the Integral Zero Theorem

a) Factor $2x^3 + 3x^2 - 3x - 2$ fully.

b) Describe how to use the factors of the polynomial expression to determine the zeros of the corresponding polynomial function.

Solution

a) Let $P(x) = $ _____. Find a factor by evaluating $P(x)$ for values of x that are

factors of _____ : _____ and _____.

Test the values until you find one that gives a remainder of zero.

$P($ _____ $) = $

Since $P($ _____ $) = 0$, _____ is a factor of $P(x)$.

Use synthetic or long division to find the other factors.

> Which method of division do you prefer? Why?

Therefore, $2x^3 + 3x^2 - 3x - 2 = ($ _____ $)($ _____ $)($ _____ $)$.

b) Since the factors of $2x^3 + 3x^2 - 3x - 2$ are _____, _____, and

_____, the corresponding zeros of the function are _____, _____, and

_____.

> For an explanation of how the zeros can be confirmed, refer to Example 2b) on page 130 of *Pre-Calculus 12*.

Working Example 3: Factor Higher–Degree Polynomials

Fully factor $x^4 + 3x^3 - 7x^2 - 27x - 18$.

Solution

Let $P(x) = $ _____.

Find a factor by testing factors of _____: _____.
Test the values until you find one that gives a remainder of zero.

$P($_____$) = $

Since $P($_____$) = 0$, _____ is a factor of $P(x)$.
Use division to find the other factors.

The remaining factor is _____.

Let $f(x) = $ _____.
Use the factor theorem again.

Since $f($_____$) = 0$, _____ is a second factor.
Use division to find the other factors.

Combine all the factors to write the fully factored form.

Therefore, $x^4 + 3x^3 - 7x^2 - 27x - 18 = $ _____.

> Compare this method with Method 2 of Example 3 on page 131 of *Pre-Calculus 12*. Is it possible to use factor by grouping in this situation? Explain.

Working Example 4: Solve Problems Involving Polynomial Expressions

An artist creates a carving from a block of soapstone. The soapstone is in the shape of a rectangular prism whose volume, in cubic feet, is represented by $V(x) = 6x^3 + 25x^2 + 2x - 8$, where x is a positive real number. What are the factors that represent possible dimensions, in terms of x, of the block of soapstone?

Solution

The possible integral factors correspond to the factors of the _____ term of the

polynomial, _____ : _____.

Use the factor theorem to determine which of these values correspond to the factors of the polynomial.

The values of x that result in a remainder of _____ are _____, and the

corresponding factors are _____.

The possible dimensions of the block of soapstone are _____.

> See Example 4 on page 132 of *Pre-Calculus 12* for another method of solving this problem.

Check Your Understanding

Practise

1. What is the corresponding binomial factor of a polynomial, $P(x)$, given the value of the zero?

a) $P(2) = 0$

b) $P(-4) = 0$

c) $P(b) = 0$

d) $P(-d) = 0$

2. Determine whether $x + 1$ is a factor of each polynomial.

a) $x^3 + x^2 - x - 1$

b) $x^4 - 3x^3 - 4x^2 + x + 1$

c) $2x^3 - x^2 - 3x - 1$

d) $4x^4 + 7x + 3$

3. State whether each polynomial has $x + 3$ as a factor.

a) $x^3 + x^2 - x + 6$

b) $2x^3 + 9x^2 + 10x + 3$

c) $x^3 + 27$

d) $x^4 - 9x^2 + 2x + 6$

4. What are the possible integral zeros of each polynomial?

a) $x^3 - 3x^2 + 4x - 16$

b) $x^3 + 2x^2 + 8x + 12$

c) $x^3 - 3x^2 + 10x - 32$

d) $x^4 + 8x^3 - 9x^2 + 2x + 18$

5. Factor fully.

a) $x^3 - x^2 - 4x + 4$

b) $x^3 - 2x^2 - 4x + 8$

c) $x^3 + 3x^2 + 3x + 1$

d) $x^4 + 2x^3 - x - 2$

6. Factor fully.

a) $x^3 + 2x^2 - 9x - 18$

b) $4x^3 - 8x^2 + x + 3$

c) $6x^3 + x^2 - 31x + 10$

d) $x^4 + x^3 - 13x^2 - 25x - 12$

Apply

7. Determine the value(s) of k so that the binomial is a factor of the polynomial.

    a) $P(x) = x^3 + 5x^2 + kx + 6$ $x + 2$

        If $x + 2$ is a factor, then $P(\underline{\hspace{1.5cm}}) = \underline{\hspace{1cm}}$.

    b) $P(x) = kx^3 - 10x^2 + 2x + 3$ $x - 3$

8. The product of four integers is $x^4 + 7x^3 + 7x^2 - 15x$, where x is one of the integers. What are the possible expressions for the other three integers?

9. A sculptor creates a carving from a block of marble. The marble is in the shape of a rectangular prism whose volume, in cubic feet, is represented by $V(x) = 3x^3 + 2x^2 - 7x + 2$, where x is a positive real number. What are the factors that represent possible dimensions, in terms of x, of the block of marble?

Connect

10. Describe the steps required to factor the polynomial $x^4 - 10x^3 + 24x^2 + 10x - 25$.

3.4 Equations and Graphs of Polynomial Functions

Sketching Graphs of Polynomial Functions
- To sketch the graph of a polynomial function, use the x-intercepts, the y-intercept, the degree of the function, and the sign of the leading coefficient.
- The x-intercepts of the graph of a polynomial function are the roots of the corresponding polynomial equation.
- Determine the zeros of a polynomial function from the factors.
- Use the factor theorem to express a polynomial function in factored form.

Multiplicity of a Zero
- If a polynomial has a factor $x - a$ that is repeated n times, then $x = a$ is a zero of multiplicity n.
- The multiplicity of a zero or root can also be referred to as the *order* of the zero or root.
- The shape of a graph of a polynomial function close to a zero of $x = a$ (multiplicity n) is similar to the shape of the graph of a function with degree equal to n of the form $y = (x - a)^n$.
- Polynomial functions change sign at x-intercepts that correspond to *odd* multiplicity. The graph crosses over the x-axis at these intercepts.
- Polynomial functions do not change sign at x-intercepts of *even* multiplicity. The graph touches, but does not cross, the x-axis at these intercepts.

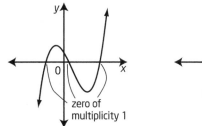

zero of
multiplicity 1

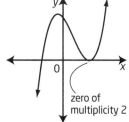

zero of
multiplicity 2

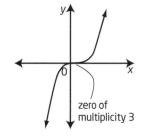

zero of
multiplicity 3

Transformation of Polynomial Functions
To sketch the graph of a polynomial function of the form $y = a[b(x - h)]^n + k$ or $y - k = a[b(x - h)]^n$, where $n \in \mathbb{N}$, apply the following transformations to the graph of $y = x^n$.
Note: You may apply the transformations represented by a and b in any order before the transformations represented by h and k.

Parameter	Transformation
k	• Vertical translation up or down • $(x, y) \rightarrow (x, y + k)$
h	• Horizontal translation left or right • $(x, y) \rightarrow (x + h, y)$
a	• Vertical stretch about the x-axis by a factor of $|a|$ • For $a < 0$, the graph is also reflected in the x-axis • $(x, y) \rightarrow (x, ay)$

b	• Horizontal stretch about the y-axis by a factor of $\frac{1}{\|b\|}$ • For $b < 0$, the graph is also reflected in the y-axis • $(x, y) \rightarrow \left(\frac{x}{b}, y\right)$

Working Example 1: Analyse Graphs of Polynomial Functions

For each graph of a polynomial function, determine
• the least possible degree
• the sign of the leading coefficient
• the x-intercepts and the factors of the function with least possible degree
• the intervals where the function is positive and the intervals where it is negative

a)

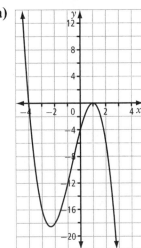

b)

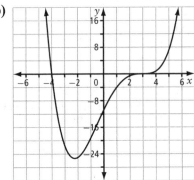

Solution

a) There are _____ x-intercepts; they are _____.

The x-intercept of multiplicity 1 is _____.

The x-intercept of multiplicity 2 is _____.

The least possible degree of the graph is _____.

The graph extends from quadrant _____ to quadrant _____.

The leading coefficient is _____.
(positive or negative)

The factors are _____.

The function is positive for values of x in the interval(s) _____.

The function is negative for values of x in the interval(s) _____.

b) The x-intercepts are _____.

The x-intercept of multiplicity _____ is _____.

The x-intercept of multiplicity _____ is _____.

The least possible degree of the graph is _____.

The graph extends from quadrant _____ to quadrant _____.

The leading coefficient is _____.
                             (*positive* or *negative*)

The factors are _____.

The function is positive for values of x in the interval(s) _____.

The function is negative for values of x in the interval(s) _____.

> 📖 To see additional graphs, refer to Example 1 on page 138 of *Pre-Calculus 12*.

Working Example 2: Analyse Equations to Sketch Graphs of Polynomial Functions

Sketch the graph of each polynomial function.

a) $y = -(x + 1)^3(x - 3)$

b) $y = 2x^5 + x^4 - 18x^3 - 9x^2$

Solution

a) The function $y = -(x + 1)^3(x - 3)$ is in _____ form.

Degree	
Leading coefficient	
End behaviour	
Zeros/x-intercepts	
Multiplicity of zeros	
y-intercept	
Interval(s) where the function is positive	
Interval(s) where the function is negative	

Use the information from the table to sketch the graph.

How can you check whether the function is positive or negative?

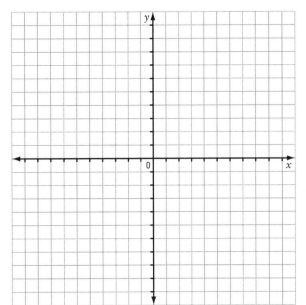

b) The function $y = 2x^5 + x^4 - 18x^3 - 9x^2$ is not in

_____ form.

First, factor out the common factor.

What zero corresponds to the common factor? What multiplicity does it have?

Next, use the integral zero theorem and the factor theorem to factor the polynomial.

The factored form of $y = 2x^5 + x^4 - 18x^3 - 9x^2$ is _____.

Degree	
Leading coefficient	
End behaviour	
Zeros/x-intercepts	
Multiplicity of zeros	
y-intercept	
Interval(s) where the function is positive	
Interval(s) where the function is negative	

Use the information from the table to sketch the graph.

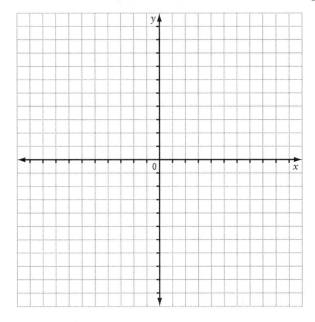

Working Example 3: Apply Transformations to Sketch a Graph

The graph of $y = x^4$ is transformed to obtain the graph of $y = 3\left[-\frac{1}{2}(x + 1)\right]^4 - 4$.

a) State the parameters and describe the corresponding transformations.

b) Complete a table to show what happens to the given points under each transformation.

c) Sketch the graph of $y = 3\left[-\frac{1}{2}(x + 1)\right]^4 - 4$.

Solution

a)

Parameter	Description of Transformation
$b =$	
$a =$	
$h =$	
$k =$	

b) Complete the table to show what happens to the given points under each transformation.

$y = x^4$	$y = \left(-\dfrac{1}{2}x\right)^4$	$y = 3\left(-\dfrac{1}{2}x\right)^4$	$y = 3\left[-\dfrac{1}{2}(x + 1)\right]^4 - 4$
$(-2, 16)$			
$(-1, 1)$			
$(0, 0)$			
$(1, 1)$			
$(2, 16)$			

c) To sketch the graph, plot the points from column 4 and draw a smooth curve through them.

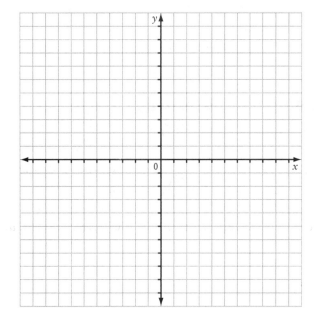

Check Your Understanding

Practise

1. Solve.

   a) $4x^3(x + 2)(2x - 1) = 0$

   b) $(x + 1)^2(x - 3)(x - 5) = 0$

   c) $x^3 - 8 = 0$

2. Use the graph of the given function to write the corresponding polynomial equation. State the roots of the equation. The roots are all integral values.

   a)

   The graph of the function has _____ x-intercepts.

   It crosses the x-axis at each of the x-intercepts. All the

   x-intercepts are of _____ multiplicity.
                      (*even* or *odd*)

   The least possible multiplicity of each x-intercept is _____,

   so the least possible degree is _____.

   The graph extends up into quadrant _____ and down into quadrant _____,

   so the leading coefficient is _____.
                               (*positive* or *negative*)

   The y-intercept is _____; this is the _____ term in the equation of the function.

   The zeros, or x-intercepts, are _____, _____, and _____. The product of the

   roots is _____.

   Compare the product of the roots to the y-intercept to determine the vertical stretch, a.

   $a =$ _____

   The equation of the polynomial function is

   $f(x) =$ _____ (_____)(_____)(_____).

b)

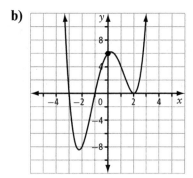

c)

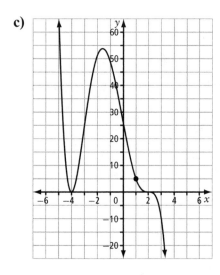

In this case, use the coordinates of the point (1, 5) to solve for *a*.

3. For each graph,
- state the x-intercepts
- state the intervals where the function is positive and the intervals where the function is negative
- explain whether the graph might represent a polynomial that has zero(s) of multiplicity 1, 2, or 3.

a)

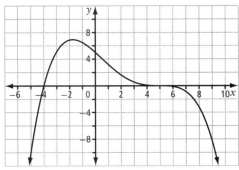

b)

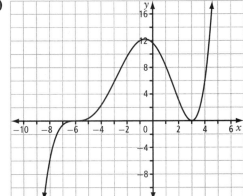

c)

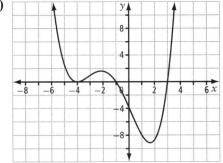

4. Without using technology, sketch the graph of each function. Label all intercepts. (Hint: Factor.)

a) $f(x) = -2x^3 + 3x^2 + 11x - 6$

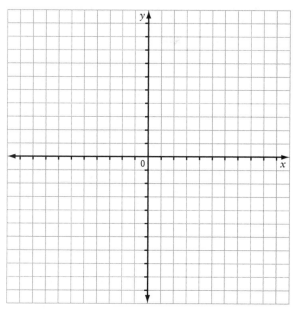

b) $g(x) = x^4 + 5x^3 + 6x^2 - 4x - 8$

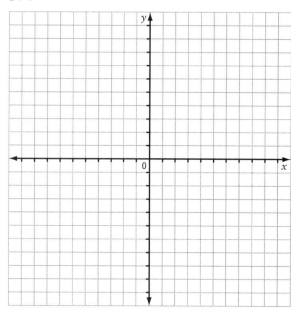

Apply

5. Determine the equation for each graph of a polynomial function shown.

a)

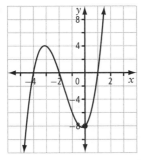

b)

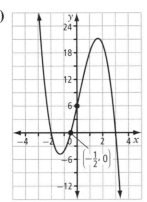

c)

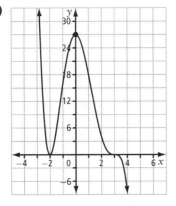

6. **a)** Given the function $y = x^3$, list the parameters of the transformed polynomial function $y = \frac{1}{2}(3(x + 4))^3 - 5$ and describe how each parameter transforms the graph of the function $y = x^3$.

b) Determine the domain and range for the transformed function.

7. Determine the equation with least degree for each polynomial function.

a) quartic function with zeros 2 (multiplicity 3) and -5, and y-intercept 30

b) quintic function with zeros -1 (multiplicity 2), 3 (multiplicity 1), and -2 (multiplicity 2), and constant term -12

8. An interlocking stone path that is x feet wide is built around a rectangular garden. The garden is 20 ft wide and 40 ft long. The combined surface area of the garden and the walking path is 1196 ft². What are the dimensions of the stone path?

> For help with #8, see Example 4 on page 145 of *Pre-Calculus 12* for an example of how to solve a problem involving polynomial functions.

Connect

9. Given a polynomial function of the form $y = a[b(x - h)]^n + k$, which parameters do not change the shape of the graph of the function? Explain.

Chapter 3 Review

3.1 Characteristics of Polynomial Functions, pages 66–77

1. Complete the chart for each polynomial function.

Polynomial Function	Degree	Type	Leading Coefficient	Constant Term
a) $f(x) = -2x^4 - x^3 + 3x - 7$				
b) $y = 3x^5 + 2x^4 - x^3 + 3$				
c) $g(x) = 0.5x^3 - 8x^2$				
d) $p(x) = 10$				

2. For each of the following,
   - determine whether the graph represents on odd-degree or an even-degree polynomial function
   - determine whether the leading coefficient of the corresponding function is positive or negative
   - state the number of x-intercepts
   - state the domain and range

a)

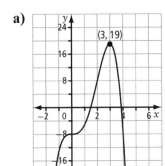

b)

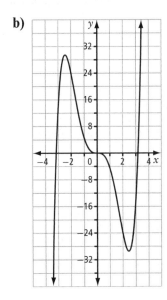

3. The distance, d, in metres, travelled by a boat from the moment it leaves shore can be modelled by the function $d(t) = 0.002t^3 + 0.05t^2 + 0.3t$, where t is the time, in seconds.

   a) What is the degree of the function $d(t)$?

   b) What are the leading coefficient and constant of this function? What does the constant represent?

   c) Describe the end behaviour of the graph of this function.

   d) What are the restrictions on the domain of this function? Explain why you selected those restrictions.

   e) What distance has the boat travelled after 15 s?

   f) Make a sketch of what you think the function will look like. Then, graph the function using technology. How does it compare to your sketch?

3.2 The Remainder Theorem, pages 78–83

4. a) Use long division to divide $5x^3 - 7x^2 - x + 6$ by $x - 1$.

   Express the result in the form $\frac{P(x)}{x - a} = Q(x) + \frac{R}{x - a}$.

   b) Identify any restrictions on the variable.

c) Write the corresponding statement that can be used to check the division. Then, verify your answer.

5. Determine the remainder resulting from each division.

a) $(x^3 + 2x^2 - 3x + 9) \div (x + 3)$

b) $(2x^3 + 7x^2 - x + 1) \div (x + 2)$

c) $(x^3 + 2x^2 - 3x + 5) \div (x - 3)$

d) $(2x^4 + 7x^2 - 8x + 3) \div (x - 4)$

6. a) Determine the value of m such that when $f(x) = x^4 - mx^3 + 7x - 6$ is divided by $x - 2$, the remainder is -8.

b) Use the value of m from part a) to determine the remainder when $f(x)$ is divided by $x + 2$.

7. When a polynomial $P(x)$ is divided by $x - 2$, the quotient is $x^2 + 4x - 7$ and the remainder is -4. What is the polynomial?

3.3 The Factor Theorem, pages 84–90

8. What is the corresponding binomial factor of a polynomial, $P(x)$, given the value of the zero?

a) $P(7) = 0$

b) $P(-6) = 0$

c) $P(c) = 0$

9. Determine whether $x + 2$ is a factor of each polynomial.

a) $x^3 + 2x^2 - x - 2$

b) $x^4 + 2x^3 - 4x^2 + x + 10$

10. What are the possible integral zeros of each polynomial?

    a) $x^3 - 5x^2 + 3x - 27$ **b)** $x^3 + 6x^2 + 2x + 36$

11. Factor fully.

    a) $x^3 - 4x^2 + x + 6$ **b)** $3x^3 - 5x^2 - 26x - 8$

    c) $5x^4 + 12x^3 - 101x^2 + 48x + 36$ **d)** $2x^4 + 5x^3 - 8x^2 - 20x$

12. Rectangular blocks of ice are cut up and used to build the front entrance of an ice castle. The volume, in cubic feet, of each block is represented by $V(x) = 5x^3 + 7x^2 - 8x - 4$, where x is a positive real number. What are the factors that represent possible dimensions, in terms of x, of the blocks?

3.4 Equations and Graphs of Polynomial Functions, pages 91–102

13. For each graph of a polynomial function, determine
- the least possible degree
- the sign of the leading coefficient
- the x-intercepts and their multiplicity
- the intervals where the function is positive and the intervals where it is negative
- the equation for the polynomial function

a)

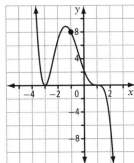

b)

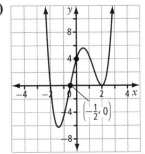

14. a) Given the function $y = x^5$, list the parameters of the transformed polynomial function $y = -2\left(\frac{1}{3}(x - 1)\right)^5 + 4$ and describe how each parameter transforms the graph of the function $y = x^5$.

b) Determine the domain and range for the transformed function.

15. Determine the equation with least degree for a cubic function with zeros −2 (multiplicity 2) and 3 (multiplicity 1), and y-intercept 36.

Chapter 3 Skills Organizer

Make note of some of the key details and things to remember about the processes you have learned in this unit. Use your class notes, textbook, or questions from this workbook to help you choose examples (or create your own). Some information is provided below to help you get started.

Process	Example	Things to Remember
Analysing graphs of odd-degree polynomial functions		
Analysing graphs of even-degree polynomial functions		
Using synthetic division		
Applying the remainder theorem		
Using the factor theorem		
Factoring using the integral zero theorem		
Determining the multiplicity of zeros		
Applying transformations of functions $y = a[b(x - h)]^n + k$		a: vertical stretch/reflection b: horizontal stretch/reflection h: horizontal translation k: vertical translation

Chapter 4 Trigonometry and the Unit Circle

4.1 Angles and Angle Measure

- One radian is the measure of the central angle subtended in a circle by an arc equal in length to the radius of the circle.

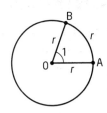

- Travelling one rotation around the circumference of a circle causes the terminal arm to turn $2\pi r$. Since $r = 1$ on the unit circle, $2\pi r$ can be expressed as 2π, or 2π radians.

You can use this information to translate rotations into radian measures. For example,

1 full rotation (360°) is 2π radians	$\frac{1}{6}$ rotation (60°) is $\frac{\pi}{3}$ radians
$\frac{1}{2}$ rotation (180°) is π radians	$\frac{1}{8}$ rotation (45°) is $\frac{\pi}{4}$ radians
$\frac{1}{4}$ rotation (90°) is $\frac{\pi}{2}$ radians	$\frac{1}{12}$ rotation (30°) is $\frac{\pi}{6}$ radians

- Angles in standard position with the same terminal arms are coterminal. For an angle in standard position, an infinite number of angles coterminal with it can be determined by adding or subtracting any number of full rotations.

- Counterclockwise rotations are associated with positive angles. Clockwise rotations are associated with negative angles.

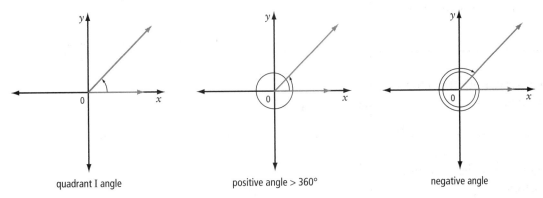

quadrant I angle   positive angle > 360°   negative angle

- The general form of a coterminal angle (in degrees) is $\theta \pm 360°n$, where n is a natural number (0, 1, 2, 3, …) and represents the number of revolutions. The general form (in radians) is $\theta \pm 2\pi n$, $n \in \mathbb{N}$.

- Radians are especially useful for describing circular motion. Arc length, a, means the distance travelled along the circumference of a circle of radius r. For a central angle θ, in radians, $a = \theta r$.

Working Example 1: Convert Between Degree and Radian Measure

Draw each angle in standard position. Convert each degree measure to radian measure and each radian measure to degree measure. Give answers as both exact and, if necessary, approximate measures to the nearest hundredth of a unit.

a) 135°

b) $\dfrac{5\pi}{6}$

c) 4

Solution

a) Draw the angle 135° in standard position. What is its reference angle? _____

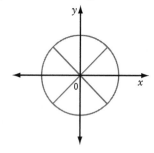

> The angle 135° is $\dfrac{3}{4}$ of a half circle, or $\dfrac{3}{4} \times \pi$.

Convert the degree measure to radian measure.

$$360° = 2\pi$$

$$1° = \dfrac{\boxed{}}{\boxed{}}$$

$$= \underline{\qquad}$$

$$135° = 135 \underline{\qquad}$$

> When expressing an angle measure in radians, no unit is necessary.

$$= \underline{\qquad} \quad \text{(exact measure in terms of } \pi\text{)}$$

$$= \underline{\qquad} \quad \text{(approximate measure, to two decimal places)}$$

> Use the π button on your calculator.

Is your answer reasonable? Verify using the diagram.

b) Draw the angle $\dfrac{5\pi}{6}$ in standard position.

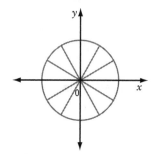

> Each half circle (π) is divided into 6 segments.

Convert the radian measure to degree measure.

$2\pi =$ _____ °

$\pi =$ _____ °

$\dfrac{5\pi}{6} = \dfrac{5\left(\boxed{}^{\circ}\right)}{6}$

$\dfrac{5\pi}{6} =$ _____ °

> When expressing an angle measure in degrees, the degree symbol ° is used.

Is your answer reasonable? Verify using the diagram.

c) The measure 4 has no units shown, so it represents an angle in radians.

Draw the angle 4 in standard position. Hint: $\pi \approx 3.14$ is equivalent to 180°.

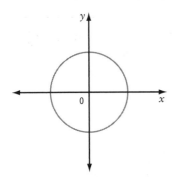

Convert the radian measure to degree measure.

2π radians $= 360°$

1 radian $= \dfrac{\boxed{}^{\circ}}{\boxed{}}$

4 radians $=$ _____ ° (exact measure)

$=$ _____ ° (approximate measure, to two decimal places)

Is your answer reasonable? Verify using the diagram.

> 📖 Refer to pages 168–169 of *Pre-Calculus 12* for two other valid procedures for converting between degrees and radians. Use whichever method makes the most sense to you.

Working Example 2: Identify Coterminal Angles and Express Them in General Form

a) Identify the angles coterminal with 210° that satisfy the domain −720° ≤ θ < 720°. Express the angles coterminal with 210° in general form.

b) Identify the angles coterminal with $-\frac{3\pi}{4}$ within the domain $-4\pi \le \theta < 4\pi$. Express angles coterminal with $-\frac{3\pi}{4}$ in general form.

Solution

a) To determine angles coterminal with 210°, add and subtract multiples of 360° (1 full rotation).

The given domain of 0° ± 720° is ± 2 rotations. Determine the coterminal angles and cross out any that fall outside the given domain.

θ − 2(360°)	θ − 360°	θ + 360°	θ + 2(360°)

The values that satisfy the domain −720° ≤ θ < 720° are _____.

For *n* rotations, the general form for angles coterminal with 210° is _____, $n \in \text{N}$.

b) To determine coterminal angles, add and subtract multiples of 2π (1 full rotation).

$$2\pi = \frac{\boxed{}\pi}{4}$$

The given domain of 0 ± 4π is ± _____ rotations.

Determine the coterminal angles and cross out any that fall outside the given domain.

θ − 2(2π)	θ − 2π	θ + 2π	θ + 2(2π)

The values that satisfy the domain _____ ≤ θ < _____ are

_____.

For *n* rotations, the general form for angles coterminal with $-\frac{3\pi}{4}$ is _____, $n \in \text{N}$.

📖 See Examples 2 and 3 on pages 170–172 of *Pre-Calculus 12* for more examples.

Working Example 3: Determine Arc Length in a Circle

The ring road around the eastern part of the city of Regina is almost a semicircle. Estimate the length of the ring road (from A to B) if the radius of the circle is 4.9 km.

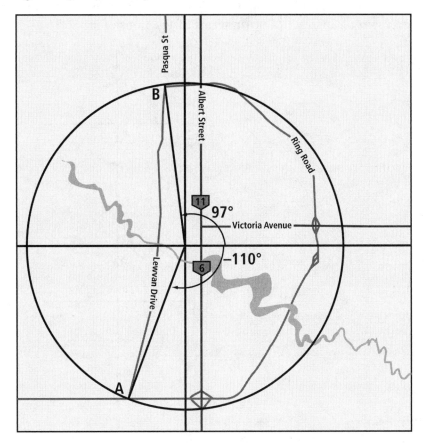

Solution

Determine the measure of the central angle in radians. Then, use the formula $a = \theta r$ to determine the arc length.

The central (obtuse) angle is _____ (in degrees).

Convert the degree measure to radian measure.

$$360° = \underline{\hspace{2cm}}$$

$$1° = \underline{\hspace{2cm}}$$

$$\underline{\hspace{2cm}} \times 1° = \underline{\hspace{2cm}} \times \frac{2\pi}{360}$$

$$\approx \underline{\hspace{3cm}}$$

> Write down a decimal approximation, but keep all digits in your calculator.

For central angles θ expressed in radians, the arc length of a circle of radius r is $a = \theta r$.

Therefore, the length of the ring road is approximately _____.

> What are the units?

The actual distance is 17.6 km. How accurate is your estimate?

📖 For a similar problem on a larger scale, try #20 on page 178 of *Pre-Calculus 12*.

Practise

1. Sketch each angle in standard position. Change each degree measure to radian measure. Express your answer as an exact value (in terms of fractions of π).

   a) 60°

   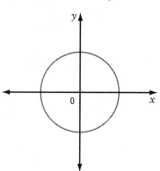

   b) 315°

   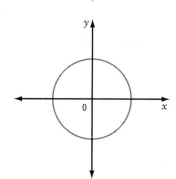

   c) −210°

   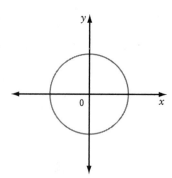

   d) 600°

   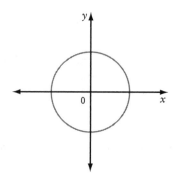

2. Draw each angle in standard position. Change each degree measure to radian measure. Express your answer as a decimal rounded to two decimal places.

a) 101°

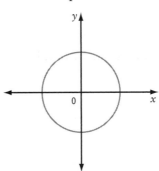

b) 57.3°

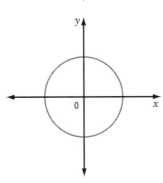

📖 For additional practice, see #3 on page 175 of *Pre-Calculus 12*.

3. Sketch each angle in standard position. Change each radian measure to degree measure. If necessary, round your answer to two decimal places.

a) $\frac{\pi}{2}$

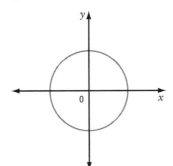

b) $\frac{4\pi}{3}$

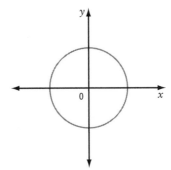

c) $-\dfrac{2\pi}{9}$

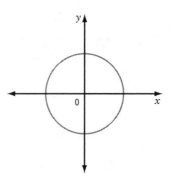

d) 2

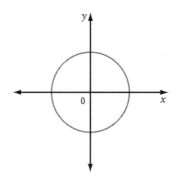

4. Determine one positive and one negative angle coterminal with each angle given.

   a) 349°

   b) −487°

   c) $\dfrac{2\pi}{3}$

   d) $\dfrac{9\pi}{4}$

5. For each angle θ, determine all coterminal angles within the given domain. Write an expression for all angles coterminal with θ in general form.

a) θ = 255° within the domain −720° ≤ θ < 720°

θ − 2(360°)	θ − 360°	θ + 360°	θ + 2(360°)

For *n* rotations, the general form for angles coterminal with 255° is

_____, $n \in$ N.

b) θ = π within the domain −4π ≤ θ < 4π

θ − 4π	θ − 2π	θ + 2π	θ + 4π

For *n* rotations, the general form for angles coterminal with π is

_____, $n \in$ N.

c) $\theta = \frac{5\pi}{6}$ within the domain −2π ≤ θ < 6π

For *n* rotations, the general form for angles coterminal with $\frac{5\pi}{6}$ is

_____, $n \in$ N.

📖 Also try #11 on page 176 of *Pre-Calculus 12*.

6. Determine the arc length subtended by each central angle. Give answers to the nearest hundredth of a unit.

a) radius 20 cm, central angle $\frac{2\pi}{3}$

b) radius 15 mm, central angle 195°

Apply

7. Angular velocity describes the rate of change in a central angle over time. For example, the change could be expressed in revolutions per minute (rpm), radians per minute, or degrees per second. To determine linear velocity from angular velocity, use the formula $v = \omega r$, where ω is the angular velocity in radians per unit of time and r is the radius of the circular motion.

   a) How does the angular velocity formula compare to the formula for arc length?

   b) The Great Beijing wheel, a Ferris wheel with a diameter of 198 m, makes 1 revolution in 20 min. What is its angular velocity, in radians per minute? What is the linear velocity of a passenger, in m/s?

   c) A bicycle wheel turns at 60 rpm. If the wheels of the bicycle measure 650 mm across, what distance, in metres, does the bicycle travel in 1.00 min?

   d) The mean distance from Earth to the moon is 385 000 km. The moon travels around Earth once every 27.2 days. Assuming a circular orbit, what is the linear velocity of the moon, in km/h?

Connect

8. Label the given angles (including the axes) in both degrees and radians, $0° \leq \theta < 720°$ and $0 \leq \theta < 4\pi$.

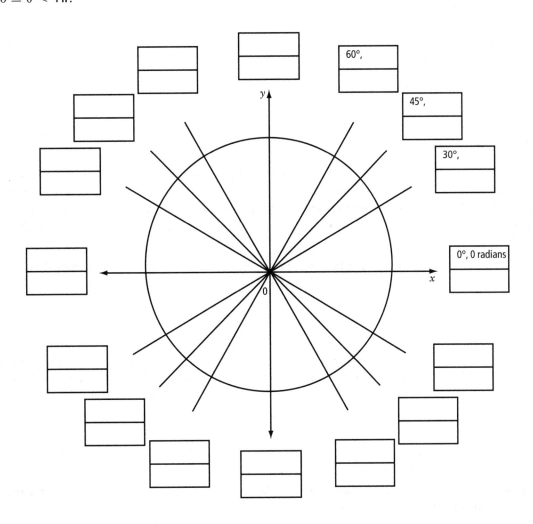

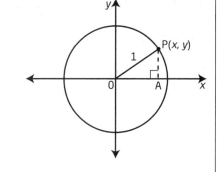

KEY IDEAS

- In general, a circle of radius r centred at the origin has equation $x^2 + y^2 = r^2$.

- The unit circle has radius 1 and is centred at the origin. The equation of the unit circle is $x^2 + y^2 = 1$. All points $P(x, y)$ on the unit circle satisfy this equation.

- An arc length measured along the unit circle equals the measure of the central angle (in radians).

In other words, when $r = 1$, the formula $a = \theta r$ simplifies to $a = \theta$.

- Recall the special right triangles you learned about previously.

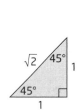
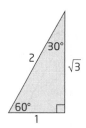

These special triangles can be scaled to fit within the unit circle ($r = 1$).

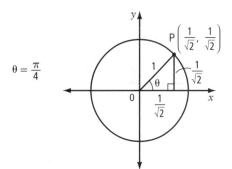
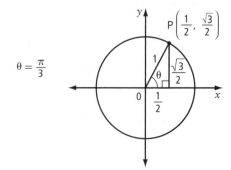

Working Example 1: Determine Coordinates for a Point on the Unit Circle

Determine the missing y-coordinate for each point on the unit circle.

a) point A $\left(-\frac{4}{5}, y\right)$ in quadrant II

b) point B $\left(\frac{3}{10}, y\right)$ in quadrant IV

Solution

a) Start by sketching the point on the unit circle. Then, solve for y in the equation of the unit circle.

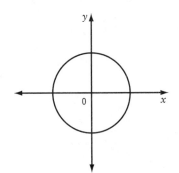

The equation of the unit circle is $x^2 + y^2 = 1$.
Substitute in the known value of x.

$$\boxed{}^2 + y^2 = 1$$

Solve for y.

> Isolate y^2. Then, take the square root of both sides.

Since quadrant _____ is specified, take only the _____ root.
(*positive* or *negative*)

Therefore, $y =$ _____.

b) Start by sketching the point on the unit circle. Then, solve for y in the equation of the unit circle.

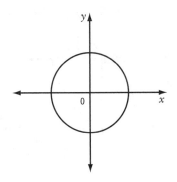

$$x^2 + y^2 = 1$$

> Check that your answer is reasonable using the fact that $|y| \le 1$ on the unit circle.

Since quadrant _____ is specified, take only the _____ root.
(*positive* or *negative*)

Therefore, $y =$ _____.

Working Example 2: Reflections of $\frac{\pi}{6}$ on the Unit Circle

Determine the coordinates of all points on the unit circle for which the reference angle is $\frac{\pi}{6}$.

Solution

Start by drawing a diagram showing $\frac{\pi}{6}$ reflected in all four quadrants.

What is $\frac{\pi}{6}$ in degrees?

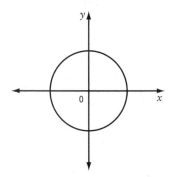

The angles (in radians) are $\frac{\pi}{6}$,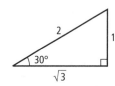

The points are A $\left(\frac{\pi}{6}\right)$, B $\left(\boxed{}\right)$, C $\left(\boxed{}\right)$, and D $\left(\boxed{}\right)$.

The appropriate special triangle is:

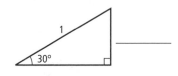

Scaled down to fit within a unit circle ($r = 1$):

Therefore, point A $\left(\frac{\pi}{6}\right)$ has coordinates _____.

- Point B $\left(\boxed{}\right)$ is a reflection in the y-axis of point A.

  The x-coordinate changes sign and the y-coordinate stays the same.

  Therefore, point B has coordinates _____.

- Point C $\left(\boxed{}\right)$ is a reflection in the x-axis and y-axis of point A.

  The x-coordinate is _____ and the y-coordinate is _____.

  Therefore, point C has coordinates _____.

- D $\left(\boxed{}\right)$ is a reflection in the x-axis of point A.

  The x-coordinate is _____ and the y-coordinate is _____.

  Therefore, point D has coordinates _____.

Check Your Understanding

Practise

1. Determine the equation of a circle centred at (0, 0) with each radius.

   a) 25 units

   b) 1.1 units

2. Is each point on the unit circle? Give evidence to support your answer.

   a) $(0.65, -0.76)$ The equation of the unit circle is _____.

Left Side	Right Side

   Conclusion: _____

   b) $\left(-\dfrac{\sqrt{2}}{2}, -\dfrac{\sqrt{2}}{2}\right)$

   c) $\left(\dfrac{\sqrt{7}}{2}, -\dfrac{1}{7}\right)$

   > What information could you use to answer part c) other than a left side/right side proof?

3. Determine the missing coordinate for each point on the unit circle. Draw a diagram to support your answer.

a) point $A\left(x, \dfrac{5}{13}\right)$ in quadrant II

$x^2 + y^2 = 1$

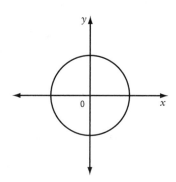

Since quadrant _____ is specified, take only the _____ root.
(*positive* or *negative*)

Therefore, $x = $ _____.

b) point $B\left(\dfrac{1}{6}, y\right)$ in quadrant IV

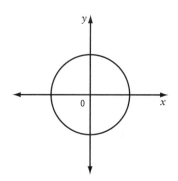

Since quadrant _____ is specified, take only the _____ root.
(*positive* or *negative*)

Therefore, $y = $ _____.

c) point $C\left(x, -\dfrac{1}{2}\right)$ in quadrant III

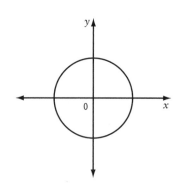

Do you recognize this pair of values?
What angle is associated with it?

4. If $P(\theta)$ is the point at which the terminal arm of angle θ in standard position intersects the unit circle, determine the exact coordinates of each of the following.

The word *exact* in the question is a clue to use special triangles.

a) $P\left(\dfrac{\pi}{2}\right)$

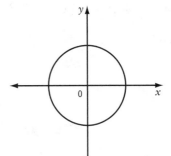

b) $P(2\pi)$

c) $P\left(\dfrac{2\pi}{3}\right)$

d) $P\left(\dfrac{5\pi}{4}\right)$

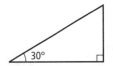

30°

e) $P\left(-\dfrac{\pi}{4}\right)$

f) $P\left(\dfrac{23\pi}{6}\right)$

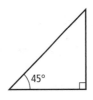

45°

5. Determine the value of angle θ in standard position, $0 \le \theta < 2\pi$, given the coordinates of P(θ), the point at which the terminal arm intersects the unit circle.

> The domain is given in radians, so your answers should also be in radians.

a) P(θ) = (−1, 0)   θ = _____

b) $P(\theta) = \left(\dfrac{\sqrt{3}}{2}, \dfrac{1}{2} \right)$ θ = _____

c) $P(\theta) = \left(-\dfrac{1}{\sqrt{2}}, \dfrac{1}{\sqrt{2}} \right)$ θ = _____

d) $P(\theta) = \left(-\dfrac{1}{2}, -\dfrac{\sqrt{3}}{2} \right)$ θ = _____

 This question should help you complete #5 and #6 on page 187 of *Pre-Calculus 12*.

6. Determine the arc length on the unit circle from (1, 0) to each point.

a) $P\left(\dfrac{\pi}{2} \right)$

θ = _____

On the unit circle, r = 1.

So, a = _____.

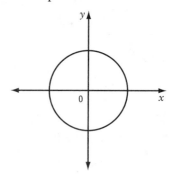

b) $P(\theta) \left(-\dfrac{\sqrt{3}}{2}, \dfrac{1}{2} \right)$

θ = _____

On the unit circle, r = 1.

So, a = _____.

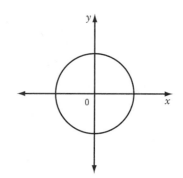

Apply

7. Earth moves in a roughly circular orbit around the sun at a distance of approximately 150 000 000 km. To estimate longer distances in space, scientists measure in multiples of the Earth–sun radius, or astronomical units (1 AU = 149 597 870.691 km). NASA defines 1 AU as the radius of an unperturbed circular orbit of a massless theoretical body revolving about the sun in $\frac{2\pi}{k}$ days, where k is a constant exactly equal to 0.017 202 098 95.

a) Placing the sun at the origin, write an equation representing Earth's orbit, in kilometres, assuming a circular orbit.

b) Placing the sun at the origin, write an equation representing Earth's orbit (in AU), assuming a circular orbit.

c) Mars is 1.38 AU from the sun. If the unit circle shown at right describes Earth's orbit, sketch the orbit of Mars.

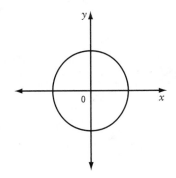

d) One year on Mars represents one complete rotation. How long (in radians) is 1 Mars-year on Earth? How long is this in Earth-days?

Connect

8. Give the exact coordinates of each P(θ) listed on the diagram below.

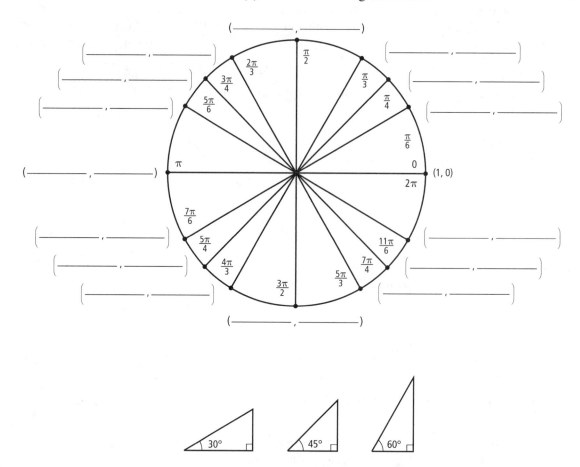

📖 Check your work by referring to the Key Ideas on page 186 of *Pre-Calculus 12*.

4.3 Trigonometric Ratios

KEY IDEAS

- These are the primary trigonometric ratios:

sine	cosine	tangent
$\sin \theta = \dfrac{y}{r}$	$\cos \theta = \dfrac{x}{r}$	$\tan \theta = \dfrac{y}{x}$

- For points on the unit circle, $r = 1$. Therefore, the primary trigonometric ratios can be expressed as:

$$\sin \theta = \frac{y}{1} = y \qquad \cos \theta = \frac{x}{1} = x \qquad \tan \theta = \frac{y}{x}$$

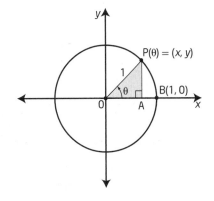

- Since $\cos \theta$ simplifies to x and $\sin \theta$ simplifies to y, you can write the coordinates of $P(\theta)$ as $P(\theta) = (\cos \theta, \sin \theta)$ for any point $P(\theta)$ at the intersection of the terminal arm of θ and the unit circle.

- These are the reciprocal trigonometric ratios:

cosecant	secant	cotangent
$\csc \theta = \dfrac{1}{\sin \theta}$	$\sec \theta = \dfrac{1}{\cos \theta}$	$\cot \theta = \dfrac{1}{\tan \theta}$
$\csc \theta = \dfrac{r}{y}$	$\sec \theta = \dfrac{r}{x}$	$\cot \theta = \dfrac{x}{y}$

- Recall from the CAST rule that
  - $\sin \theta$ and $\csc \theta$ are positive in quadrants I and II
  - $\cos \theta$ and $\sec \theta$ are positive in quadrants I and IV
  - $\tan \theta$ and $\cot \theta$ are positive in quadrants I and III

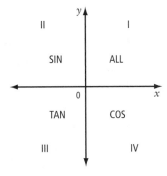

Working Example 1: Determine the Trigonometric Ratios for Angles in the Unit Circle

Point A $\left(-\frac{12}{13}, \frac{5}{13}\right)$ is on the unit circle and on the terminal arm of an angle θ in standard position. Determine the values of the six trigonometric ratios for angle θ.

Solution

Method 1: Use the Unit Circle

Start by sketching point A on the unit circle.

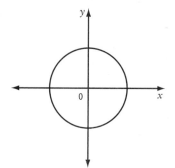

Since point A is on the unit circle,

- the _____-coordinate is defined as cos θ

- the y-coordinate is defined as _____

The primary trigonometric ratios are

$\sin \theta =$ _____ $\cos \theta =$ _____ $\tan \theta = \frac{y}{x}$

$=$ _____

$=$ _____

Now, take the reciprocal of each ratio to determine the reciprocal trigonometric ratios.

$\csc \theta = \frac{1}{\sin \theta}$ $\sec \theta = \frac{1}{\boxed{}}$ _____ $\theta = \frac{1}{\tan \theta}$

$=$ _____ $=$ _____ $=$ _____

$=$ _____ $=$ _____ $=$ _____

> Leave your answer as a fraction in lowest terms, unless "approximate" (meaning decimal) value is specified.

Method 2: Use a Right Triangle

Start by sketching point A on the unit circle. Draw a vertical line from point A to the x-axis to form right △ABO.

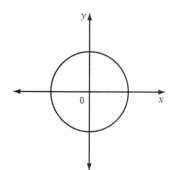

The angle is in quadrant _____.

$x =$ _____ $y =$ _____ $r = 1$

> How could you determine r for a point not on the unit circle?

Substitute these values into the definitions of the primary trigonometric ratios.

$\sin \theta = \frac{y}{r}$ $\cos \theta = \frac{x}{r}$ $\tan \theta = \frac{y}{x}$

$=$ _____ $=$ _____ $=$ _____

Take the reciprocal of each ratio to determine the reciprocal trigonometric ratios.

$\csc \theta = \frac{1}{\sin \theta}$ $\sec \theta = \frac{1}{\cos \theta}$ $\cot \theta = \frac{1}{\tan \theta}$

$=$ _____ $=$ _____ $=$ _____

Note that this process can be followed for points that are not on the unit circle.

Working Example 2: Exact and Approximate Values for Trigonometric Ratios

a) Determine the exact value of $\csc \dfrac{5\pi}{4}$.

b) Determine the value of $\cot(-0.5)$ to four decimal places.

Solution

a) Sketch the angle $\dfrac{5\pi}{4}$ in standard position on the unit circle.

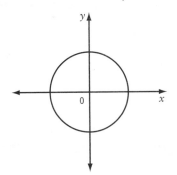

Point $P\left(\dfrac{5\pi}{4}\right)$ is in quadrant _____. The reference angle

for $\dfrac{5\pi}{4}$ is $\theta_R =$ _____.

Sketch the special triangle for the reference angle.
Determine the values of x ($\cos \theta_R$) and y ($\sin \theta_R$).

For the reference angle θ_R (in quadrant I), $P\left(\dfrac{\pi}{4}\right) =$ (_____, _____).

Therefore, for the angle $\dfrac{5\pi}{4}$, $P\left(\dfrac{5\pi}{4}\right) =$ (_____, _____).

$\csc \theta$ is the reciprocal of _____.

$\csc \theta =$ _____.

> The expression *exact value* is a clue that you should be thinking in terms of special triangles and fractions of π.

b) Draw the angle -0.5 in standard position on the unit circle.

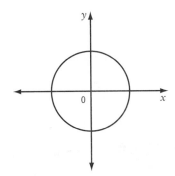

-0.5 is in quadrant _____. The reference angle

θ_R is _____.

$\cot \theta$ is the reciprocal of _____.

> Is the angle in radians or degrees? Make sure your calculator is on the correct setting.

This is not one of the special angles for which you know exact values of x and y using special triangles. Therefore, calculate the primary trigonometric ratio of the reference angle using your calculator.

Then, take the reciprocal.

Determine the sign (+ or −).

Final answer: $\cot(-0.5) \approx$ _____

> Your scientific or graphing calculator has a reciprocal button, usually labelled $\dfrac{1}{x}$ or x^{-1}. Do not round until the final answer.

Working Example 3: Determine Angles Given Their Trigonometric Ratios

Determine the measure of all angles that satisfy the following conditions. Give exact answers where possible. Otherwise, round to two decimal places.

a) $\sec \theta = \sqrt{2}$ in the domain $0 \le \theta < 4\pi$

b) $\csc \theta = -1.5557$ in the domain $-360° \le \theta < 360°$

Solution

a) $\sec \theta = \sqrt{2}$. Therefore, $\cos \theta = \underline{\hspace{2cm}}$.

Draw the special triangle.

$\boxed{\text{Degrees or radians?}}$

Then, draw the angle on the unit circle.

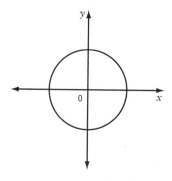

The reference angle θ_R is $\underline{\hspace{2cm}}$.

Cosine and secant are positive in quadrants $\underline{\hspace{2cm}}$ and $\underline{\hspace{2cm}}$.

Add the associated angles to your diagram of the unit circle.

quadrant I angle: $\underline{\hspace{2cm}}$

quadrant IV angle: $\underline{\hspace{2cm}}$

Now, check the domain and determine all additional relevant coterminal angles.

Therefore, $\sec \theta = \sqrt{2}$ when $\theta = \underline{\hspace{1.5cm}}$, $\underline{\hspace{1.5cm}}$, $\underline{\hspace{1.5cm}}$, and $\underline{\hspace{1.5cm}}$, $0 \le \theta < 4\pi$.

b) $\csc \theta = -1.5557$. Therefore, $\sin \theta = \underline{\hspace{2cm}}$.

Draw the angle on the unit circle and calculate θ_R.

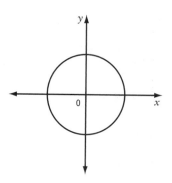

The reference angle θ_R is $\underline{\hspace{2cm}}$.

Sine and cosecant are negative in quadrants $\underline{\hspace{2cm}}$ and $\underline{\hspace{2cm}}$.

Add the associated angles to your diagram of the unit circle.

quadrant III angle: $\underline{\hspace{2cm}}$

quadrant IV angle: $\underline{\hspace{2cm}}$

Now, check the domain and determine all additional relevant coterminal angles.

Therefore, $\csc \theta = -1.5557$ when $\theta = \underline{\hspace{1.5cm}}$, $\underline{\hspace{1.5cm}}$, $\underline{\hspace{1.5cm}}$, and $\underline{\hspace{1.5cm}}$, $-360° \le \theta < 360°$.

Check Your Understanding

Practise

1. Point P $\left(\dfrac{7}{25}, -\dfrac{24}{25}\right)$ is on the unit circle and on the terminal arm of an angle θ in standard position. Determine the values of the six trigonometric ratios for angle θ.

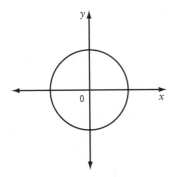

sin θ = _____ cos θ = _____ tan θ = _____

csc θ = _____ sec θ = _____ cot θ = _____

2. Without using a calculator, determine the sign (+ or −) of each of the following.

a) sin 580°

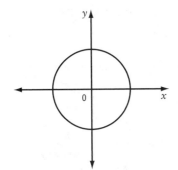

quadrant _____

sign is _____

b) tan 1

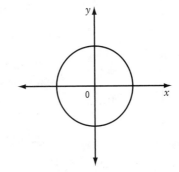

quadrant _____

sign is _____

c) csc θ = $\dfrac{2\pi}{3}$

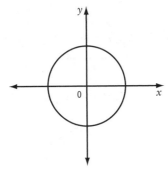

quadrant _____

sign is _____

d) sec θ = $\dfrac{5\pi}{4}$

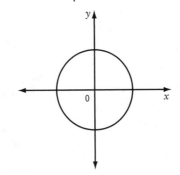

quadrant _____

sign is _____

3. In which quadrant(s) is (are) the terminal arm(s) of angle θ given the following conditions?

a) cot θ is positive _____

b) cot θ is positive and sin θ is negative _____

c) csc θ = 1.2 _____

d) csc θ = 1.2 and cos θ = -0.574 _____

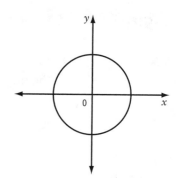

4. What is the exact value for each trigonometric ratio?

a) cos $\frac{\pi}{3}$

$P\left(\frac{\pi}{3}\right)$ is in quadrant _____.

θ_R = _____

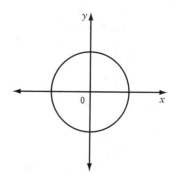

b) sin $\frac{\pi}{4}$

$P\left(\frac{\pi}{4}\right)$ is in quadrant _____.

θ_R = _____

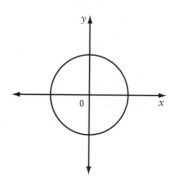

c) tan 3π

$P(3\pi)$ is a quadrantal angle.

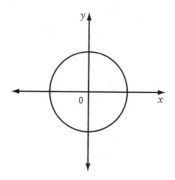

d) $\cot\left(-\dfrac{2\pi}{3}\right)$

  $P\left(-\dfrac{2\pi}{3}\right)$ is in quadrant _____.

  $\theta_R =$ _____

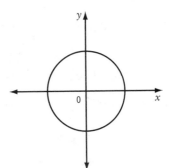

e) $\sec\dfrac{5\pi}{6}$

  $P\left(\dfrac{5\pi}{6}\right)$ is in quadrant _____.

  $\theta_R =$ _____

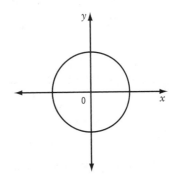

f) $\csc\left(-\dfrac{9\pi}{4}\right)$

  $P\left(-\dfrac{9\pi}{4}\right)$ is in quadrant _____.

  $\theta_R =$ _____

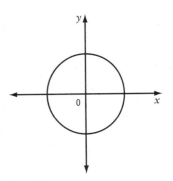

5. Determine the approximate value for each trigonometric ratio, to three decimal places.

  a) $\sec 74°$

  $\sec\theta$ is the reciprocal of _____

  quadrant: _____

  sign (+ or –): _____

  b) $\cot 104°$

  c) $\csc 2.8$

  d) $\sec\left(-\dfrac{7\pi}{10}\right)$

These questions are similar to #1 and #2 on page 201 of *Pre-Calculus 12*.

Apply

6. Determine the measure of all angles that satisfy the following conditions. Round your answers to the nearest degree.

a) $\tan \theta = -3.078$ in the domain $0° \le \theta < 720°$

$\theta_R = \tan^{-1}(+3.078)$

$\approx$ _____

Tangent is negative in quadrants _____ and _____.

Therefore, $\tan \theta = -3.078$ when $\theta \approx$ _____,

_____, _____, and _____, $0° \le \theta < 720°$.

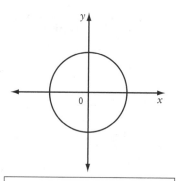

Which other coterminal angles fall within the domain?

b) $\sec \theta = -1.046$ in the domain $-360° \le \theta < 360°$

$\sec \theta$ is the reciprocal of _____.

$\theta_R \approx$ _____

Secant is negative in quadrants _____ and _____.

Therefore, $\sec \theta = -1.046$ when $\theta \approx$ _____,

_____, _____, and _____, $-360° \le \theta < 360°$.

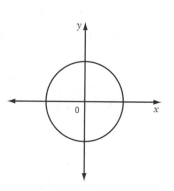

7. Determine the measure of all angles that satisfy the following conditions. Give exact answers.

Drawing the special triangle may help.

a) $\sin \theta = -\dfrac{\sqrt{3}}{2}$ in the domain $0 \le \theta < 4\pi$

$\theta_R =$ _____

Sine is negative in quadrants _____ and _____.

Therefore, $\sin \theta = -\dfrac{\sqrt{3}}{2}$ when $\theta =$ _____, _____,

_____, and _____, $0 \le \theta < 4\pi$.

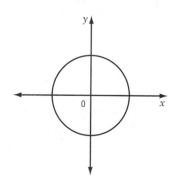

b) $\csc \theta = 2$ in the domain $-2\pi \le \theta < 2\pi$

$\csc \theta$ is the reciprocal of _____.

What is the reciprocal of 2?

$\theta_R =$ _____

Cosecant is positive in quadrants _____ and _____.

Therefore, $\csc \theta = 2$ when $\theta =$ _____, _____,

_____, and _____, $-2\pi \le \theta < 2\pi$.

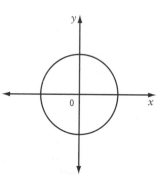

8. Determine the value of the five other trigonometric ratios if $\csc \theta = \frac{5}{3}$, $90° \le \theta < 180°$.

The angle is in quadrant _____.

$x =$ _____ $y =$ _____ $r =$ _____

$\sin \theta =$ _____ $\cos \theta =$ _____ $\tan \theta =$ _____

$\sec \theta =$ _____ $\cot \theta =$ _____

> 📖 This question will help you with #12 on page 202 of *Pre-Calculus 12.*

Connect

9. Choose any two of the special angles $\frac{\pi}{6}$, $\frac{\pi}{4}$, and $\frac{\pi}{3}$. Complete the table below. You may also choose the quadrantal angles (on the axes), but then you will have to change the headings on the table.

$\theta_R =$		Quadrant I	Quadrant II	Quadrant III	Quadrant IV
	sin				
	csc				
	cos				
	sec				
	tan				
	cot				
$\theta_R =$		Quadrant I	Quadrant II	Quadrant III	Quadrant IV
	sin				
	csc				
	cos				
	sec				
	tan				
	cot				

KEY IDEAS

- Solving an equation means to determine the value (or values) of a variable that make an equation true (Left Side = Right Side).
  For example, $\sin \theta = \frac{1}{2}$ is true when $\theta = 30°$ or $\theta = 150°$, and for every angle coterminal with 30° or 150°. These angles are solutions to a very simple trigonometric equation.

- The variable θ is often used to represent the unknown angle, but any other variable is allowed.

- In general, solve for the trigonometric ratio, and then determine
  – all solutions within a given domain, such as $0 \leq \theta < 2\pi$

  or

  – all possible solutions, expressed in general form, $\theta + 2\pi n, n \in I$

- Unless the angle is a multiple of 90° or $\frac{\pi}{2}$, there will be two angles per solution of the equation within each full rotation of 360° or 2π. As well, there will be two expressions in general form per solution, one for each angle. It is sometimes possible to write a combined expression representing both angles in general form.

- If the angle is a multiple of 90° or $\frac{\pi}{2}$ (that is, the terminal arm coincides with an axis), then there will be at least one angle within each full rotation that is a correct solution to the equation.

- Note that $\sin^2 \theta = (\sin \theta)^2$. Also, recall that
  – $\sin \theta$ and $\csc \theta$ are positive in quadrants I and II
  – $\cos \theta$ and $\sec \theta$ are positive in quadrants I and IV
  – $\tan \theta$ and $\cot \theta$ are positive in quadrants I and III

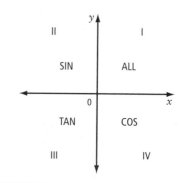

Working Example 1: Solve a First-Degree Trigonometric Equation

Solve for the angle (in degrees). Round answers to the nearest tenth of a degree.

a) $7 \cos \theta + 5 = 2 - 3 \cos \theta$, $0° \leq \theta < 360°$

b) $17 + 3 \cot \theta = 29$, in general form

Solution

a) Start by solving for the trigonometric ratio.

$$7 \cos \theta + 5 = 2 - 3 \cos \theta$$

> Treat $\cos \theta$ as a variable and isolate it on one side of the equation.

$$\cos \theta = \underline{\hspace{2cm}}$$

Determine the reference angle.

$$\theta_R = \cos^{-1}(+0.3)$$

$$\approx \underline{\hspace{2cm}}$$

Cosine is negative in quadrants _____ and _____.

Add the associated angles to your diagram of the unit circle.

quadrant II angle: _____

quadrant III angle: _____

Therefore, the solutions are $\theta = $ _____ and _____, $0° \leq \theta < 360°$.

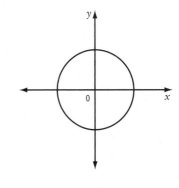

b) Start by solving for the trigonometric ratio.

$$17 + 3 \cot \theta = 29$$

$$3 \cot \theta = \underline{\hspace{2cm}}$$

$$\cot \theta = \underline{\hspace{2cm}}$$

$\cot \theta$ is the reciprocal of _____. Therefore, $\tan \theta = $ _____.

Determine the reference angle.

$$\theta_R = \underline{\hspace{2cm}}$$

Tangent and cotangent are positive in quadrants _____

and _____.

Add the associated angles to your diagram of the unit circle.

$$\theta_1 = \underline{\hspace{2cm}} \qquad \theta_2 = \underline{\hspace{2cm}}$$

Can θ_1 and θ_2 be generalized in a single expression?

Notice on your diagram that $\theta_2 = \theta_1 + 180°$. There is a solution every $180°$.

The general form is _____ $+ 180°n$, $n \in I$.

Working Example 2: Solve Second-Degree Equations

Solve for the unknown value. If necessary, round your answer to two decimal places.

a) $2 \sin^2 \theta = 1, 0 \le \theta < 2\pi$

b) $\tan^2 \theta - 4 \tan \theta + 3 = 0, 0 \le \theta < 2\pi$

Solution

a) Isolate the trigonometric ratio $\sin^2 \theta$. Then, take the square root of both sides.

$$2 \sin^2 \theta = 1$$

$$\sin^2 \theta = \underline{\hspace{2cm}}$$

What is the degree of the equation? How many solutions are there?

$$\sin \theta = \underline{\hspace{1.5cm}} \text{ or } \sin \theta = \underline{\hspace{1.5cm}}$$

Determine the reference angles for both solutions.

$\theta_R = \underline{\hspace{1.5cm}} \qquad \theta_R = \underline{\hspace{1.5cm}}$

$\sin > 0$ (positive) in Q $\underline{\hspace{1.5cm}}$ and Q $\underline{\hspace{1.5cm}}$

$\theta_1 = \underline{\hspace{1.5cm}} \qquad \theta_2 = \underline{\hspace{1.5cm}}$

or

$\sin < 0$ (negative) in Q $\underline{\hspace{1.5cm}}$ and Q $\underline{\hspace{1.5cm}}$

$\theta_3 = \underline{\hspace{1.5cm}} \qquad \theta_4 = \underline{\hspace{1.5cm}}$

Therefore, the solutions are $\underline{\hspace{4cm}}$, $0 \le \theta < 2\pi$.

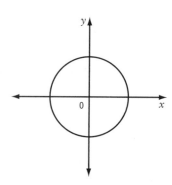

b) Factor and solve for $\tan \theta$.

$$\tan^2 \theta - 4 \tan \theta + 3 = 0$$

$$(\tan \theta - \underline{\hspace{1.5cm}})(\tan \theta - \underline{\hspace{1.5cm}}) = 0$$

Treat $\tan \theta$ as a variable.

Determine the reference angles for both solutions.

Is your calculator in radians?

$\theta_R = \underline{\hspace{1.5cm}} \qquad \theta_R = \underline{\hspace{1.5cm}}$

$\tan > 0$ (positive) in Q $\underline{\hspace{1.5cm}}$ and Q $\underline{\hspace{1.5cm}}$

$\theta_1 = \underline{\hspace{1.5cm}} \qquad \theta_2 = \underline{\hspace{1.5cm}}$

or

$\tan < 0$ (negative) in Q $\underline{\hspace{1.5cm}}$ and Q $\underline{\hspace{1.5cm}}$

$\theta_3 = \underline{\hspace{1.5cm}} \qquad \theta_4 = \underline{\hspace{1.5cm}}$

Therefore, the solutions are $\underline{\hspace{4cm}}$, $0 \le \theta < 2\pi$.

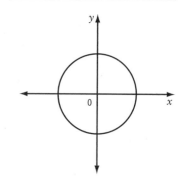

📖 Also see Example 2 on page 208–209 of *Pre-Calculus 12*.

Practise

1. Determine the exact solutions for each trigonometric equation in the specified domain.

   a) $4 \sin \theta - 5 = 3, 0° \le \theta < 360°$

   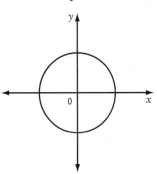

   b) $7 \cot \theta - 4 = 6 \cot \theta - 5, 0 \le \theta < 4\pi$

   $\cot \theta$ is the reciprocal of _____.

   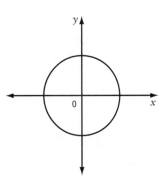

   Therefore, the solutions are

   $\theta =$ _____, $0 \le \theta < 4\pi$.

2. Solve for θ within the domain $0° \le \theta < 360°$. Round answers to one decimal place.

   a) $-3(5 - 4 \sec \theta) = \sec \theta$

   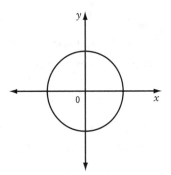

   b) $\csc \theta + \dfrac{3}{4} = -\dfrac{2}{3}$

   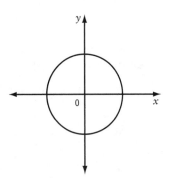

3. Solve for θ within the given domain. Give exact answers where possible. Otherwise, round your answer to two decimal places.

a) $4 \cos^2 \theta = 3, 0 \leq \theta < 2\pi$

Determine the reference angles for both solutions.

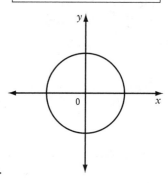

Treat $\cos \theta$ as a variable.

The solutions are _____, $0 \leq \theta < 2\pi$.

b) $\csc^2 \theta - 3 \csc \theta - 10 = 0, 0 \leq \theta < 360°$

Determine the reference angles for both solutions.

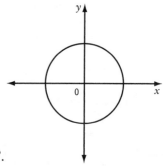

Degrees or radians?

The solutions are _____, $0 \leq \theta < 360°$.

4. The equation $\cos \theta = \dfrac{\sqrt{3}}{2}, 0 \leq \theta < 2\pi$, has solutions $\dfrac{\pi}{6}$ and $\dfrac{11\pi}{6}$.
Suppose the domain is not restricted.

a) Write the general solution corresponding to $\dfrac{\pi}{6}$.

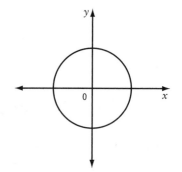

b) Write the general solution corresponding to $\dfrac{11\pi}{6}$.

5. The equation $\tan \theta = 1, 0 \leq \theta < 2\pi$, has solutions $\dfrac{\pi}{4}$ and $\dfrac{5\pi}{4}$.

a) Write the solutions for $\tan \theta = 1$ if the domain is $0 \leq \theta < 4\pi$.

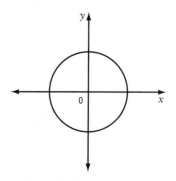

b) Suppose the domain is unrestricted. Write the general solution.

Apply

6. The following solution contains one or more errors. Identify the errors and correct them.

Solve $\tan^2 \theta - 3 \tan \theta = 0$ in the domain $0 \leq \theta < 2\pi$.
Round answers to two decimal places.

$$\tan^2 \theta - 3 \tan \theta = 0$$

$$\tan^2 \theta = 3 \tan \theta \quad (\div \tan \theta)$$

$$\tan \theta = 3$$

$$\theta = \tan^{-1}(3)$$

$$= 1.25$$

Correct solution:

$\therefore$ The solution is 1.25 radians.

7. a) Solve $\cos^2 \theta = \cos \theta$, $0 \leq \theta < 2\pi$. Give exact answers.

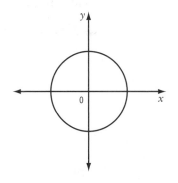

b) Suppose the domain of solutions to $\cos^2 \theta = \cos \theta$ is unrestricted. Write a general expression representing each solution. Can the expressions be combined to a single general expression representing all solutions? Why or why not?

📖 Also try #13 on page 212 of *Pre-Calculus 12*.

8. Verify whether the expression $\dfrac{(1 + 2n)\pi}{3}$, $n \in I$ represents the general form for solutions to $\sec \theta = 2$.

Try various cases, such as $n = 0$.

Connect

9. Fill in the table with information related to solving trigonometric equations.

				Diagram
If	$\sin \theta$ $\csc \theta$	< 0	the solutions will be in quadrants _____ and _____.	
If	$\sin \theta$ $\csc \theta$	> 0	the solutions will be in quadrants _____ and _____.	
If	$\cos \theta$ _____ θ	< 0	the solutions will be in quadrants _____ and _____.	
If	$\cos \theta$ _____ θ	> 0	the solutions will be in quadrants _____ and _____.	
If	$\tan \theta$ _____ θ	> 0	the solutions will be in quadrants _____ and _____.	
If	$\tan \theta$ _____ θ	< 0	the solutions will be in quadrants _____ and _____.	

Chapter 4 Review

4.1 Angles and Angle Measure, pages 109–119

1. Convert each degree measure to radian measure and each radian measure to degree measure. Give exact values.

   a) 270°

   b) $\dfrac{5\pi}{3}$

   c) 300°

   d) −4

   e) 495°

   f) $\dfrac{13\pi}{4}$

2. Identify one positive and one negative angle measure that is coterminal with each angle. Then, write a general expression for all the coterminal angles in each case.

   a) $\dfrac{11\pi}{6}$

   b) −375°

3. Determine the measure of the central angle subtended by each arc to one decimal place.

   a) arc length 31.4 cm, radius 5.0 cm, in radians

   b) arc length 11.3 m, radius 22.6 m, in degrees

4.2 The Unit Circle, pages 120–128

4. Determine the missing coordinate for point $P\left(x, -\frac{2}{3}\right)$ in quadrant III on the unit circle.

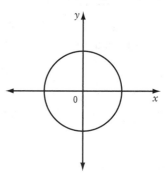

5. Determine the value of angle θ in standard position, $0 \le \theta < 2\pi$, given the coordinates of $P(\theta)$, the point at which the terminal arm of θ intersects the unit circle.

a) $P\left(\frac{1}{2}, \frac{\sqrt{3}}{2}\right)$ $\theta =$

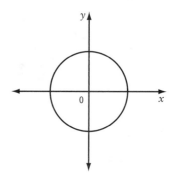

b) $P\left(\frac{1}{\sqrt{2}}, -\frac{1}{\sqrt{2}}\right)$ $\theta =$

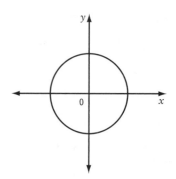

4.3 Trigonometric Ratios, pages 129–137

6. Determine the measure of all angles that satisfy $\sec \theta = 1.788$, $0° \le \theta < 720°$. Round your answers to the nearest degree.

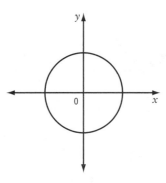

7. Determine the exact value of

a) $\cot\left(\dfrac{5\pi}{6}\right)$

b) $\csc\left(\dfrac{5\pi}{3}\right)$

4.4 Introduction to Trigonometric Equations, pages 138–144

8. Write the general form of the solutions to $\sec \theta + 10 = 2 - 4 \sec \theta$ (in degrees).

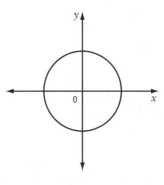

$\theta_1 \approx$ _____, $n \in I$

$\theta_2 \approx$ _____, $n \in I$

9. Solve $2 \sin^2 \theta + \sin \theta = 1$, $0 \le \theta < 2\pi$. Give exact solutions.

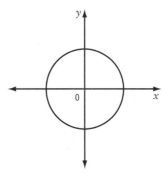

Chapter 4 Skills Organizer

Make note of some of the key things you remember about the processes you have learned in this chapter. Use your class notes, textbook, or questions from this workbook to help you choose examples (or create your own).

Process	Example	Things to Remember
Converting angle measures • from degrees to radians • from radian to degrees		
Determining coterminal angles		
Determining the six trigonometric ratios for angles in the unit circle		
Solving trigonometric equations • for a restricted domain • a general solution		

Chapter 5 Trigonometric Functions and Graphs

5.1 Graphing Sine and Cosine Functions

> ## KEY IDEAS

- Sine and cosine functions are *periodic* or *sinusoidal functions*. The values of these functions repeat in a regular pattern. These functions are based on the unit circle.
- Consider the graphs of $y = \sin \theta$ and $y = \cos \theta$.

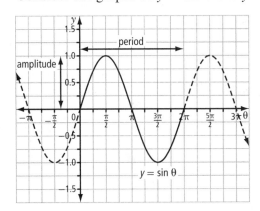

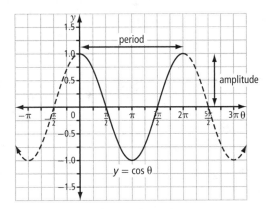

– The maximum value is $+1$.	– The maximum value is $+1$.
– The minimum value is -1.	– The minimum value is -1.
– The amplitude is 1.	– The amplitude is 1.
– The period is 2π.	– The period is 2π.
– The y-intercept is 0.	– The y-intercept is 1.
– The θ-intercepts on the given domain are $-\pi$, 0, π, 2π, and 3π.	– The θ-intercepts on the given domain are $-\frac{\pi}{2}$, $\frac{\pi}{2}$, $\frac{3\pi}{2}$, and $\frac{5\pi}{2}$.
– The domain of $y = \sin \theta$ is $\{\theta \mid \theta \in \mathbf{R}\}$.	– The domain of $y = \cos \theta$ is $\{\theta \mid \theta \in \mathbf{R}\}$.
– The range of $y = \sin \theta$ is $\{y \mid -1 \leq y \leq 1, y \in \mathbf{R}\}$.	– The range of $y = \cos \theta$ is $\{y \mid -1 \leq y \leq 1, y \in \mathbf{R}\}$.

- For sinusoidal functions of the form $y = a \sin bx$ or $y = a \cos bx$, a represents a vertical stretch of factor $|a|$ and b represents a horizontal stretch of factor $\frac{1}{|b|}$. Use the following key features to sketch the graph of a sinusoidal function.
  - the maximum and minimum values
  - the amplitude, which is one half the total height of the function

  $$\text{Amplitude} = \frac{\text{maximum value} - \text{minimum value}}{2}$$

  The amplitude is given by $|a|$.
  - the period, which is the horizontal length of one cycle on the graph of a function

  $$\text{Period} = \frac{2\pi}{|b|} \text{ or } \frac{360°}{|b|}$$

  Changing the value of b changes the period of the function.
  - the coordinates of the horizontal intercepts

Working Example 1: Graph the Sine and Cosine Functions

Graph each function for the domain $0 \le \theta \le 3\pi$.

a) $y = \sin \theta$ **b)** $y = \cos \theta$

Solution

a) Complete the table of values. Round values to three decimal places.

θ	$y = \sin \theta$	θ	$y = \sin \theta$	θ	$y = \sin \theta$	θ	$y = \sin \theta$
0		$\dfrac{6\pi}{6} = \pi$		$\dfrac{12\pi}{6} = 2\pi$		$\dfrac{18\pi}{6} = 3\pi$	
$\dfrac{\pi}{6}$		$\dfrac{7\pi}{6}$		$\dfrac{13\pi}{6}$			
$\dfrac{2\pi}{6} = \dfrac{\pi}{3}$		$\dfrac{8\pi}{6} = \dfrac{4\pi}{3}$					
		$\dfrac{9\pi}{6} = \dfrac{3\pi}{2}$		$\dfrac{15\pi}{6} = \dfrac{5\pi}{2}$			
$\dfrac{4\pi}{6} = \dfrac{2\pi}{3}$				$\dfrac{16\pi}{6} = \dfrac{8\pi}{3}$			
$\dfrac{5\pi}{6}$							

> Make sure your calculator is in radian mode.

Plot the points and join them with a smooth curve.

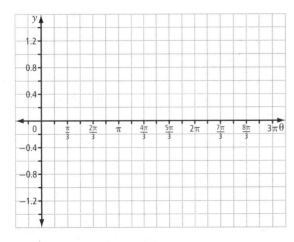

b) Complete the table of values.

θ	$y = \cos \theta$	θ	$y = \cos \theta$	θ	$y = \cos \theta$	θ	$y = \cos \theta$
0		π		2π		3π	
$\dfrac{\pi}{6}$		$\dfrac{7\pi}{6}$					
$\dfrac{\pi}{3}$		$\dfrac{4\pi}{3}$					
$\dfrac{\pi}{2}$		$\dfrac{3\pi}{2}$					
$\dfrac{2\pi}{3}$		$\dfrac{5\pi}{3}$					
$\dfrac{5\pi}{6}$		$\dfrac{11\pi}{6}$					

> What will the value for 2π be? Which angle is coterminal with 2π?

Plot the points and join them with a smooth curve.

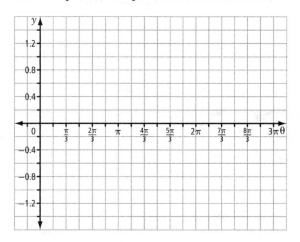

Working Example 2: Determine the Period of a Sine Function

Graph $y = \sin(3\theta)$ on the domain $0 \le \theta \le 3\pi$.

Solution

First consider the key features of the basic sine function, $y = \sin \theta$.
Use the key features to sketch the graph of the basic sine function, $y = \sin \theta$.

Now consider the function $y = \sin(3\theta)$.

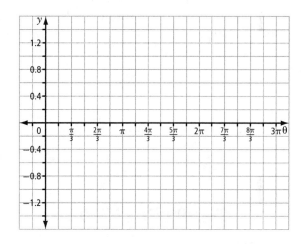

- The amplitude of $y = \sin(3\theta)$ is _____.

- The maximum value of $y = \sin(3\theta)$

  is _____.

- The minimum value of $y = \sin(3\theta)$

  is _____.

- The period of $y = \sin(3\theta)$ is $\dfrac{2\pi}{|b|}$, or _____.

- The θ-intercepts of $y = \sin(3\theta)$ on the domain

  $0 \le \theta \le 3\pi$ are _____.

- The y-intercept of $y = \sin(3\theta)$ is _____.

How can you use the period of
$y = \sin(3\theta)$ and the θ-intercepts of
the basic sine function to determine
the θ-intercepts of $y = \sin(3\theta)$?

Use the key features to sketch the graph of the function $y = \sin(3\theta)$ on the coordinate grid above.

Working Example 3: Determine the Amplitude of a Cosine Function

Graph $y = -4 \cos \theta$ on the domain $0 \le \theta \le 3\pi$.

Solution

Complete the table. First, determine the key features of $y = \cos \theta$ on the specified domain.

	$y = \cos \theta$	$y = -4 \cos \theta$
Maximum value		
Minimum value		
Amplitude		
Period		
θ-intercepts		
y-intercept		

How does the amplitude of $y = -4 \cos \theta$ compare to the amplitude of $y = \cos \theta$?

How do the θ-intercepts of $y = -4 \cos \theta$ compare to the θ-intercepts of $y = \cos \theta$?

Use the key features to sketch the graph of the basic cosine function, $y = \cos \theta$. Then, sketch the graph of $y = -4 \cos \theta$ on the same coordinate grid.

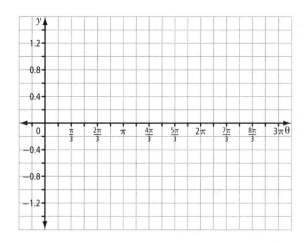

Check Your Understanding

Practise

1. State the amplitude of each trigonometric function.

   a) $y = 2 \cos \theta$

   b) $y = \frac{1}{4} \sin \theta$

   c) $y = 5 \sin (2\theta)$

   d) $y = -3 \cos \left(\frac{1}{2} \theta \right)$

2. State the period of each trigonometric function in degrees and in radians.

a) $y = 3 \sin \theta$

Degrees: $\dfrac{360°}{|b|} =$ _____

Radians: $\dfrac{2\pi}{|b|} =$ _____

b) $y = \cos (2\theta)$

c) $y = 0.25 \sin (0.25\theta)$

d) $y = -1.5 \cos (1.5\theta)$

3. State the period, in radians, and the amplitude of each trigonometric function.

a)
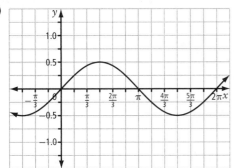

b)
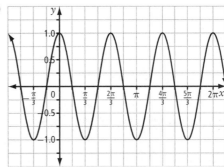

c)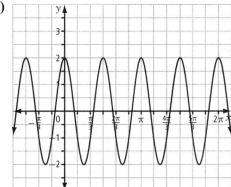

d)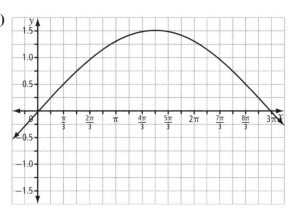

4. Identify the key features of $y = \sin \theta$ and the transformed sine function. Then, graph at least two cycles of the transformed sine function.

a) $y = \sin\left(\frac{1}{3}\theta\right)$

Identify the key features of $y = \sin \theta$.

$a =$ _____; the amplitude is _____.

Maximum value: _____   Minimum value: _____

$b =$ _____; the period is _____.

θ-intercepts: _____ y-intercept: _____

Identify the key features of $y = \sin\left(\frac{1}{3}\theta\right)$.

$a =$ _____; the amplitude is _____.

The graph _____ reflected in the x-axis.
       (*is* or *is not*)

Maximum value: _____   Minimum value: _____

$b =$ _____; the period is _____.

The graph is stretched _____ by a factor of _____.
       (*horizontally* or *vertically*)

θ-intercepts: _____ y-intercept: _____

Use the key features to sketch the graph of the function.

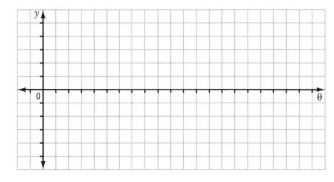

> Consider the key features of the function when choosing the scales.

b) $y = 1.5 \sin (2\theta)$

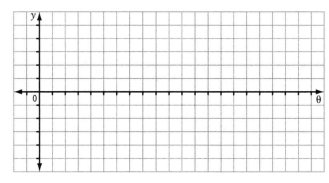

c) $y = -2 \sin (4\theta)$

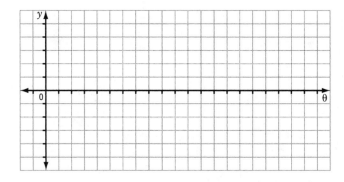

5. Identify the key features of each cosine function. Then, graph at least two cycles of each cosine function.

a) $y = 2 \cos \left(\dfrac{1}{2} \theta \right)$

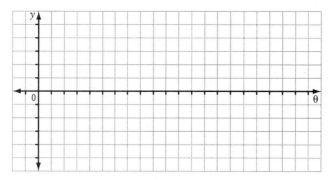

b) $y = -\cos (2\theta)$

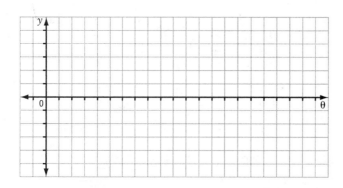

Connect

6. Consider the graphs of $y = \sin x$ and $y = \cos x$ below.

   a) Divide the graph of each trigonometric function into quadrants. Label the quadrants on the graphs and on the unit circles.

   b) Shade in the regions where $\sin x$ or $\cos x$ is positive on each graph and on each unit circle. Identify the maximum values.

   c) Using a different colour, shade in the regions where $\sin x$ or $\cos x$ is negative on each graph and on each unit circle. Identify the minimum values.

   d) Identify the x-intercepts and the corresponding angles on the unit circle.

Sine Function

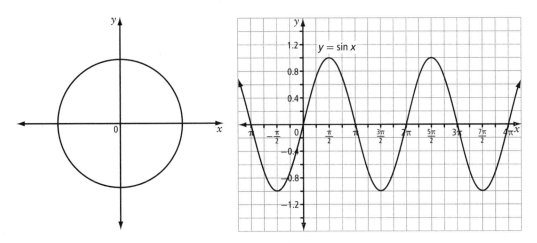

Cosine Function

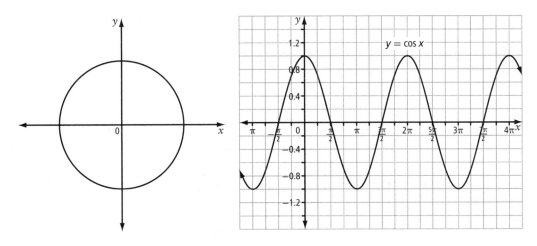

KEY IDEAS

- You can apply the same transformation rules to sinusoidal functions of the form
  $y = a \sin b(\theta - c) + d$ or $y = a \cos b(\theta - c) + d$.
  - A vertical stretch by a factor of $|a|$ changes the amplitude to $|a|$.

    $y = a \sin \theta$ $\qquad\qquad\qquad\qquad$ $y = a \cos \theta$

    If $a < 0$, the function is reflected through the horizontal mid-line of the function.
  - A horizontal stretch by a factor of $\frac{1}{|b|}$ changes the period to $\frac{360°}{|b|}$ or $\frac{2\pi}{|b|}$ radians.

    $y = \sin (b\theta)$ $\qquad\qquad\qquad\qquad$ $y = \cos (b\theta)$

    If $b < 0$, the function is reflected in the y-axis.
  - For sinusoidal functions, a horizontal translation is called the *phase shift*.

    $y = \sin (\theta - c)$ $\qquad\qquad\qquad\qquad$ $y = \cos (\theta - c)$

    If $c > 0$, the function shifts c units to the right.
    If $c < 0$, the function shifts c units to the left.
  - The *vertical displacement* is a vertical translation.

    $y = \sin \theta + d$ $\qquad\qquad\qquad\qquad$ $y = \cos \theta + d$

  - If $d > 0$, the function shifts d units up.
  - If $d < 0$, the function shifts d units down.

    $$d = \frac{\text{maximum value} + \text{minimum value}}{2}$$

  - The *sinusoidal axis* is defined by the line $y = d$. It represents the mid-line of the function.

- Apply transformations of sinusoidal functions in the same order as for any other functions:
  - **i)** horizontal stretches and reflections, $\frac{1}{|b|}$
  - **ii)** vertical stretches and reflections, $|a|$
  - **iii)** translations, c and d

- The domain of a sinusoidal function is not affected by transformations.

  The range of a sinusoidal function, normally $\{y \mid -1 \le y \le 1, y \in R\}$, is affected by changes to the amplitude and vertical displacement.

  Consider the graph of $y = 2 \sin 2\left(x - \frac{\pi}{2}\right) + 1$.

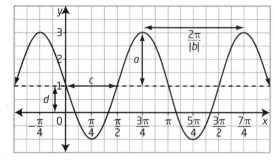

  $a = 2$, so the amplitude is 2

  $b = 2$, so the period is $\frac{2\pi}{2}$, or π

  $c = \frac{\pi}{2}$, so the graph is shifted $\frac{\pi}{2}$ units right

  $d = 1$, so the graph is shifted 1 unit up

  domain: $\{x \mid x \in R\}$

  range: $\{y \mid -1 \le y \le 3, y \in R\}$

Working Example 1: Graph $y = \sin(\theta - c) + d$

a) Sketch the graph of the function $y = \sin\left(\theta + \frac{\pi}{2}\right) + 3$.

b) State the domain and range.

Solution

a) Sketch two cycles of the graph of the base function, $y = \sin \theta$.

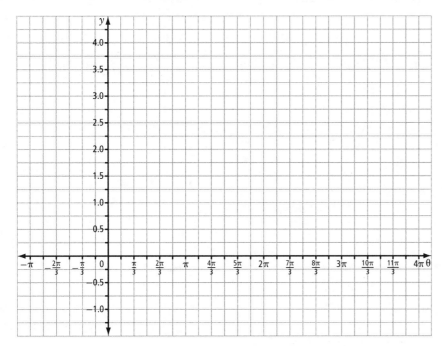

Next, consider the transformed function $y = \sin\left(\theta + \frac{\pi}{2}\right) + 3$.

The amplitude is _____ and the period is _____.

$c =$ _____. This represents a phase shift of _____ units to the _____.
(*left* or *right*)

$d =$ _____. This represents a vertical displacement of _____ units _____.
(*up* or *down*)

On the grid above, sketch the sinusoidal axis at $y = 3$.

Use the sinusoidal axis, amplitude, period, and phase shift to sketch the graph of $y = \sin\left(\theta + \frac{\pi}{2}\right) + 3$ on the grid above.

b) The domain of $y = \sin\left(\theta + \frac{\pi}{2}\right) + 3$

is _____.

The range of $y = \sin\left(\theta + \frac{\pi}{2}\right) + 3$ is

_____.

> Compare the graph of
> $y = \sin\left(\theta + \frac{\pi}{2}\right) + 3$ to
> the graph of $y = \cos \theta$.
> What do you notice?

Working Example 2: Determine an Equation From a Graph

Write two sinusoidal equations of the form $y = a \sin b(\theta - c) + d$ and $y = a \cos b(\theta - c) + d$ to represent the function shown in the graph below.

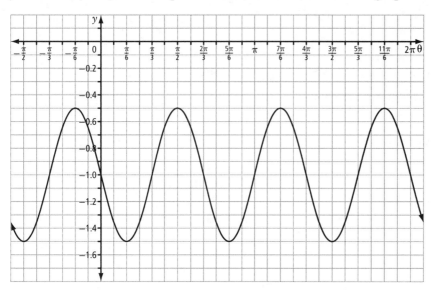

Solution

Determine the equation of a sine function.
In $y = a \sin b(\theta - c) + d$, there are four parameters to determine: a, b, c, d.

• Determine the amplitude, a.

$$|a| = \frac{\text{maximum value} - \boxed{}}{2}$$

$$= \frac{\boxed{} - \boxed{}}{2}$$

$$= \underline{}$$

• Determine the displacement, d.

   The equation of the sinusoidal axis is $y = $ _____. Therefore, $d = $ _____.

• Determine the value of b.

   The period of the graphed function is _____ radians.

   $$\text{Period} = \frac{2\pi}{|b|}$$

   $$\underline{} = \frac{2\pi}{|b|}$$

   $$b = \underline{}$$

Choose b to be positive.

- Determine the phase shift, *c*.

   The graph is shifted _____ units to the right, so *c* = _____.

A sine equation that represents the graphed function is *y* = _____.

To determine an equation of a cosine function, $y = a \cos b(\theta - c) + d$, the values for *a*, *b*, and *d* are the same, but the phase shift is different.

The graph is shifted _____ units to the right, so *c* = _____.

A cosine equation that represents the graphed function is *y* = _____.

Check Your Understanding

Practise

1. Determine the phase shift and the vertical displacement. Then, graph the function. Choose appropriate scales for the axes.

   a) $y = \cos\left(\theta - \frac{\pi}{3}\right) - 1$

   Phase shift: _____   Vertical displacement: _____

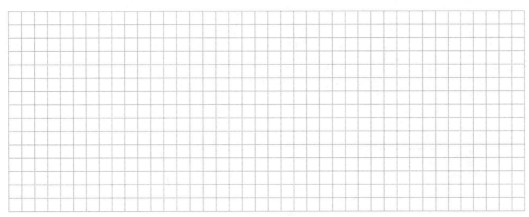

   b) $y = \sin\left(\theta + \frac{\pi}{4}\right) + 2$

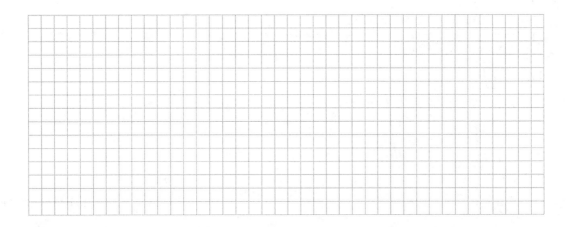

For more practice, see #1 and #2 on page 250 of *Pre-Calculus 12*.

2. Determine the key features of each sine function.

a) $y = -5 \sin\left(\frac{1}{2}(\theta - 90°)\right) + 15$

Amplitude: _____ Period: _____

Phase shift: _____ Vertical displacement: _____

Domain: _____ Range: _____

b) $y = 0.1 \sin(2\theta + 90°) - 1$

c)

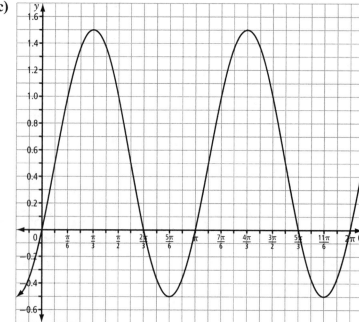

d)

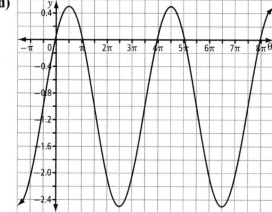

3. Write the equation of each sine function in the form $y = a \sin b(x - c) + d$ given its characteristics.

a) amplitude 2, period π, phase shift $\frac{\pi}{3}$ to the left, vertical displacement 1 unit down

b) amplitude $\frac{1}{4}$, period 6π, phase shift π to the left, vertical displacement 2 units up

c) amplitude 4, period 540°, phase shift 60° to the right, no vertical displacement

4. Graph each function in the space provided. Show at least two cycles.

a) $y = 5 \sin 0.5(\theta + \pi) + 3$

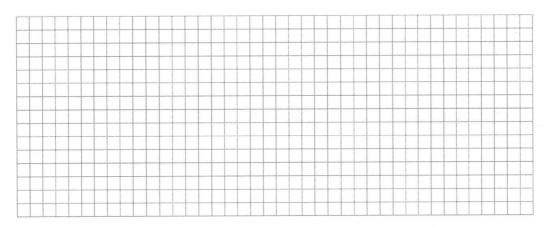

b) $y = -2 \sin 2\left(\theta - \frac{\pi}{3}\right) + 4$

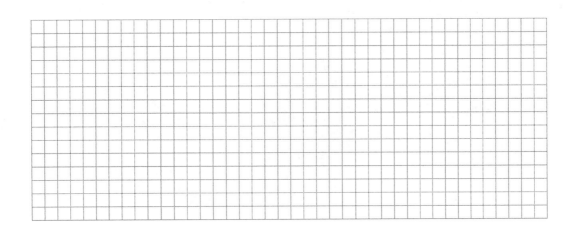

c) $y = 1.5 \cos 3\left(\theta + \dfrac{\pi}{2}\right) - 1$

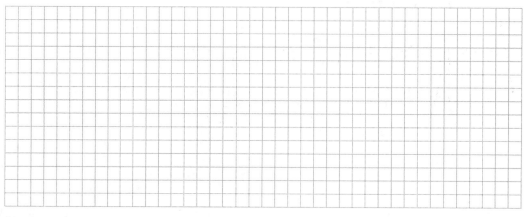

d) $y = -\cos \dfrac{1}{3}(\theta - \pi) + 3$

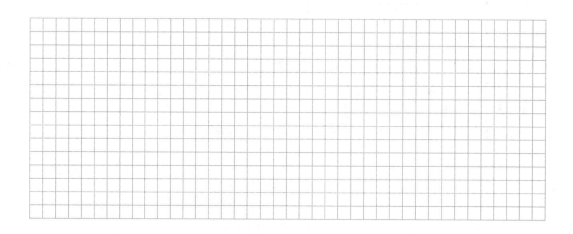

Apply

5. Write two different equations of the form $y = a \sin b(\theta - c) + d$ for the function graphed below. Use technology to check that your equations are correct.

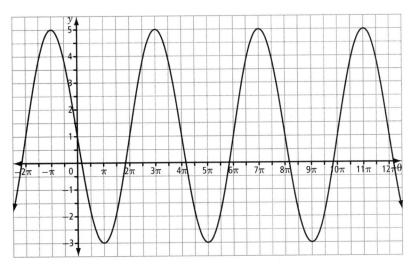

6. Write two different equations of the form $y = a \cos b(\theta - c) + d$ to represent the function graphed below. Use technology to verify that your equations are correct.

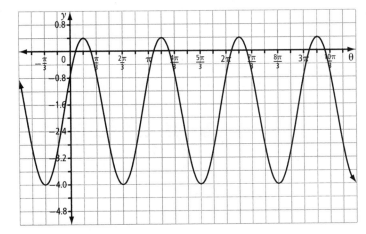

7. Write an equation of the form $y = a \sin b(\theta - c) + d$ and an equation of the form $y = a \cos b(\theta - c) + d$ to represent the function graphed below.

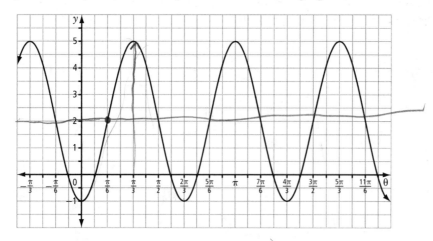

$a = \dfrac{\max - \min}{2}$

$a = \dfrac{5 - -1}{2}$

$a = \dfrac{6}{2}$

$a = 3$

$\text{Period} = \dfrac{2\pi}{b}$

$\dfrac{2\pi}{3} = \dfrac{2\pi}{b}$

$2\pi(b) = 2\pi(3)$

$b = 3$

$\boxed{c = \dfrac{\pi}{6}}$ ← b/c sin starts

$d = \dfrac{\max + \min}{2}$

$d = \dfrac{5 + -1}{2}$

$d = \dfrac{4}{2}$

$d = 2$

$y = 3 \sin 3\left(\theta - \dfrac{\pi}{6}\right) + 2$

so sp has to go ↑ 15°

Connect

8. The graphed function is represented by an equation of each of the following forms. Determine the values of a, b, c, and d.

a) $y = a \sin b(\theta - c) + d;\ a > 0$

$a = 3$

$d = \dfrac{\max + \min}{2}$

$\qquad = \dfrac{5 + -1}{2}$

$d = 2$

$c = \dfrac{\pi}{2}$

$\text{Period} = \dfrac{2\pi}{b}$

$\pi = \dfrac{2\pi}{b}$

$\pi b = 2\pi$

$b = 2$

$y = 3 \sin 2\left(\theta - \dfrac{\pi}{2}\right) + 2$

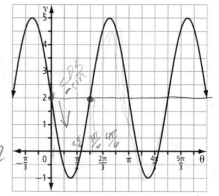

b) $y = a \sin b(\theta - c) + d;\ a < 0$

c) $y = a \cos b(\theta - c) + d;\ a > 0$

KEY IDEAS

- The graph of the tangent function, $y = \tan x$, is periodic, but it is *not* sinusoidal.

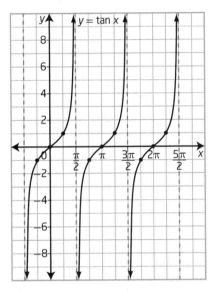

- These are the characteristics of the tangent function graph, $y = \tan x$:
  - It has period π or 180°.
  - It is discontinuous where $\tan x$ is undefined, that is, when $x = \dfrac{\pi}{2}, \dfrac{3\pi}{2}, \dfrac{5\pi}{2}, \ldots, \dfrac{\pi}{2} + n\pi$, $n \in \mathrm{I}$. The discontinuity is represented on the graph of $y = \tan x$ as *vertical asymptotes*.
  - The domain is $\left(x \mid x \neq \dfrac{\pi}{2} + n\pi, x \in \mathrm{R}, n \in \mathrm{I} \right)$.
  - It has no maximum or minimum values.
  - The range is $\{ y \mid y \in \mathrm{R} \}$.
  - It has x-intercepts at every multiple of π: 0, π, 2π, $\ldots$, $n\pi$, $n \in \mathrm{I}$. Each of the x-intercepts is a turning point, where the slope changes from decreasing to increasing.

- On the unit circle, you can express the coordinates of the point P on the terminal arm of angle θ as (x, y) or $(\sin \theta, \cos \theta)$. The slope of the terminal arm is represented by the tangent function:

$$\text{slope} = \frac{\Delta y}{\Delta x}$$
$$= \frac{y - 0}{x - 0} \qquad\qquad \text{OR} \qquad\qquad \text{slope} = \frac{\sin \theta}{\cos \theta}$$
$$= \frac{y}{x} \qquad\qquad\qquad\qquad\qquad\qquad\qquad = \tan \theta$$
$$= \tan \theta$$

Therefore, you can use the tangent function to model the slope of a line from a fixed point to a moving object as the object moves through a range of angles.

Working Example 1: Graph $y = \tan\theta$ Using Key Points

Graph $y = \tan\theta$ over the domain $-\pi \le \theta \le 4\pi$.

Solution

The key features needed to sketch the graph of the tangent function are the zeros, ones, and asymptotes.

> The *ones* of a tangent function are the values of θ when $y = \pm 1$.

Determine the Zeros

Given $\tan\theta = \dfrac{\sin\theta}{\cos\theta}$, when $\sin\theta = 0$, $\tan\theta =$ _____.

Therefore, $y = \tan\theta$ has the same zeros (*x*-intercepts) as $y = \sin\theta$.

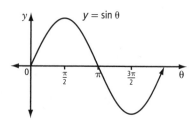

The zeros of $y = \tan\theta$ over the domain $-\pi \le \theta \le 4\pi$ are _____, _____, _____,

_____, _____, and _____.

Determine the Ones

The tangent function represents the slope of the terminal arm of an angle in standard position.

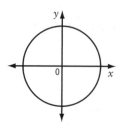

Given slope $= \dfrac{\sin\theta}{\cos\theta}$, the slope is 1 when $\sin\theta =$ _____.

Over the domain $-\pi \le \theta \le 4\pi$, the slope of the terminal arm is 1 when $\theta =$ _____, _____,

_____, _____, and _____.

Given slope $= \dfrac{\sin\theta}{\cos\theta}$, the slope is -1 when $\sin\theta =$ _____.

Over the domain $-\pi \le \theta \le 4\pi$, the slope of the terminal arm is -1 when $\theta =$ _____,

_____, _____, _____, and _____.

Determine the Asymptotes

Given $\tan \theta = \dfrac{\sin \theta}{\cos \theta}$, $\tan \theta$ is undefined when _____ = 0.

Therefore, $y = \tan \theta$ has non-permissible values wherever $y =$ _____ has zeros (*x*-intercepts).

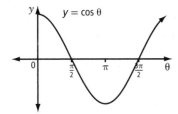

The non-permissible values of $y = \tan \theta$ over the domain $-\pi \le \theta \le 4\pi$ are _____, _____,

_____, _____, and _____.

Use a broken line to draw a vertical asymptote on the graph at each non-permissible value of $y = \tan \theta$.

Plot the zeros and the ones.

Draw the tangent function starting at the lower edge of your graph near an asymptote, passing through the points plotted, and continuing to the upper edge of your graph near an asymptote. Be sure not to cross the asymptotes. In the given domain, how many cycles are shown?

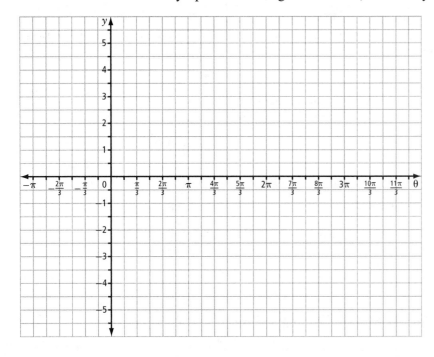

Working Example 2: Model a Problem Using the Tangent Function

An airplane is flying at a constant altitude of 9700 m in a straight line directly above a radar station. How does the horizontal distance between the plane and the radar station change as the plane crosses overhead?

Solution

Draw a diagram to illustrate the situation.

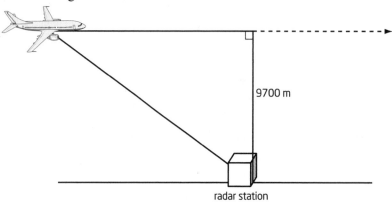

radar station

Label the complementary angle to the angle of elevation as θ, and label the horizontal distance as h.

Write an equation expressing h in terms of θ.

$\tan \theta =$

$\quad h =$

As θ approaches 0, what happens to the horizontal distance?
Indicate this point on the graph of $y = 9700 \tan \theta$ below, and on the diagram above.

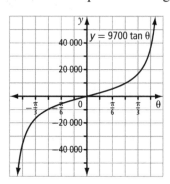

As the plane continues its flight away from the radar station,
• what happens to θ?

• what happens to h? Indicate this region on the graph and on the diagram.

Check Your Understanding

Practise

1. Use the graph of $y = \tan \theta$ to determine each value.

a) $\tan 2\pi$

b) $\tan \dfrac{3\pi}{2}$

c) $\tan \dfrac{\pi}{4}$

d) $\tan \left(-\dfrac{\pi}{4}\right)$

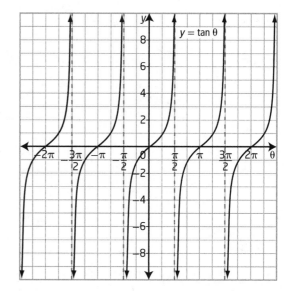

2. Use the graph of $y = \tan \theta$ from #1 and your knowledge of the properties of the tangent function to determine each value.

a) $\tan (-\pi)$

b) $\tan (-3\pi)$

c) $\tan (-100\pi)$

3. Use the graph of $y = \tan \theta$ from #1 and your knowledge of the properties of the tangent function to determine each value.

a) $\tan \left(\dfrac{9\pi}{4}\right)$

b) $\tan \left(\dfrac{13\pi}{4}\right)$

c) $\tan \left(\dfrac{17\pi}{4}\right)$

4. Refer to your answers in #2 and #3. Write a general expression for all solutions in each case.

   a) $\tan \theta = 0$ **b)** $\tan \theta = 1$

5. Use graphing technology to graph $y = \tan x$, where x is measured in degrees. Trace along the graph to locate the approximate value of the function when $x = 35°$. Predict the following values. Verify your predictions by tracing along the graph.

   $\tan 35° \approx$ _____

   a) $\tan (-325°)$ **b)** $\tan 395°$ **c)** $\tan (-35°)$

Apply

6. An observer watches a hot-air balloon pass directly overhead at a constant altitude of 640 m.

   a) Determine the relation between the horizontal distance, d, in metres, from the observer to the hot-air balloon and the angle, in degrees, formed from the vertical to the balloon.

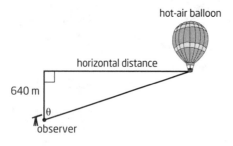

hot-air balloon

horizontal distance

640 m

θ

observer

b) Graph the function. What are reasonable limits on the domain and range?

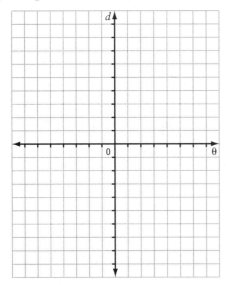

7. A simple sundial has a gnomon 10 cm high. Suppose the angle of the sun with respect to the gnomon changes from −75° at 7:00 a.m. to +75° at 5:00 p.m.

   a) Write an expression for the length of the shadow in terms of the angle of the sun.

   b) Describe any assumptions you made in creating this model.

   c) Determine the length of the shadow at 9:00 a.m.

   d) Determine the length of the shadow at 4:00 p.m.

📖 For more practice modelling using the tangent function, try #9 to #12 on pages 264–265 of *Pre-Calculus 12*.

Connect

8. a) For each labelled point on the graph of $y = \tan \theta$, sketch the terminal arm of angle θ on a unit circle.

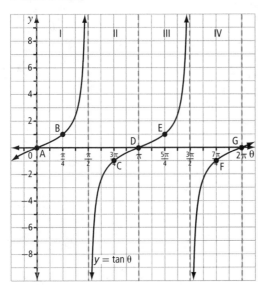

A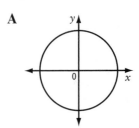

B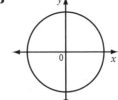

C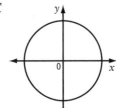

D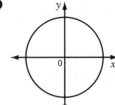

E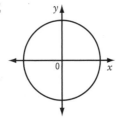

F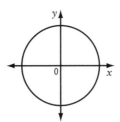

G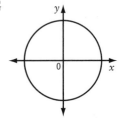

b) For each asymptote of $y = \tan \theta$, sketch the terminal arm of angle θ on a unit circle.

i) $\theta = \dfrac{\pi}{2}$ **ii)** $\theta = \dfrac{3\pi}{2}$

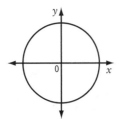 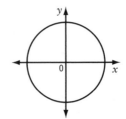

KEY IDEAS

- You can use sinusoidal functions to model periodic phenomena that do not involve angles as the independent variable. Examples of such phenomena include
  - wave shapes, such as a heartbeat or ocean waves
  - pistons in a machine or the swing of a pendulum
  - circular motion, such as a Ferris wheel

- You can adjust the parameters a, b, c, and d in sinusoidal equations of the form $y = a \sin b(\theta - c) + d$ or $y = a \cos b(\theta - c) + d$ to fit the characteristics of the phenomenon being modelled.

- Graphing technology allows you examine how well the model represents the data. It also allows you to extrapolate or interpolate solutions from the model.

- You can find approximate solutions to trigonometric equations using the graphs of the trigonometric functions. Express solutions over a specific interval or give a general solution.

Working Example 1: Solve Simple Trigonometric Equations

Solve each equation over the specified interval.

a) $\sin x = 0.5, 0° \le x \le 720°$

b) $\sin 2x = 0.5, 0° \le x \le 720°$

Solution

a) Method 1: Use the Unit Circle and Special Triangles

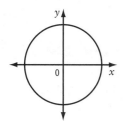

$\theta_R = \sin^{-1}(0.5) = \underline{\hspace{2cm}}$

The solutions are $x = \underline{\hspace{1.5cm}}, \underline{\hspace{1.5cm}}, \underline{\hspace{1.5cm}}, \underline{\hspace{1.5cm}}, 0° \le x \le 720°$.

Method 2: Use a Graph

Graph $y = \sin x$ (Left Side) and $y = 0.5$ (Right Side) on the same set of axes on the domain $0° \leq x \leq 720°$.

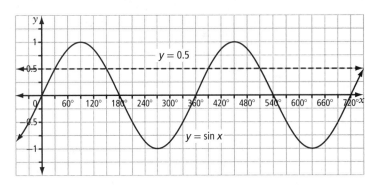

Determine the coordinates of the points of intersection of the two functions.

The solutions are $x =$ _____, _____, _____, _____, $0° \leq x < 720°$.

> Check that your calculator is set to the correct mode.

b) Graph $y = \sin 2x$ (Left Side) and $y = 0.5$ (Right Side) on the same set of axes over the domain $0° \leq x \leq 720°$.

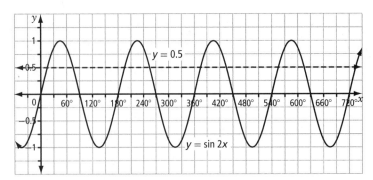

> How many solutions are there?

The solutions are $x =$ _____, $0° \leq x < 720°$.

Working Example 2: Solve a Trigonometric Equation by Graphing

Solve $3 = 16 \cos [5(x + 1)] - 5$, $0 \leq x \leq \pi$.

Solution

Collect all terms on the same side of the equation.
$3 = 16 \cos [5(x + 1)] - 5$

$0 =$ _____

Substitute y for 0.

$y =$ _____

Graph the related function using graphing technology.

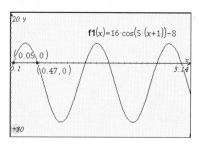

How many solutions are there within the given domain?

The solutions within the first cycle are $x_1 \approx$ _____ and $x_2 \approx$ _____.

Additional solutions are of the form $x + n$ (period).

The solutions are $x \approx$ _____, $0 \leq x \leq \pi$.

Working Example 3: Model Average Temperature

Write a sinusoidal function that models the average temperature each month in Whitehorse, Yukon, in a given year.

Month	Temperature (°C)	Month	Temperature (°C)	Month	Temperature (°C)
1	−18.4	5	6.8	9	7.5
2	−13.4	6	11.9	10	0.6
3	−7.3	7	14.0	11	−9.1
4	0.1	8	12.3	12	−15.7

Solution

Use graphing technology to create a scatter plot of the data.

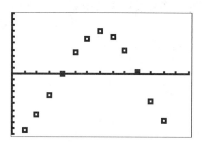

Let x represent _____. Let y represent _____.

Use a cosine model, $y = a \cos b(x - c) + d$, where $a < 0$.

$$|a| = \frac{\text{maximum value} - \text{minimum value}}{2}$$

$$= $$

Period: _____

Use the period to determine b, where $\dfrac{2\pi}{|b|}$ = period.

Determine the phase shift.

$c =$ _____

$d = \dfrac{\text{maximum value} + \text{minimum value}}{2}$

$=$

At what x-value does the minimum of $y = -\cos x$ occur? At what x-value does the minimum of the table data occur?

Write your equation: _____

Use graphing technology. Graph the equation with the scatter plot to check that it is a reasonable representation of the data.

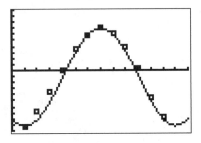

Check Your Understanding

Practise

1. Use the graph of $y = 6 \cos (4x)$ to solve each trigonometric equation.

   a) $6 \cos (4x) = 3, 0 \leq x \leq \pi$

   b) $6 \cos (4x) = -6$, general solution in radians

2. Use the graph of $V = 170 \sin (120\pi t)$ to approximate the solutions to each trigonometric equation.

   a) $50 = 170 \sin (120\pi t), 0 \leq x \leq 0.030$

   b) $170 \sin (120\pi t) = -120, 0 \leq x \leq 0.030$

   c) $170 \sin (120\pi t) = 0$, general solution in radians

3. Sound travels in waves. You can see the sinusoidal patterns of sound waves using a device called an oscilloscope.

   a) Orchestra members tune their instruments to $A = 440$ Hz, meaning the sound wave repeats 440 times per second. What is the period of this sound wave, in seconds?

   b) Write a simple sine function representing the waveform of the note $A = 440$.
$$\frac{2\pi}{|b|} = \text{period}$$

   c) "Middle C" has a frequency of 261.63 Hz. What sine function could represent middle C?

4. Electricity comes into your home or school as alternating current, which can be modelled by a sinusoidal function. Electrical devices operate at the root mean square voltage, which is $\frac{1}{\sqrt{2}}$ of the peak voltage.

   a) In Canada, many electrical devices require 120 V and 60 Hz. Write a sine function that represents the peak voltage in Canada.

   > To get the amplitude of the wave, multiply the required voltage by $\sqrt{2}$ (≈ 1.4).

   b) In Europe (and in most of Asia, Africa, and parts of South America), many appliances require 220 V and 50 Hz. Write a sine function that represents the peak voltage in Europe.

Apply

5. The London Eye has diameter 122 m and height 135 m. It takes approximately 30 min for one rotation of the wheel. Passengers board at the bottom of the ride. The ride moves slowly enough that it is usually not necessary for the wheel to stop to let passengers on or off.

   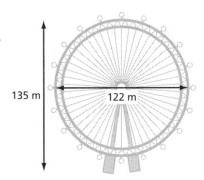

   135 m   122 m

   a) Sketch a sinusoidal function representing the height of a passenger riding the London Eye. What assumptions do you have to make?

   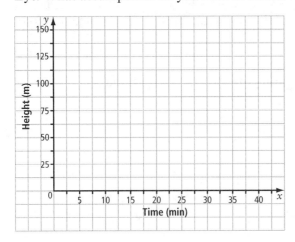

b) Write a sinusoidal function that represents the height of a passenger riding the London Eye. Over what domain is the function valid?

6. One particular afternoon, the tide in Victoria, BC, reached a maximum height of 3.0 m at 2:00 p.m. and a minimum height of 0.2 m at 8:00 p.m.

a) Sketch a sinusoidal function based on these data. What assumptions do you have to make?

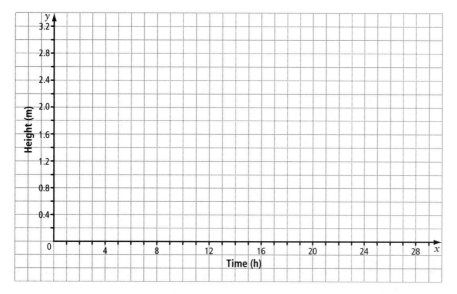

b) Write a sinusoidal function that represents the tide in Victoria, BC, on this day. Over what domain is the function valid?

7. Write a sinusoidal function that models the average temperature in Brandon, Manitoba. Use graphing technology to verify that your function is a good representation of the data.

	Jan 1	Feb 2	Mar 3	Apr 4	May 5	Jun 6	Jul 7	Aug 8	Sep 9	Oct 10	Nov 11	Dec 12
°C	−18.3	−15.8	−7.9	3.5	10.8	16.0	18.9	17.4	11.8	5.1	−5.3	−13.7

Connect

8. Using examples from class, from your textbook, and from this workbook, brainstorm a list of situations that can be modelled using a sinusoidal function in the form $y = a \sin b(x - c) + d$ or $y = a \cos b(x - c) + d$. Next to each item, list any helpful information for constructing the model. One example has been provided to help you get started.

Situation	Notes
Circular motion	• $|a|$ = radius of the circle

Chapter 5 Review

5.1 Graphing Sine and Cosine Functions, pages 149–157

1. Graph at least two cycles of $y = 3 \cos \left(\frac{1}{2}\theta \right)$. State the amplitude and period in degrees.

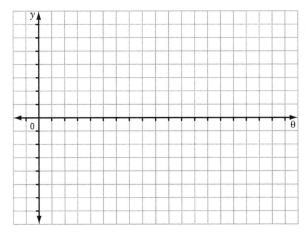

2. Graph at least two cycles of $y = -0.5 \sin (2\theta)$. State the amplitude and period in radians.

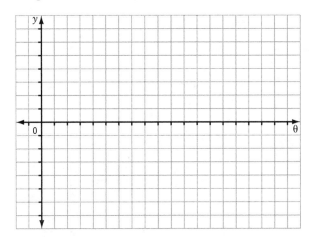

3. Without graphing, determine the amplitude and period, in radians and in degrees, of each function.

   a) $y = 2 \sin 3x$

   b) $y = \frac{1}{3} \cos x$

   c) $y = \frac{3}{4} \cos 2x$

   d) $y = -4 \sin \frac{2}{3} x$

5.2 Transformations of Sinusoidal Functions, pages 158–166

4. Determine the amplitude, period, phase shift, and vertical displacement with respect to $y = \sin x$ or $y = \cos x$ for each function.

   a) $y = 5 \sin \frac{1}{4}\left(x + \frac{\pi}{3}\right) - 1$

   b) $y = -\frac{1}{2} \cos 2(x - \pi) - 3$

   c) $y = 3 \cos 4(x + 50°) + 6$

5. Graph at least two cycles of $y = \sin 2\left(x + \frac{\pi}{12}\right) - 0.4$.

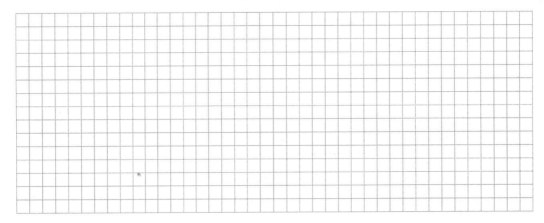

6. Write two equations of the form $y = a \cos b(\theta - c) + d$ that represent the function shown below.

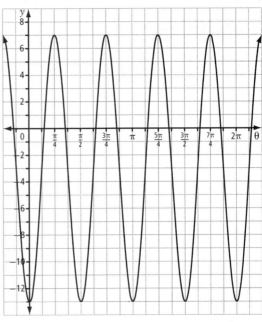

5.3 The Tangent Function, pages 167–174

7. Graph $y = \tan x$ over the domain $-\dfrac{3\pi}{2} \le x \le \dfrac{5\pi}{2}$.

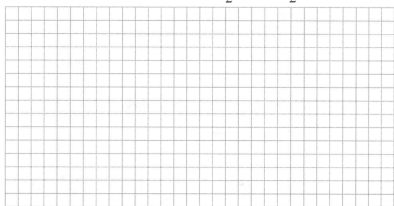

8. For each diagram, determine $\tan \theta$ and the value of θ, in degrees. If necessary, round your answer to the nearest tenth.

a)

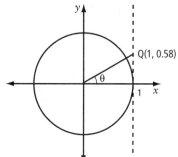

b)

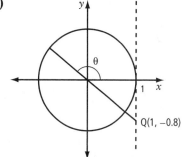

5.4 Equations and Graphs of Trigonometric Functions, pages 175–182

9. Write a sinusoidal function to model the average temperature in Nanaimo, BC.

	Jan	Feb	Mar	Apr	May	Jun	Jul	Aug	Sep	Oct	Nov	Dec
°C	1.9	3.6	5.3	8.1	11.8	14.9	17.3	17.2	14.2	9.4	5.1	2.8

10. Solve each equation by graphing.

a) $\sin 2x = 0, 0 \le x \le 2\pi$

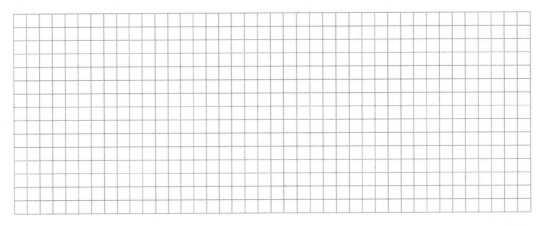

b) $\cos\left(x + \frac{\pi}{2}\right) + 1 = 0, 0 \le x \le 2\pi$

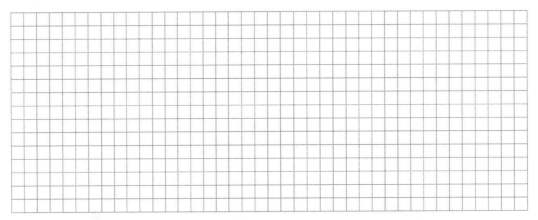

c) $\sin 2(x - 30°) + 0.5 = 0$, general solution in degrees

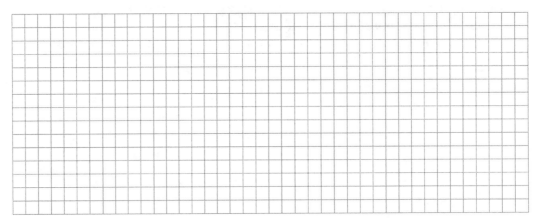

Chapter 5 Skills Organizer

Complete the table for each trigonometric function.

	$y = a \sin b(\theta - c) + d$	$y = a \cos b(\theta - c) + d$	$y = \tan \theta$
Sketch			
Key points			
Zeros			
Maximum values			
Minimum values			
Period			
Amplitude			
Domain			
Range			

Chapter 6 Trigonometric Identities

6.1 Reciprocal, Quotient, and Pythagorean Identities

<< **KEY IDEAS** >>

Trigonometric Identities

A trigonometric identity is a trigonometric equation that is true for *all* permissible values of the variable in the expressions on both sides of the equation.

- **Reciprocal Identities**

$$\csc x = \frac{1}{\sin x} \qquad \sec x = \frac{1}{\cos x} \qquad \cot x = \frac{1}{\tan x}$$

- **Quotient Identities**

$$\tan x = \frac{\sin x}{\cos x} \qquad \cot x = \frac{\cos x}{\sin x}$$

- **Pythagorean Identities**
  There are three forms of the Pythagorean identity:

  – Form 1: Derived from the Pythagorean theorem, $a^2 + b^2 = c^2$, and applied to a right triangle in the unit circle where angle θ is in standard position. The hypotenuse is 1, the adjacent side is $x = \cos \theta$, and the opposite side is $y = \sin \theta$. Therefore, $\cos^2 \theta + \sin^2 \theta = 1$.

  – Form 2: Divide both sides of form 1 by $\sin^2 \theta$ and apply the quotient and reciprocal identities.

$$\frac{\cos^2 \theta}{\sin^2 \theta} + \frac{\sin^2 \theta}{\sin^2 \theta} = \frac{1}{\sin^2 \theta}$$
$$\cot^2 \theta + 1 = \csc^2 \theta$$

  – Form 3: Divide both sides of form 1 by $\cos^2 \theta$ and apply the quotient and reciprocal identities.

$$\frac{\cos^2 \theta}{\cos^2 \theta} + \frac{\sin^2 \theta}{\cos^2 \theta} = \frac{1}{\cos^2 \theta}$$
$$1 + \tan^2 \theta = \sec^2 \theta$$

Verification and Use of Trigonometric Identities

- Trigonometric identities can be verified in two ways:
  i) numerically, by substituting specific values for the variable
  ii) graphically, using technology

- Verifying that two sides of an equation are equal for given values, or that they appear equal when graphed, is not sufficient to conclude that the equation is an identity.

- You can use trigonometric identities to simplify more complicated trigonometric expressions.

Working Example 1: Verify a Potential Identity Numerically and Graphically

a) Determine the non-permissible values, in degrees, for the equation $\csc \theta = \frac{\cot \theta}{\cos \theta}$.

b) Numerically verify that $\theta = 45°$ is a solution for the equation.

c) Numerically verify that $\theta = \frac{\pi}{6}$ is a solution for the equation.

d) Use technology to graphically determine whether the equation could be an identity over the domain $-360° < \theta \le 360°$.

Solution

a) Assess each trigonometric function in the equation individually. Are there values for which the denominators are zero or the numerators are undefined? Visualize the graph of each function to help you determine the non-permissible values.

For the left side of the equation, $\csc \theta$, the non-permissible values are _____.

For the right side of the equation, $\frac{\cot \theta}{\cos \theta}$, the non-permissible values for $\cot \theta$ are

_____. The denominator is zero when $\cos \theta = 0$. Therefore, the non-

permissible values for the denominator are _____.

Combined, the non-permissible values for $\csc \theta = \frac{\cot \theta}{\cos \theta}$ are _____.

b) Substitute $\theta = 45°$ into each side of the equation.

Left Side	Right Side
$\csc \theta$	$\dfrac{\cot \theta}{\cos \theta}$
$= \csc \mathbf{45°}$	
$= \dfrac{1}{\boxed{} \mathbf{45°}}$	$= \dfrac{\dfrac{1}{\boxed{} \mathbf{45°}}}{\cos \mathbf{45°}}$
$= \dfrac{\boxed{}}{\boxed{}}$	$= \dfrac{\boxed{}}{\boxed{}}$
$= \underline{}$	$= \underline{}$

This equation _____ true for $\theta = 45°$.
(is or is not)

c) Substitute $\theta = \frac{\pi}{6}$.

Left Side	Right Side

d) Use technology to graph $y = $ _____ and

$y = $ _____ with domain $-360° < \theta \le 360°$.

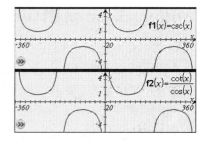

The two graphs look _____, so
(identical or *different)*

$\csc \theta = \dfrac{\cot \theta}{\cos \theta}$ _____ be an _____.
(could or *could not)*

Working Example 2: Use Identities to Simplify Expressions.

a) Determine the non-permissible values, in radians, of the variable in the expression $\dfrac{\tan x \cos x}{\sec x \cot x}$.

b) Simplify the expression.

Solution

a) Consider non-permissible values, if any.

The non-permissible values of $\tan x$ are _____.

The non-permissible values of $\sec x$ are _____.

The non-permissible values of $\cot x$ are _____.

Combined, the non-permissible values for $\dfrac{\tan x \cos x}{\sec x \cot x}$ are _____.

> Explain why you need to consider the non-permissible values for $\tan x$ in the numerator, but you do not consider the non-permissible values for $\cos x$.

b) To simplify the expression, use the reciprocal identity for $\sec x$ and quotient identities for $\tan x$ and $\cot x$ to write trigonometric functions in terms of cosine and sine.

$$\dfrac{\tan x \cos x}{\sec x \cot x} = \dfrac{\dfrac{\boxed{}}{\boxed{}} \cos x}{\dfrac{1}{\boxed{}} \, \boxed{}}$$

$$= \dfrac{\sin x}{\dfrac{\boxed{}}{\boxed{}}}$$

$$= \underline{} \, (\underline{})$$

$$= \underline{}$$

📖 To see a similar question, refer to Example 2 on pages 293 and 294 of *Pre-Calculus 12*.

Working Example 3: Use the Pythagorean Identity

a) Verify that the equation $\cot^2 x - \csc^2 x = -1$ is true when $x = \frac{\pi}{4}$.

b) Use the quotient identities to express the Pythagorean identity $\cos^2 x + \sin^2 x = 1$ as the equivalent identity $\cot^2 x - \csc^2 x = -1$.

Solution

a) Substitute $x = \frac{\pi}{4}$.

Left Side	Right Side
$\cot^2 x - \csc^2 x$	-1

$= \cot^2 \boxed{} - \csc^2 \boxed{}$

$= \dfrac{1}{\boxed{} \frac{\pi}{4}} - \dfrac{1}{\boxed{} \frac{\pi}{4}}$

$= \dfrac{1}{\boxed{}} - \dfrac{1}{\boxed{}}$

$= \underline{\hspace{3cm}}$

$= \underline{\hspace{3cm}}$

Left Side $\underline{\hspace{2cm}}$ Right Side
$(= \text{ or } \neq)$

The equation $\cot^2 x - \csc^2 x = -1$ is $\underline{\hspace{3cm}}$ when $x = \frac{\pi}{4}$.
$(true \text{ or } not \text{ } true)$

b) $\cos^2 x + \sin^2 x = 1$

Multiply both sides by $\dfrac{1}{\boxed{}}$, $x \neq \pi n$, where $n \in I$.

$\left(\dfrac{1}{\boxed{}} \right) \cos^2 x + \left(\dfrac{1}{\boxed{}} \right) \sin^2 x = \left(\dfrac{1}{\boxed{}} \right) 1$

$\dfrac{\cos^2 x}{\boxed{}} + \dfrac{\sin^2 x}{\boxed{}} = \dfrac{1}{\boxed{}}$

$\underline{\hspace{2cm}} + 1 = \underline{\hspace{2cm}}$ Use the quotient identities.

$\underline{\hspace{2cm}} - \underline{\hspace{2cm}} = -1$ Rearrange the terms.

📖 To see a similar example, refer to Example 3 on page 295 of *Pre-Calculus 12*.

Check Your Understanding

Practise

1. Determine the non-permissible values of x, in radians, for each expression.

   a) $\dfrac{\sin x}{\cos x}$

   b) $\dfrac{\cos x}{\tan x}$

   c) $\dfrac{\cot x}{1 + \sin x}$

   d) $\dfrac{\tan x}{\cos x - 1}$

   > In parts c) and d), explain whether it is possible to write a single restriction.

2. Simplify each expression to one of the three primary trigonometric functions, $\sin x$, $\cos x$, or $\tan x$.

   a) $\cot x \sin x$

   b) $\dfrac{\sec^2 x \cos x}{\csc x}$

   c) $\dfrac{\cot x \tan x}{\csc x}$

3. Simplify. Then, rewrite each expression as one of the three reciprocal trigonometric functions, $\csc x$, $\sec x$, or $\cot x$.

   a) $\dfrac{\csc x}{\sec x}$

   b) $\csc x \tan x \sec x \cos x$

   c) $\dfrac{\sin x}{1 - \cos^2 x}$

4. a) Verify that the equation $\dfrac{\csc x}{\tan x + \cot x} = \cos x$ is true for $x = 60°$ and for $x = \dfrac{\pi}{6}$.

b) What are the non-permissible values of the equation in the domain $0° \le x < 360°$.

> What determines if a value is permissible when it is in the denominator?

5. Consider the equation $\tan x + \dfrac{1}{\tan x} = \dfrac{1}{\cos x \sin x}$.

a) What are the non-permissible values, in radians, for this equation?

b) Using technology, graph the two sides of the equation over the domain $0 \le x \le 2\pi$. Sketch the graphs below. Could this equation be an identity? Explain.

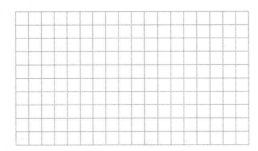 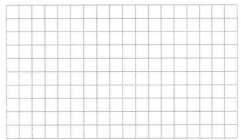

c) Verify that the equation is true when $x = \dfrac{\pi}{4}$. Use exact values for each expression in the equation.

Apply

6. When a polarized lens is rotated through angle θ over a second lens, the amount of light passing through both lenses decreases by $(1 - \cos \theta)(1 + \cos \theta)$.

   a) Determine an equivalent expression for this decrease, using only $\sin \theta$.

   $(1 - \cos \theta)(1 + \cos \theta)$

   $= 1 +$ _____ $-$ _____ $- \cos^2 \theta$

   $=$ _____ $-$ _____

   $=$ _____

   b) What fraction of light is lost when $x = \frac{\pi}{3}$?

   c) What percent of light is lost when $\theta = 30°$?

7. Compare $y = \cos x$ and $y = \sqrt{1 - \sin^2 x}$ by completing the following.

   a) Verify that $\cos x = \sqrt{1 - \sin^2 x}$ for $x = \frac{\pi}{6}$, $x = \frac{4\pi}{3}$, and $x = \pi$.

   b) Using technology, graph $y = \cos x$ and $y = \sqrt{1 - \sin^2 x}$ in the same window. Sketch the graphs below.

   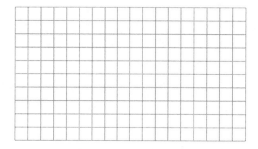

   c) State whether $\cos x = \sqrt{1 - \sin^2 x}$ is possibly an identity. Justify your answer.

8. Simplify $\frac{\cot x + \tan x}{\sec x}$ to one of the three reciprocal trigonometric ratios. What are the non-permissible values of the original expression in the domain $0 \le x < 2\pi$?

9. a) Use technology to determine, graphically, whether the expression $\csc x - \frac{\cot x}{\sec x}$ appears to be equivalent to $\cos x$ or $\sin x$. Sketch the graphs. Write the identity below.

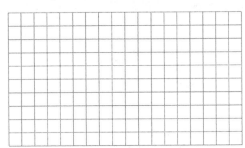 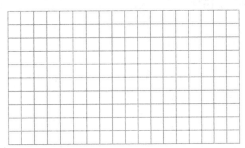

b) What are the non-permissible values of the identity in part a), expressed in radians?

c) Express $\csc x - \frac{\cot x}{\sec x}$ as the single primary trigonometric ratio that you identified in part a).

10. Simplify $(\cos x - \sin x)^2 - (\sin x - \cos x)^2$.

Connect

11. a) Complete the table for non-permissible values for each trigonometric ratio.

Trigonometric Ratio	Non-Permissible Values (degrees)	Non-Permissible Values (radians)
tan x		
csc x		
sec x		
cot x		

b) Explain why the table does not include sin x and cos x.

c) If sin x or cos x is the only term in the denominator, do you need to consider non-permissible values? Explain.

12. a) Complete the chart with the zeros of each trigonometric ratio in the first column.

Trigonometric Ratio	Zero Values (degrees)	Zero Values (radians)
sin x		
cos x		
tan x		
cot x		

b) When are the zeros non-permissible values?

c) Why are there no zero values for csc x and sec x?

13. Do all identities have non-permissible values? Explain.

> ## KEY IDEAS

Sum and Difference Identities

The sum and difference identities are used to simplify expressions and to determine exact trigonometric values of some angles.

- **Sum Identities**

  $\sin (A + B) = \sin A \cos B + \cos A \sin B$

  $\cos (A + B) = \cos A \cos B - \sin A \sin B$

  $\tan (A + B) = \dfrac{\tan A + \tan B}{1 - \tan A \tan B}$

  Examples:

  $\sin (12° + 23°) = \sin 12° \cos 23° + \cos 12° \sin 23°$

  $\cos \left(\dfrac{\pi}{6} + \dfrac{\pi}{4} \right) = \cos \dfrac{\pi}{6} \cos \dfrac{\pi}{4} - \sin \dfrac{\pi}{6} \sin \dfrac{\pi}{4}$

  $\tan (40° + 25°) = \dfrac{\tan 40° + \tan 25°}{1 - \tan 40° \tan 25°}$

- **Difference Identities**

  $\sin (A - B) = \sin A \cos B - \cos A \sin B$

  $\cos (A - B) = \cos A \cos B + \sin A \sin B$

  $\tan (A - B) = \dfrac{\tan A - \tan B}{1 + \tan A \tan B}$

  $\sin (52° - 33°) = \sin 52° \cos 33° - \cos 52° \sin 33°$

  $\cos \left(\dfrac{\pi}{3} - \dfrac{\pi}{4} \right) = \cos \dfrac{\pi}{3} \cos \dfrac{\pi}{4} + \sin \dfrac{\pi}{3} \sin \dfrac{\pi}{4}$

  $\tan (70° - 35°) = \dfrac{\tan 70° - \tan 35°}{1 + \tan 70° \tan 35°}$

Double-Angle Identities

Double-angle identities are special cases of the sum identities when the two angles are equal.

$\sin 2A = 2 \sin A \cos A$

Examples:

$\sin \dfrac{\pi}{4} = 2 \sin \dfrac{\pi}{8} \cos \dfrac{\pi}{8}$

The double-angle identity for cosine can be expressed in three different forms:

$\cos 2A = \cos^2 A - \sin^2 A$
$\cos 2A = 2 \cos^2 A - 1$
$\cos 2A = 1 - 2 \sin^2 A$

$\cos 140° = \cos^2 70° - \sin^2 70°$
$\cos 140° = 2 \cos^2 70° - 1$
$\cos 140° = 1 - 2 \sin^2 70°$

$\tan 2A = \dfrac{2 \tan A}{1 - \tan^2 A}$

$\tan \dfrac{\pi}{6} = \dfrac{2 \tan \dfrac{\pi}{12}}{1 - \tan^2 \dfrac{\pi}{12}}$

Special Angles and Their Exact Trigonometric Values

Degrees	Radians	$\sin \theta$	$\cos \theta$	$\tan \theta$
30°	$\dfrac{\pi}{6}$	$\dfrac{1}{2}$	$\dfrac{\sqrt{3}}{2}$	$\dfrac{1}{\sqrt{3}}$
45°	$\dfrac{\pi}{4}$	$\dfrac{\sqrt{2}}{2}$	$\dfrac{\sqrt{2}}{2}$	1
60°	$\dfrac{\pi}{3}$	$\dfrac{\sqrt{3}}{2}$	$\dfrac{1}{2}$	$\sqrt{3}$

Working Example 1: Simplify Expressions Using Sum, Difference, and Double-Angle Identities

Write each expression as a single trigonometric function.

a) $\cos 32° \cos 50° + \sin 32° \sin 50°$

b) $\dfrac{2 \tan \frac{\pi}{6}}{1 - \tan^2 \frac{\pi}{6}}$

Solution

a) The expression $\cos 32° \cos 50° + \sin 32° \sin 50°$ has the same form as the right side of the

difference identity for _____:

_____$(A - B) =$ _____ A _____ B + _____ A _____ B

Thus,

$\cos 32° \cos 50° + \sin 32° \sin 50° =$ _____ $(32°$ _____ $50°)$

$=$ _____

> How can you verify your solution?

b) The expression $\dfrac{2 \tan \frac{\pi}{6}}{1 - \tan^2 \frac{\pi}{6}}$ has the same form as the right side of the _____

identity for tangent: $\tan 2A = \dfrac{\boxed{}}{\boxed{}}$.

Therefore,

$\dfrac{2 \tan \frac{\pi}{6}}{1 - \tan^2 \frac{\pi}{6}} = $ _____ $2\left(\dfrac{\pi}{6}\right)$

$= $ _____ $\dfrac{\boxed{}}{\boxed{}}$

📖 To see a similar example, refer to Example 1 on page 301 of *Pre-Calculus 12*.

Working Example 2: Simplify Expressions Using Identities

Consider the expression $\dfrac{\sin 2x}{\cos 2x - 1}$.

a) What are the permissible values for the expression?

b) Simplify the expression to one of the three reciprocal trigonometric ratios.

c) How can you verify your answer from part b) in the interval $[0, 2\pi)$?

Solution

a) Identify any non-permissible values. The expression $\dfrac{\sin 2x}{\cos 2x - 1}$ is undefined when _____.

Use a double-angle identity to simplify $\cos 2x$: $\cos 2x =$ _____.

Solve _____ $= 0$.

> Does it matter which double-angle identity for $\cos 2x$ you select? Explain.

There are two sets of non-permissible values: _____.

When these two sets of non-permissible values are combined, the permissible values are all

real numbers except _____.

> To see a second method for determining the permissible values in part a), refer to Example 3 on pages 302 and 303 of *Pre-Calculus 12*.

b) $\dfrac{\sin 2x}{\cos 2x - 1} = \dfrac{\boxed{}}{\boxed{} - 1}$

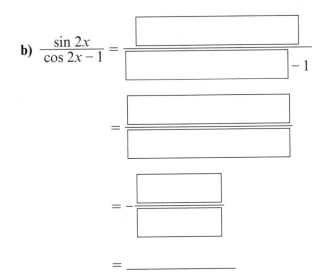

> How does the -1 in the denominator help you to determine which double-angle identity for $\cos 2x$ is best in this situation?

$$= \dfrac{\boxed{}}{\boxed{}}$$

$$= -\dfrac{\boxed{}}{\boxed{}}$$

$$= \underline{\qquad\qquad}$$

The expression $\dfrac{\sin 2x}{\cos 2x - 1}$ is equivalent to _____.

c) I can verify my answer by _____.

Use the method you have described to verify your answer. Does your verification prove your answer? Explain.

> To see a similar example, refer to Example 3 on pages 302 and 303 of *Pre-Calculus 12*.

Working Example 3: Determine Exact Trigonometric Values for Angles

Determine the exact value for each expression, stating your answer in the most simplified form.

a) $\cos \dfrac{7\pi}{12}$

b) $\tan 165°$

Solution

a) Use the _____ identity for cosine with two

special angles that can be _____ to get $\dfrac{7\pi}{12}$.
(added or subtracted)

$$\cos \frac{7\pi}{12} = \cos \left(\frac{\square}{\square} + \frac{\square}{\square} \right)$$

$$=$$

b) Rewrite $\tan 165°$ as the sum of special angles:

$$\tan 165° = \tan (\rule{1cm}{0.4pt}° + \rule{1cm}{0.4pt}°).$$

Use the tangent _____ identity:
(sum or difference)

$$\tan (A \rule{0.8cm}{0.4pt} B) = \frac{\tan A \rule{0.8cm}{0.4pt} \tan B}{1 \rule{0.8cm}{0.4pt} \tan A \tan B}.$$

$$\tan (\rule{1cm}{0.4pt}° + \rule{1cm}{0.4pt}°) = \frac{\boxed{} + \boxed{}}{1 - \boxed{} \; \boxed{}}$$

$$=$$

> Describe a second method that you could use to answer part b).

To see a similar example, refer to Example 4 on pages 304–305 of *Pre-Calculus 12*.

Check Your Understanding

Practise

1. Write each expression as a single trigonometric function.

a) $\cos 87° \cos 22° + \sin 87° \sin 22°$

b) $\sin 72° \cos 46° - \cos 72° \sin 46°$

c) $\dfrac{\tan 28° + \tan 33°}{1 - \tan 28° \tan 33°}$

d) $6 \sin \dfrac{\pi}{10} \cos \dfrac{\pi}{10}$

e) $1 - 2 \sin^2 \dfrac{\pi}{8}$

f) $\dfrac{2 \tan \dfrac{\pi}{3}}{1 - \tan^2 \dfrac{\pi}{3}}$

2. Simplify. Then, give an exact value for each expression.

a) $2 \sin \dfrac{\pi}{4} \cos \dfrac{\pi}{4}$

b) $\cos \dfrac{\pi}{3} \cos \dfrac{\pi}{12} + \sin \dfrac{\pi}{3} \sin \dfrac{\pi}{12}$

c) $\dfrac{\tan 80° + \tan 40°}{1 - \tan 80° \tan 40°}$

d) $2 \cos^2 \dfrac{\pi}{2} - 1$

3. Write each as a single trigonometric function.

a) $\sin 80° \cos 40° - \cos 80° \sin 40°$

b) $\cos \frac{2\pi}{3} \cos \frac{\pi}{12} - \sin \frac{2\pi}{3} \sin \frac{\pi}{12}$

c) $\dfrac{\tan \frac{2\pi}{3} - \tan \frac{\pi}{12}}{1 + \tan \frac{2\pi}{3} \tan \frac{\pi}{12}}$

4. Simplify each expression to a single primary trigonometric function.

a) $\dfrac{\cos 2x - 1}{\sin 2x}$

b) $1 - 2 \sin^2 \frac{\theta}{4}$

c) $\frac{1}{2} \sin \frac{\theta}{2} \cos \frac{\theta}{2}$

$\frac{1}{2} \sin \frac{\theta}{2} \cos \frac{\theta}{2} = 2\,(\underline{\hspace{2cm}})$

$= \frac{1}{4} \sin 2(\underline{\hspace{2cm}})$

$= \underline{\hspace{2cm}}$

d) $8 \sin^2 2\theta - 4$

$8 \sin^2 2\theta - 4 = -4(1 - \underline{\hspace{1.5cm}})$

$= -4 \underline{\hspace{1.5cm}}$

5. Consider the expression $\dfrac{1 - \cos 2x}{\sin x}$.

a) State the permissible values.

b) Simplify the expression to one of the three primary trigonometric ratios.

6. Determine the exact value of each trigonometric expression.

   a) $\sin 105°$

   b) $\cos 165°$

   c) $\tan \dfrac{23\pi}{12}$

   d) $\csc \dfrac{5\pi}{12}$

Apply

7. Simplify $\sin (x + y) + \sin (x - y)$.

8. Angle θ is in quadrant III and $\tan \theta = \dfrac{7}{24}$. Determine an exact value for each of the following.

   a) $\sin 2\theta$

   b) $\cos 2\theta$

   c) $\tan 2\theta$

9. Angle x is in quadrant II, angle y is in quadrant III, $\cos x = -\dfrac{5}{13}$, and $\tan y = \dfrac{4}{3}$. Determine the value of each of the following.

   a) $\sin (x + y)$

   b) $\cos (x - y)$

   c) $\tan (x - y)$

10. Simplify each expression to the equivalent expression shown.

a) $\dfrac{\sin 2x}{1 - \cos 2x}$; cot x

b) $\sin (x + y) \sin (x - y)$; $\sin^2 x - \sin^2 y$

11. Simplify each of the following.

a) $\cos \left(\dfrac{3\pi}{4} + x \right) + \sin \left(\dfrac{3\pi}{4} + x \right)$

b) $\cos \left(\dfrac{\pi}{4} - x \right) \sec \dfrac{\pi}{4} - \sin \left(\dfrac{\pi}{4} - x \right) \csc \dfrac{\pi}{4}$

Connect

12. a) Explain how the double-angle identities are related to the sum identities.

b) Explain why there are three forms of the double-angle identity for cosine. How are they related to each other?

❬❬ KEY IDEAS ❭❭

Guidelines for Proving Identities

- To prove that an identity is true for all permissible values, express both sides of the identity in equivalent forms. One or both sides of the identity must be algebraically manipulated into an equivalent form to match the other side.

- There is a major difference between solving a trigonometric equation and proving a trigonometric identity:

  – *Solving* a trigonometric equation determines the value that makes a particular case true. You perform equivalent operations on both sides of the equation (that is, perform operations across the = sign) to isolate the variable and solve for the variable.

  – *Proving* an identity shows that the expressions on each side of the equal sign are equivalent for *all* values for which the variable is defined. Therefore, you work on each side of the identity independently, and you *do not* perform operations across the = sign.

Tips for Proving Identities

- It is easier to simplify a complicated expression than to make a simple expression more complicated, so start with the more complicated side of the identity.

- Use known identities to make substitutions.

- If a quadratic is present, consider the Pythagorean identity first. It, or one of its alternative forms, can often be used.

- Rewrite the expression using sine and cosine only.

- Multiply the numerator and the denominator by the conjugate of an expression.

- Factor to simplify expressions.

Verifying Identities

- Identities can be verified using a specific value, but this validates that the identity is true for that value only.

- Graphing each side of a possible identity may show the identity might be true, but it does not prove the identity formally.

Working Example 1: Verify Versus Prove That an Equation Is an Identity

a) Verify numerically that $1 - \cos^2 x = \sin x \cos x \tan x$ for some values of x. Work in degrees.

b) Prove that $1 - \cos^2 x = \sin x \cos x \tan x$ for all permissible values of x.

Solution

a) First, determine the non-permissible values. The only function in the equation that has

non-permissible values in its domain is _____. The non-permissible values are

_____.

Verify the identity numerically. Use $x =$ _____.

> Does it matter what choice of angle measure you make to verify the identity numerically? Explain.

Left Side	Right Side
$1 - \cos^2 x$	$\sin x \cos x \tan x$
$= 1 - \cos^2 \underline{\quad}°$	$= \sin \underline{\quad}° \cos \underline{\quad}° \tan \underline{\quad}°$
$= 1 - \left(\dfrac{\square}{\square}\right)^2$	$=$
$= 1 - \dfrac{\square}{\square}$	
$= \underline{\quad}$	

> Describe how you could verify this identity graphically.

Left Side = Right Side

b) To prove the identity algebraically, examine both sides of the equation and simplify each side to a common expression.

Left Side $= 1 - \cos^2 x$ Right Side $= \sin x \cos x \tan x$

$=$ $=$

The simplified forms of the two sides _____ equal. Therefore,

(*are* or *are not*)

$1 - \cos^2 x = \sin x \cos x \tan x$ _____.

> To see an example similar to the above, refer to Example 1 on pages 310 and 311 of *Pre-Calculus 12*.

Working Example 2: Prove an Identity Using Double-Angle Identities

Prove that $\dfrac{1 + \cos 2x}{\sin 2x} = \cot x$ is an identity for all permissible values of x.

Solution

Left Side $= \dfrac{1 + \cos 2x}{\sin 2x}$ Right Side $= \cot x$

$=$

> Which double-angle identity should be selected for cos 2x? Explain.

The Left Side $\underset{(= \text{ or } \neq)}{\underline{\hspace{2cm}}}$ Right Side. Therefore, $\dfrac{1 + \cos 2x}{\sin 2x} = \cot x \underset{(\textit{is} \text{ or } \textit{is not})}{\underline{\hspace{2cm}}}$ an identity for all permissible values of x.

> To see another example similar to the above, refer to Example 2 on page 311 of *Pre-Calculus 12*.

Working Example 3: Prove More Complicated Identities

Prove that $\dfrac{\cos \theta}{1 - \sin \theta} + \dfrac{\cos \theta}{1 + \sin \theta} = \dfrac{2}{\cos \theta}$

Solution

Left Side $= \dfrac{\cos \theta}{1 - \sin \theta} + \dfrac{\cos \theta}{1 + \sin \theta}$ Right Side $= \dfrac{2}{\cos \theta}$

$= \dfrac{\cos \theta \left(\boxed{} \right) + \cos \theta \left(\boxed{} \right)}{(1 - \sin \theta)(1 + \sin \theta)}$

$=$

> Which identity is used to simplify the denominator?

The Left Side $\underline{\hspace{2cm}}$ Right Side. Therefore, $\dfrac{\cos \theta}{1 - \sin \theta} + \dfrac{\cos \theta}{1 + \sin \theta} = \dfrac{2}{\cos \theta}. \underset{(\textit{is} \text{ or } \textit{is not})}{\underline{\hspace{2cm}}}$ an identity for all permissible values of x.

> To see a similar example, refer to Example 3 on page 312 of *Pre-Calculus 12*.

Working Example 4: Prove an Identity That Requires Factoring

Prove the identity $\cos^4 x - \sin^4 x = \cos 2x$.

Solution

Left Side $= \cos^4 x - \sin^4 x$

$= ($ _____ $-$ _____ $)($ _____ $+$ _____ $)$

$= ($ _____ $)($ _____ $)$

$=$ _____

> How do you factor a difference of squares?

> Which identity did you use to simplify the first factor? Which identity did you use to simplify the second factor?

To see another example similar to the above, refer to Example 4 on page 313 of *Pre-Calculus 12*.

Check Your Understanding

Practise

1. Factor and simplify each rational trigonometric expression.

a) $\dfrac{\cos x - \sin^2 x \cos x}{\cos^2 x}$

b) $\dfrac{\cos^2 x - 3\cos x - 10}{8 + 4\cos x}$

c) $\dfrac{3\sec x + 6\sec x \sin x}{4\sin^2 x - 1}$

2. Use factoring to help to prove each identity for all permissible values of x.

a) $\dfrac{\sin x + \sin^2 x}{\cos x + \sin x \cos x} = \tan x$

b) $1 - \tan x = \dfrac{\cos^2 x - \sin^2 x}{\cos^2 x + \sin x \cos x}$

c) $\dfrac{3\cos^2 x + 5\cos x - 2}{9\cos^2 x - 1} = \dfrac{\cos x + 2}{3\cos x + 1}$

3. Use a common denominator to express the rational expressions as a single term.

a) $\dfrac{\cos x}{\sin x} + \sec x$

b) $\dfrac{1}{1 - \cos x} - \dfrac{1}{1 + \cos x}$

c) $\dfrac{\cos x}{1 + \sin x} + \dfrac{\sin x}{\cos x}$

4. Prove each identity.

a) $\dfrac{1 - \sin^2 x}{\cos x} = \dfrac{\sin 2x}{2 \sin x}$

b) $\dfrac{\csc^2 x - 1}{\csc^2 x} = \cos^2 x$

$$\text{Left Side} = \dfrac{\csc^2 x - 1}{\csc^2 x}$$

$$= \dfrac{\boxed{}}{\boxed{}} = \dfrac{1}{\boxed{}}$$

$$= 1 - \underline{}$$

$$= \underline{}$$

$$\text{Right Side} = \underline{}$$

c) $(\cos x - \sin x)^2 = 1 - \sin 2x$

5. Match each expression on the left with an equivalent expression on the right. Justify your answer.

a) $\sin x \cot x$

A $\sin^2 x + \cos^2 x + \tan^2 x$

b) $1 - 2 \sin^2 x$

B $1 + 2 \sin x \cos x$

c) $(\sin x + \cos x)^2$

C $\cos x$

d) $\sec^2 x$

D $2 \cos^2 x - 1$

Apply

6. a) Use technology to verify graphically that $\tan x = \dfrac{\sin x + \sin 2x}{\cos 2x + 1 + \cos x}$ could be an identity. Sketch the graphs below.

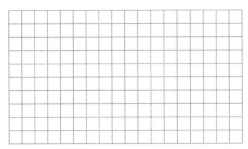 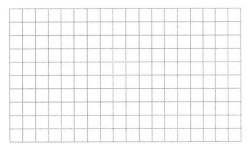

b) Prove the identity using double-angle identities.

c) Determine any non-permissible values.

7. Prove each identity.

a) $\sec x = \dfrac{2(\cos x \sin 2x - \sin x \cos 2x)}{\sin 2x}$

Right Side $= \dfrac{2(\cos x \sin 2x - \sin x \cos 2x)}{\sin 2x}$

$= \dfrac{2\boxed{}(2 \sin x \cos x) - \boxed{}(2 \cos^2 x - 1)}{2 \sin x \cos x}$

$= \dfrac{2\boxed{} - 2\boxed{} + \sin x}{\sin x \cos x}$

$=$

Left Side $= \sec x$

b) $\sec x = \dfrac{2 \csc 2x \tan x}{\sec x}$

c) $\tan 2x - \sin 2x = 2 \tan 2x \sin^2 x$

d) $\dfrac{1 + \tan x}{1 + \cot x} = \dfrac{1 - \tan x}{\cot x - 1}$

8. Prove each identity.

a) $\sin (45° + x) + \sin (45° - x) = \sqrt{2} \cos x$

Left Side $= \sin (45° + x) + \sin (45° - x)$

$= ($ _____ $+$ _____ $) + ($ _____ $-$ _____ $)$

$= 2$ _____ $\cos x$

$= 2 \dfrac{\square}{\square} \cos x$

$=$ _____ $\cos x$

Right Side $=$ _____

b) $\sin (x + \pi) = -\cos \left(x + \dfrac{3\pi}{2} \right)$

9. Consider the equation $\sin^4 x - \cos^4 x = 2 \sin^2 x + 1$.

a) Graph each side of the equation. Sketch your graphs below. Could the equation be an identity? Explain.

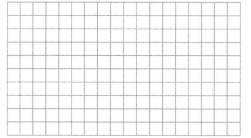 

b) Either prove that the equation is an identity or find a counterexample to show that it is not an identity.

10. Prove that $2 \sin (x + y) \cos (x + y) = \sin 2x \cos 2y + \sin 2y \cos 2x$.

Connect

11. Consider the equation $\sin^4 x + \cos^2 x = \sin^2 x + \cos^4 x$.

    a) Using technology, graph each side of the equation. Could the equation be an identity?

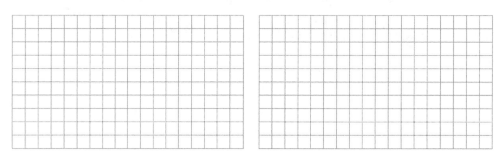

    b) Either prove that the equation is an identity or find a counterexample to show that it is not an identity.

    c) Explain the difference between the verification you made in part a) and the proof you provided in part b).

6.4 Solving Trigonometric Equations Using Identities

KEY IDEAS

Solving Trigonometric Equations

Solving a trigonometric equation means to find all the possible angle values that make the equation true within the given or restricted domain. When the domain is not restricted, you provide a general solution.

Strategies for Solving Trigonometric Equations

Description	Example
Isolate the trigonometric ratio, if possible.	$2 \sin x = 1$ $\sin x = \dfrac{1}{2}$
Factor and then set each factor equal to 0.	Common factoring: $\sin x \tan x + \sin x = 0$ $\sin x (\tan x + 1) = 0$ $\sin x = 0$ or $\tan x = -1$ Difference of squares: $\sin^2 x - 1 = 0$ $(\sin x - 1)(\sin x + 1) = 0$ $\sin x = 1$ or $\sin x = -1$ Trinomial factoring: $2 \sin^2 x - \sin x - 1 = 0$ $(2 \sin x + 1)(\sin x - 1) = 0$ $\sin x = -0.5$ or $\sin x = 1$
Simplify the given equation or change the given equation to one common ratio (such as $\sin x$ or $\cos x$) by using one or more of the following: – reciprocal identities – quotient identities – Pythagorean identities – double-angle identities Then, solve.	$\begin{aligned} \cos 2x - 2 \sin x + 3 &= 0 \\ (1 - 2 \sin^2 x) - 2 \sin x + 3 &= 0 \quad \text{Replace } \cos 2x \text{ with } 1 - 2 \sin^2 x. \\ -2 \sin^2 x - 2 \sin x + 4 &= 0 \quad \text{Simplify.} \\ \sin^2 x + \sin x - 2 &= 0 \\ (\sin x + 2)(\sin x - 1) &= 0 \quad \text{Factor.} \\ \sin x = -2 \text{ or } \sin x &= 1 \quad \text{Solve.} \end{aligned}$ It is important to consider all possible solutions to ensure that they are not non-permissible values. In this example, the root $x = -2$ is rejected because the minimum value for $\sin x$ is -1.

Checking Trigonometric Equations

- The algebraic solution can be verified graphically.
- Check that solutions for an equation do not include non-permissible values from the original equation.

Working Example 1: Solve by Substituting Trigonometric Identities and Factoring

Solve each equation algebraically over the domain $0 \leq x < 2\pi$.

a) $\sin 2x + \sin x = 0$

b) $6 \sin^2 x = \cos x + 4$

Solution

a) $\sin 2x + \sin x = 0$

$2\underline{\hspace{1cm}}\ \underline{\hspace{1cm}} + \sin x = 0$

$\sin x\ (\underline{\hspace{1cm}} + \underline{\hspace{1cm}}) = 0$

$\sin x = 0$ $\qquad\qquad$ or $\qquad \underline{\hspace{1.5cm}} = 0$

> Explain why a double-angle formula is needed.

$x = \underline{\hspace{1cm}}$ or $x = \underline{\hspace{1cm}}$ $\qquad\qquad$ $\cos x = -\dfrac{\boxed{}}{\boxed{}}$

$\qquad\qquad\qquad\qquad\qquad\qquad\qquad x = \underline{\hspace{1cm}}$ or $x = \underline{\hspace{1cm}}$

State the non-permissible value(s) for this equation, if any: $\underline{\hspace{5cm}}$.

The solutions over the given domain are $\underline{\hspace{6cm}}$.

b) $6 \sin^2 x = \cos x + 4$

> Which term in the equation might lead you to consider using the Pythagorean identity?

$6(\underline{\hspace{1cm}} - \underline{\hspace{1cm}}) - \cos x - 4 = 0$

$6 - 6\underline{\hspace{1cm}} - \cos x - 4 = 0$

$-6\underline{\hspace{1cm}} - \cos x + \underline{\hspace{1cm}} = 0$

$6\underline{\hspace{1cm}} + \cos x - \underline{\hspace{1cm}} = 0$

$(\underline{\hspace{2.5cm}})(\underline{\hspace{2.5cm}}) = 0$

$\underline{\hspace{2.5cm}} = 0$ or $\underline{\hspace{2.5cm}} = 0$

$\cos x = \underline{\hspace{2cm}}$ $\qquad\qquad$ $\cos x = \underline{\hspace{2cm}}$

$x = \underline{\hspace{1cm}}$ or $x = \underline{\hspace{1cm}}$ $\qquad$ $x \approx \underline{\hspace{1cm}}$ or $x \approx \underline{\hspace{1cm}}$

State the non-permissible value(s) for this equation, if any: $\underline{\hspace{4cm}}$.

The solutions over the given domain are $\underline{\hspace{6cm}}$.

📖 To see a similar example, refer to Example 1 on page 317 of *Pre-Calculus 12*.

Working Example 2: Solve an Equation With a Quotient Identity Substitution

Solve the equation $\sin^2 x = \tan x \cos x$ algebraically in the domain $0° \le x < 360°$.

Solution

$$\sin^2 x = \tan x \cos x$$

$$\sin^2 x = \frac{\boxed{}}{\boxed{}} \cos x$$

$$\sin^2 x = \underline{\hspace{1.5cm}}$$

$$\underline{\hspace{3cm}} = 0$$

$\sin x = 0$ or $\sin x = \underline{\hspace{1.5cm}}$

For $\sin x = 0$, $x = \underline{\hspace{1.2cm}}°$ or $x = \underline{\hspace{1.2cm}}°$.

For $\sin x = \underline{\hspace{1.2cm}}$, $x = \underline{\hspace{1.2cm}}°$.

> How could you verify your answer graphically?

State the non-permissible value(s) for this equation, if any: $\underline{\hspace{4cm}}$.

The solutions over the given domain are $\underline{\hspace{4cm}}$.

Working Example 3: Determine the General Solution for a Trigonometric Equation

Solve $\cos 2x = \sqrt{3} \cos x - 1$ algebraically. Give the general solution in radians.

Solution

> Which double-angle identity should you select for $\cos 2x$? Explain.

$$\cos 2x = \sqrt{3} \cos x - 1$$

$$\underline{\hspace{3cm}} = \sqrt{3} \cos x - 1$$

$$\underline{\hspace{3cm}} - \sqrt{3} \cos x + 1 = 0$$

$$\underline{\hspace{3cm}} - \sqrt{3} \cos x = 0$$

$$\cos x \,(\underline{\hspace{2.5cm}}) = 0$$

$\cos x = 0$ or $\underline{\hspace{2.5cm}} = 0$

$$\cos x = \underline{\hspace{1.2cm}}$$

For $\cos x = 0$, $x = \underline{\hspace{2.5cm}}$, where $n \in I$.

For $\cos x = \underline{\hspace{1.2cm}}$, $x = \underline{\hspace{2.5cm}}$, and $x = \underline{\hspace{2.5cm}}$, where $n \in I$.

State the non-permissible value(s) for this equation, if any: $\underline{\hspace{4cm}}$.

The general solution is $x = \underline{\hspace{5cm}}$, where $n \in I$.

📖 To see a similar example, refer to Example 3 on page 319 of *Pre-Calculus 12*.

Working Example 4: Determine the General Solution Using Reciprocal Identities

Algebraically solve $2 \csc^2 x + \csc x - 1 = 0$. Give general solutions expressed in radians.

Solution

$$2 \csc^2 x + \csc x - 1 = 0$$

$$(\underline{\hspace{3cm}})(\underline{\hspace{3cm}}) = 0$$

$$\underline{\hspace{3cm}} = 0 \text{ or } \underline{\hspace{3cm}} = 0$$

$$\csc x = \underline{\hspace{2cm}} \qquad \csc x = \underline{\hspace{2cm}}$$

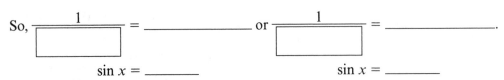

So, $\dfrac{1}{\boxed{}} = \underline{\hspace{2cm}}$ or $\dfrac{1}{\boxed{}} = \underline{\hspace{2cm}}$.

$$\sin x = \underline{\hspace{2cm}} \qquad\qquad \sin x = \underline{\hspace{2cm}}$$

For $\sin x = \underline{\hspace{2cm}}$ there is no solution.

For $\sin x = \underline{\hspace{2cm}}$, $x = \underline{\hspace{3cm}}$, where $n \in \mathrm{I}$.

The non-permissible values are $\underline{\hspace{4cm}}$.

The solution is $\underline{\hspace{4cm}}$, where $n \in \mathrm{I}$.

> How does factoring help to solve this equation?

Check Your Understanding

Practise

1. Solve each equation algebraically over the domain $0° \le x < 360°$.

   a) $2 \sin x = \sqrt{3}$

   b) $2 \cos x - 1 = 0$

   c) $\tan x - 1 = 0$

   d) $\cot x + 1 = 0$

2. Solve each equation algebraically over the domain $0 \le x < 2\pi$.

   a) $4 \sin^2 x - 1 = 0$

   b) $4 \cos^2 x = 3$

   c) $\tan^2 x - 3 = 0$

   d) $3 \csc^2 x - 4 = 0$

3. Solve each equation algebraically over the domain $0 \leq x < 2\pi$. Use technology to verify your solution graphically.

a) $\sin^2 x - \sin x = 0$

b) $\cos^2 x + \cos x = 0$

c) $\tan x + \tan^2 x = 0$

d) $\cos^2 x + 2\cos x = 0$

4. Solve each equation algebraically over the domain $0 \leq x < 2\pi$. Verify your solution graphically.

a) $\sin 2x - 1 = \cos 2x$

b) $\sqrt{2} \sin^2 x = \tan x \cos x$

c) $\cos 2x = \cos^2 x$

$$\cos 2x = \cos^2 x$$

$$2 \underline{\hspace{3cm}} - 1 = \cos^2 x$$

$$\underline{\hspace{3cm}} = 1$$

$$\underline{\hspace{3cm}} = 1 \text{ or } \underline{\hspace{3cm}} = -1$$

$$x = \underline{\hspace{2cm}} \qquad \text{or} \qquad x = \underline{\hspace{2cm}}$$

d) $\cos 2x = 2\sin^2 x$

e) $\sin 2x \tan x = 1$

5. Rewrite each equation in terms of sine or cosine only. Then, solve algebraically for $0 \le x < 2\pi$.

a) $\sin^2 x - \cos^2 x = \dfrac{1}{2}$

b) $2 \sin^2 x - 3 \cos 2x = 3$

c) $3 \cos 2x + \cos x + 1 = 0$

d) $3 + \sin x = 5 \cos 2x$

Apply

6. Solve each equation algebraically over the domain $0 \le x < 2\pi$.

a) $8 \sin^2 x - 6 \sin x + 1 = 0$

b) $\cos x + 1 = 2 \sin^2 x$

c) $2 \cos^2 x - 3 \cos x + 1 = 0$

d) $\sin^2 x + 2 \sin x - 3 = 0$

e) $2 \tan^2 x = 3 \tan x - 1$

f) $\sin x = -\cos 2x$

7. a) Solve $2 \sin^2 x = -3 \cos x$ algebraically over each domain. Verify your answers graphically.

    i) $0 \le x < 2\pi$ **ii)** $-2\pi \le x < 2\pi$ **iii)** $-\pi \le x < \pi$

b) Describe the relationship between the domain and the number of solutions.

c) What is the general solution for this equation?

8. Solve each equation algebraically over the domain $0 \leq x < 2\pi$.

   a) $\csc^2 x - \csc x - 2 = 0$

   b) $2\sec^2 x + \sec x - 1 = 0$

   c) $3\csc^2 x - 5\csc x - 2 = 0$

   d) $\sec^2 x + 5\sec x + 6 = 0$

9. Assume that $\cos x = -\dfrac{2}{3}$ and $\cos x = \dfrac{1}{4}$ are the solutions of a trigonometric equation. What are the values of B and C if the equation is of the form $12\cos^2 x + B\cos x + C = 0$?

10. Solve $\sin x \cos 2x + \sin x = 0$ algebraically over the domain of real numbers. Give your answer(s) in radians.

11. Solve the equation $\sin 2x = -\sqrt{2} \cos x$ algebraically. Give the general solution expressed in radians.

Connect

12. Explain if it is possible to solve the equation $\sin^2 x - 5 \sin x + 3 = 0$ by factoring?

13. Determine the mistake that Brooke made in the following work. Then, complete a correct solution.

Solve $\cos 2x = -\cos x$. Express your answers in degrees.

Solution

$\cos 2x = -\cos x$
$\cos 2x + \cos x = 0$
$\cos x (\cos x + 1) = 0$
$\cos x = 0 \text{ or } \cos x = -1$
$x = 90° + 180°n \text{ or } x = 180° + 360°n, \text{ where } n \in I$

Chapter 6 Review

6.1 Reciprocal, Quotient, and Pythagorean Identities, pages 188–196

1. Determine the non-permissible values of x, in radians, for each expression.

   a) $\dfrac{\sec x}{\sin x}$

   b) $\dfrac{\cos x}{\csc x}$

   c) $\dfrac{\sec x}{1 + \cos^2 x}$

2. Simplify each expression to one of the three primary trigonometric functions: $\sin x$, $\cos x$, or $\tan x$.

   a) $\dfrac{\cos x \csc x}{\sec x \cot x}$

   b) $\dfrac{\cot x \tan x}{\csc x}$

3. Simplify. Then, rewrite each expression as one of the three reciprocal trigonometric functions: $\csc x$, $\sec x$, or $\cot x$.

   a) $\cot x \sec x$

   b) $\dfrac{\cos x}{(1 - \sin x)(1 + \sin x)}$

4. **a)** Verify that the equation $(\sec x + \tan x) \cos x - 1 = \sin x$ is true for $x = 30°$ and for $x = \dfrac{\pi}{3}$.

   b) What are the non-permissible values of the equation in part a) in the domain $0° \le x < 360°$?

6.2 Sum, Difference, and Double-Angle Identities, pages 197–204

5. Write each expression as a single trigonometric ratio. Then, give an exact value for the expression.

   a) $\cos^2 15° - \sin^2 15°$

   b) $\sin 35° \cos 100° + \cos 35° \sin 100°$

   c) $1 - 2\sin^2 75°$

6. Determine the exact value of each trigonometric expression.

   a) $\sin\left(-\dfrac{\pi}{12}\right)$

   b) $\cos\dfrac{\pi}{12}$

   c) $\cos 105°$

   d) $\sin\dfrac{23\pi}{12}$

7. Angle θ is in quadrant II and $\sin\theta = \dfrac{7}{25}$. Determine an exact value for each of the following.

   a) $\sin 2\theta$

   b) $\cos 2\theta$

   c) $\tan 2\theta$

6.3 Proving Identities, pages 205–214

8. Prove $\sin(\pi - x) - \tan(\pi + x) = \dfrac{\sin x\,(\cos x - 1)}{\cos x}$.

9. Consider the equation $\sin^2 x + \tan^2 x + \cos^2 x = \sec^2 x$.

  a) Graph each side of the equation. Could the equation be an identity? Explain.

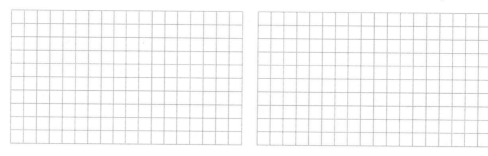

  b) Either prove that the equation is an identity or find a counterexample to show that it is not an identity.

10. Prove each identity.

  a) $\cos x \tan^2 x = \sin x \tan x$

  b) $\sin 2x = \tan x + \tan x \cos 2x$

6.4 Solving Trigonometric Equations Using Identities, pages 215–223

11. Rewrite each equation in terms of sine or cosine. Then, solve algebraically for $0 \le x < 2\pi$.

a) $2 \cos^2 x - \sin x = -1$

b) $\sin^2 x = 2 \cos x - 2$

c) $\cos x + \cos 2x = 0$

12. Solve each equation algebraically over the domain $0 \le x < 2\pi$.

a) $2 \cos^2 x + 3 \cos x + 1 = 0$

b) $\sin^2 x + 3 \sin x + 2 = 0$

c) $\sin^2 x + 5 \sin x + 6 = 0$

d) $\cos^2 x + 3 \cos x + 2 = 0$

13. Solve the equation $2 \cos^2 x = 1 - \sin x$ algebraically. Give the general solution expressed in radians.

Chapter 6 Skills Organizer

Use the following organizer to summarize what you have learned about trigonometric identities.

Key Identities

Strategies for Proving

Trigonometric Identities

Examples

Non-Examples

Chapter 7 Exponential Functions

7.1 Characteristics of Exponential Functions

- An exponential function models a type of non-linear change. These types of functions have the form $y = c^x$, where c is a constant ($c > 0$). All exponential functions of this form have a y-intercept of 1.

> Why does c have to be positive?

> Why is the y-intercept for all exponential functions of this form equal to 1?

- When $c > 1$ in an exponential function of the form $y = c^x$, the exponential function is increasing.

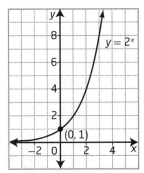

> How can you tell from the graph that this is an increasing function? Does this situation represent growth or decay?

- When c is between 0 and 1 (that is, $0 < c < 1$) in an exponential function of the form $y = c^x$, the exponential function is decreasing.

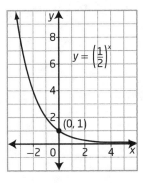

> How can you tell from the graph that this is a decreasing function? Does this situation represent growth or decay?

- When $c = 1$ in an exponential function of the form $y = c^x$, the exponential function is neither increasing nor decreasing.

> How does the graph of $y = 1^x$ reflect a function that is neither increasing nor decreasing?

- Exponential functions of the form $y = c^x$ have domain $\{x \mid x \in \mathrm{R}\}$, range $\{y \mid y > 0, y \in \mathrm{R}\}$, no x-intercepts, and horizontal asymptote at $y = 0$.

> How do the graphs above reflect the domain, range, and horizontal asymptote?

Working Example 1: Properties of Exponential Functions

Graph each exponential function. Then, identify the following:
- the domain and range
- the x-intercept and y-intercept, if they exist
- whether the graph represents an increasing or decreasing function
- the equation of the horizontal asymptote

a) $y = 3^x$

b) $y = \left(\dfrac{1}{3}\right)^x$

Solution

a) Use technology to graph the function.

The function is defined for all real values of x, so the

domain is _____.

All of the y-values of the function are positive, so the

range is {_____, $y \in R$}.

The graph has no x-intercept because the graph never intersects the x-axis.

Since $3^0 = 1$, the y-intercept of the graph is _____.

The function values get larger as x-values get larger, so the graph is _____.
(increasing or *decreasing)*

The graph of the function gets closer and closer to the _____ as the x-values

decrease, so there is a horizontal asymptote at _____.

b) Use technology to graph the function.

The domain of the function is _____.

The range of the function is _____.

The graph has no x-intercept because the graph never intersects the x-axis.

The y-intercept of the graph is _____

because $\left(\dfrac{1}{3}\right)^0 =$ _____.

The function values get _____ as x-values get larger, so the graph is decreasing.

There is a horizontal asymptote at _____.

 See pages 336–338 of *Pre-Calculus 12* for an example using similar concepts.

Working Example 2: Determine an Exponential Function From Its Graph

What exponential function can be used to describe the graph below?

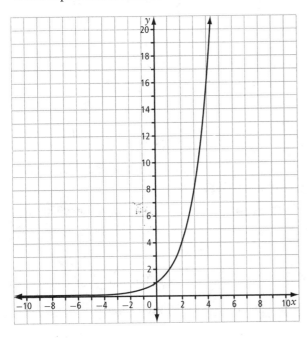

Solution

An exponential function has the form $y = c^x$. When $x = 1$, the value of the function is c.

The given graph includes the ordered pair (1, _____), so you can conclude that $c =$ _____.

Therefore, the exponential function that can be used to describe the graph is _____.

Choose a point other than (0, 1) to substitute into the function to verify if the function is correct. Try (4, 16).

Check:

Left Side	Right Side
y	2^x
= _____	$= 2^{\square}$
	= _____

The left side _____ right side, so _____.
      ($=$ or $\neq$)

📖 See pages 338–340 of *Pre-Calculus 12* for a similar example.

Working Example 3: An Application of Exponential Functions

Fong has just graduated from university and wants to begin her retirement planning. Her investment advisor suggests an investment that he expects to double in value every decade. The estimated growth rate is modelled by the exponential graph shown.

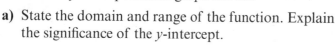

a) State the domain and range of the function. Explain the significance of the y-intercept.

b) Write an exponential equation that expresses the value of each dollar invested, after t decades.

c) What is the value of a dollar invested for ten years?

d) How long will it take for $1 in this investment to be worth $8?

e) Use a table of values to determine how long it will take for $1 in this investment to be worth $26.

Solution

a) Since time is graphed on the t-axis, the domain is _____. The range of the

function is _____. The y-intercept at (0, 1) represents the initial value of each dollar.

b) Since the point (1, _____) is on the graph, the equation is $y = \boxed{}^t$.

c) Ten years is one decade. The point (1, 2) is on the graph, so in ten years the value of $1 is 2^1,

or $_____.

d) The point (_____, 8) is on the graph, so it will take _____ decades, or _____ years,

for each dollar of the investment to be worth $8.

> How might you use the equation to solve part d)?

e) Create a table of values for $V(t) = \boxed{}^t$.

t	$V(t)$
1	
2	
3	
4	
5	

The table shows that the number of decades is between _____ and _____. You can determine a better estimate for t by looking at values between these numbers. Use systematic trial to find a value for t where $V \approx 26$:

Therefore, it will take approximately _____ decades, or _____ years, for $1 in this investment to be worth $26.

 See pages 340–341 of *Pre-Calculus 12* for more examples.

Check Your Understanding

Practise

1. State whether each of the following is an exponential function. Justify your answers.

    a) $y = x^5$

    b) $y = 0.1^x$

    c) $y = 12^x$

    d) $y = \sqrt[3]{x}$

            $y = x^{1/3}$

    e) $y = x^{0.5}$

2. Match each exponential function to its graph.

    a) $y = 5^x$
    b) $y = 7^x$
    c) $y = \left(\dfrac{3}{4}\right)^x$
    d) $y = 0.2^x$

A
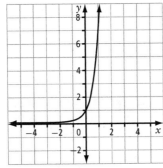

B
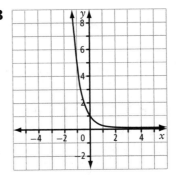

C
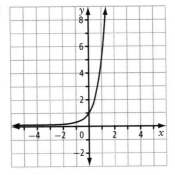

D
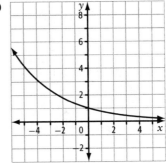

3. Write the equation of each exponential function graphed below.

a)

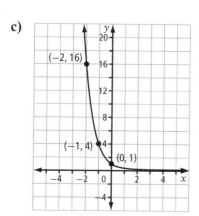

The point (0, 1) does not help determine the equation because _____.

However, since you know that _____² = 100, you can conclude that the base of the exponential function is _____. Thus, the equation is _____.

b)

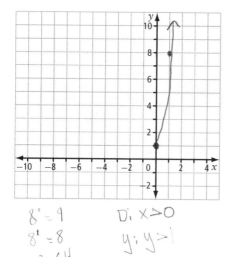

c)

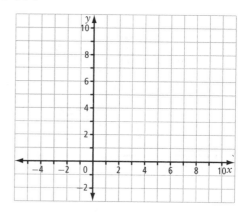

4. Sketch the graph of each exponential function. Identify the domain and range, the *y*-intercept, whether the graph is increasing or decreasing, and the equation of the horizontal asymptote.

a) $f(x) = 8^x$

b) $f(x) = 0.5^x$

$8^0 = 1$ D: x > 0
$8^1 = 8$ y: y > 1
$8^2 = 64$

c) $g(x) = \left(\dfrac{2}{3}\right)^x$

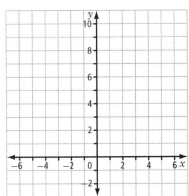

d) $g(x) = \left(\dfrac{3}{2}\right)^x$

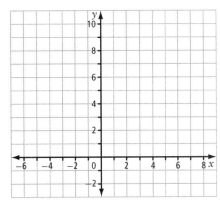

Apply

5. The number of transistors on a computer chip, N, doubles approximately every two years. If originally there is one transistor on a chip, then this can be modelled by the function $N = 2^t$, where t is the number of two-year periods that have passed.

a) Graph the function. Is the function increasing or decreasing?

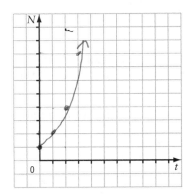

$y = ac^x$

$y = 2^+$

$1 = 2^0$

$2 = 2^1$

$4 = 2^2$

$8 = 2^3$

Increasing

b) What are the domain and range of the function?

D: $\{x \mid x \geq 0, x \in R\}$

R: $\{y \mid y \geq 1, y \in R\}$

c) How many transistors are on a chip after 2 years? 10 years? 20 years?

$y = 2^1$ $y = 2^5$ $y = 2^{16}$
$y = 2$ $y = 32$ $y = 1024$

> How many 2-year periods are there in 10 years? 20 years? How might you use a table of values to solve this question?

6. A filter removes 75% of the impurities of water that is passed through it. Multiple filters can be used together to increase the purity of the water. This situation is represented by $A = 0.25^n$, where A is the proportion of impurities remaining and n is the number of filters used.

a) Explain why the base of the exponential function is 0.25.

Because you have to minus 75% from 100% to make 25% → 0.25
y = ac^x

b) Graph the exponential function.

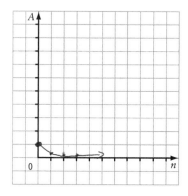

$A = 0.25^n$

$1 = 0.25^0$

$0.25 = 0.25^1$

$\frac{1}{16} = 0.25^2$

$\frac{1}{64} = 0.25^3$

> What are the benefits and drawbacks of using a graph? What other methods could you use? What are the benefits and drawbacks of using an equation or table of values?

c) What are the domain and range?

D: {x | x ≥ 0, x∈R}

R: {y | y ≥ 1, y∈R}

d) What proportion of impurities remains when four filters are used, to the nearest ten thousandth?

7. The population of a particular insect decreases by half each night that the temperature drops below freezing.

a) Write an exponential function to model the proportion of the population remaining, P, after n nights of freezing temperatures.

b) Graph the function.

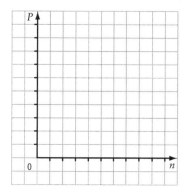

c) What percent of the population is remaining after five freezing nights, to the nearest hundredth of a percent? After eight freezing nights?

d) Will the population ever reach zero? Explain.

8. One dollar is invested at 4.5% interest compounded annually.

   a) Write an exponential function to represent the value of the investment, V, after t years.

   b) Graph the function from part a).

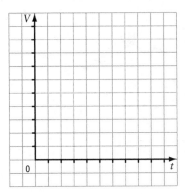

   c) Determine the value of the investment after 15 years.

   d) Use the graph to determine the time needed for the value of the investment to reach $3. Round your answer to the nearest year.

Connect

9. Consider the exponential function $y = c^x$, where $c > 0$.

   a) Explain why the domain and range of all such exponential functions are the same.

   b) Explain why every exponential function of this form has the same y-intercept, 1.

   c) State one characteristic of exponential functions that depends on the value of c.

KEY IDEAS

- You can use transformed exponential functions to model real-world applications of exponential growth or decay.

- To graph an exponential function of the form $y = a(c)^{b(x-h)} + k$, apply transformations to the base function, $y = c^x$, where $c > 0$. Each of the parameters, a, b, h, and k, is associated with a particular transformation.

Parameter	Transformation	Example
a	• vertical stretch about the x-axis by a factor of $|a|$ • $a < 0$ results in a reflection in the x-axis • $(x, y) \rightarrow (x, ay)$	For $a = 2$, the equation of the transformed base function is $y = 2(3)^x$.
b	• horizontal stretch about the y-axis by a factor of $\frac{1}{|b|}$ • $b < 0$ results in a reflection in the y-axis • $(x, y) \rightarrow \left(\frac{x}{b}, y\right)$	For $b = 2$, the equation of the transformed base function is $y = (3)^{2x}$.

Parameter	Transformation	Example
h	• horizontal translation left or right, depending on the sign: $+h$ shifts the graph left, and $-h$ shifts the graph right • $(x, y) \rightarrow (x + h, y)$	For $h = \pm 2$, the equation of the transformed base function is $y = (3)^{(x \pm 2)}$.
k	• vertical translation up or down, depending on the sign: $+k$ shifts the graph up, and $-k$ shifts the graph down • $(x, y) \rightarrow (x, y + k)$	For $k = \pm 2$, the equation of the transformed base function is $y = (3)^x \pm 2$.

• When applying transformations, you must apply parameters a and b before parameters h and k.

Working Example 1: Translations of Exponential Functions

Consider the exponential function $y = 2^x$. For each of the following transformed functions,
• state the parameter and describe the transformation
• graph the base function and the transformed function on the same grid
• describe any changes to the domain, range, intercepts, and equation of the horizontal asymptote
• explain the effect of the transformation on an arbitrary point, (x, y), on the graph of the base function

a) $y = 2^x + 3$

b) $y = 2^{x-5}$

c) $y - 4 = 2^{x+1}$

Solution

a) Compare the function $y = 2^x + 3$ to $y = a(c)^{b(x-h)} + k$ to determine the value of the

parameter: $k =$ _____. This transformation indicates a _____ translation

of _____ units _____ compared to the graph of $y = 2^x$.
         (up or down)

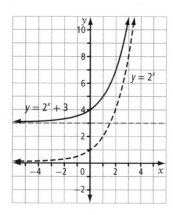

The domain is the same for both graphs: _____.

The range for the transformed graph is $\{y \mid y > 3, y \in R\}$.

Since the graph is translated up, the _____

asymptote is also translated up. Thus, the equation of the

horizontal asymptote for $y = 2^x + 3$ is _____. Similarly,

the y-intercept of the transformed graph is translated up to

become _____.

Since each point on the graph of the base function moves up three units, each y-coordinate

increases by _____. So, $(x, y) \rightarrow (x, y + \underline{\quad})$.

b) Compare the function $y = 2^{x-5}$ to $y = a(c)^{b(x-h)} + k$ to determine the value of the

parameter: $h =$ _____. This parameter corresponds to a _____ translation

of _____ units to the _____ compared to the graph of $y = 2^x$.
         (right or left)

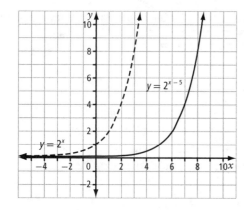

The domain is $\{x \mid x \in R\}$ for both graphs. The

range, which is unchanged for the transformed

graph, is _____. A horizontal

translation has no effect on the horizontal

asymptote. The y-intercept of $y = 2^{x-5}$

corresponds to the point $\left(5, \frac{1}{32}\right)$ on $y = 2^x$, so the

y-intercept of the transformed function is $\frac{1}{32}$.

Since each point on the graph of the base function moves right five units, each x-coordinate

moves _____ by _____ units. So, $(x, y) \rightarrow (\underline{\qquad}, \underline{\qquad})$.
       (right or left)

c) Begin by writing $y - 4 = 2^{x+1}$ in the form $y =$ _____. The parameters in the transformed function are

- $h =$ _____, which corresponds to a _____ translation by _____ units to

  the _____.
  (*right* or *left*)

- $k =$ _____, which corresponds to a _____ translation by _____

  units _____.
  (*up* or *down*)

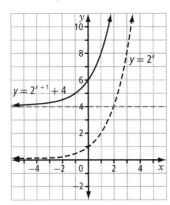

The domain is _____ for both graphs. The range of the transformed graph is _____. The equation of the horizontal asymptote for the transformed function is _____. You can determine the y-intercept of the transformed function, $y = 2^{x+1} + 4$, by substituting $x =$ _____ into the equation to calculate the new y-intercept: _____.

For this transformation, each point $(x, y) \rightarrow$ (_____, _____).

Working Example 2: Stretches of Exponential Functions

Consider the exponential function $y = 3^x$. For each of the following transformations,
- state the parameter and describe the corresponding transformation
- graph the base function and the transformed function on the same grid
- describe any changes to the domain, range, intercepts, and equation of the horizontal asymptote
- show what happens to an arbitrary point, (x, y), on the graph of the base function

a) $y = 2(3)^x$ **b)** $y = 3^{2x}$

Solution

a) Compare the function $y = 2(3)^x$ with $y = a(c)^{b(x-h)} + k$ to determine the value of the parameter:

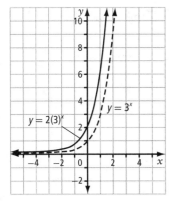

$a =$ _____, which corresponds to a _____ stretch by a factor of _____.

The domain, range, and equation of the horizontal asymptote are unchanged under this transformation. However, the y-intercept of the transformed graph is

_____ because the y-coordinates of every point on the base function are multiplied by 2.

For this transformation, $(x, y) \rightarrow$ (_____, _____).

b) Compare the function $y = 3^{2x}$ with $y = a(c)^{b(x-h)} + k$ to determine the value of the parameter:

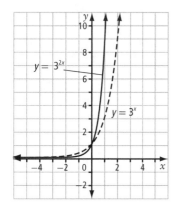

$b =$ _____, which corresponds to a _____

stretch by a factor of _____.

The domain and range are unchanged. The y-intercept is the invariant point of the transformation, so it remains the same. A horizontal stretch has no effect on the horizontal asymptote.

For this transformation, $(x, y) \rightarrow ($_____, _____$)$.

Working Example 3: Combining Transformations of Exponential Functions

Describe the transformations of $y = 4^x$ caused by $y = -4^{\frac{1}{3}(x+2)} - 1$. Then, graph the base function and transformed function on the same axes.

Solution

Compare the function $y = -4^{\frac{1}{3}(x+2)} - 1$ to $y = a(c)^{b(x-h)} + k$ to determine the values of the parameters.

• $a =$ _____, which corresponds to a _____ in the _____-axis.

• $b =$ _____, which corresponds to a _____ stretch by a factor of _____.

• $h =$ _____, which corresponds to a _____ translation of _____ units _____.

• $k =$ _____, which corresponds to a _____ translation of _____ units _____.

The figure on the right shows the graph of the base function. Sketch the transformed function and the horizontal asymptote on the same grid as the base function. When combining transformations, recall that you must first perform stretches and reflections, in any order, and then translations.

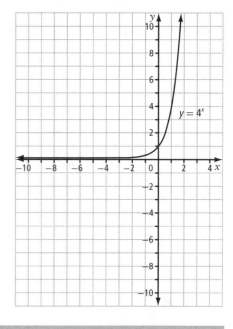

📖 See pages 349–351 of *Pre-Calculus 12* for an example that explores transformations.

Working Example 4: Use Transformations of an Exponential Function to Model a Situation

The real estate board in a city announces that the current average price of a house in the city is $400 000. It predicts that average prices will double every 15 years.

a) Write a transformed exponential function in the form $y = a(c)^{b(x-h)} + k$ to model this situation. Justify your answer.

b) Describe how each of the parameters in the transformed function relates to the information provided.

c) Use technology to graph the function. Use the graph to predict the value of a house after 10 years.

Solution

a) Since the average price of a house doubles over a certain time interval, the base function is $P(t) = 2^t$, where P is the price of the house and t is the time. The time is in intervals of _____ years, so t can be replaced by the rational exponent $\dfrac{r}{\boxed{}}$, where r represents the number of years. Therefore the function becomes $P(r) = $ _____.

The current price of a home is _____, so the P-intercept is (_____, _____).

This means that there must be a vertical stretch by a factor of _____. Therefore, the transformed function that models the price of the house is $P(r) = $ _____.

b) Based on the function $y = a(c)^{b(x-h)} + k$, the parameters of the function are

- $b = \dfrac{\boxed{}}{\boxed{}}$, representing _____

- $a = $ _____, representing _____

c) The graph represents the change in value of a house in this city.

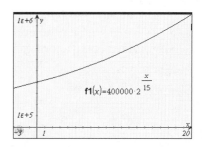

Determine the point on the curve corresponding to $x = 10$.

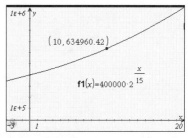

When $r = 10$, $y = $ _____. So, in 10 years, the average value of a house in this city will be _____.

📖 See pages 352–353 of *Pre-Calculus 12* for more examples.

Check Your Understanding

Practise

1. State whether each function shows a vertical translation of $y = 5^x$.

   a) $y = 5^{x-2}$ **b)** $y = 5^x - 2$

   c) $y = 2(5)^x$ **d)** $y = 5^{3x}$

2. State whether each function shows a horizontal stretch of $y = 5^x$.

   a) $y = 5^{x-2}$ no   **b)** $y = 5^x - 2$ no

   c) $y = 2(5)^x$ no   **d)** $y = 5^{3x}$ yes

3. State whether each function shows a reflection in the y-axis of $y = 5^x$.

   a) $y = 5^{x-2}$ **b)** $y = -5^x - 2$

   c) $y = 2(5)^{-x}$ **d)** $y = 5^{\frac{x}{3}}$ hor.

4. Identify all transformations for each function.

   a) $y = 4^{2(x-5)} - 6$ **b)** $y = \frac{2}{3}\left(\frac{1}{2}\right)^{-x} + 9$

vertical stretch = 4

HSF $= \frac{1}{2}$

HT $= 5$

VT $= -6$

   c) $y = -2(1.06)^{\frac{1}{4}x}$ **d)** $y = 500\left(\frac{5}{2}\right)^{2x+6} - 8$

5. Sketch the graph of each exponential function without using technology. For each function,
- state the domain and range
- identify the y-intercept
- indicate whether the graph is increasing or decreasing
- write the equation of the horizontal asymptote

   a) $f(x) = 8^{x-2} + 4$

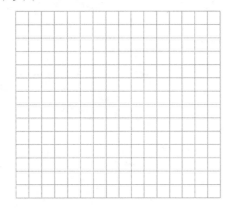

b) $g(x) = -2^x + 3$

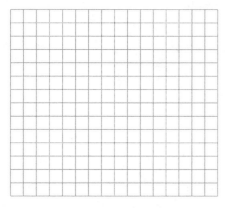

c) $f(x) = 0.5(3)^{x+2} - 5$

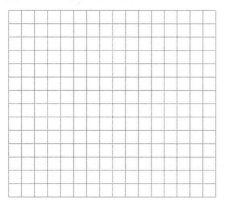

Apply

6. Iodine-131 has a half-life of 8 days. This means that after 8 days, half of the original mass of the isotope will have decayed. Suppose a sample of iodine-131 has a mass of 250 grams.

a) Write an exponential equation that models the amount, M, of iodine-131 remaining after d days. State the transformations that are represented by your function.

The equation is $M(d) = \underline{250}\ \left(\dfrac{1}{2}\right)^{\boxed{\frac{d}{8}}}$. This represents a $\underline{vertical}$
                                                                                (horizontal or vertical)

stretch about the $\underline{X}$-axis by a factor of $\underline{\frac{1}{2}}$, and a horizontal stretch about

the $\underline{y}$-axis by a factor of $\underline{8}$.

b) Graph the exponential equation you wrote. State the domain, range, equation of the horizontal asymptote, and *M*-intercept of the graph.

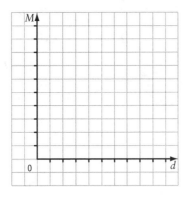

c) What mass of iodine-131 remains after 3 days? Explain how you arrived at your answer.

$$y = 250\left(\tfrac{1}{2}\right)^{\frac{d}{8}}$$

$$y = 250\left(\tfrac{1}{2}\right)^{\frac{3}{8}}$$

$$y = 192.8$$

📖 Question 9 on page 356 of *Pre-Calculus 12* is related to this question.

$$A = P(1+i)^n$$

7. Lyndsay bought a classic car 15 years ago for $12 500. The car has tripled in value in that time.

a) Write an exponential function that models the value, *V*, of Lyndsay's car after *t* years. State the transformations represented by the function.

$$V = 12\,500\,(3)^{\frac{t}{15}}$$

b) Graph the exponential function. What are the domain and range?

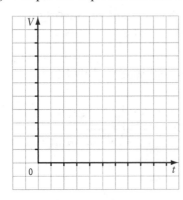

Domain: $x \geq 0$

Range: $y \geq 12\,500$

c) What might Lyndsay expect her car to be worth in 40 years? What assumption are you making?

$$V = 12500(3)^{\frac{40}{15}}$$

$$V = 234009.43$$

d) Use your graph to approximate when the car will be worth $50 000.

$$50000 = 12500(3)^{\frac{t}{15}}$$

$$4 = (3)^{\frac{t}{15}}$$

$$3^{1.262} = 3^{\frac{t}{15}}$$

$$1.262 = \frac{t}{15}$$

$$18.93 = t$$

$$\approx 19$$

8. The population of a town is decreasing by 2% per year. The current population of the town is 11 568.

a) Write an exponential function to model the population remaining, P, after t years. Graph the function.

$$P = 11568(0.98)^t$$

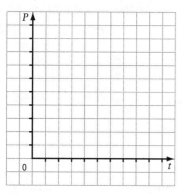

b) State the transformations in your exponential function.

c) Use your equation to determine the population remaining after 5 years.

$$P = 11\,568\,(0.98)^5$$
$$P = 10\,456$$

d) Use the graph to approximate the population of the town after 20 years.

e) According to your equation, will the population ever reach zero? Is this reasonable? Explain.

9. The exponential function $V = 500(1.0225)^{2t}$ models the value of $500, after t years, that is invested at 4.5% compounded semi-annually.

a) State the transformations represented by the function. Graph the function.

VSF of 500
HSF of $\frac{1}{2}$

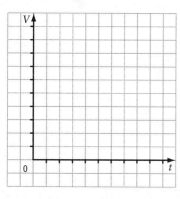

b) State the V-intercept of the function. Explain what this point represents in this situation.

50V

c) Determine the value of the investment after 15 years.

d) Use the graph to determine the time needed for the value of the investment to reach $1000.

Completing #7 to #9 should help you complete #10 to #12 on page 356 of *Pre-Calculus 12*.

Connect

10. Two students are discussing the exponential functions graphed below.

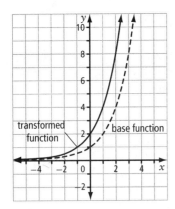

a) David says that he believes that the functions graphed are $y = 2^x$ and $y = 2(2)^x$. Jodi believes that the functions graphed are $y = 2^x$ and $y = 2^{x+1}$. Who is correct? Explain.

b) Show algebraically why $y = 2^{x+1}$ and $y = 2(2)^x$ have the same graph.

$2(2)^x = 2^{x+1}$ $(2^2)^x =$

$2(2^x)$ $2^{2x} = 2^{x+1}$

$4^x = 2^{x+1}$ $2x = x+1$

c) Write two other transformations that look different but have the same graph. Show algebraically that the two transformations are equivalent.

See pages 354–357 of *Pre-Calculus 12* for more questions.

7.3 Solving Exponential Equations

<table>
<tr><td colspan="2" align="center">

KEY IDEAS

</td></tr>
<tr><td colspan="2" align="center">**Strategies for Solving Exponential Equations With a Common Base**</td></tr>
<tr><td align="center">**Description**</td><td align="center">**Example**</td></tr>
<tr>
<td>For equations that begin with terms on both sides of the equal sign that have the same base ...</td>
<td>

$11^{(2x + 6)} = 11^2$ Bases are the same.

$2x + 6 = 2$ Equate the exponents.

$2x = -4$ Solve for x.

$x = -2$

</td>
</tr>
<tr>
<td>For equations that begin with terms on each side of the equal sign that have different bases, but that can be rewritten as the same base ...</td>
<td>

$9^{(x + 3)} = 81^{(2x + 9)}$

$3^{2(x + 3)} = 3^{4(2x + 9)}$ Rewrite terms so they have the same base.

$2(x + 3) = 4(2x + 9)$ Equate the exponents.

$2x + 6 = 8x + 36$ Solve for x.

$-6x = 30$

$x = -5$

</td>
</tr>
<tr><td colspan="2" align="center">**Strategies for Solving Exponential Equations That Do Not Have a Common Base**</td></tr>
<tr><td align="center">**Description**</td><td align="center">**Example**</td></tr>
<tr>
<td>Systematic trial</td>
<td>

Consider the equation $7 = 1.4^x$.

Guess 1: $x = 5$: $1.4^5 = 5.37824$ (less than 7)

Guess 2: $x = 7$: $1.4^7 = 10.5413504$ (greater than 7)

Guess 3: $x = 6$: $1.4^6 = 7.529536$ (approximately 7)

So, x is approximately 6.

</td>
</tr>
<tr>
<td>

Graphing
- Method 1: Point of Intersection
  Graph $y = 7$ and $y = 1.4^x$ on the same axes, and find the point of intersection.

- Method 2: x-Intercept
  Graph $y = 1.4^x - 7$, and determine the x-intercept.

</td>
<td>

Consider the equation $7 = 1.4^x$.

So, $x = 5.7832711$.

</td>
</tr>
</table>

Working Example 1: Rewriting Powers With a Specified Base

Rewrite each of the following with a base of 2.

a) 32   b) 16^3 c) $\sqrt[3]{16}$ d) $\left(\frac{1}{64}\right)^{\frac{1}{3}}$

Solution

a) $32 = 2^5$

b) Since $16 = 2^4$, $16^3 = ($_____$)^3$. Thus, $16^3 = 2^{\square}$.

c) $\sqrt[3]{16} = (2^4)^{\boxed{}} = $ _____

d) Since $64 = $ _____, $\frac{1}{64} = 2^{\square}$. So $\left(\frac{1}{64}\right)^{\frac{1}{3}} = ($_____$)^{\frac{1}{3}} = 2^{-2}$.

Working Example 2: Solving Exponential Equations by Changing Bases

Solve each equation.

a) $10^{x+4} = 1000^{x-4}$ b) $25^{2x} = 125^{x-1}$

Solution

a) Express both sides of the equation as powers with base 10.

$10^{x+4} = 1000^{x-4}$

$10^{x+4} = (10^3)^{x-4}$

$10^{x+4} = 10^{3x-12}$

Equate the powers:

$x + 4 = 3x - 12$

_____ = _____

$x = $ _____

b) Express both sides of the equation as powers with base 5.

$25^{2x} = 125^{x-1}$

$\left(5^{\square}\right)^{2x} = \left(5^{\square}\right)^{x-1}$

$5^{\square} = 5^{\square}$

_____ = _____

Equate the powers:

$4x = $ _____

$x = $ _____

See pages 360–361 of *Pre-Calculus 12* for similar examples.

Working Example 3: Solving Exponential Equations With Different Bases

Solve for x. Express your answer to the nearest tenth.

$7^x = 3579$

Solution

3579 is not an integer power of 7, so you cannot use the same techniques as in Working Examples 1 and 2. Both sides cannot be expressed with the same base. Instead, you can either use systematic trial or technology. When using technology, you can determine x by graphing one or two functions.

Method 1: Systematic Trial

Use systematic trial to find the approximate value of x that satisfies the equation.

Try $x = 4$.   Try $x = 5$.

$7^4 = 2401$ (less than 3570) $7^5 = 16\,807$ (greater than 3570)

The solution is between 4 and 5, but is obviously closer to 4 than 5.

Try $x = 4.2$.   Try $x = 4.3$.

$7^{4.2} \approx 3543$ (less than 3579) $7^{4.3} \approx 4304$ (greater than 3579)

The solution is between $x = 4.2$ and 4.3, and probably much closer to $x = 4.2$. You could continue this process to get an even closer approximation, but this is probably close enough.

Method 2: Using Technology, Find the x-Intercept of a Single Function

Use your graphing calculator to graph the function $f(x) = 7^x - 3579$. Find the x-intercept of the graph:

$x =$ _____.

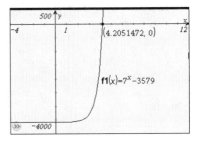

Method 3: Using Technology, Find the Point of Intersection of the Graphs of Two Functions

Graph the functions $f(x) = 7^x$ and $g(x) = 3579$ in the same calculator window. Use the trace or intersection feature of the graphing calculator to determine the coordinates of the point of intersection:

$x =$ _____.

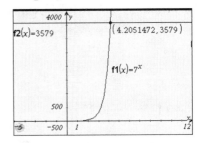

> Which method do you prefer?

📖 See pages 362–363 of *Pre-Calculus 12* for more examples.

Check Your Understanding

Practise

1. Express each of the following with base 3.

   a) 81

     3^4

   b) 27^5

     $(3^3)^5$ 3^{15}

   c) $3\sqrt{3}$

     $3^1 \times 3^{\frac{1}{2}}$

     $3^{1.5}$

   d) $\sqrt[3]{243}$

     $243^{\frac{1}{3}}$

     $(3^5)^{\frac{1}{3}}$

     $3^{\frac{5}{3}}$

   e) $9\sqrt[3]{81^2}$

     Work with 9 and $\sqrt[3]{81^2}$ separately.

     $9 = 3^{\boxed{2}}$

     $\sqrt[3]{81^2} = \left(\left(3^{\boxed{4}}\right)^{\boxed{2}}\right)^{\boxed{\frac{1}{3}}}$

     $= \underline{3^{\frac{8}{3}}}$

     Thus, $9\sqrt[3]{81^2} = 3^{\boxed{2}}3^{\boxed{8/3}}$.

     $= \underline{3^{\frac{14}{3}}}$

   f) $\left(\dfrac{1}{27}\right)^2$

   g) $\left(\dfrac{\sqrt{3}}{81}\right)^{-3}$

2. Rewrite each pair of expressions to have the same base.

   a) 8 and 64

   b) 3^2 and 9^3

   c) 5^{x+6} and 125

   d) 2^{3x} and 8^{2x+4}

   e) 27^{5x+4} and $\left(\dfrac{1}{9}\right)^{x+3}$

   f) $\left(\dfrac{1}{4}\right)^{x+7}$ and 8^{-3x}

3. Solve using systematic trial. Round answers to one decimal place. Check your answers using technology.

a) $175 = 5^x$

b) $12 = 2.1^x$

4. Solve the following.

a) $4^{2x} = 4096$

$$4^{2x} = 4^6$$
$$2x = 6$$
$$x = 3$$

b) $2^{3x-5} = 128$

c) $6^{x+3} = \dfrac{1}{216}$

$$6^{x+3} = \dfrac{1}{6^3}$$
$$6^{x+3} = 6^{-3}$$
$$x+3 = -3$$
$$x = -6$$

d) $10^{5x+6} = 0.0001$

$$10^{5x+6} = \dfrac{1}{10000}$$
$$10^{5x+6} = 10^{-4}$$
$$5x+6 = -4$$
$$5x = -10$$
$$x = -2$$

5. Solve the following.

a) $64^{4x} = 16^{x+5}$

b) $9^{x-7} = 27^{2x-9}$

c) $125^{6x+2} = 25^{8x+1}$

d) $8^{x+2} = \left(\dfrac{1}{4}\right)^{x+3}$

e) $5(3)^x = 135$

$$3^x = 3^3 \qquad x = 3$$

_____ = _____ Divide each side by 5.

$3^x =$ _____ Express as base 3.

_____ = _____ Equate powers and solve.

6. Solve each of the following graphically, using technology. Sketch a diagram of the graph. Where necessary, round answers to the nearest hundredth. Use both methods described in Working Example 3 at least once.

a) $5^x = 32$

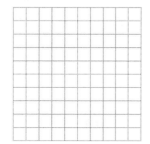

b) $10^{2x} = 439$

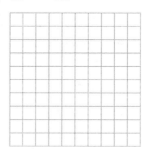

c) $25\left(\frac{1}{2}\right)^{4x} = 5$

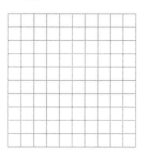

d) $200(1.05)^{12x} = 1250$

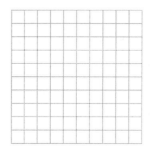

Apply

7. A type of bacterium doubles each hour.

   a) If there are 4 bacteria in a sample, write a exponential function that models the sample's growth over time.

   $$y = 4(2)^t$$

   b) Use your equation to determine the time it takes for the sample to become 4096 bacteria.

   $$4096 = 4(2)^t \qquad t = 10$$
   $$1024 = 2^t$$
   $$2^{10} = 2^t$$

8. A painting doubles in value every 8 years. It is currently worth $1000.

   a) Write an exponential function that models the value of the painting.

   $$y = 1000(2)^{\frac{x}{8}}$$

   b) Use your equation to determine the time needed for the painting to be worth $3200.

   $$3200 = 1000(2)^{\frac{x}{8}} \qquad 1.679 = \frac{x}{8}$$
   $$3.2 = 2^{\frac{x}{8}} \qquad 13.43 = x$$
   $$2^{1.679} = 2^{\frac{x}{8}}$$

9. The student council of a school notices that their membership is growing by 3% per year.

   a) The membership is currently 350 students. Write an exponential function to model the size of the student council.

   $$y = 350(1.03)^t$$

   b) Use your equation to determine the time needed until the student council has 560 members. Round your answer to the nearest whole number.

   $$560 = 350(1.03)^t$$
   $$1.6 = 1.03^t$$
   $$1.03^{15.91} = 1.03^t$$
   $$15.91 = t$$
   16 years

Connect

10. Keegan invests $1000 at 3.75% compounded annually.

    a) Write an exponential function to model the growth of Keegan's investment.

    b) Describe the two methods that you have learned that you can use to find an approximate solution to this equation.

    c) Use your preferred method to determine the time needed, to the nearest year, that it would take for Keegan's investment to be worth $2500. If you choose a graphical method, sketch your graph.

    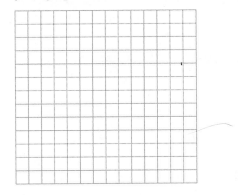

    d) Why are you unable to solve your equation algebraically more precisely? Describe the difficulty that arises. (You will learn to overcome this difficulty in the Chapter 8.)

Chapter 7 Review

7.1 Characteristics of Exponential Functions, pages 229–237

1. For each exponential function, state the domain, range, y-intercept, horizontal asymptote, and whether a graph of the function would be increasing or decreasing. Verify your answers by using technology to graph the functions.

   a) $y = 4.5^x$

   b) $y = \left(\dfrac{2}{3}\right)^x$

2. State the exponential function represented by each graph.

   a)
   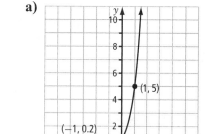

   b)
   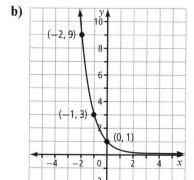

3. A photographer uses filters to change the look of the photographs she takes. A particular filter reduces the light transmitted through it by 15%. The photographer may use more than one of this type of filter at a time.

   a) Write an exponential function that shows the proportion of light, P, passing through n filters.

   b) Graph your function and use the graph to estimate the number of filters needed to reduce the light transmitted to half the original intensity.

   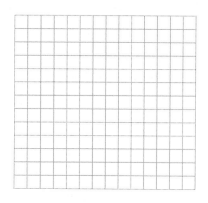

7.2 Transformations of Exponential Functions, pages 238–248

4. Identify all the transformations in each exponential function below.

a) $y = 2(3)^x - 3$

b) $y = 5^{x+3}$

c) $y = 10^{2x-8} + 1$

d) $y = 5(8)^{6x+12}$

5. Write the equation for each of the following transformations to the function $y = 4^x$. Then, state the domain and range of the transformed function.

a) vertically stretched by a factor of $\frac{1}{2}$, translated 2 units left and 6 units down

b) horizontally stretched by a factor of $\frac{1}{3}$, vertically stretched by a factor of 5

c) horizontally stretched by a factor of 2, translated 3 units right and 1 unit down

7.3 Solving Exponential Equations, pages 249–255

6. Solve each of the following equations algebraically. Use graphing technology to check your answer.

a) $5^{x+2} = 3125$

b) $2^{3x-2} = 16^x$

c) $\left(\frac{1}{9}\right)^{x-6} = 27^{2x-1}$

d) $(\sqrt{3})^x = 9^{2x+5}$

7. The half-life of a radioactive substance is 4 days.

   a) Write an exponential function that models the proportion, *P*, of the substance remaining after *t* days.

$$y = ac^x$$
$$y = \left(\tfrac{1}{2}\right)^{\frac{x}{4}} \qquad P = \left(\tfrac{1}{2}\right)^{\frac{x}{4}}$$

   b) Use your function to determine the time that must pass until there is 25% of the substance remaining.

$$0.25 = \left(\tfrac{1}{2}\right)^{\frac{x}{4}} \qquad 2 = \tfrac{x}{4}$$
$$\left(\tfrac{1}{2}\right)^{2} = \left(\tfrac{1}{2}\right)^{\frac{x}{4}} \qquad 8 = x \qquad 8 \text{ days}$$

   c) Use graphing technology to determine the time that must pass until there is 7% of the substance remaining. State your answer to the nearest tenth. Sketch the graph.

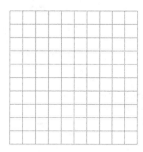

8. The number of bacteria in a sample doubles every 10 h. Initially, there are 64 colonies present.

   a) Write an exponential function that models the number of bacteria colonies, *N*, present after *t* hours.

$$y = ac^x$$
$$y = 64(2)^{\frac{x}{10}} \qquad N = 64(2)^{\frac{x}{10}}$$

   b) Use your function to determine the number of colonies present after 24 h.

$$N = 64(2)^{\frac{24}{10}}$$
$$N \approx 337 \qquad 337 \text{ colonies}$$

   c) Determine the time that must pass until there are 1024 colonies present.

$$1024 = 64(2)^{\frac{x}{10}} \qquad 4 = \tfrac{x}{10}$$
$$16 = 2^{\frac{x}{10}} \qquad 40 = x \qquad 40 \text{ hours}$$
$$(2^{4} = 2^{\frac{x}{10}}$$

   d) Use graphing technology to determine the time, correct to the nearest hour, that passes before 1500 colonies are present. Sketch the graph.

Chapter 7 Skills Organizer

Complete the organizer to review the concepts you have learned in this chapter.

Graphs and Transformations

$y = c^x$
domain: $x \in R$
range: $y > 0$
y-intercept: _____
horizontal asymptote: _____

$y = a(c)^x$
transformation: _____
domain: _____
range: _____

$y = c^{x - h}$
transformation: _____
domain: _____
range: _____

$y = c^{bx}$
transformation: _____
domain: _____
range: _____

$y = c^x + k$
transformation: _____
domain: _____
range: _____

Solving Exponential Equations

If the bases are the same,

If the powers can be rewritten to have the same base,

If the powers cannot be written with the same base,

Chapter 8 Logarithmic Functions

8.1 Understanding Logarithms

- A logarithm is the exponent to which a fixed base must be raised to obtain a specific value.

  Example: $5^3 = 125$. The logarithm of 125 is the exponent that must be applied to base 5 to obtain 125. In this example, the logarithm is 3: $\log_5 125 = 3$.

- Equations in exponential form can be written in logarithmic form and vice versa.

Exponential Form	**Logarithmic Form**
$x = c^y$	$y = \log_c x$

- The inverse of the exponential function $y = c^x$, $c > 0$, $c \neq 1$, is $x = c^y$ or, in logarithmic form, $y = \log_c x$. Conversely, the inverse of the logarithmic function $y = \log_c x$, $c > 0$, $c \neq 1$, is $x = \log_c y$ or, in exponential form, $y = c^x$.

- The graphs of an exponential function and its inverse logarithmic function are reflections of each other in the line $y = x$.

- For the logarithmic function $y = \log_c x$, $c > 0$, $c \neq 1$,
  – the domain is $\{x \mid x > 0, x \in \mathbf{R}\}$
  – the range is $\{y \mid y \in \mathbf{R}\}$
  – the x-intercept is 1
  – the vertical asymptote is $x = 0$, or the y-axis

- A common logarithm has base 10. It is not necessary to write the base for common logarithms: $\log_{10} x = \log x$

Working Example 1: Graph the Inverse of an Exponential Function

The graph of $y = 2^x$ is shown at right. State the inverse of the function. Then, sketch the graph of the inverse function and identify the following characteristics of the graph:
- domain and range
- x-intercept, if it exists
- y-intercept, if it exists
- the equation of any asymptotes

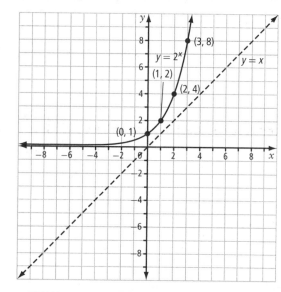

Solution

The inverse of $y = 2^x$ is $x = 2^y$.

In logarithmic form, the inverse function is $y = \log_{\square} x$.

The inverse of a function is its reflection in the line $y = x$. To graph the inverse, sketch this reflection. Alternatively, interchange each pair of coordinates on the graph of the function to obtain coordinates on the inverse graph.

For example, the point $(1, 0)$ is on the graph of $y = 2^x$. Therefore, the point _____ is on the graph of the inverse.

Add the graph of the inverse of the function to the grid on the previous page.

- The domain is _____.

- The range is _____.

- The graph has no y-intercept.

- The x-intercept is _____.

- The vertical asymptote is _____.

Working Example 2: Change the Form of an Expression

For each expression in exponential form, rewrite it in logarithmic form. For each expression in logarithmic form, rewrite it in exponential form.

a) $3^4 = 81$

b) $36^{\frac{1}{2}} = 6$

c) $\log_5 125 = 3$

d) $\log 10\ 000 = 4$

Solution

a) The base is 3 and the exponent is 4. The logarithmic form is $\log_{\square} 81 =$ _____.

b) 36 is the base, so the logarithmic form is $\log_{36}$ _____ $=$ _____.

c) The base is 5 and the exponent is 3. The exponential form is $5^3 =$ _____.

d) When a base is not stated, the base of a logarithm is 10. The exponential form of this

   expression is _____ $=$ _____.

Working Example 3: Evaluate and Determine a Value in Logarithmic
Expressions

Evaluate each expression.

a) $\log_2 32$

b) $\log_{100} 10$

c) $\log_3 \sqrt{27}$

d) $\log_4 x = 3$

e) $\log_x 125 = 3$

f) $\log 0.01 = x$

Solution

a) This logarithmic expression asks which exponent is applied to base 2 to produce a result of 32. Since $2^5 = 32$, the value of the logarithmic expression is _____.

b) Since $100^{\frac{1}{2}} = 10$, the value of $\log_{100} 10$ is _____.

c) Written as a power of 3, 27 is equal to _____ and $\sqrt{}$ is written as an exponent of _____. This means that $\log_3 \sqrt{27} = \frac{3}{2}$.

d) In exponential form, $\log_4 x = 3$ is equivalent to _____ = _____. So, $x =$ _____.

e) In exponential form, $\log_x 125 = 3$ is equivalent to _____ = _____. So, $x =$ _____.

f) 0.01 can be written as $\frac{1}{100}$, which is $10^{\square}$. So, $\log 0.01 =$ _____.

Working Example 4: An Application of Logarithmic Functions

The intensity of sound is measured in decibels (dB). The level of a sound, L, in decibels, is given by $L = 10 \log \left(\frac{I}{I_0} \right)$, where I is the intensity of the sound and I_0 is the faintest sound detectable to humans. The sound level inside a particular car is 39 dB when it is idling, and 80 dB at full throttle. How many times more intense is the sound at full throttle?

Solution

Let I_i be the intensity of the sound at idle and I_f be the intensity at full throttle.

$39 = 10 \log \left(\frac{I_i}{I_0} \right)$ or $3.9 = \log \left(\frac{I_i}{I_0} \right)$ $80 = 10 \log \left(\frac{I_f}{I_0} \right)$ or $8 =$ _____

Rewrite each expression in exponential form.

$\frac{I_i}{I_0} =$ _____ $\frac{I_f}{I_0} =$ _____

Then, multiply by I_0 to obtain $I_i = I_0 \, 10^{3.9}$ and $I_f =$ _____.

To compare the intensities, divide I_f by I_i.

$\frac{I_f}{I_i} = \frac{I_0 \, 10^{\square}}{I_0 \, 10^{\square}}$

$\frac{I_f}{I_i} =$ _____

The I_0 terms divide out, leaving $10^{\square} =$ _____.

Therefore, the sound at full throttle is about 12 589 times as intense as the sound at idle.

📖 See pages 375–379 of *Pre-Calculus 12* for more examples.

Practise

1. For each exponential graph below, sketch the inverse function and state the domain, range, *x*-intercept, and equation of the vertical asymptote. Then, write the equation of the inverse function.

a)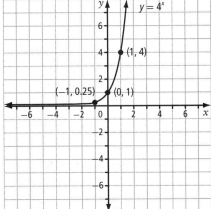

b)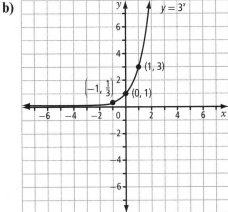

2. Express in logarithmic form.

a) $3^5 = 243$

b) $10^4 = 10\,000$

c) $16^{\frac{1}{2}} = 4$

d) $8^{-2} = \dfrac{1}{64}$

e) $10^{-2} = 0.01$

f) $27^{\frac{2}{3}} = 9$

g) $12^x = 2y$

h) $2^{2x-5} = y - 1$

3. Express in exponential form.

    a) $\log_2 32 = 5$ **b)** $\log_8 512 = 3$

    c) $\log_5 625 = 4$ **d)** $\log 1000 = 3$

    e) $\log 0.0001 = -4$ **f)** $\log_{\frac{1}{2}} 8 = -3$

    g) $\log_3 (x + 1) = y$ **h)** $\log_4 2x = y + 1$

4. Evaluate.

    a) $\log_6 36$ **b)** $\log_2 64$

    c) $\log 100$ **d)** $\log_3 \dfrac{1}{9}$

> This expression asks for the exponent of 3 that gives a value of $\dfrac{1}{9}$.

    e) $\log_5 \dfrac{1}{125}$ **f)** $\log_7 7$

    g) $\log_5 5^4$ **h)** $\log_2 \left(8\sqrt{32} \right)$

                                                  Writing as powers of 2,

                                                 $8 = $ _____ and $\sqrt{32} = $ _____.

                                                 By the exponent laws, $\left(8\sqrt{32} \right) = 2^{\boxed{}}$.

                                                 $\log_2 \left(8\sqrt{32} \right) = $ _____

    i) $\log_{12} 1$ **j)** $\log_{25} 5$

📖 Completing these will help you to complete #1–#4 on page 380 of *Pre-Calculus 12*.

5. Put the following in ascending order: $\log_6 400$, $\log_2 100$, $\log_{10} 300$.

Apply

6. Determine the value of x in each of the following.

a) $4^x = 64$

b) $10^{2x} = 1\ 000\ 000$

c) $\log_2 x = 4$

d) $\log_5 x = -2$

e) $\log_4 256 = x$

f) $\log_{16} 4 = x$

g) $\log_x 81 = 4$

h) $\log_x 6 = \dfrac{1}{2}$

i) $\log_x \dfrac{1}{25} = -2$

j) $\log_x \dfrac{1}{64} = -3$

7. Evaluate each expression.

a) 10^y, where $y = \log_{10} 216$

b) 8^y, where $y = \log_8 4$

c) 6^y, where $y = \log_6 12$

d) $\log_2 2^7$

e) $\log_5 5^{-8}$

f) $\log_7 7^{10}$

8. The intensity of sound is measured in decibels (dB). The level of a sound, L, in decibels, is given by $L = 10 \log \left(\frac{I}{I_0} \right)$, where I is the intensity of the sound and I_0 is the faintest sound detectable to humans.

   a) Determine the level of a sound that is 20 times more intense than I_0, correct to the nearest decibel.

   b) The level of sound in a quiet bedroom at night might be 30 dB, while normal conversation has a sound level of about 60 dB. How many times more intense is normal conversation than the quiet room?

Connect

9. Refer to the graph of the logarithmic function $y = \log_2 x$ in Working Example 1, page 260.

   a) Predict how the graph of $y = \log_5 x$ will compare to the original graph.

   b) Using technology, compare the graph of $y = 2^x$ to the graph of $y = 5^x$.

   c) Use your work in part b) to justify or change your prediction in part a).

   d) Generalize to explain how logarithmic graphs with different bases will compare.

10. Consider the logarithmic function $y = \log_c x$.

   a) Explain why $c > 0$ for all such functions.

   b) Explain why $c \neq 1$ for all such functions.

8.2 Transformations of Logarithmic Functions

KEY IDEAS

- To represent real-life situations, you may need to transform the basic logarithmic function, $y = \log_b x$, by applying reflections, stretches, and translations. These transformations should be performed in the same manner as those applied to any other function.

- The effects of the parameters a, b, h, and k in $y = a \log_c (b(x - h)) + k$ on the graph of the logarithmic function $y = \log_c x$ are described in the table.

Parameter	Effect
a	Vertically stretch by a factor of $|a|$ about the x-axis. Reflect in the x-axis if $a < 0$.
b	Horizontally stretch by a factor of $\left|\dfrac{1}{b}\right|$ about the y-axis. Reflect in the y-axis if $b < 0$.
h	Horizontally translate h units.
k	Vertically translate k units.

- Only parameter h changes the vertical asymptote and the domain. None of the parameters changes the range.

Working Example 1: Translations of a Logarithmic Function

a) Sketch the graph of $y = \log_4 (x + 4) - 5$.

b) State the
- domain and range
- x-intercept
- y-intercept
- equation of the asymptote

Solution

a) Begin with the graph of $y = \log_4 x$. Identify key points, such as $(1, 0)$, $(4, 1)$, and $(16, 2)$.

Identify the transformations.

The graph moves _____ units to the left and 4 units _____.

In mapping notation, the key points are transformed as follows:

Key points: (x, y) maps to $(x - 4, y - 5)$

(x, y)	$\rightarrow$	$(x - 4, y - 5)$
$(1, 0)$	$\rightarrow$	$(-3, -5)$
$(4, 1)$	$\rightarrow$	$(0, -4)$
$(16, 2)$	$\rightarrow$	$(12, -3)$

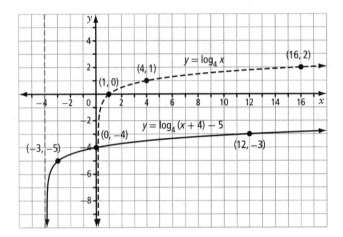

b) The domain of $y = \log_4 x$ is _____. Since the graph is translated 4 units left, this changes the domain to $\{x \mid x > -4, x \in R\}$. The range of the transformed function is not changed and is _____.

To determine the x-intercept, set $\log_4 (x + 4) - 5 = 0$. Then, solve for x.

$\log_4 (x + 4) = 5$

$\quad x + 4 = $ _____ (write in exponential form)

$\quad\quad x = $ _____

To confirm that the y-intercept is -4, substitute $x = 0$.

$y = \log_4 (0 + 4) - 5$

$y = $ _____ $- 5$

$y = $ _____

The graph of $y = \log_4 x$ has a vertical asymptote at $x = 0$. Since the graph is translated 4 units left, the asymptote is translated as well.

Thus, $y = \log_4 (x + 4) - 5$ has a vertical asymptote at _____.

Working Example 2: Reflections and Stretches of Logarithmic Functions

Sketch the graph of each of the following. State any invariant points.

a) $y = 2 \log_9 x$ **b)** $y = -\log_2 4x$

Solution

a) The coefficient of 2 indicates a vertical stretch by a factor of 2. Choose key points on the graph of $y = \log_9 x$. Then, use mapping notation to show the transformation of those points.

Key points: (x, y) maps to $(x, 2y)$

(x, y)	$\rightarrow$	$(x, 2y)$
$(1, 0)$	$\rightarrow$	$(1, 0)$
$\left(3, \dfrac{1}{2}\right)$	$\rightarrow$	$(3, 1)$
$(9, 1)$	$\rightarrow$	$(9, 2)$

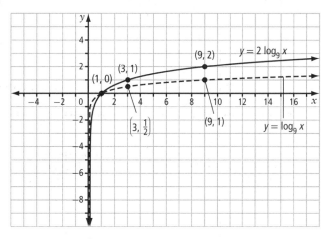

The invariant point is _____.

b) The transformations are a reflection in _____ and a _____ stretch by a factor of $\dfrac{1}{4}$. Using key points on $y = \log_2 x$, use mapping notation to express the transformations.

Key points: (x, y) maps to $\left(\dfrac{1}{4}x, -y\right)$

(x, y)	$\rightarrow$	$\left(\dfrac{1}{4}x, -y\right)$
$(1, 0)$	$\rightarrow$	$\left(\dfrac{1}{4}, 0\right)$
$(2, 1)$	$\rightarrow$	$\left(\dfrac{1}{2}, -1\right)$
$(4, 2)$	$\rightarrow$	
$(8, 3)$	$\rightarrow$	

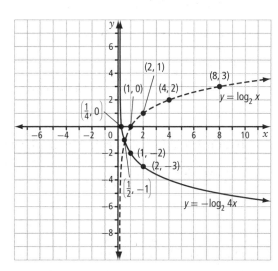

There are no invariant points on the graph.

Why does this set of transformations have no invariant points?

Working Example 3: Combine Transformations

Sketch the graph of $y = -2 \log_3 (x - 3) + 5$.

Solution

First, apply all stretches and reflections to $y = \log_3 x$, in any order. Then, apply translations. Consider the effect of a reflection in the x-axis and a vertical stretch by a factor of 2 on the key points $(1, 0)$, $(3, 1)$, and $(9, 2)$.

Key points: (x, y) maps to $(x, -2y)$

$y = \log_3 x$	$y = -2 \log_3 x$
$(1, 0)$	$(1, 0)$
$(3, 1)$	$(3, -2)$
$(9, 2)$	

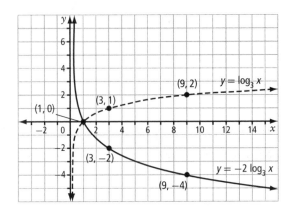

Since the graph is translated 3 units right and 5 units up, apply these translations to the points.

Key points: (x, y) maps to $(x + 3, y + 5)$

$y = -2 \log_3 x$	$y = -2 \log_3 (x - 3) + 5$
$(1, 0)$	$(4, 5)$
$(3, -2)$	
$(9, -4)$	

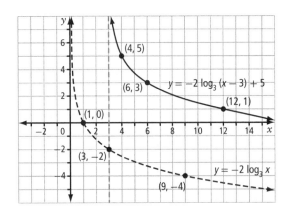

📖 See pages 384–389 of *Pre-Calculus 12* for more examples.

Check Your Understanding

Practise

1. State the transformations, in order of application, to transform $y = \log_c x$ to each of the following.

   a) $y = \log_4 (x + 1) - 8$ **b)** $y = 2 \log (4x)$

   c) $y = -\log_2 (3x)$ **d)** $y = 5 \log_6 (-2(x + 4))$

2. Write the equations that correspond to the following transformations of $y = \log_5 x$.

   a) vertically stretched by a factor of 3 and translated 2 units to the right

   b) reflected in the x-axis and translated 1 unit down and 4 units left

   c) vertically stretched by a factor of $\frac{1}{2}$ and horizontally stretched by a factor of $\frac{1}{2}$

   d) vertically stretched by a factor of 4, reflected in the y-axis, and translated 2.5 units down

3. Sketch each of the following transformations of $y = \log_c x$.

   a) $y = \log_2 (x + 2) - 3$ **b)** $y = 2 \log_8 x + 4$

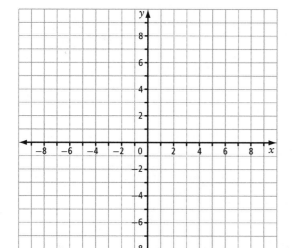 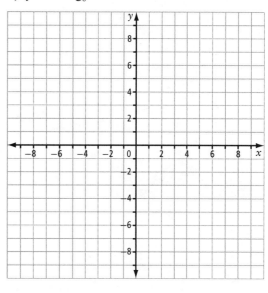

c) $y = -\log_5 (x - 1) - 2$

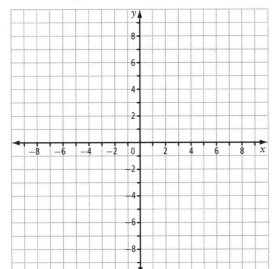

d) $y = \log (2x) + 5$

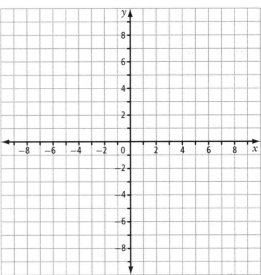

Completing these will help you complete #1–#4 on pages 389 and 390 of *Pre-Calculus 12*.

4. Describe how the graph of each logarithmic function could be obtained from the graph of its base function, $y = \log_c x$.

   a) $y = \log_6 (2x + 6)$

   The graph has been horizontally stretched by a factor of _____.

   However, before determining the horizontal translation, factor 2 out of the argument of the logarithm.

   > The *argument* of a function is the *input* value. For $y = f(x)$, the argument for the function, f, is x.

   $y = \log_6 (2(_____))$

   This shows that the graph is translated _____ units to the _____.

   b) $y = \log_2 (3x - 12)$

   c) $y = \log \left(\frac{1}{2}x - 3 \right)$

   d) $y = \log_3 \left(\frac{1}{3}x + 6 \right)$

Apply

5. The Shannon-Hartley theorem is used to determine the highest possible rate for transmitting information. The formula is $C = B \log_2 (r + 1)$, where r is the signal-to-noise ratio, B is the bandwidth in hertz, and C is the rate in bits per second.

   a) Describe the transformations in the theorem, compared to the graph of $C = \log_2 r$.

   There is a VSF, and a horizontal translation of 1 left.

   b) If the bandwidth is 10 000 Hz and the signal-to-noise ratio is 31, determine the transmission rate.

   $C = 10\ 000 \cdot \log_2 (31 + 1)$

   $C = 9.1 \times 10^4$

6. For each of the following, state the domain, range, intercepts to the nearest tenth (if they exist), and equation of the vertical asymptote.

   a) $y = \log_5 (x - 8) - 12$

   $x \in R \quad x > 8$

   $y \in R$

   x-intercept: $(26.3, 0.8)$
   y-intercept: $(0.5, -17.2)$

   b) $y = -3 \log_9 (4(x - 1)) + 2$

   c) $y = \frac{1}{2} \log_{12} (6x) - 4$

   d) $y = \log_2 \left(\frac{1}{4}(x + 3)\right) - 5$

7. Each graph has been translated from $y = \log_3 x$. State the translation(s) in each case.

   a)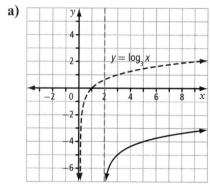

   b)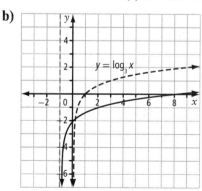

8. Each graph below has been vertically stretched from $y = \log_4 x$. State the stretch in each case.

a)

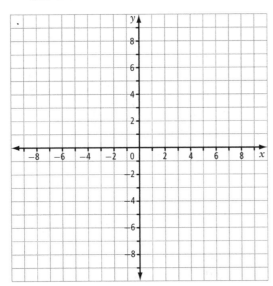

b)

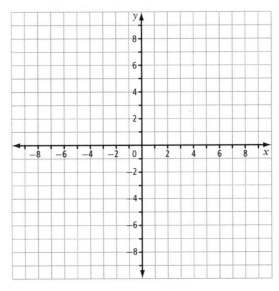

Connect

9. Consider the following transformations of $y = \log_2 x$.

a) Sketch the result when the graph is vertically stretched by a factor of 2 and then translated 4 units left.

b) Sketch the result when the graph of $y = \log_2 x$ is translated 4 units left and then vertically stretched by a factor of 2.

c) Compare the transformed graphs in parts a) and b). Does the order of performing a vertical stretch and a horizontal translation matter?

d) Give two other transformations of the graph of $y = \log_2 x$ for which the order of the transformations does not matter.

e) Make a general statement about when the order of performing transformations matters.

8.3 Laws of Logarithms

- Let P be any real number, and M, N, and c be positive real numbers with $c \neq 1$. Then, the following laws of logarithms are valid.

Name	Law	Description
Product	$\log_c MN = \log_c M + \log_c N$	The logarithm of a product of numbers is the sum of the logarithms of the numbers.
Quotient	$\log_c \dfrac{M}{N} = \log_c M - \log_c N$	The logarithm of a quotient of numbers is the difference of the logarithms of the dividend and divisor.
Power	$\log_c M^P = P \log_c M$	The logarithm of a power of a number is the exponent times the logarithm of the number.

- Many quantities in science are measured using a logarithmic scale. Two commonly used logarithmic scales are the decibel scale and the pH scale.

Working Example 1: Use the Laws of Logarithms to Expand Expressions

Expand each expression using the laws of logarithms.

a) $\log_4 \dfrac{x^3 y}{4z}$

b) $\log_5 \sqrt{xy^3}$

c) $\log \dfrac{100\sqrt[3]{x^4}}{y^2}$

Solution

a) $\log_4 \dfrac{x^3 y}{4z} = \log_4 \underline{x^3 y} - \log_4 \underline{4z}$ *factored out*

$= \log_4 x^3 + \log_4 y - (\log_4 4 + \log_4 z)$

$= 3 \log_4 x + \log_4 y - 1 - \log_4 z$

> Why does $\log_4 4 = 1$?

b) $\log_5 \sqrt{xy^3} = \log_5 (xy^3)^{\boxed{1/2}}$

$= \frac{1}{2} \log_5 (xy^3)$

$= \frac{1}{2} (\log_5 \underline{x} + \log_5 \underline{y^3})$

$= \frac{1}{2} (\log_5 \underline{x} + \underline{\log_5 y} \log_5 \underline{3})$

$= \frac{1}{2} \log_5 \underline{\hspace{1cm}} + \underline{\hspace{1cm}} \log_5 \underline{\hspace{1cm}}$

c) $\log \dfrac{100\sqrt[3]{x^4}}{y^2} = \log 100\sqrt[3]{x^4} - \log y^2$

$$= \log 100 + \log x^{\boxed{}} - \underline{\hspace{2cm}}$$

$$= 2 + \underline{\hspace{2cm}} - \underline{\hspace{2cm}}$$

Working Example 2: Write Expressions With a Single Logarithm

Rewrite each expression using a single logarithm. State the restrictions on the variable.

a) $\log_2 x^3 - 4 \log_2 x - \log_2 \sqrt{x}$

b) $4 \log_6 y^2 + \log_6 y - \dfrac{2}{3} \log_6 y$

c) $\log (x - 3) + \log (x + 4)$

Solution

a) $\log_2 x^3 - 4 \log_2 x - \log_2 \sqrt{x}$

$$= \log_2 x^3 - \log_2 \underline{\hspace{1.5cm}} - \log_2 x^{\frac{1}{2}}$$

$$= \log \dfrac{x^3}{\boxed{}}$$

$$= \log \dfrac{1}{x^{\frac{3}{2}}}, x > 0$$

b) $4 \log_6 y^2 + \log_6 y - \dfrac{2}{3} \log_6 y$

$$= \log_6 \underline{\hspace{1.5cm}} + \log_6 y - \log_6 \underline{\hspace{1.5cm}}$$

$$= \log_6 \dfrac{y^8 y}{y^{\frac{2}{3}}}$$

$$= \underline{\hspace{1.5cm}}, y > 0$$

c) $\log (x - 3) + \log (x + 4)$

$$= \log [(x - 3)(x + 4)]$$

$$= \log \underline{\hspace{2.5cm}}, x > 3$$

Working Example 3: Evaluate Expressions With the Laws of Logarithms

Evaluate each expression.

a) $\log_4 8 + \log_4 32$

b) $\log_6 216 \sqrt[4]{36}$

Solution

a) $\log_4 8 + \log_4 32$

$$= \log_4 (8 \times 32)$$

$$= \log_4 \underline{\hspace{1.5cm}}$$

$$= \underline{\hspace{1cm}}$$

b) $216 = 6^{\boxed{}}$ and $\sqrt[4]{36} = 6^{\boxed{}}$

Rewrite $\log_6 216 \sqrt[4]{36}$.

$$\log_6 216 \sqrt[4]{36} = \log_6 6^3 6^{\frac{1}{2}}$$

$$= \underline{\hspace{2.5cm}}$$

$$= \underline{\hspace{1.5cm}}$$

📖 See pages 395–399 of *Pre-Calculus 12* for more examples.

Check Your Understanding

Practise

1. Use the laws of logarithms to evaluate.

a) $\log_4 8 + \log_4 2$

b) $\log_5 250 - \log_5 2$

c) $\log_2 96 - \log_2 3$

d) $\log_6 3 + \log_6 12$

e) $\log_5 10 + \log_5 10 - \log_5 4$

f) $\log 25 + 2\log 4 + \log 5 - \log 2$

g) $\log_4 4^5$

h) $\log_9 9^{11}$

| Since $\log_2 16 =$ _____, this means that $2^{\log_2 16} =$ _____. |

i) $2^{\log_2 16}$

$\log_2 16$
$= 2^4$
$2^y = 16$
$= 16$
$2^x = 2^4$
$x = 4$

j) $10^{\log 1000}$

$\log 1000$
$10^x = 1000$
$10^x = 10^3$

$= 10^3$
$= 1000$

2. Expand each expression using the laws of logarithms.

a) $\log_7 x^4\sqrt{y^3}$

Use the product law to rewrite $\log_7 x^4\sqrt{y^3}$.

$\log_7$ _____ $+ \log_7$ _____

Rewrite $\sqrt{y^3}$ using exponents: _____

Use the power law to rewrite $\log_7 x^4$ and $\log_7 \sqrt{y^3}$.

$\log_7 x^4 =$ _____ and $\log_7 \sqrt{y^3} =$ _____ $\log_7 y$

Thus, the expanded expression for $\log_7 x^4\sqrt{y^3}$ is _____.

b) $\log_{12}(xy^2z^5)^3$

$\log_{12}(x^3y^6z^{15})$

$\log_{12}x^3 + \log_{12}y^6 + \log_{12}z^{15}$

$3\log_{12}x + 6\log_{12}y + 15\log_{12}z$

c) $\log_8 \dfrac{x^3}{\sqrt{yz^5}}$

$\log_8 x^3 - \log_8\sqrt{yz^5}$

$3\log_8 x - \log_8(yz^5)^{\frac{1}{2}}$

$3\log_8 x - \log_8 y^{\frac{1}{2}} - \log_8 z^{\frac{5}{2}}$

$3\log_8 x - \frac{1}{2}\log_8 y - \frac{5}{2}\log_8 z$

d) $\log\sqrt{\dfrac{x}{y^3}}$

$\log\dfrac{x^{\frac{1}{2}}}{y^{3(\frac{1}{2})}} - \log$

$\log x^{\frac{1}{2}} - \log y^{\frac{3}{2}}$

$\frac{1}{2}\log x - \frac{3}{2}\log y$

3. Expand each expression using the laws of logarithms. Then, evaluate and simplify where possible.

a) $\log_7 49\sqrt[3]{x^5}$

$\log_7 49(x^5)^{\frac{1}{3}}$

$\log_7 49(x^{\frac{5}{3}})$

$\log_7 49 + \log_7 x^{\frac{5}{3}}$

$2 + \frac{5}{3}\log_7 x$

b) $\log \dfrac{100}{x^2y^2}$

$10^? = 100$
$10^2 = 100$

$\log 100 - \log x^2y^2$

$\log 100 - \log x^2 + \log y^2$

$\log_{10} 100 - 2\log x + 2\log y$

$2 - 2\log x + 2\log y$

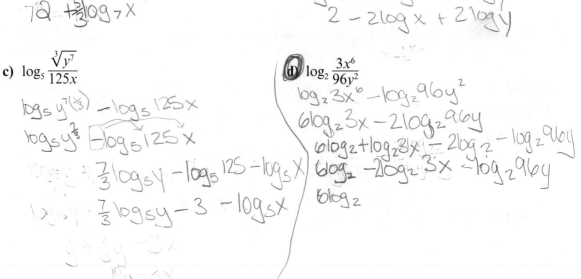

c) $\log_5 \dfrac{\sqrt[3]{y^7}}{125x}$

$\log_5 y^{7(\frac{1}{3})} - \log_5 125x$

$\log_5 y^{\frac{7}{3}} - \log_5 125x$

$\frac{7}{3}\log_5 y - \log_5 125 - \log_5 x$

$\frac{7}{3}\log_5 y - 3 - \log_5 x$

d) $\log_2 \dfrac{3x^6}{96y^2}$

$\log_2 3x^6 - \log_2 96y^2$

$6\log_2 3x - 2\log_2 96y$

$6\log_2 + \log_2 3x - 2\log_2 - \log_2 96y$

$6\log_2 - 2\log_2 3x - \log_2 96y$

$6\log_2$

4. Write each expression as a single logarithm in simplest form.

a) $\log_6 2x^7 + \log_6 3x^2 + \log_6 \frac{9}{x^5}$

$\log_6 \left(2x^7 \cdot 3x^2 \cdot \frac{9}{x^5}\right)$

$\log_6 \left(\frac{54x^9}{x^5}\right)$ (9-5)

$\log_6 (54x^4)$

b) $\log_2 5x^2y^3 - \log_2 20x^4y + \log_2 2xy^6$

$\log_2 \left(\frac{5x^2y^3 \cdot 2xy^6}{20x^4y}\right)$

$\log_2 \left(\frac{10x^3y^9}{20x^4y}\right)$

$\log_2 \left(\frac{y^8}{2x}\right)$

c) $\log_4 (x^2y)^2 + 5\log_4 x^3y^4 + \log_4\left(\frac{1}{x^3y^2}\right)$

$\log_4\left(x^4y^2 \cdot x^{15}y^{20} \cdot \frac{1}{x^3y^2}\right)$

$\log_4\left(\frac{x^{19}y^{22}}{x^3y^2}\right)$

$\log_4 x^{16}y^{20}$

d) $6\log_3 xy - \log_3 xy^2 - \log_3 \sqrt[3]{x^4y}$

$\log_3 x^6y^6 - \log_3 xy^2 + \log_3 (x^4y)^{\frac{1}{3}}$

$\log_3\left(\frac{x^6y^6}{xy^2 \cdot x^{4/3}}\, y^{1/3}\right)$

$\log_3(\,\ldots\,)$

e) $\frac{1}{2}\log 4x\sqrt{y} - \log 25x^2\sqrt{y}$

$\frac{1}{2}\log 4xy^{\frac{1}{2}} - \log 25x^2y^{\frac{1}{2}}$

$\log 2x^{\frac{1}{2}}y^{\frac{1}{4}} - \log 25x^2y^{\frac{1}{2}}$

$\log\left(\frac{2x^{\frac{1}{2}}y^{\frac{1}{4}}}{25x^2y^{\frac{1}{2}}}\right)$ $\log\left(\frac{2y}{25x^{3/2}y^{1/4}}\right)$

$-1.5 \approx \frac{3}{2}$

f) $\log_7 x^4 + \frac{1}{3}(\log_7 x^2 - \log_7 \sqrt{5x})$

$\log_7 x^4 \,(\log_7 3\,)$

g) $\dfrac{\log 16x^8}{4} - \dfrac{\log 27x}{3}$

$\dfrac{\log 4x^2}{\log 9x^3}$ $2 - 3$

$\log\left(\frac{4x^6}{9}\right)$

$\frac{1}{3}\ \frac{2}{7}$

$\frac{3}{4}\ \frac{7}{2}$

$\frac{1}{4} = \frac{2}{4} = \frac{-1}{4}$

h) $\dfrac{\log_9 x^4y^8}{2} + \dfrac{\log_9 x^{12}y^{15}}{3}$

$\log_9\left(x^2y^4 \cdot x^4y^5\right)$

$\log_9 x^6y^9$

📖 Completing #1–#4 will help you with #1–#3 on page 400 of *Pre-Calculus 12*.

Apply

5. The loudness of a sound, L, in decibels, is given by $L = 10\log\frac{I}{I_0}$, where I is the intensity of the sound, in watts per square metre, and I_0 is 10^{-12} W/m².

a) Use the laws of logarithms to rewrite the right-hand side of the equation as a difference.

$L = 10\log\frac{I}{10^{-12}}$

b) Rearrange the equation in part a) to isolate I.

6. The pH scale is used to measure the acidity or alkalinity of a substance. The formula for pH is $pH = -\log [H_3O^+]$, where $[H_3O^+]$ is the concentration of the hydronium ion.

  a) Rewrite the equation to isolate $[H_3O^+]$.

$$\frac{PH}{-\log} = [H_3O^+]$$

  b) A textbook defines pH as $\log \dfrac{1}{[H_3O^+]}$. Use the laws of logarithms to show that this is equivalent to the definition given above.

$$\frac{PH}{-\log} = [H_3O^+]$$

7. Decide whether each of the following is true or false. Justify your answer.

  — must be mult.

  a) $\log_5 (x \oplus 10) = \log_5 x + \log_5 10$

$$\log_5 x + \log_5 10 = \log_5 x + \log_5 10$$

  ✗

  b) $\dfrac{\log_2 18}{\log_2 9} = \log_2 2$

$$\log_2 9 = \log_2 2$$

  ✗

  c) $4^{\log_4 y} = y$

$$4^{\log y} = 4^{y}$$

  d) $\log_c 1 = 0$

$$c^0 = 1$$

  ✓

  e) $\log_c xy^2 = 2 \log_c xy$

8. Use the laws of logarithms to isolate x in each expression.

  a) $\log_6 36x = 1$

$$\log 6^1 = 36 x \qquad x = 1$$
$$\frac{6}{6} = x \qquad x = -1$$

  b) $\log_3 \dfrac{27}{x} = 2$

$$3^2 = \frac{27}{x}$$
$$9 = \frac{27}{x}$$
$$9x = 27$$
$$x = 3$$

  c) $3 \log_x 4 = 2$

$$\log x 4 = \frac{2}{3}$$
$$\log x^{2/3} = 4$$
$$\log x = 8$$

$$x = -32$$
$$6^1 = 2x$$

9. Let $\log_5 12 = P$. Write each of the following expressions in terms of P.

a) $\log_5 12^7$

P^7

b) $\log_5 60$

$\log_5 12^{1.65}$

$P^{1.65}$

c) $\log_5 144$

$\log_5 12^2$

P^2

d) $\log_5 \dfrac{12}{5}$

e) $\log_5 \dfrac{1}{12}$

$\log_5 -12$

$-P$

f) $\log_5 \sqrt{12}$

Connect

10. Consider the following transformations of $y = \log_2 x$.

a) Explain how $y = \log_2 x^2$ is a vertical stretch by a factor of 2 of the original graph.

b) Explain how $y = \log_2 3x$ is a horizontal stretch of the original graph. By what factor is the graph stretched?

c) Explain how $y = \log_2 3x$ is a vertical translation of the original graph. By what amount is the graph translated?

d) Is $y = \log_2 \dfrac{1}{x}$ the reciprocal transformation of the original function? Justify your answer.

> ### KEY IDEAS

- When solving a logarithmic equation algebraically, start by applying the laws of logarithms to express one side or both sides of the equation as a single logarithm.

- Some useful properties are listed below, where c, L, $R > 0$ and $c \neq 1$.
  - If $\log_c L = \log_c R$, then $L = R$.
  - The equation $\log_c L = R$ can be written with logarithms on both sides of the equation as $\log_c L = \log_c c^R$.
  - The equation $\log_c L = R$ can be written in exponential form as $L = c^R$.
  - The logarithm of zero or a negative number is undefined. To identify whether a root is extraneous, substitute the root into the original equation and check whether all of the logarithms are defined.

- You can solve an exponential equation algebraically by taking logarithms of both sides of the equation. If $L = R$, then $\log_c L = \log_c R$, where c, L, $R > 0$ and $c \neq 1$. Then, apply the power law for logarithms to solve for an unknown.

- You can solve an exponential equation or a logarithmic equation using graphical methods.

- Many real-world situations can be modelled with an exponential or a logarithmic equation. A general model for many problems involving exponential growth or decay is

$$\text{Final quantity} = \text{initial quantity} \times (\text{change factor})^{\text{number of changes}}$$

Working Example 1: Solve Logarithmic Equations

Solve.

a) $\log_4 (5x + 1) = \log_4 (x + 17)$

b) $\log (5x) - \log (x - 1) = 1$

c) $\log_6 (x - 3) + \log_6 (x + 6) = 2$

Solution

a) Since $\log_4 (5x + 1) = \log_4 (x + 17)$, $5x + 1 = x + 17$.
So, $4x = 16$ and $x = 4$.
Check $x = 4$ in the original equation.

Left Side	Right Side
$\log_4 (5(4) + 1)$ $= \log_4 21$	$\log_4 (4 + 17)$ $= \log_4 21$

Left Side = Right Side

b) Method 1: Solve Algebraically by Rewriting in Exponential Form

Using the laws of logarithms, rewrite $\log (5x) - \log (x - 1)$ as $\log$ _____.

Then, rewrite $\log \dfrac{5x}{x - 1} = 1$ in exponential form.

$\dfrac{5x}{x - 1} =$ _____

Multiply both sides by $(x - 1)$.

$$\dfrac{5x}{x - 1}(x - 1) = 10(x - 1)$$
$$5x = 10x - 10$$
$$-5x = -10$$
$$x = 2$$

Check:

Left Side	Right Side
$\log (5(\mathbf{2})) - \log (\mathbf{2} - 1)$ $= \log 10 - \log 1$ $= 1 - 0$ $= 1$	1

Left Side = Right Side

Method 2: Solve Algebraically by Writing Each Side as a Logarithm

Begin by rewriting 1 as $\log_{10}$ _____.

So, the equation is $\log (5x) - \log (x - 1) = \log 10$.

Solve for x.

$$\log (5x) - \log (x - 1) = 10$$
$$\log \dfrac{5x}{x - 1} = \log 10$$
$$\dfrac{5x}{x - 1} = 10$$
$$5x = 10(x - 1)$$
$$5x = 10x - 10$$
$$-5x = -10$$
$$x = 2$$

> Compare the algebra in Method 1 to the algebra in Method 2. How are the methods similar? How are they different?

Method 3: Solve Graphically

Use technology to graph the equations $y = \log (5x) - \log (x - 1)$ and $y = 1$ in the same window. Then, find the point of intersection.

The solution is $x = 2$.

c) Using the laws of logarithms, rewrite the left side of the equation.

$$\log_6 (x - 3) + \log_6 (x + 6) = 2$$
$$\log_6 (x - 3)(x + 6) = \underline{\hspace{3cm}}$$

Method 1: Rewrite in Exponential Form

In exponential form, the equation is equivalent to $(x - 3)(x + 6) = 6^2$.

Expand and simplify the left side of the equation.

$$\underline{\hspace{5cm}} = 36$$

Subtract 36 from each side.

$$\underline{\hspace{5cm}} = 0$$

Factor the left side.

$$(x + \underline{\hspace{1.5cm}})(x - \underline{\hspace{1.5cm}}) = 0$$
$$x = \underline{\hspace{1.5cm}} \text{ or } x = \underline{\hspace{1.5cm}}$$

The original equation is defined for $x > 3$ and $x > -6$. In other words, both conditions are met when $x > 3$. Thus, $x = -9$ is an extraneous root. Check $x = 6$.

Left Side	Right Side
$\log_6 (\mathbf{6} - 3) + \log_6 (\mathbf{6} + 6)$	2
$= \log_6 3 + \log_6 12$	
$= \log_6 36$	
$= 2$	

Left Side = Right Side

Method 2: Rewrite as a Logarithm

Written as a logarithm with base 6, $2 = \underline{\hspace{1.5cm}}$.

$$\log_6 (x - 3) + \log_6 (x + 6) = \log_6 36$$
$$\log_6 (x - 3)(x + 6) = \log_6 36$$
$$(x - 3)(x + 6) = 36$$
$$\underline{\hspace{5cm}} = 36$$
$$\underline{\hspace{5cm}} = 0$$

Factoring,

$$\underline{\hspace{5cm}} = 0$$

So, $x = -9$ or $x = 6$.
Since $x > 3$, the solution is $x = 6$.

Working Example 2: Solve Exponential Equations

Solve. Express your answer as an exact value and as a decimal correct to two decimal places.

a) $5^x = 200$ **b)** $8^{2x-3} = 15\ 109$ **c)** $3^{2x} = 7^{x+1}$

Solution

a) Method 1: Use the Power Law of Logarithms

Take the logarithms of both sides of the equation:

$\log 5^x = \log 200$

$x \log 5 = \log 200$

$x = \dfrac{\log 200}{\log 5}$

As a decimal, $x \approx 3.29$.

Method 2: Write in Logarithmic Form

$5^x = 200$ is the same as $\log_5 200 = x$. An exact value for x is $\log_5 200$.

Use technology to calculate the value to two decimal places: $\log_5 200 = 3.29$.

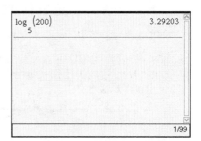

$\log_5 (200) \qquad\qquad 3.29203$

1/99

b) Take the logarithm of each side: $\log 8^{2x-3} = \log 15\ 109$.
Then, use the power law of logarithms.

$$\underline{} = \log 15\ 109$$

$$2x - 3 = \dfrac{\log 15\ 109}{\log 8}$$

$$x = \dfrac{1}{2}\left(\dfrac{\log 15\ 109}{\log 8} + 3\right)$$

$$x \approx 3.81$$

c) Since $3^{2x} = 7^{x+1}$, $\log 3^{2x} = \log 7^{x+1}$.

Use the power law of logarithms.

$$\underline{} = \underline{}$$

$$2x \log 3 = x \log 7 + \log 7$$

$$2x \log 3 - x \log 7 = \log 7$$

Factor.

$$x(2 \log 3 - \log 7) = \log 7$$

$$x = \dfrac{\log 7}{2 \log 3 - \log 7}$$

Written as a decimal, $x \approx 7.74$.

Working Example 3: Model Exponential Growth

A town has a current population of 12 468. The population is growing by 2% per year.

a) Write an exponential equation to model the population growth.

b) What will be the town's population in eight years?

c) When will the population first reach 20 000?

Solution

a) If P is the population of the town and t is time, in years, then $P = 12\,468(1.02)^t$.

b) In eight years, the population will be $P =$ _____, or 14 608.

c) When the population reaches 20 000, $12\,468(1.02)^t = 20\,000$.

Divide each side by 12 468: $1.02^t =$ _____

Take the logarithm of each side: $\log 1.02^t =$ _____

Apply the power law of logarithms: _____ $=$ _____

$$t = \text{_____}$$

Written as a decimal, t is approximately 23.86. It will take about 23.9 years until the town reaches a population of 20 000.

Working Example 4: Model Exponential Decay

A business invests $450 000 in new equipment. For tax purposes, the equipment is considered to depreciate in value by 20% each year.

a) Write an exponential equation to model the value of the equipment.

b) What will be the value of the equipment in three years?

c) When will the value first drop to $100 000?

Solution

a) If V denotes the value of the equipment, and t is time, in years, then $V = 450\,000(0.8)^t$.

b) $V = 450\,000(0.8)^3$
   $= 230\,400$

The equipment will be worth $230 400 in three years.

c) $450\,000(0.8)^t = 100\,000$

Divide each side by 450 000: _____ $=$ _____

Take the logarithm of each side: _____ $=$ _____

Use the power law of logarithms to rewrite the equation: _____ $=$ _____

Divide each side by log 0.8: _____ $=$ _____

After 6.74 years, the equipment will have a value of $100 000 for tax purposes.

See pages 406–411 of *Pre-Calculus 12* for more examples.

Check Your Understanding

Practise

1. Solve. Give exact answers.

   a) $\log_4 x = 5$

   $4^5 = x$

   $1024 = x$

   b) $\log_5 x + 6 = 8$

   $\log_5 x = 2$

   $5^2 = x$

   $25 = x$

   c) $2 \log_2 x = 10$

   $\log_2 x = 5$

   $2^5 = x$

   $32 = x$

   d) $\log_6 (x + 3) + 2 = 5$

   $\log_6 (x+3) = 3$

   $6^3 = x + 3$

   $216 = x + 3$

   $213 = x$

   e) $3 \log_5 x = \log_5 125$

   $\log_5 x^3 = \log_5 125$

   $\log_5 x^3 = 3$

   $5^3 = x^3$

   $5 = x$

   f) $2 \log (x - 5) = 6$

   $\log(x-5) = 3$

   $10^3 = x - 5$

   $1000 = x - 5$

   $1005 = x$

2. Solve. Round your answers to two decimal places.

   a) $12^{3x} = 1000$

   $12^x =$

   b) $7^{x + 2} = 441$

   $Y_1 = 7^{x+2}$

   $Y_2 = 441$

   $x = 1.13$

   c) $2^{3 - x} = 100$

   d) $3^{\frac{2x}{3}} = 350$

3. Solve. Express your answers as exact values.

   a) $5^x = 205$

   Take the logarithm of each side of the equation: _____ = _____

   Then, use the power law of logarithms: _____ = _____

   Divide each side by log 5: $x =$ _____

   b) $4^{x-3} = 311$

   c) $10^{2x+1} = 7539$

   d) $5(4)^{x+2} = 200$

   e) $6^{\frac{x}{2}} = 85$

4. Solve.

   a) $3 \log_6 x = \log_6 9 + \log_6 24$

   $\log_6 x^3 = \log_6 9 + \log_6 24$

   $\log_6 x^3 = 1.23 + 1.8$

   $\log_6 x^3 = 3.03$

   $6^{3.03} = x^3 \qquad x = 6.1$

   b) $\log_2 x^2 - \log_2 5 = \log_2 20$

   c) $\log_4 x + 2 \log_4 x = 6$

   d) $5 \log_3 x - \log_3 x = 8$

   📖 Completing #1–#4 will help you with #1–#3 on page 412 of *Pre-Calculus 12*.

5. Identify the values of x for which each equation is defined.

   a) $\log_9 (x + 4) = \log_9 (2x)$

   Since logarithms are only defined for positive values, $x + 4 > 0$, or $x > $ ___4 (?)___.

   Similarly, since $2x > 0$, $x > $ ___0___.

   If $x > 0$, both statements are true. So, the equation is defined when $x > $ _____.

b) $\log_7 (3x + 1) - \log_7 (x - 2) = 1$

$\log_7 3x + \log_7 - \log_7 x + \log_7 2 = 1$

$\log_7 3x + \log_7 2 = 1$

$\log_7 (3x \cdot 2) = 1 \qquad x = \dfrac{7}{6}$

$\log_7 6x = 1$

$7^1 = 6x$

c) $\log_6 (3 - x) + \log_6 (x - 3) = 2$

Apply

6. Solve. Express your answers as exact values and as decimal values correct to the nearest hundredth.

a) $5^{x-3} = 10^x$

5^{x-3}

b) $8^{2x + 3} = 12^{2x}$

c) $2^{2x-5} = 6^{x+2}$

d) $2(6)^{x+2} = 3^{2x-3}$

$2(3$

7. Solve.

a) $\log_2 (4x + 10) - \log_2 x = 3$

$\log_2 4x + \log_2 \left(\dfrac{4x + 10}{x}\right) = 3$

$2^3 = \dfrac{4x + 10}{x}$

$8x = 4x + 10$

$4x = 10$

$x = 2.5$

b) $\log_3 (x + 7) - \log_3 (x - 3) = 2$

c) $\log (2x + 6) = 1 + \log (x - 1)$

d) $\log_5 (4x - 6) - 3 = \log_5 (2x - 3)$

8. Solve.

   a) $\log x + \log (x + 3) = 1$

   b) $\log_4 (x - 4) + \log_4 (x + 2) = 2$

   c) $\log_6 (x + 3) - 2 = -\log_6 (x - 2)$

   d) $\log (x + 2) = 2 - \log (7x - 1)$

9. The half-life of plutonium-238 is 88 years. Suppose that a sample of plutonium has a mass of 65 grams.

   a) Write an exponential equation to model the mass of plutonium, m, present after t years.

   $$y = 65\left(\tfrac{1}{2}\right)^{\frac{x}{88}} \qquad m = 65\left(\tfrac{1}{2}\right)^{\frac{x}{88}}$$

   b) Determine the mass of plutonium in the sample after 50 years. Round your answer to two decimal places.

   $$y = 65\left(\tfrac{1}{2}\right)^{\frac{50}{88}} \qquad y = 43.84 \text{ g}$$

   c) Determine the time needed for the sample to decay to a mass of 20 grams, to the nearest tenth of a year.

   $$20 = 65\left(\tfrac{1}{2}\right)^{\frac{x}{88}}$$
   $$\tfrac{4}{13} = \left(\tfrac{1}{2}\right)^{\frac{x}{88}} \qquad x = 149.6 \text{ years}$$

10. The population of a high school is growing by 1.5% per year. Currently there are 974 students in the school.

   a) Write an exponential equation to model the population of the school, p, after t years.

   $$y = ac^x \qquad y = 974(1.015)^x$$

   b) What population should be expected at the high school in five years?

   c) When will the population of the school reach 1200 students?

Connect

11. Describe two methods to solve each equation algebraically. Then, solve the equations using each method. Check your solutions numerically or graphically.

Equation	Method	Solution
a) $5^{2x(x-1)} = 5^{(3x-3)}$		
b) $\log(2x^2 + 3x) = \log 9$		

8.1 Understanding Logarithms, pages 260–266

1. Sketch the graph of each logarithmic function. Then, state the domain, range, x-intercept, and vertical asymptote.

a) $y = \log_2 x$

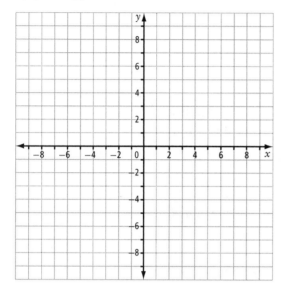

b) $y = \log_5 x$

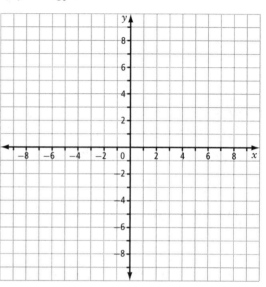

2. Write each expression in logarithmic form.

a) $6^3 = 216$

b) $2^{10} = 1024$

c) $10^{-3} = 0.001$

d) $5^x = 125$

3. Write each expression in exponential form.

a) $\log_3 81 = 4$

b) $\log_{25} 5 = \dfrac{1}{2}$

c) $\log 1 = 0$

d) $\log_2 (3x - 4) = 9$

8.2 Transformations of Logarithmic Functions, pages 267–274

4. Identify the transformations in each logarithmic function. State the domain, range, and intercepts of the graph of each. Round your answers to one decimal place if necessary.

a) $y = 2 \log_4 (x + 1)$

b) $y = \log_7 (x - 3) + 5$

5. Write the equation for each of the following transformations to the function $y = \log x$. Then, state the domain and range of the transformed function.

a) translation 5 units right and 4 units down

b) vertical stretch by a factor of 3, translation 2 units left and 6 units down

c) horizontal stretch by a factor of $\frac{1}{3}$, translation 1 unit up

8.3 Laws of Logarithms, pages 275–281

6. Use the laws of logarithms to evaluate each of the following.

a) $\log_6 9 + \log_6 4$

b) $\log 2000 - \log 2$

c) $\log_{12} 9 + \log_{12} 2 + \log_{12} 8$

d) $\log_7 100 - \log_7 25 - \log_7 4$

7. Expand each of the following.

a) $\log_5 \left(25x^4 \sqrt[4]{y^3} \right)$

b) $\log \dfrac{\sqrt{x}\, y^5}{100x}$

8. Write each of the following as a single logarithm.

a) $\log_4 x^2y^5 + \log_4 xy^{-2}$

b) $\log \dfrac{x^4}{\sqrt{y}} - \log \dfrac{y^2}{x}$

8.4 Logarithmic and Exponential Equations, pages 282–291

9. Solve. Express each answer as an exact value and as a decimal rounded to two places.

a) $3^x = 100$

b) $7^{x-3} = 517$

c) $10^{2x+1} = 5500$

d) $5^x = 2^{x-4}$

10. Solve.

a) $\log_2 x = 7$

b) $\log_3 (4x + 9) = 5$

c) $\log_2 (6x - 3) - \log_2 x = 4$

d) $\log_8 (6x + 2) + \log_8 (x - 3) = 2$

11. The intensity of sound is measured in decibels (dB). The level of a sound, L, is given by $L = 10 \log \frac{I}{I_0}$, where I is the intensity of the sound and I_0 is the faintest sound detectable to humans. A sound engineer increases the volume at a concert from 90 decibels (dB) to 93 dB. Show that this increase approximately doubles the intensity of the sound.

12. A strain of bacteria doubles every 4 hours. A sample contains 40 bacteria.

a) Write an exponential equation to determine the number of bacteria present, N, after t hours.

b) Determine the time needed until 1000 bacteria are present. Round your answer to two decimal places.

c) Determine the time needed for the number of bacteria in the sample to triple. Does your answer depend on the number of bacteria present at the beginning?

13. A water filter removes 40% of the impurities in a sample of water.

a) Write an exponential equation to determine the percent of impurities remaining, P, after the water has passed through n filters.

b) What percent of impurities will remain after the water has passed through 3 filters?

c) How many filters are needed to remove at least 99% of impurities in the water?

Chapter 8 Skills Organizer

Complete the following graphic organizer to summarize your knowledge of logarithms.

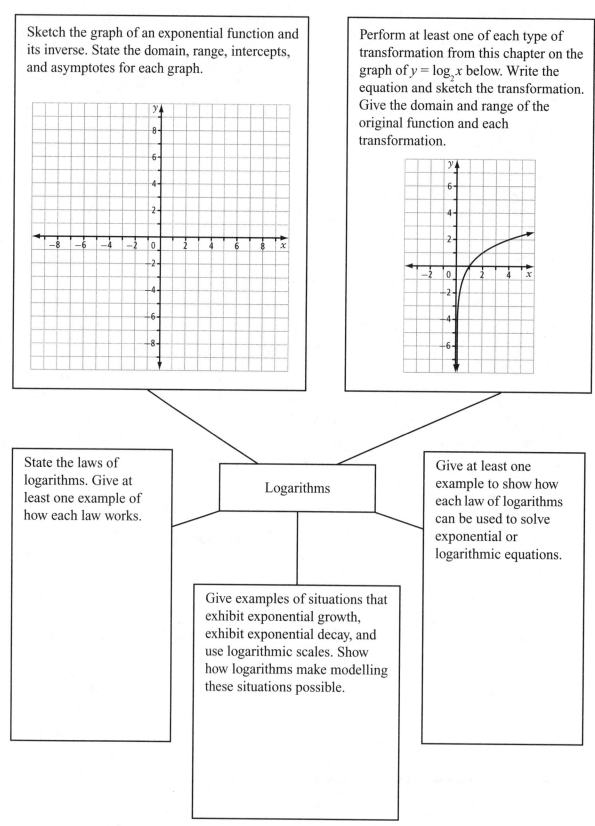

Sketch the graph of an exponential function and its inverse. State the domain, range, intercepts, and asymptotes for each graph.

Perform at least one of each type of transformation from this chapter on the graph of $y = \log_2 x$ below. Write the equation and sketch the transformation. Give the domain and range of the original function and each transformation.

State the laws of logarithms. Give at least one example of how each law works.

Logarithms

Give at least one example to show how each law of logarithms can be used to solve exponential or logarithmic equations.

Give examples of situations that exhibit exponential growth, exhibit exponential decay, and use logarithmic scales. Show how logarithms make modelling these situations possible.

Chapter 9 Rational Functions

9.1 Exploring Rational Functions Using Transformations

KEY IDEAS

- Rational functions are functions of the form $y = \dfrac{p(x)}{q(x)}$, where $p(x)$ and $q(x)$ are polynomial expressions and $q(x) \neq 0$.

- You can graph a rational function by creating a table of values and then graphing the points in the table. To create a table of values,
  - identify the non-permissible value(s)
  - write the non-permissible value in the middle row of the table
  - enter positive values above the non-permissible value and negative values below the non-permissible value
  - choose small and large values of x to give you a spread of values

- You can use what you know about the base function $y = \dfrac{1}{x}$ and transformations to graph equations of the form $y = \dfrac{a}{x - h} + k$.

  Example:

  For $y = \dfrac{3}{x + 4} + 5$, the values of the parameters are

  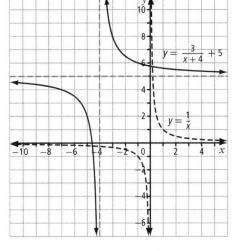

  $a = 3$, representing a vertical stretch by a factor of 3
  $h = 4$, representing a horizontal translation 4 units to the left
  $k = 5$, representing a vertical translation 5 units up
  vertical asymptote: $x = -4$
  horizontal asymptotes: $y = 5$

- Some equations of rational functions can be manipulated algebraically into the form $y = \dfrac{a}{x - h} + k$ by creating a common factor in the numerator and the denominator.

  Example:

  $y = \dfrac{3x + 6}{x - 4}$

  $y = \dfrac{3x - 12 + 12 + 6}{x - 4}$

  $y = \dfrac{3x - 12 + 18}{x - 4}$

  $y = \dfrac{3(x - 4)}{x - 4} + \dfrac{18}{x - 4}$

  $y = \dfrac{18}{x - 4} + 3$

Working Example 1: Graph a Rational Function Using a Table of Values

Graph $y = \frac{4}{x}$ using a table of values.

Solution

Begin by identifying any non-permissible values: what value(s) can x not equal? $x \neq$ _____.

Graphs of rational functions of the form $y = \frac{4}{x}$ approach asymptotes at $x =$ _____ and

$y =$ _____. Plot the vertical and horizontal asymptotes on the grid below.

Create a table of values. Plot and connect the points from the table of values to generate the general shape of the graph. It is often easier to create a table of values if you rearrange the formula so that rather than being a quotient, it is a product of polynomials: $xy = 4$.

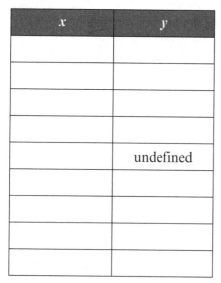

x	y
	undefined

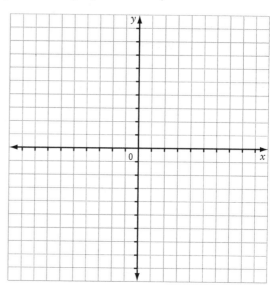

Check your graph using your graphing calculator. How do the graphs compare?

Summarize the characteristics of the function using a table.

Characteristic	$y = \frac{4}{x}$
Non-permissible value	
Behaviour near non-permissible value	
End behaviour	
Domain	
Range	
Equation of vertical asymptote	
Equation of horizontal asymptote	

📖 To see a similar example, see Example 1 on pages 432–434 of *Pre-Calculus 12*.

Working Example 2: Graph a Rational Function Using Transformations

Graph $y = \dfrac{3}{x-3} + 2$ using transformations.

Solution

Compare the function $y = \dfrac{3}{x-3} + 2$ to the form $y = \underline{\hspace{2cm}} + k$ to determine the value of the parameters. Then, describe the effect that each parameter has on the graph of $y = \dfrac{1}{x}$.

If the asymptotes of $y = \dfrac{1}{x}$ are $x = 0$ and $y = 0$, use the above transformation to determine the asymptotes of $y = \dfrac{3}{x-3} + 2$. Explain your reasoning.

Will the graph of $y = \dfrac{3}{x-3} + 2$ have an x-intercept or y-intercept? Explain how you know.

What are the x-intercept and y-intercept?

> Which variable is set to 0 to find the x-intercept? the y-intercept?

Use all of the above information to graph $y = \dfrac{3}{x-3} + 2$.

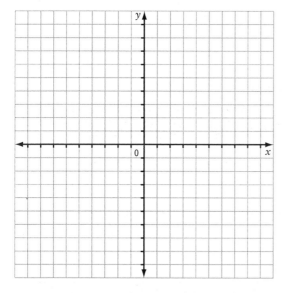

> Check your graph using your graphing calculator. How do the two graphs compare?

📖 To see a similar example, see Example 2 on pages 434–435 of *Pre-Calculus 12*.

Working Example 3: Graph a Rational Function With Linear Expressions in the Numerator and the Denominator

Graph $y = \dfrac{4x + 2}{x - 1}$. Identify any asymptotes and intercepts.

Solution

Let $x = 0$. Solve for y to determine the y-intercept.

The y-intercept is at $(0, \underline{\hspace{1.5cm}})$.

Let $y = 0$. Solve for x to determine the x-intercept.

$$0 = \frac{4x + 2}{x - 1}$$

$$(\underline{\hspace{1cm}})(0) = (\underline{\hspace{1cm}})\frac{4x + 2}{x - 1}$$

$$\underline{\hspace{1.5cm}} = \underline{\hspace{1.5cm}}$$

$$\underline{\hspace{1.5cm}} = 4x$$

$$\underline{\hspace{1.5cm}} = x$$

The x-intercept is at $(\underline{\hspace{1.5cm}}, 0)$.

Manipulate the equation of the function algebraically to obtain the form $y = \dfrac{a}{x - h} + k$.

$$y = \frac{4x + 2}{x - 1}$$

$$y = \frac{4x - 4 + 4 + 2}{x - 1}$$

$$y =$$

> Why is 4 subtracted and added to the numerator?

> Which parameters determine the vertical and horizontal asymptotes of the transformed function?

The parameters are $a = \underline{\hspace{1.5cm}}$, $h = \underline{\hspace{1.5cm}}$, and $k = \underline{\hspace{1.5cm}}$. State the effect of each parameter on the graph of $y = \frac{1}{x}$. Then, use the information you have generated to sketch the transformed function on the grid above.

📖 To see a similar example, see Example 3 on pages 435–437 of *Pre-Calculus 12*.

Check Your Understanding

Practise

1. Graph each function using a table of values. Identify the asymptotes.

a) $y = \dfrac{6}{x}$

b) $y = \dfrac{-4}{x}$

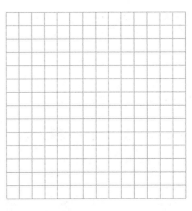

2. Graph each function using transformations. Label the asymptotes and intercepts.

a) $y = \dfrac{2}{x + 1} - 3$

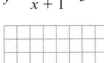

b) $y = \dfrac{-3}{x - 2} + 1$

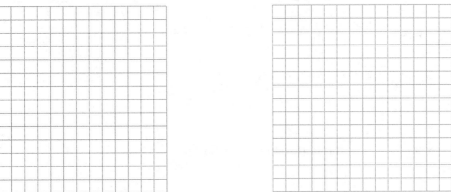

3. Graph each function using technology. Identify any asymptotes and intercepts. Sketch the graph.

a) $y = \dfrac{2x + 1}{x - 2}$

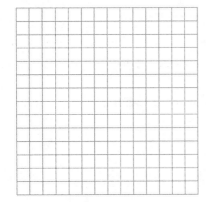

b) $y = \dfrac{-3x - 4}{x + 2}$

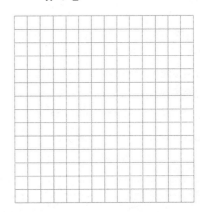

Apply

4. Match each graph with its equation.

a) $y = \dfrac{3}{x-2}$

b) $y = \dfrac{3}{x+2}$

c) $y = \dfrac{3}{x} - 2$

d) $y = \dfrac{3}{x} + 2$

A
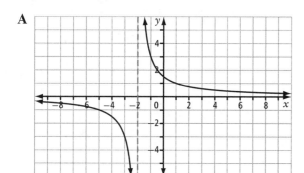

B
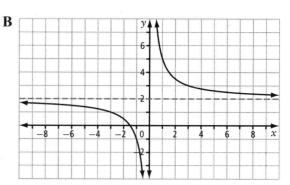

C
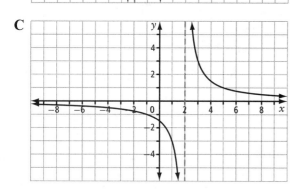

D
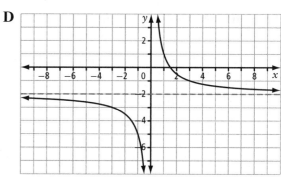

5. Write the equation of each function in the form of $y = \dfrac{a}{x-h} + k$.

a)
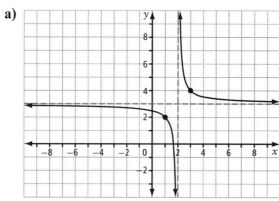

For the graph of $y = \frac{1}{x}$, what is the relationship between the intersection of the asymptotes and the point (1, 1)? How can you use this knowledge to determine a vertical stretch?

The vertical asymptote provides the _____ parameter. The horizontal asymptote provides the _____ parameter.

b)

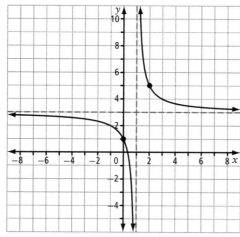

c)

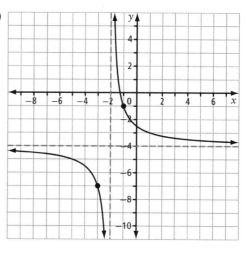

6. Write each equation in the form $y = \dfrac{a}{x - h} + k$. Then, graph the function using transformations. Indicate the asymptotes.

a) $y = \dfrac{7x - 23}{x - 4}$

b) $y = \dfrac{-5x - 1}{x + 2}$

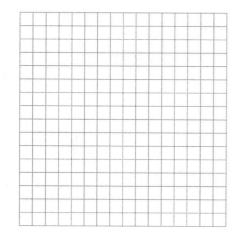

Connect

7. a) Determine an equation of a rational function that has an asymptote at $x = -3$ and $y = -4$. Explain the rationale for your equation.

b) Sketch the graph of your function. Identify the asymptotes on your graph.

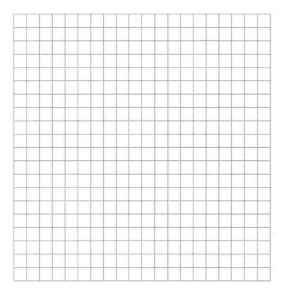

c) What is the domain and range of your function?

d) Is there another possible function with these asymptotes? Explain.

8. Describe the similarities and differences between graphing $y = \dfrac{2}{x-4} - 3$, $y = 2(x-4)^2 - 3$, and $y = 2\sqrt{x-4} - 3$ without technology.

9.2 Analysing Rational Functions

>> **KEY IDEAS** >>

Determining Asymptotes and Points of Discontinuity
The graph of a rational function may have an asymptote, a point of discontinuity, or both.
To establish these important characteristics of a graph, begin by factoring the numerator and
denominator fully.

• **Asymptotes: No Common Factors** If the numerator and denominator do not have a common factor, the function has an asymptote. – The vertical asymptotes are identified by the non-permissible values of the function. – For a function that can be rewritten in the form $y = \dfrac{a}{x-h} + k$, the k parameter identifies the horizontal asymptote.	**Example:** $y = \dfrac{x+4}{x-3}$ Since the non-permissible value is $x = 3$, the vertical asymptote is at $x = 3$. $y = \dfrac{x+4}{x-3}$ $y = \dfrac{x-3+3+4}{x-3}$ $y = \dfrac{x-3}{x-3} + \dfrac{7}{x-3}$ $y = \dfrac{7}{x-3} + 1$ Since $k = 1$, the horizontal asymptote is at $y = 1$.
• **Points of Discontinuity: At Least One Common Factor** If the numerator and denominator have at least one common factor, there is at least one point of discontinuity in the graph. – Equate the common factor(s) to zero and solve for x to determine the x-coordinate of the point of discontinuity. – Substitute the x-value in the simplified expression to find the y-coordinate of the point of discontinuity.	**Example:** $y = \dfrac{(x-4)(x+2)}{x+2}$ $x + 2 = 0$: the x-coordinate of the point of discontinuity is -2. Substitute $x = -2$ into the simplified equation: $y = x - 4$ $y = -2 - 4$ $y = -6$ point of discontinuity: $(-2, -6)$
• **Both Asymptote(s) and Point(s) of Discontinuity** If a rational expression remains after removing the common factor(s), there may be both a point of discontinuity and asymptotes.	**Example:** $y = \dfrac{(x-4)(x+2)}{(x+2)(x-1)}$ $y = \dfrac{(x-4)}{(x-1)}$ – common factor: $x + 2$, so there is a point of discontinuity at $(-2, 2)$ – non-permissible value: $x = 1$, so the vertical asymptote is at $x = 1$ – simplified function can be rewritten as $y = -\dfrac{3}{x-1} + 1$, so the horizontal asymptote is at $y = 1$

Working Example 1: Graph a Rational Function With a Point of Discontinuity

Sketch the graph of $f(x) = \dfrac{x^2 - 3x - 4}{x - 4}$.

Solution

Fully factor the numerator and denominator of the rational function.

There is a common factor, so the graph of the function has a _____.

Simplify the rational function. What type of equation remains after the function is simplified?

Equate the common factor to zero and solve for x. Doing so identifies the _____-value of the

_____.

Substitute the value of x into the simplified function and solve for y. Doing so identifies the

_____-value of the point of discontinuity in the graph.

The point of discontinuity is _____.

Graph the rational function, labelling the point of discontinuity.

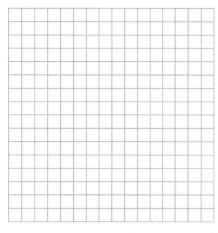

> Does it matter if you graph the original equation or the simplified equation? Explain.

📖 To see a similar example, see Example 1 on pages 447–448 of *Pre-Calculus 12*.

Working Example 2: Compare Points of Discontinuity and Asymptotes in Rational Functions

Compare the graphs of $f(x) = \dfrac{x^2 + 4x + 3}{x + 1}$ and $g(x) = \dfrac{x^2 - 4x + 3}{x + 1}$.

Solution

Fully factor the numerator and denominator of each rational function. Simplify the rational functions, if possible. How do the two simplified equations differ?

When simplified, $f(x)$ is a _____ function. It has a(n) _____.
(*point of discontinuity* or *asymptote*)

When simplified, $g(x)$ is a _____ function. It has a(n) _____.
(*point of discontinuity* or *asymptote*)

With the help of technology, sketch the graph of each function on the grids below. Draw and label any asymptotes that exist.

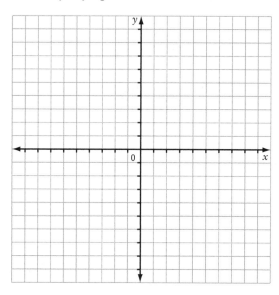
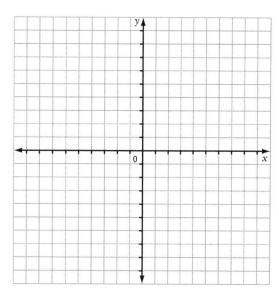

Both $f(x)$ and $g(x)$ have a non-permissible value at $x =$ _____. Describe what happens to each function as the graph approaches this non-permissible value.

To see a similar example, see Example 2 on pages 448–449 of *Pre-Calculus 12*.

Working Example 3: Sketch a Discontinuous Rational Function

Sketch the graph of $f(x) = \dfrac{x^2 + 2x - 8}{x^2 + 5x + 4}$. Label all important parts of the graph.

Solution

Fully factor the numerator and denominator of the rational function. Simplify the rational function.

Equate the common factor to zero and solve for x to establish the _____ of the point of discontinuity. Substitute the value of x into the simplified function and solve for y to establish the _____ of the point of discontinuity in the graph.

The point of discontinuity is at _____.

Find the x-intercept and y-intercept of the simplified function.

Find the horizontal and vertical asymptotes of the simplified function. Then, use the information you have generated to graph the general shape of the rational function. Label the point of discontinuity, the asymptotes, and the intercepts. Check your sketch using technology.

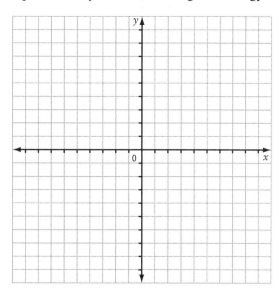

📖 To see a similar example, see Graph 2 in Example 3 on page 449 of *Pre-Calculus 12*.

Check Your Understanding

Practise

1. Determine whether the following functions have points of discontinuity, vertical asymptotes, or both. Explain how you made your determination.

a) $f(x) = \dfrac{x + 5}{x + 4}$

b) $f(x) = \dfrac{x^2 - 5x + 6}{x - 3}$

c) $f(x) = \dfrac{x^2 - x - 12}{x^2 - 5x + 4}$

d) $f(x) = \dfrac{x^2 - 4x - 5}{x^2 - 5x + 6}$

2. For each function, predict the location of any points of discontinuity, vertical asymptotes, x-intercepts, and y-intercepts.

a) $f(x) = \dfrac{x + 1}{x - 4}$

b) $f(x) = \dfrac{x^2 + 7x + 12}{x + 3}$

c) $f(x) = \dfrac{x^2 - 7x + 10}{x^2 - 4x - 5}$

d) $f(x) = \dfrac{x^2 + 6x + 8}{x^2 - 5x - 6}$

3. Match each function with its graph.

a) $f(x) = \dfrac{x + 4}{x + 8}$

b) $f(x) = \dfrac{x^2 + 12x + 32}{x + 8}$

c) $f(x) = \dfrac{x^2 + 12x + 32}{x^2 + 10x + 16}$

d) $f(x) = \dfrac{x^2 + 5x + 4}{x^2 + 10x + 16}$

A

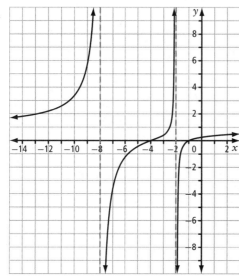

B

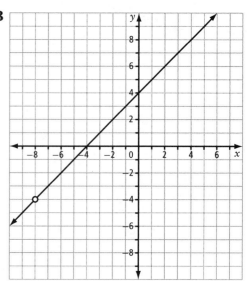

C

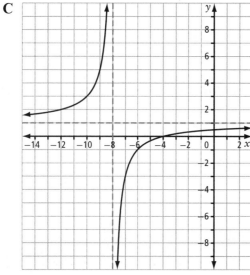

D

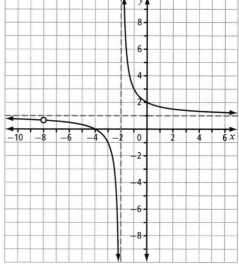

4. Identify any characteristics that are needed to sketch the graph. Then, sketch the function.

a) $f(x) = \dfrac{x + 3}{x - 2}$

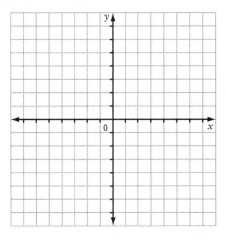

b) $f(x) = \dfrac{x^2 - 5x + 6}{x - 2}$

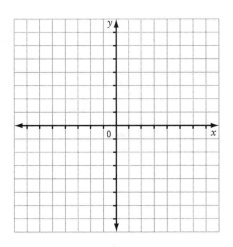

c) $f(x) = \dfrac{x^2 + 3x - 4}{x^2 + 2x - 8}$

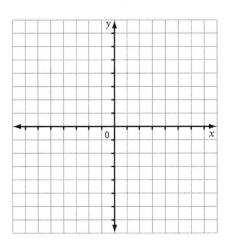

Apply

5. Write an equation for each rational function graphed below.

a)

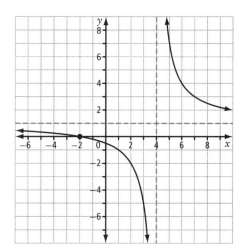

b)

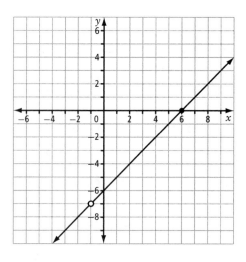

c)

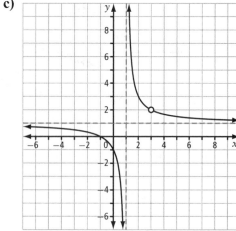

6. Write an equation of a possible rational function with the following characteristics.

a) point of discontinuity: $(-4, -6)$
x-intercept: 2

b) point of discontinuity: $(3, 2)$
vertical asymptote: $x = 1$
x-intercept: -1

c) vertical asymptotes: $x = 4$ and $x = -3$
x-intercept: 0

d) vertical asymptote: $x = 7$
x-intercepts: -1 and -3

Connect

7. a) Where is the point of discontinuity on the graph of $y = \dfrac{2x^2 + 5x - 12}{2x - 3} - 5$?

b) Explain why the point of discontinuity is sometimes referred to as a "hole" in the graph. What does this mean?

8. Explain how you can determine whether a function has the following:

a) a point of discontinuity only

b) a vertical asymptote only

c) both a point of discontinuity and a vertical asymptote

9. Is it possible for a rational function to have neither a vertical asymptote nor a point of discontinuity? Explain.

KEY IDEAS

Solving Rational Equations
You can solve rational equations algebraically or graphically.

• **Algebraically** Solving algebraically determines the exact solution and any extraneous roots. To solve algebraically, – Equate to zero and list the restrictions. – Factor the numerator and denominator fully (if possible). – Multiply each term by the lowest common denominator to eliminate the fractions. – Solve for x. – Check the solution(s) against the restrictions. – Check the solution(s) in the original equation.	**Example:** $$\frac{16}{x+6} = 4 - x$$ $$x + \frac{16}{x+6} - 4 = 0, \; x \neq -6$$ $$(x+6)\left(x + \frac{16}{x+6} - 4\right) = (x+6)(0)$$ $$(x+6)(x) + \left(x+6\right)\left(\frac{16}{x+6}\right) - (x+6)(4) = 0$$ $$x^2 + 6x + 16 - 4x - 24 = 0$$ $$x^2 + 2x - 8 = 0$$ $$(x+4)(x-2) = 0$$ roots: $x = -4$ and $x = 2$
• **Graphically** There are two methods for solving equations graphically. **Method 1: Use a System of Two Functions** – Graph each side of the equation on the same set of axes. – The solution(s) will be the x-coordinate(s) of any point(s) of intersection. **Method 2: Use a Single Function** – Rearrange the equation so that one side is equal to zero. – Graph the corresponding function. – The solution(s) will be the x-intercept(s).	**Example:** $\dfrac{16}{x+6} = 4 - x$ Graph $y = \dfrac{16}{x+6}$ and $y = 4$ on the same axes. 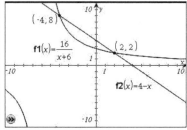 The points of intersection are $(-4, 8)$ and $(2, 2)$, so the roots are $x = -4$ and $x = 2$. Graph $y = x + \dfrac{16}{x+6} - 4$. 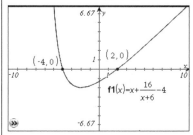 x-intercepts: $x = -4$ and $x = 2$

Working Example 1: Relate Roots and *x*-Intercepts

a) Find the solution to $\frac{3}{x} = 1 + \frac{x-13}{6}$ algebraically.

b) Verify your solutions graphically.

Solution

$$\frac{3}{x} = 1 + \frac{x-13}{6}$$

$$0 = 1 + \frac{x-13}{6} - \frac{\boxed{}}{\boxed{}}, \; x \neq 0 \quad \text{State restrictions and equate to 0.}$$

$$0 = (\underline{\hspace{1cm}})(1) + (\underline{\hspace{1cm}})\left(\frac{x-13}{6}\right) - (\underline{\hspace{1cm}})\left(\frac{\boxed{}}{\boxed{}}\right) \quad \text{Multiply by LCD.}$$

$$0 = (\underline{\hspace{1cm}}) + (\underline{\hspace{2cm}}) - (\underline{\hspace{1cm}})$$

$$0 = \underline{\hspace{4cm}} \qquad\qquad \text{Combine like terms.}$$

$$0 = (\underline{\hspace{1cm}})(\underline{\hspace{1cm}}) \qquad\qquad \text{Factor.}$$

$$(\underline{\hspace{1cm}}) = 0 \qquad \text{or} \qquad (\underline{\hspace{1cm}}) = 0$$

$$x = \underline{\hspace{1.5cm}} \qquad\qquad x = \underline{\hspace{1.5cm}} \qquad \text{Solve.}$$

Is either value a non-permissible value? _____

Check by substitution:

b) Use technology to graph the original function using a single function or a system of two functions. Sketch the graph on the grid. Label the asymptote(s). If you used two functions, label the point(s) of intersection. If you used one function, label the *x*-intercept(s).

$x =$ _____

Compare the solution(s) obtained algebraically and graphically. What can you conclude?

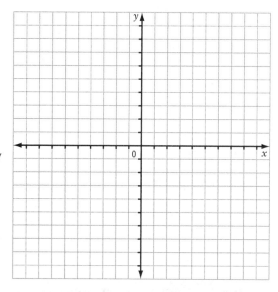

📖 To see a similar example, see Example 1 on pages 459–460 of *Pre-Calculus 12*.

Working Example 2: Compare the Accuracy of Graphical and Algebraic Solutions

a) Solve $\dfrac{3}{2x} - \dfrac{2x}{x+1} = -2$ graphically, using either one or two functions. (Use a different graphical method than the one you used in Working Example 1.)

b) Verify your solution(s) algebraically.

Solution

Use technology to graph the function, using either a single function or a system of two functions. Sketch the graph below. Label the asymptote(s) and the point(s) of intersection or the x-intercept(s).

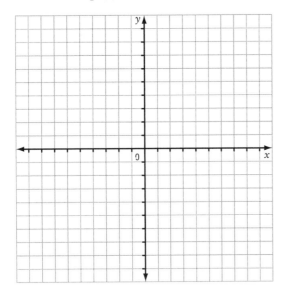

b) Solve algebraically. Describe your solution strategy to the right of each step.

$$\dfrac{3}{2x} - \dfrac{2x}{x+1} = -2$$

Compare the solutions you obtained graphically and algebraically. Which is more accurate?

To see a similar example, see Example 2 on pages 460–461 of *Pre-Calculus 12*.

Working Example 3: Solve a Rational Equation With an Extraneous Root

Solve $\dfrac{x}{x-1} - 2x = \dfrac{x+1}{2x-2}$ algebraically and graphically. Compare the solutions.

Solution

List the restriction(s) of the function.

Solve algebraically.

$$\dfrac{x}{x-1} - 2x = \dfrac{x+1}{2x-2}$$

Check the solution(s) against the restriction(s).

Check your solution in the original equation.

Use technology to graph the function using either graphical method. Sketch the graph on the grid. Label the asymptote(s) and point(s) of intersection or x-intercept(s).

$x = $ _____

Compare the solution you obtained algebraically to the one you obtained graphically. What do you notice?

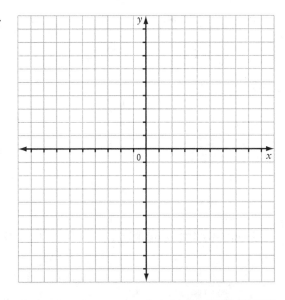

To see a similar example, see Example 3 on pages 462–463 of *Pre-Calculus 12*.

Check Your Understanding

Practise

1. Solve each rational equation algebraically. Check your solutions.

a) $\dfrac{x+1}{2} = \dfrac{3x+7}{x}$

b) $\dfrac{6}{x} - \dfrac{9}{x-1} = \dfrac{1}{4}$

c) $\dfrac{2x}{x+3} + \dfrac{x}{x-3} = \dfrac{18}{x^2-9}$

d) $\dfrac{3}{x^2-4} + \dfrac{3}{x+2} = 2$

2. Solve each rational equation graphically. Sketch the graphs on the grids.

a) $\dfrac{4x}{3x-2} + \dfrac{2x}{3x+2} = 2$

b) $\dfrac{2x-3}{x-3} - 2 = \dfrac{12}{x+3}$

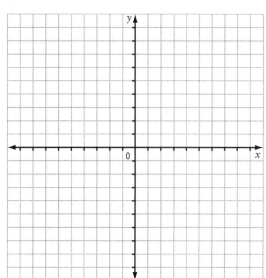

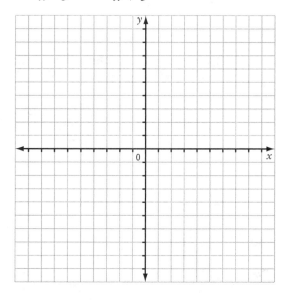

c) $\dfrac{2x-5}{x-1} - 2 = \dfrac{3}{x+2}$

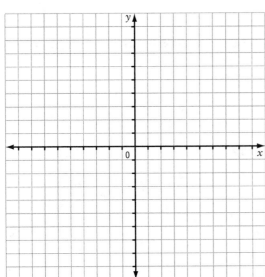

d) $\dfrac{5x}{x+2} + \dfrac{2}{x} = 5$

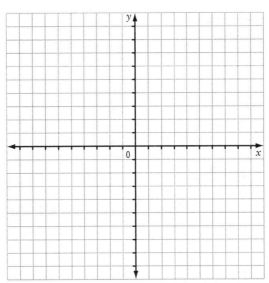

3. Solve each equation algebraically. Then, solve graphically using technology. Compare the solutions found using each method.

a) $\dfrac{x}{x+1} + \dfrac{5}{x-1} = 1$

b) $\dfrac{x^2-4}{x^2-1} = \dfrac{x}{x+3}$

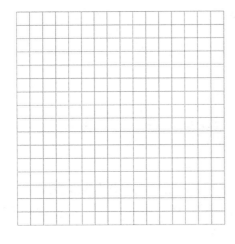

Apply

4. Solve. State any extraneous root(s).

   a) $\dfrac{1}{x-2} = \dfrac{x}{10-5x}$

   b) $\dfrac{x^2}{x-1} + 2 = \dfrac{1}{x-1}$

   c) $\dfrac{x}{x-2} + \dfrac{2}{x+3} = \dfrac{10}{x^2+x-6}$

   d) $\dfrac{x^2}{x+2} = \dfrac{4}{x+2}$

5. Amber and Matteo are travelling separately from their home in Calgary to a wedding 400 km away. Amber leaves 1 h earlier than Matteo, but Matteo drives at an average speed 20 km/h faster than Amber. If they arrive at the wedding at the exact same time, what was the average speed at which each of them travelled?

   a) Let x represent the time it takes Amber to travel to the wedding. Write an expression for the average speed that each person travels.

   b) Write and solve an equation that represents the difference in their average speeds.

Connect

6. Explain why solving a rational equation graphically gives an approximate solution, while solving a rational equation algebraically gives an exact solution.

7. Explain why solving a rational equation graphically does not show extraneous roots.

9.1 Exploring Rational Functions Using Transformations, pages 297–304

1. Graph each function using transformations. Label the important parts of the graph.

a) $y = \dfrac{3}{x-4} + 2$

b) $y = \dfrac{7}{x-1} - 2$

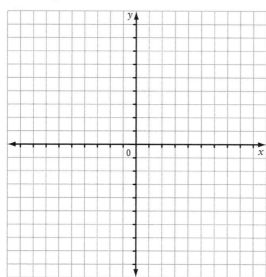

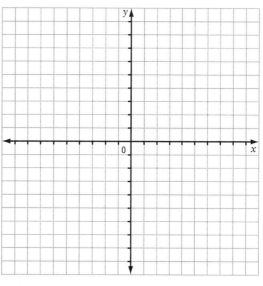

2. Graph the following functions without technology. Label all the important parts.

a) $f(x) = \dfrac{4x+5}{x-3}$

b) $f(x) = \dfrac{-2x+5}{x-3}$

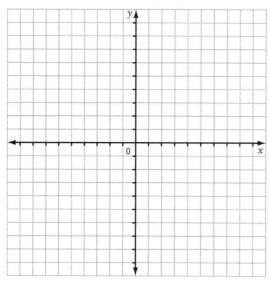

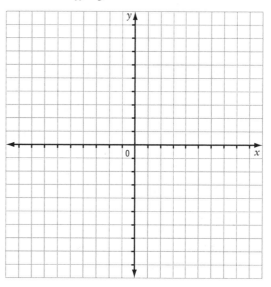

9.2 Analysing Rational Functions, pages 305–313

3. Match the graph of each rational function with the most appropriate equation. Give reasons for each choice.

a)

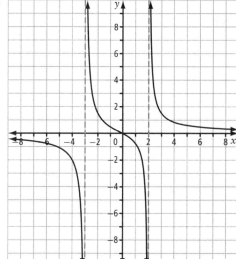

b)

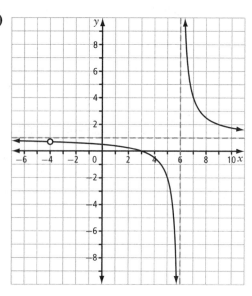

c)

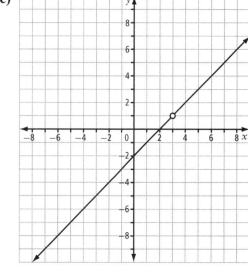

d)

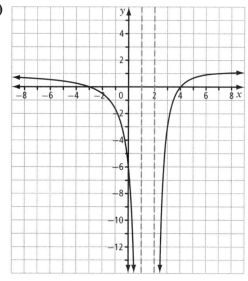

A $f(x) = \dfrac{x^2 + x - 12}{x^2 - 2x - 24}$

B $g(x) = \dfrac{x^2 - x - 12}{x^2 - 3x + 2}$

C $h(x) = \dfrac{x^2 - 5x + 6}{x - 3}$

D $j(x) = \dfrac{3x}{x^2 + x - 6}$

4. For each function, predict the location of any points of discontinuity, vertical asymptotes, and intercepts.

a) $f(x) = \dfrac{2x + 1}{x + 5}$

b) $f(x) = \dfrac{x^2 - 8x + 12}{x - 2}$

9.3 Connecting Graphs and Rational Equations, pages 314–320

5. Solve each rational equation algebraically.

a) $\dfrac{3}{x} - \dfrac{6}{x - 2} = \dfrac{1}{4}$

b) $\dfrac{x - 2}{3} = \dfrac{2x - 4}{x}$

c) $\dfrac{x + 1}{x + 3} = \dfrac{x + 4}{x + 5}$

b) $\dfrac{x + 2}{x - 2} = \dfrac{2x + 4}{x + 1}$

6. Use technology to solve each rational equation graphically. Sketch and label a graph of the solution. Provide answers to the nearest tenth.

a) $\dfrac{4}{x} + \dfrac{3}{x + 1} = \dfrac{1}{2}$

b) $\dfrac{3x - 1}{x + 4} + 3 = \dfrac{6}{x - 4}$

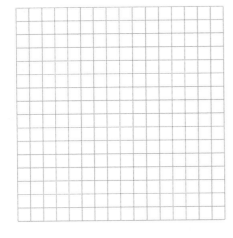

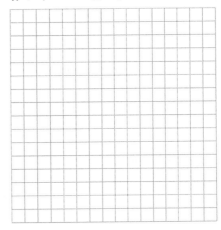

$x = $ _____

$x = $ _____

Think of all the material presented in Chapter 9. Compare and contrast solving rational equations algebraically and graphically. Use explanations and examples to complete the Venn diagram.

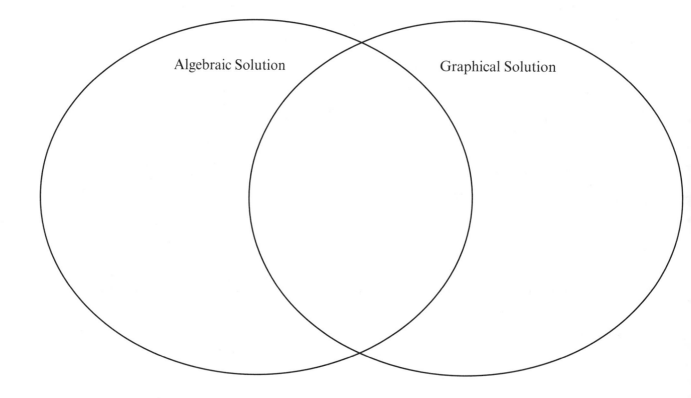

Algebraic Solution

Graphical Solution

Chapter 10 Function Operations

10.1 Sums and Differences of Functions

• You can form new functions by performing operations with functions.

Sum of Functions	Difference of Functions
$h(x) = f(x) + g(x)$ or $h(x) = (f + g)(x)$	$h(x) = f(x) - g(x)$ or $h(x) = (f - g)(x)$
Example $f(x) = x^2$ and $g(x) = -x + 5$ $h(x) = f(x) + g(x)$ $h(x) = x^2 + (\boldsymbol{-x + 5})$ $h(x) = x^2 - x + 5$	**Example** $f(x) = -2x$ and $g(x) = x - 4$ $h(x) = f(x) - g(x)$ $h(x) = \boldsymbol{-2x - (x - 4)}$ $h(x) = -3x + 4$
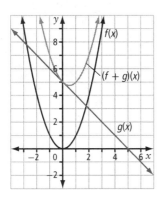	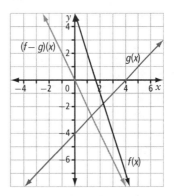

• The domain of the combined function formed by the sum or difference of two functions is the domain common to the individual functions.

Example

If the domain of $f(x)$ is $\{x \mid x \geq 0, x \in \mathbb{R}\}$ and the domain of $g(x)$ is $\{x \mid x \leq 10, x \in \mathbb{R}\}$, the domain of $(f + g)(x)$ is $\{x \mid 0 \leq x \leq 10, x \in \mathbb{R}\}$.

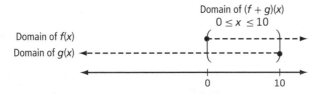

• The range of a combined function can be determined using its graph.

Working Example 1: Determine the Sum of Two Functions

Consider $f(x) = x + 1$ and $g(x) = 2x - 5$.

a) Determine the equation of the function $h(x) = (f + g)(x)$.

b) Sketch the graphs of $f(x)$, $g(x)$, and $h(x)$ on the same set of coordinate axes.

c) State the domain and range of $h(x)$.

d) Determine the values of $f(x)$, $g(x)$, and $h(x)$ when $x = -3$.

Solution

a) $h(x) = (f + g)(x)$

$h(x) = f(\underline{\hspace{1.5cm}}) + g(\underline{\hspace{1.5cm}})$

$h(x) = x + 1 + \underline{\hspace{1.5cm}}$

$h(x) = \underline{\hspace{1.5cm}} x + \underline{\hspace{1.5cm}}$

b) Use the slope-intercept form of the equation of a line to graph the functions $g(x)$ and $h(x)$.

For $g(x)$, the slope of the line $y = 2x - 5$ is $\underline{\hspace{1.5cm}}$ and the y-intercept is $\underline{\hspace{1.5cm}}$.

For $h(x)$, the slope of the line $y = 3x - 4$ is $\underline{\hspace{1.5cm}}$ and the y-intercept is $\underline{\hspace{1.5cm}}$.

Add the graphs of $g(x)$ and $h(x)$ to the grid shown.

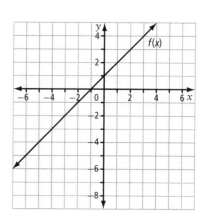

c) The domain of $f(x)$ is $\{x \mid x \in R\}$. The domain of $g(x)$ is $\{x \mid x \in R\}$.

Therefore, the domain of $h(x)$ is $\underline{\hspace{4cm}}$.

The range of $f(x)$ is $\{y \mid y \in R\}$. The range of $g(x)$ is $\{y \mid y \in R\}$.

Therefore, the range of $h(x)$ is $\underline{\hspace{4cm}}$.

d) Substitute $x = -3$ into $f(x)$, $g(x)$, and $h(x)$.

$f(x) = x + 1$	$g(x) = 2x - 5$	$h(x) = 3x - 4$
$f(-3) = \underline{\hspace{1cm}} + 1$	$g(-3) = \underline{\hspace{1.5cm}}$	$h(-3) = \underline{\hspace{1.5cm}}$
$f(-3) = \underline{\hspace{1.5cm}}$	$g(-3) = \underline{\hspace{1.5cm}}$	$h(-3) = \underline{\hspace{1.5cm}}$

📖 This example should help you complete #1 on page 483 of *Pre-Calculus 12*.

Working Example 2: Determine the Difference of Two Functions

Consider $f(x) = x^2$ and $g(x) = 4x - 4$.

a) Determine the equation of the function $h(x) = (f - g)(x)$.

b) Sketch the graphs of $f(x)$, $g(x)$, and $h(x)$ on the same set of coordinate axes.

c) State the domain and range of $h(x)$.

Solution

a) $h(x) = (f - g)(x)$

$h(x) = f(x) - g(x)$

$h(x) = x^2 - (\underline{\hspace{3cm}})$

$h(x) = \underline{\hspace{5cm}}$

b) Generate a table of values using a spreadsheet. Enter four column headings into a spreadsheet: x, $f(x)$, $g(x)$, and $h(x)$. Enter the integer values -4 to 4 into the first column. Enter the formula for x^2 into the second column and copy down to fill in the values. Enter the formula for $4x - 4$ into the third column and copy down. Enter the formula for $x^2 - 4x + 4$ into the fourth column and copy down. Fill in the values in the table below.

Use the spreadsheet graphing function to generate the three graphs. Sketch and label them below.

x	$f(x)$	$g(x)$	$h(x)$
-4			
-3			
-2			
-1			
0			
1			
2			
3			
4			

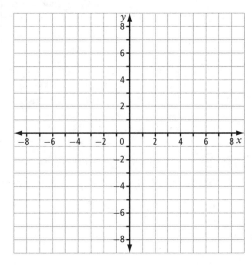

c) The function $f(x) = x^2$ has domain $\{x \mid \underline{\hspace{2cm}}\}$.

The function $g(x) = 4x - 4$ has domain $\{x \mid \underline{\hspace{2cm}}\}$.

Therefore, the function $h(x) = x^2 - 4x + 4$ has domain $\{x \mid \underline{\hspace{2cm}}\}$.

The function $f(x) = x^2$ has range $\{y \mid \underline{\hspace{2cm}}\}$.

The function $g(x) = 4x - 4$ has range $\{y \mid \underline{\hspace{2cm}}\}$.

Therefore, the function $h(x) = x^2 - 4x + 4$ has range $\{y \mid \underline{\hspace{2cm}}\}$.

> 📖 This example should help you complete #2 on page 483 of *Pre-Calculus 12*.

Working Example 3: Determine a Combined Function From Graphs

Use the graphs of $f(x)$ and $g(x)$ to sketch the graph of $h(x) = (f + g)(x)$.

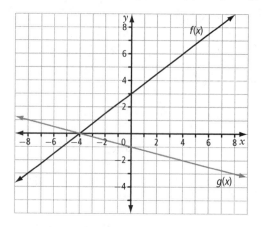

Solution

Method 1: Add the y-Coordinates of Corresponding Points

Complete the second and third columns of the table below using the graphs of $f(x)$ and $g(x)$.
Add the y-values of $f(x)$ and $g(x)$ at each x-value to determine the points on the graph of $h(x)$.

x	$f(x)$	$g(x)$	$h(x) = (f + g)(x)$
-8			
-4			
0			
4			
8			

Plot the points for $h(x)$ and draw the graph of $h(x)$ on the grid below.

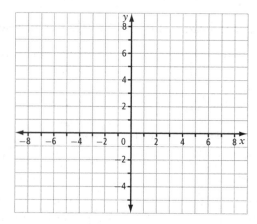

Method 2: Determine the Equations

For the graph of $f(x)$, the y-intercept is _____ and the slope is _____.

Therefore, the equation is $f(x) =$ _____.

For the graph of $g(x)$, the y-intercept is _____ and the slope is _____.

Therefore, the equation is $g(x) =$ _____.

Determine the equation of $h(x)$ algebraically.

$h(x) = f(x) + g(x)$

$h(x) =$ _____ + _____

$h(x) =$ _____

Graph $h(x) = \frac{1}{2}x + 2$ on the grid.

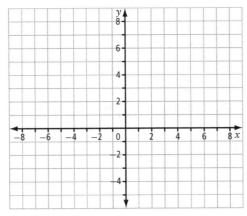

Verify by graphing $f(x)$, $g(x)$, and $h(x)$ on a graphing calculator.

> 📖 This example should help you complete #7 and #8 on page 484 of *Pre-Calculus 12*.

Working Example 4: Application of the Differences of Two Functions

The yearbook committee prepares the annual book to sell to students. The fixed cost is $800 and the printing cost for each yearbook is $15. The committee plans to sell the yearbooks for $20 each.

a) Write an equation to represent
- the total cost, C, as a function of the number, n, of yearbooks printed
- the revenue, R, as a function of the number, n, of yearbooks sold

b) Graph $C(n)$ and $R(n)$ on the same set of axes. What does the point of intersection represent?

c) Profit, P, is the difference between revenue and cost. Write a function representing $P(n)$. How many yearbooks need to be sold before the committee can start making a profit?

d) What is the domain of $C(n)$, $R(n)$, and $P(n)$?

Solution

a) The total cost of printing the yearbooks can be represented by the function

$C(n) = 15n +$ _____.

The revenue can be represented by the function $R(n) =$ _____n.

b) Graph and label $C(n) = 15n + 800$ and $R(n) = 20n$.

The point of intersection of the graphs of $C(n)$ and $R(n)$ is

(_____, _____). The point of intersection represents the

point at which total cost equals the _____. This is

also called the break-_____ point. When 160 yearbooks are

sold, the revenue is $_____.

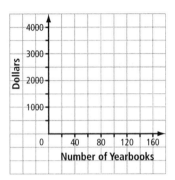

c) $P(n) = R(n) - C(n)$

$P(n) = \mathbf{20n} -$ _____

$P(n) =$ _____

The committee will start making a profit after _____ yearbooks have been sold.

d) The domain for $C(n)$, $R(n)$, and $P(n)$ is $\{n \mid n \geq$ _____$, n \in W\}$.

The range of $C(n)$ is $\{C \mid C$ _____$\}$.

The range of $R(n)$ is $\{R \mid R$ _____$\}$.

The range of $P(n)$ is _____.

Check Your Understanding

Practise

1. Complete the table.

x	$f(x)$	$g(x)$	$(f + g)(x)$	$(f - g)(x)$
–6	2			–2
–4	4	2		
–2	6		6	
0		–2	6	
2		–4		14
4	12		6	
6		–8		22

2. Let $f(x) = \{(-6, 4), (-4, 2), (-2, 0), (0, -2)\}$ and $g(x) = \{(-2, 9), (-6, 3), (-4, 6), (0, 12)\}$. Determine each of the following.

   a) $(f + g)(x) =$

   b) $(f - g)(x) =$

3. Let $f(x) = 3x - 2$ and $g(x) = 2x + 1$. Determine the equation of each combined function.

   a) $(f + g)(x) =$

   b) $(f - g)(x) =$

   c) $(g - f)(x) =$

4. Let $f(x) = x^2 - 3x$ and $g(x) = |2x|$. Determine the value of each combined function.

   a) $(f + g)(-4) =$

   b) $(f - g)(6) =$

   c) $(g - f)(1) =$

5. Let $f(x) = 5x^2$ and $g(x) = \sqrt{x^2 - 4}$. Determine each combined function and state its domain.

   a) $y = (f + g)(x)$ Domain:

   b) $y = (f - g)(x)$ Domain:

   c) $y = (g - f)(x)$ Domain:

6. Let $f(x) = \sqrt{x}$ and $g(x) = \sin x$. Use graphing technology to graph the following combined functions. Sketch the graphs on the grids provided. State the domain and range of each function.

   a) $y = (f + g)(x)$

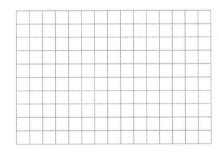

   Domain:

   Range:

b) $y = (f - g)(x)$

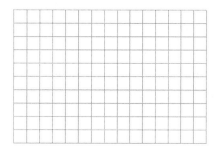

Domain:

Range:

7. Use the graphs of $f(x)$ and $g(x)$ to evaluate the following.

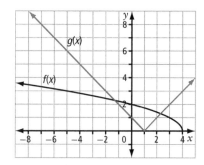

a) $(f + g)(-5) =$

b) $(f - g)(3) =$

c) $(g - f)(4) =$

d) $(f + g)(0) =$

e) Explain why $(f + g)(5)$ cannot be evaluated.

8. Add a sketch of the combined function indicated to each graph.

a) $y = (f + g)(x)$

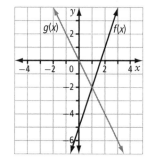

b) $y = (f - g)(x)$

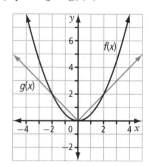

Apply

9. If $f(x) = 2x + 3$, $g(x) = -x^2 + 5$, and $h(x) = -x$, determine each combined function.

a) $y = f(x) + g(x) + h(x)$

b) $y = f(x) - g(x) - h(x)$

c) $y = h(x) + f(x) - g(x)$

10. If $h(x) = (f + g)(x)$ and $f(x) = 4x - 7$, determine $g(x)$.

a) $h(x) = x^2 - 2x$

b) $h(x) = 4 - x$

c) $h(x) = -2x^2 + x + 1$

Questions 9 and 10 should help you complete #9, #10, and #11 on page 484 of *Pre-Calculus 12*.

11. A communications company manufactures a mobile phone for $25 per unit plus a fixed operating cost of $45 000. The mobile phones are sold for $100 per unit.

a) Determine a function to represent the cost, C, of producing n units.

b) Determine a function to represent the revenue, R, from sales of n units.

c) Determine a function to represent the profit, P, from sales of n units.

d) What is the break-even point for the manufacturer of these cell phones?

12. A boat on still water generates a wave modelled by $f(x) = 2 \sin x$. A gust of wind generates a wave modelled by $g(x) = \frac{1}{2} \sin x$, where x is measured in radians.

a) Graph $f(x)$ and $g(x)$.

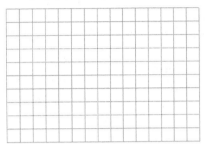

b) Sketch the graph of $h(x) = (f + g)(x)$ on the same grid as you used in part a).

c) What is the maximum height of the combined waves?

Connect

13. Create two functions, $f(x)$ and $g(x)$, to show that if the domains of $f(x)$ and $g(x)$ have no values in common, it is not possible to add or subtract the functions. Explain why this is.

$f(x) =$ _____ $g(x) =$ _____

14. Is it possible for two different functions, $f(x)$ and $g(x)$, to exist where $(f - g)(x) = (g - f)(x)$? If not, explain why not. If it is possible, give an example of $f(x)$ and $g(x)$.

KEY IDEAS

- New functions can be formed by performing the operations of multiplication and division with functions.

Product of Functions	Quotient of Functions
$h(x) = f(x) \bullet g(x)$ or $h(x) = (f \bullet g)(x)$ **Example** $f(x) = x + 3$ and $g(x) = 2x - 1$ $h(x) = f(x) \bullet g(x)$ $h(x) = (x + 3)(2x - 1)$ $h(x) = 2x^2 + 5x - 3$ 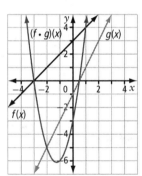	$h(x) = \dfrac{f(x)}{g(x)}$, where $g(x) \neq 0$ or $h(x) = \left(\dfrac{f}{g}\right)(x)$, where $g(x) \neq 0$ **Example** $f(x) = 3x - 1$ and $g(x) = x^2 - x$ $h(x) = \dfrac{f(x)}{g(x)}$ $h(x) = \dfrac{3x - 1}{x^2 - x}$, where $x \neq 1, 0$ 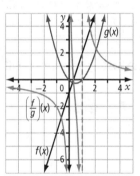

- The domain of a product or a quotient of functions is the domain common to the original functions. The domain of a quotient of functions must have the restriction that the divisor cannot equal zero. That is, for $h(x) = \dfrac{f(x)}{g(x)}$, the values of x are such that $g(x) \neq 0$.

- The range of a combined function can be determined using its graph.

Working Example 1: Determine the Product of Functions

Let $f(x) = x - 3$ and $g(x) = x^2 - 8x + 15$.

a) Determine $h(x) = (f \cdot g)(x)$.

b) State the domain and range of $h(x)$.

Solution

a) $h(x) = (f \cdot g)(x)$

$h(x) = f(x) \cdot g(x)$

$h(x) = (\boldsymbol{x - 3})(\underline{\hspace{5cm}})$

$h(x) = \underline{\hspace{4cm}}$

b) The function $f(x) = x - 3$ is a $\underline{\hspace{3cm}}$ function with domain
                                    (linear or quadratic)

$\{x \mid x \underline{\hspace{2cm}}\}$.

The function $g(x) = x^2 - 8x + 15$ is a $\underline{\hspace{3cm}}$ function with domain
                                        (linear or quadratic)

$\{x \mid \underline{\hspace{3cm}}\}$.

Therefore, the cubic function $h(x) = x^3 - 11x^2 + 39x - 45$ has domain

$\underline{\hspace{4cm}}$ and range $\underline{\hspace{4cm}}$.

Verify by using graphing technology.

Working Example 2: Determine the Quotient of Functions

Let $f(x) = x - 3$ and $g(x) = x^2 - 8x + 15$.

a) Determine the equation of $h(x) = \left(\dfrac{f}{g}\right)(x)$.

b) Sketch the graphs of $f(x)$, $g(x)$, and $h(x)$ on the same set of coordinate axes.

c) State the domain and range of $h(x)$.

Solution

a) $h(x) = \left(\dfrac{f}{g}\right)(x)$

$h(x) = \dfrac{f(x)}{g(x)}$

$h(x) = \dfrac{x - 3}{\boxed{}}$

$h(x) = \dfrac{x - 3}{\left(\boxed{}\right)(x - 3)}$

$h(x) = \dfrac{1}{\boxed{}}, x \neq \underline{\hspace{1.5cm}}, \underline{\hspace{1.5cm}}$ | Why are there two non-permissible values?

b) Use graphing technology to graph $f(x)$, $g(x)$, and $h(x)$.
Sketch and label the graphs on the grid below.

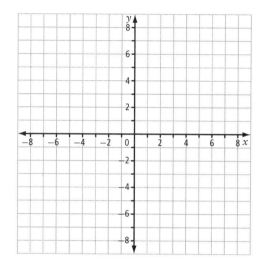

c) The function $f(x) = x - 3$ is a _____ function with domain
(linear or quadratic)
$\{x \mid$ _____ $\}$.

The function $g(x) = x^2 - 8x + 15$ is a _____ function with domain
(linear or quadratic)
$\{x \mid$ _____ $\}$.

The domain of $h(x) = \left(\dfrac{f}{g}\right)(x)$ consists of all values in both the domain of $f(x)$ and $g(x)$

excluding the values for which $g(x) = 0$. Since $g(x)$ does not exist at (_____ , -0.5) and is

undefined at $x =$ _____ , the domain is

$\{x \mid x \neq$ _____ , _____ , $x \in \mathbf{R}\}$.

The range of $h(x)$ is $\{y \mid y \neq$ _____ , _____ , $y \in \mathbf{R}\}$.

> How are the non-permissible values shown on the graph?

📖 This example should help you complete #1, #2, #4, and #6 on page 496 of *Pre-Calculus 12*.

Working Example 3: Application of Products and Quotients of Functions

An electronics store is doing a one-day promotion. Every hour, starting at 9:00 a.m., the price of a 3-D television is reduced by 5%. The price, P, of the television at t hours after 8:00 a.m. can be modelled by the function $P(t) = 1020 - 51t$. The number, N, of televisions sold at time t can be modelled by the function $N(t) = 6t$.

a) Write an expression for the revenue, R, for televisions sold t hours after 8:00 a.m.

b) What is the revenue from 3-D television sales at 12:00 p.m.?

c) The store's cost for each television is $705. Write an expression for the percent gain or loss in profit at t hours.

d) What is the percent gain or loss at 12:00 p.m.?

Solution

a) The revenue is the product of the number of televisions sold and the

_____.

$R(t) = N(t) \cdot P(t)$

$R(t) = ($_____$)($_____$)$

$R(t) = $_____

b) To determine the revenue at 12:00 p.m., replace t in the function $R(t) = 6120t - 306t^2$

with _____.

$R(t) = 6120($_____$) - 306($_____$)^2$

$R(t) = $_____ $-$ _____

$R(t) = $_____

The revenue at 12:00 p.m. is _____.

c) To determine the percent gain or loss, first determine the function for the cost, $C(t)$.

The cost of $6t$ televisions is $705($_____$)$.

$C(t) = $_____

The percent gain or loss is the quotient of revenue and cost multiplied by 100. Then, subtract 100 from this total.

Percent gain or loss $= \dfrac{R(t)}{C(t)}(100) - 100$

Percent gain or loss $= \dfrac{6120t - 306t^2}{4230t}(100) - 100$

Percent gain or loss $= $_____ $- 100$

Percent gain or loss $= $_____

d) To determine the percent gain or loss at 12:00 p.m., replace t in the Percent-gain-or-loss

function from part c) with _____.

The percent gain at 12:00 p.m. is _____.

See pages 497–498 of *Pre-Calculus 12* for more examples.

Check Your Understanding

Practise

1. Determine $h(x) = f(x) \cdot g(x)$ and $k(x) = \dfrac{f(x)}{g(x)}$ for each pair of functions.

   a) $f(x) = 2x - 1$ and $g(x) = 2x - 3$

   $h(x) =$ $k(x) =$

   b) $f(x) = 3x$ and $g(x) = -x^2 - 4$

   $h(x) =$ $k(x) =$

   c) $f(x) = \sqrt{4 - x}$ and $g(x) = 5x - 1$

   $h(x) =$ $k(x) =$

2. Use the graphs of $f(x)$ and $g(x)$ to evaluate the following.

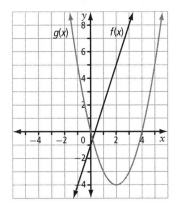

   a) $(f \cdot g)(-1) =$ b) $\left(\dfrac{f}{g}\right)(1) =$

   c) $\left(\dfrac{g}{f}\right)(0) =$ d) $(g \cdot f)(3) =$

3. Add the sketch of each combined function to the set of axes shown.

a) $h(x) = f(x) \cdot g(x)$

b) $k(x) = \dfrac{f(x)}{g(x)}$

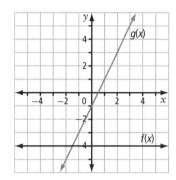
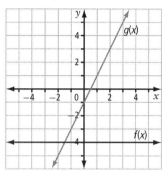

4. Consider the functions $f(x) = 2x - 1$ and $g(x) = (x + 1)^2$.

a) Determine $h(x) = f(x) \cdot g(x)$.

b) Determine $k(x) = \dfrac{f(x)}{g(x)}$.

c) Use graphing technology to graph $f(x)$, $g(x)$, $h(x)$, and $k(x)$. Sketch the graph on the grid below.

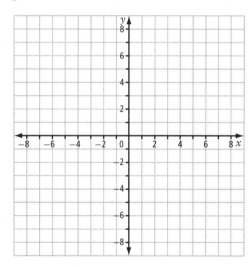

d) Determine the domain and range of each combined function.

$h(x)$: Domain: Range:

$k(x)$: Domain: Range:

Apply

5. Evaluate each combined function using $f(x) = (x^2 + 1)$ and $g(x) = -2x$.

   a) $(f \cdot g)(5) =$

   b) $\left(\dfrac{f}{g}\right)(-2) =$

   c) $\left(\dfrac{g}{f}\right)(2) =$

6. Given $f(x) = x^2$, $g(x) = 4x - 5$, and $h(x) = \sqrt{x-1}$, determine each combined function. State any restrictions on x.

   a) $y = f(x) \cdot g(x) \cdot h(x)$

   b) $y = \dfrac{g(x) \cdot h(x)}{f(x)}$

7. If $h(x) = f(x) \cdot g(x)$ and $f(x) = 2 - x$, determine $g(x)$. State any restrictions on x.

   a) $h(x) = x^2 - 2x$

   b) $h(x) = \sqrt{x^2 - 4}$

8. If $h(x) = \dfrac{f(x)}{g(x)}$ and $g(x) = -2x$, determine $f(x)$. State any restrictions on x.

   a) $h(x) = x^2 + 6x$

   b) $h(x) = -x - 3$

Questions 7 and 8 are similar to #7 and #8 on page 496 of *Pre-Calculus 12*.

9. Let $f(x) = 1$ and $g(x) = \sin x$.

   a) Write the equation of $h(x)$ as a quotient of functions that is equivalent to csc x.

   b) Use graphing technology to graph $f(x)$, $g(x)$, and $h(x)$ on the same axes. Sketch the graphs on the grid below. State any restrictions on x for $h(x)$.

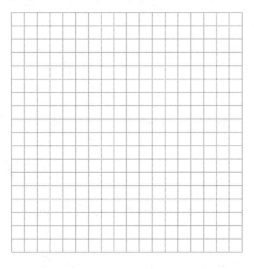

10. Consider $f(x) = \cos x$ and $g(x) = \sqrt{x}$.

   a) Use graphing technology to graph $f(x)$, $g(x)$, and $h(x) = f(x) \cdot g(x)$ on the same axes. Sketch the graphs on the grid below.

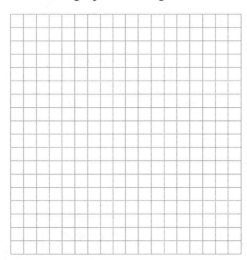

   b) State the domain and range of $h(x)$.

11. An agricultural company calculated that, during harvesting season, the total hours, T, worked per week was the number of hours worked, H, multiplied by the number of employees, E. The function $H(w) = 10 + 0.4w$ represents the hours worked per week and the function $E(w) = 30 - 2w$ represents the number of employees, where w is the number of weeks from the start of harvesting.

a) Represent $T(w)$ as a combined function.

b) What is the total number of hours worked per week after 6 weeks of harvesting?

c) During which week number will the harvesting end? Explain how you determined your answer.

d) State the domain and range of $T(w)$.

12. The total weight, W, in tonnes, of live fish in a fish farm is given by the function $W(a) = 12 + 1.41a$, where a represents the age of the fish, in weeks. The function $F(a) = a^2 + 0.25a$ represents the total weight, in tonnes, of food the fish have been fed when the fish are a weeks old.

a) Write the combined function $R(a)$ that represents the ratio of total weight of food to total weight of fish.

b) What is the total weight of the fish at 15 weeks? How much food has been fed at that age?

c) Sketch the graph of $R(a)$ on the grid below. State the domain and range of $R(a)$.

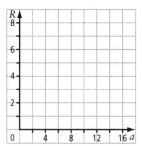

Connect

13. The volume, V, of a cylinder, in cubic inches, is given by $V(x) = \pi(25x^3 - 12.5x^2)$.

a) Write a function, $A(x)$, to represent the area of the base when the radius is $2.5x$.

b) Graph $A(x)$. State its domain and range in this context.

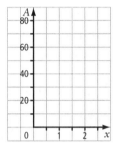

c) Determine the combined function $H(x)$ to represent the height of the cylinder when the area of the base, $A(x)$, is the function that you wrote in part a).

d) Graph $H(x)$. State its domain and range in this context.

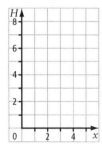

╔═══╗

KEY IDEAS

- Composite functions are functions that are formed from two functions, $f(x)$ and $g(x)$, in which the output of one of the functions is used as the input for the other function.
  - $f(g(x))$ is read as "f of g of x"
  - $(f \circ g)(x)$ is another way of writing $f(g(x))$ and is read the same way

For example, if $f(x) = 2x - 2$ and $g(x) = x^2 + 3x$, then $f(g(x))$ is shown in the mapping diagram.

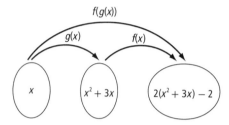

The output for $g(x)$ is the input for $f(x)$.

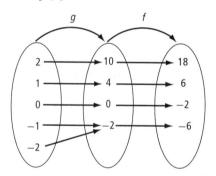

To determine the equation of a composite function, substitute the second function into the first. To determine $f(g(x))$,

$f(g(x)) = f(x^2 + 3x)$	Substitute $x^2 + 3x$ for $g(x)$.
$f(g(x)) = 2(x^2 + 3x) - 2$	Substitute $x^2 + 3x$ into $f(x) = 2x - 2$.
$f(g(x)) = 2x^2 + 6x - 2$	Simplify.

To determine $g(f(x))$,

$g(f(x)) = g(2x - 2)$	Substitute $2x - 2$ for $f(x)$.
$g(f(x)) = (2x - 2)^2 + 3(2x - 2)$	Substitute $2x - 2$ into $g(x) = x^2 + 3x$.
$g(f(x)) = 4x^2 - 8x + 4 + 6x - 6$	Simplify.
$g(f(x)) = 4x^2 - 2x - 2$	

Note that $f(g(x)) \neq g(f(x))$.

- The domain of $f(g(x))$ is the set of all values of x in the domain of g for which $g(x)$ is the domain of f. Restrictions must be considered.

╚═══╝

Working Example 1: Evaluate a Composite Function

If $f(x) = 4 - x$ and $g(x) = x^2 + x$, determine each value.

a) $f(g(2))$ b) $g(f(-3))$ c) $g(g(1))$

Solution

a) Method 1: Determine the Value of the Inner Function and Then Substitute

Evaluate the function inside the brackets for $x = 2$. Then, substitute this value into the outer function.

$g(x) = x^2 + x$

$g(2) =$ _____

$g(2) =$ _____

Substitute the value of $g(2)$ into $f(x)$.

$f(g(2)) = f(6)$

$f(g(2)) = 4 -$ _____   Substitute 6 for $g(2)$.

$f(g(2)) =$ _____   Evaluate $f(x) = 4 - x$ when x is 6.

Therefore, $f(g(2)) =$ _____.

Method 2: Determine the Composite Function and Then Substitute

$f(g(x)) = f(x^2 + x)$ Substitute $x^2 + x$ for $g(x)$.

$f(g(x)) = 4 - ($_____$)$ Substitute $x^2 + x$ into $f(x) = 4 - x$.

$f(g(x)) =$ _____

Substitute $x = 2$ into $f(g(x))$.

$f(g(2)) =$ _____ $-$ _____$^2 -$ _____

$f(g(2)) =$ _____

Therefore, $f(g(2)) =$ _____.

b) Determine $f(-3)$ and then $g(f(-3))$.

$f(x) = 4 - x$

$f(-3) =$ _____

Substitute $f(-3) = 7$ into $g(x)$.

$g(f(-3)) = g(7)$

$g(f(-3)) =$ _____

Therefore, $g(f(-3)) =$ _____.

c) Determine $g(g(x))$ and then evaluate.

$g(g(x)) = g(x^2 + x)$ Substitute $x^2 + x$ for $g(x)$.

$g(g(x)) = ($_____$)^2 + ($_____$)$ Substitute $x^2 + x$ into $g(x) = x^2 + x$.

$g(g(x)) = $ _____   Expand.

$g(g(x)) = $ _____   Simplify.

Substitute $x = 1$ into $g(g(x))$.

$g(g(1)) = $ _____$^4 + 2($_____$)^3 + 2($_____$)^2 + $ _____

$g(g(1)) = $ _____

Therefore, $g(g(1)) = $ _____.

> 📖 This example should help you complete #1 and #3 on page 507 of *Pre-Calculus 12*.

Working Example 2: Compose Functions With Restrictions

If $f(x) = x - 3$ and $g(x) = \sqrt{x}$, determine the following.

a) $(f \circ g)(x)$

b) $(g \circ f)(x)$

c) Does order matter when composing functions?

d) State the domain of $f(x)$, $g(x)$, $(f \circ g)(x)$, and $(g \circ f)(x)$.

Solution

a) Determine $(f \circ g)(x)$.

$(f \circ g)(x) = f(\sqrt{x})$ Substitute $\sqrt{x}$ for $g(x)$.

$(f \circ g)(x) = $ _____ $- 3$ Substitute $\sqrt{x}$ into $f(x) = x - 3$.

Therefore, $(f \circ g)(x) = $ _____.

b) Determine $(g \circ f)(x)$.

$(g \circ f)(x) = g($_____$)$ Substitute $x - 3$ for $f(x)$.

$(g \circ f)(x) = \sqrt{}$ Substitute $x - 3$ into $g(x) = \sqrt{x}$.

Therefore, $(g \circ f)(x) = $ _____.

c) Order _____ matter when composing functions because
       (*does* or *does not*)

$\sqrt{x} - 3$ _____ $\sqrt{x - 3}$.
      (= or ≠)

d) The domain of $f(x)$ is $\{x \mid x \in \mathbb{R}\}$.

The domain of $g(x)$ is $\{x \mid x \text{\underline{\hspace{2cm}}}, x \in \mathbb{R}\}$.

The domain of $(f \circ g)(x)$ is a combination of the restrictions for which $g(x)$ is the domain of $f(x)$. Therefore, the domain is $\{x \mid x \text{\underline{\hspace{2cm}}}, x \in \mathbb{R}\}$.

The domain of $(g \circ f)(x)$ is a combination of the restrictions for which $f(x)$ is the domain of $g(x)$. Therefore, the domain is $\{x \mid x \text{\underline{\hspace{2cm}}}, x \in \mathbb{R}\}$.

This example should help you complete #6 on page 507 of *Pre-Calculus 12*.

Working Example 3: Determine the Composition of Two Functions

Let $f(x) = x^2 + 1$ and $g(x) = 2x$. Determine the equation of each composite function, graph it, and state its domain and range.

a) $y = f(g(x))$ **b)** $y = g(f(x))$ **c)** $y = f(f(x))$ **d)** $y = g(g(x))$

Solution

a) Determine $f(g(x))$.

$f(g(x)) = f(\mathbf{2x})$

$f(g(x)) = (\text{\underline{\hspace{1.5cm}}})^2 + 1$

$f(g(x)) = \text{\underline{\hspace{2cm}}}$

Sketch the graph of $f(g(x))$ on the grid below.

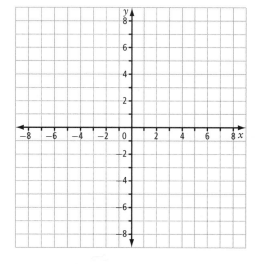

The domain is $\{x \mid x \text{\underline{\hspace{2cm}}}\}$.
The range is
$\{y \mid y \text{\underline{\hspace{2.5cm}}}\}$.

b) Determine $g(f(x))$.

$g(f(x)) = g(\mathbf{x^2 + 1})$

$g(f(x)) = 2(\text{\underline{\hspace{2cm}}})$

$g(f(x)) = \text{\underline{\hspace{3cm}}}$

Sketch the graph of $g(f(x))$ on the grid below.

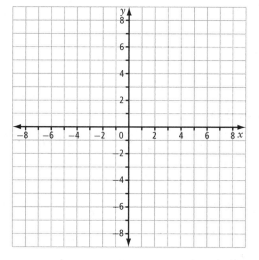

The domain is $\{x \mid x \text{\underline{\hspace{2cm}}}\}$.
The range is
$\{y \mid y \text{\underline{\hspace{2.5cm}}}\}$.

c) Determine $f(f(x))$.

$f(f(x)) = f(x^2 + 1)$

$f(f(x)) = ($ _____ $)^2 + 1$

$f(f(x)) = $ _____

Sketch the graph of $f(f(x))$ on the grid below.

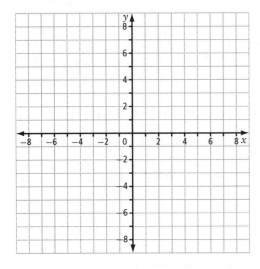

The domain is $\{x \mid x$ _____ $\}$.
The range is
$\{y \mid y$ _____ $\}$.

d) Determine $g(g(x))$.

$g(g(x)) = g(2x)$

$g(g(x)) = $ _____

$g(g(x)) = $ _____

Sketch the graph of $g(g(x))$ on the grid below.

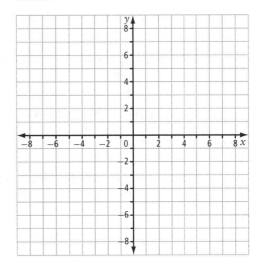

The domain is $\{x \mid x$ _____ $\}$.
The range is
$\{y \mid y$ _____ $\}$.

Working Example 4: Determine the Original Functions From a Composition

Determine two functions, $f(x)$ and $g(x)$, where $h(x) = f(g(x))$.

a) $h(x) = \sqrt{3x - 2}$

b) $h(x) = (x - 4)^2 + 3(x - 4) + 4$

c) $h(x) = x^2 - 6x + 9$

Solution

a) Let $g(x) = 3x - 2$. Then, work backward to determine $f(x)$.

$h(x) = \sqrt{3x - 2}$

$f(g(x)) = \sqrt{\boxed{}}$ 　　Replace $3x - 2$ with $g(x)$.

Therefore, $f(x) = \sqrt{x}$.

The two functions are $f(x) = $ _____ and $g(x) = $ _____.

b) Look for a function that may be common to more than one term in $h(x)$. The expression $(x - 4)$ occurs in two terms.

Let $g(x) = x - 4$. Then, work backward to determine $f(x)$.

$$h(x) = (x - 4)^2 + 3(x - 4) + 4$$

$f(g(x)) = ($_____$)^2 + 3($_____$) + 4$ Replace $x - 4$ with $g(x)$.

Therefore, $f(x) = $ _____ .

The two functions are $f(x) = $ _____ and

$g(x) = $ _____ .

c) Factor $h(x) = x^2 - 6x + 9$.

$h(x) = $ _____

Let $g(x) = x - 3$. Then, work backward to determine $f(x)$.

$h(x) = ($ _____ $)^2$

$h(g(x)) = ($ _____ $)^2$ Replace $x - 3$ with $g(x)$.

Therefore, $f(x) = $ _____ .

The two functions are $f(x) = $ _____ and $g(x) = $ _____ .

> 📖 This example should help you complete #7 on page 507 of *Pre-Calculus 12*.

Working Example 5: Application of Composite Functions

The temperature as you descend a mine shaft is a function of the depth below the surface. An equation expressing the relationships is $T = 0.01d + 20$, where T is the temperature, in degrees Celsius, and d is the depth, in metres.

a) If you go down a mine shaft at a rate of 4 m/s, express the temperature as a function of the time, t, in seconds.

b) What is the temperature after 1 min of travelling down the shaft?

Solution

a) Since the rate of travel is 4 m/s, the distance, in metres, travelled in t seconds is

$d = $ _____ . Since the temperature, T, is a function of depth, d, you can compose the two functions.

$T(d) = 0.01d + 20$

$T(d(t)) = 0.01($ _____ $) + 20$

$T(d(t)) = $ _____ $+ 20$

The temperature expressed as a function of time is $T(d(t)) = $ _____ .

b) To determine the temperature after 1 min of travel, substitute $t =$ _____ (time in seconds) in the composite function.

$$T(d(t)) = 0.04t + 20$$

$$T(d(60)) = 0.04(\underline{\hspace{1.5cm}}) + 20$$

$$T(d(60)) = \underline{\hspace{1.5cm}}$$

The temperature after one minute of travelling down the shaft is _____.

Check Your Understanding

Practise

1. Use the graphs of f and g to evaluate the functions.

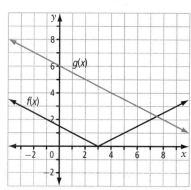

a) $f(g(6))$

b) $f(g(-2))$

c) $g(f(3))$

d) $g(f(7))$

2. If $f(x) = x + 6$ and $g(x) = -3x + 5$, determine each of the following.

a) $f(g(-4))$

b) $g(f(0))$

c) $g(g(8))$

d) $f(f(-1))$

3. Determine $(f \circ g)(x)$ and $(g \circ f)(x)$ for each pair of functions.

a) $f(x) = \sqrt{x + 4}$ and $g(x) = x^2$

$(f \circ g)(x) =$ $(g \circ f)(x) =$

b) $f(x) = |x - 4|$ and $g(x) = 3 - x$

$(f \circ g)(x) =$ $(g \circ f)(x) =$

c) $f(x) = \frac{1}{x}$ and $g(x) = x + 3$

$(f \circ g)(x) =$ $(g \circ f)(x) =$

4. For $f(x) = x^2 - 2$ and $g(x) = 4x + 1$, sketch the graph of each composite function. Determine the domain and range of the composite function.

a) $y = f(g(x))$ b) $y = g(f(x))$

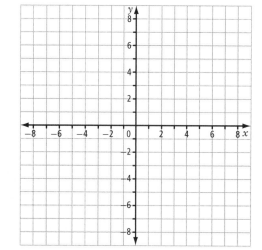

Domain:

Range:

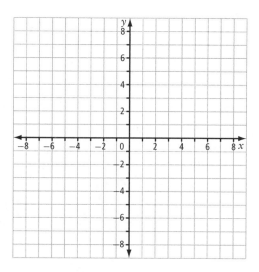

Domain:

Range:

📖 This question is similar to #6 on page 507 of *Pre-Calculus 12*.

5. If $h(x) = (f \circ g)(x)$, determine $g(x)$.

a) $h(x) = \dfrac{1}{(x-2)^2}$ and $f(x) = \dfrac{1}{x^2}$

b) $h(x) = \sqrt{x^2 - 2}$ and $f(x) = \sqrt{x}$

c) $h(x) = x^2 - 10x + 25$ and $f(x) = x^2$

6. For $f(x) = \sqrt{x-4}$ and $g(x) = 3x + 1$, determine each composite function and state its domain.

a) $(f \circ g)(x)$

b) $(g \circ f)(x)$

Apply

7. Consider $f(x) = x + 2$ and $g(x) = \dfrac{x^2 + x - 2}{x - 1}$.

a) Determine $f(g(x))$.

b) Determine $g(f(x))$.

c) What restrictions are placed on the domain of each composite function?

8. Consider $h(x) = \dfrac{1}{x}$ and $k(x) = x^2$.

a) How are $h(k(x))$ and $k(h(x))$ related?

b) What restrictions are placed on the domain of the composite functions?

9. The cost, C, of manufacturing x engines is given by the function $C(x) = 75x + 900$. The number of engines produced in t hours is given by $x(t) = 10.5x$.

a) Determine $C(x(t))$.

b) What does $C(x(t))$ represent?

c) Determine the cost incurred after 8 h of production.

d) Determine the time that must elapse for the cost to be $33 975.

10. The suggested retail price for a snowmobile is p dollars. The manufacturer offers a $1200 factory rebate, and the dealership offers a 10% discount.

a) Write a function, R, in terms of p that gives the cost of the snowmobile after receiving the rebate from the factory.

b) Write a function, D, in terms of p that gives the cost of the snowmobile after receiving the dealership discount.

c) Determine $(R \circ D)(p)$. What does it represent?

d) Determine $(D \circ R)(p)$. What does it represent?

e) Determine $(R \circ D)(10\ 750)$ and $(D \circ R)(10\ 750)$. Which gives the lower cost for the snowmobile? Explain.

11. A sales representative for a flooring company is paid a monthly salary plus a bonus of 5% of monthly sales, x, over \$50 000. Let $f(x) = x - 50\,000$ and $g(x) = 0.05x$. If x is greater than \$50 000, which represents the sales representative's bonus: $f(g(x))$ or $g(f(x))$? Explain.

12. Determine two functions, $f(x)$ and $g(x)$, such that $(f \circ g)(x) = h(x)$.

a) $h(x) = (2x + 1)^2$

b) $h(x) = \sqrt{9 - x}$

Connect

13. Do the following to determine whether the composition of functions follows the associative property.

a) Create three linear (non-horizontal) functions, $f(x)$, $g(x)$, and $h(x)$.

b) Show whether $((f \circ g) \circ h)(x)$ is equal to $(f \circ (g \circ h))(x)$.

14. Do the following to determine whether the composition of functions follows the commutative property.

a) Create two functions, $f(x)$ and $g(x)$.

b) Show whether $(f \circ g)(x)$ is equal to $(g \circ f)(x)$. What restrictions are placed on the composite functions?

Chapter 10 Review

10.1 Sums and Differences of Functions, pages 325–334

1. Given $f(x) = 2x - 1$ and $g(x) = x^2 + 4$, determine each of the following.

 a) $(f + g)(-3) =$ **b)** $(f - g)(4)$

2. Let $f(x) = \sqrt{x + 6}$ and $g(x) = 4x^2 - 1$.

 a) Determine $h(x) = f(x) + g(x)$.

 b) Use graphing technology to graph $y = h(x)$. Sketch the graph on the grid.

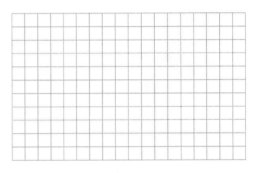

 c) State the domain of $h(x)$. Use the graph to approximate the range of $h(x)$.

 d) Determine $k(x) = f(x) - g(x)$.

 e) Use graphing technology to graph $y = k(x)$. Sketch the graph on the grid.

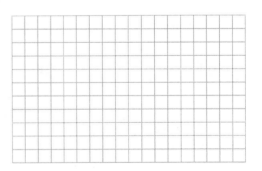

 f) State the domain of $k(x)$. Use the graph to approximate the range of $k(x)$.

3. If $h(x) = (f - g)(x)$ and $f(x) = -x + 6$, determine $g(x)$.

   a) $h(x) = 4x^2 - 12x + 9$ **b)** $h(x) = \sqrt{x} + x - 6$

4. Extreme Sports has two store locations. Between the years 2007–2012, the sales, S_1, in thousands of dollars, at the first location decreased according to the function $S_1(t) = 750 - 0.6t^2$, where t represents the number of years after the year 2000. During the same six-year period, the sales in the second store, S_2, in thousands of dollars, increased according to the function $S_2(t) = 335 + 0.8t$, where t represents the number of years after the year 2000.

   a) Graph $S_1(t)$ and $S_2(t)$ on the same set of axes.

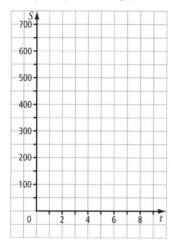

   b) Write a combined function that represents the total sales of the two stores.

   c) Graph the combined function.

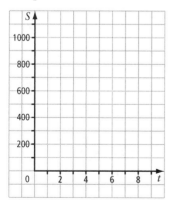

   d) Have the total sales been increasing or decreasing? Explain.

10.2 Products and Quotients of Functions, pages 335–344

5. Let $f(x) = 1 - 2x$ and $g(x) = x^2 + 3$. Determine each combined function and state any restrictions on x.

   a) $h(x) = f(x) \cdot g(x)$ **b)** $k(x) = \dfrac{g(x)}{f(x)}$

6. Use the graphs of $f(x)$ and $g(x)$ to determine the following.

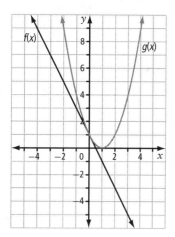

   a) $(f \cdot g)(0)$ **b)** $(f \cdot g)(-1)$

   c) $\left(\dfrac{f}{g}\right)(2)$ **d)** $\left(\dfrac{f}{g}\right)(-2)$

7. Consider $f(x) = \dfrac{1}{x - 1}$ and $g(x) = x$.

   a) Determine $h(x) = (f \cdot g)(x)$. Then, sketch the graph of $y = h(x)$ and state its domain.

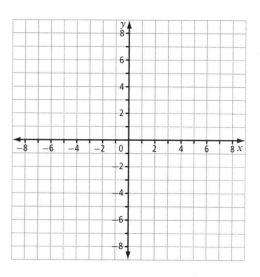

b) Determine $k(x) = \left(\dfrac{f}{g}\right)(x)$. Then, sketch the graph of $y = k(x)$ and state its domain.

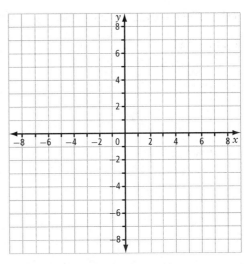

8. If $h(x) = f(x) \cdot g(x)$ and $f(x) = 2x - 3$, determine $g(x)$.

a) $h(x) = 2x^2 - 5x + 3$

b) $h(x) = 2x(\sin x) - 3(\sin x)$

c) $h(x) = -2x^3 + 3x^2$

9. Let $f(x) = \sin x$ and $g(x) = \cos x$.

a) Sketch the graphs of $f(x)$ and $g(x)$.

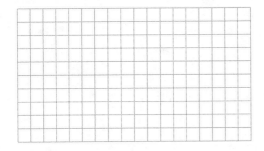

b) Sketch the graph of $y = \dfrac{g(x)}{f(x)}$.

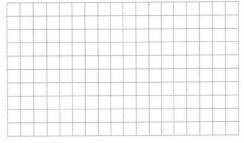

c) State the domain and range of the combined function.

d) Use your knowledge of trigonometric identities to state the equation of the function $y = \dfrac{g(x)}{f(x)}$ as a single trigonometric function.

10.3 Composite Functions, pages 345–355

10. Let $f(x) = x - 3$ and $g(x) = 1 - x^2$. Determine each of the following.

   a) $(f \circ g)(x)$ **b)** $(g \circ g)(x)$

   c) $(f \circ g)(-3)$ **d)** $(g \circ g)(2)$

11. Let $f(x) = x^2 - 9$ and $g(x) = \sqrt{x}$.

   a) Sketch the graph of $y = f(g(x))$ and state its domain and range.

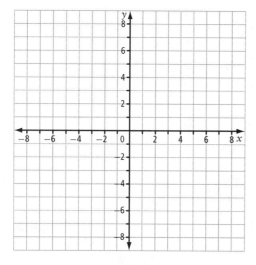

   b) Sketch the graph of $y = g(f(x))$ and state its domain and range.

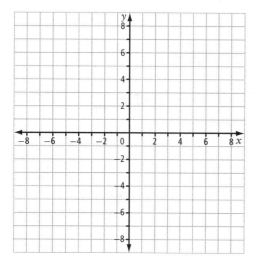

12. Given that $h(x) = (f \circ g)(x)$, determine $g(x)$.

a) $h(x) = \sqrt{9 - x}$ and $f(x) = \sqrt{x}$

b) $h(x) = \dfrac{12}{(7x - 2)^2}$ and $f(x) = \dfrac{12}{x^2}$

c) $h(x) = 4x^2 - 20x + 25$ and $f(x) = x^2$

13. The side length, d, of a cube that contains a sphere depends on the radius, r, of the sphere. Assume that the faces of the cube are tangent to the sphere.

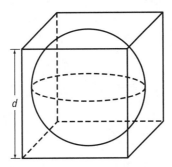

a) Write the side length of the cube as a function of the radius of the sphere.

b) Write the volume of the cube as a function of the radius of the sphere.

c) What is the volume of a cube that contains a sphere of radius 7.5 cm?

14. The number of tonnes, n, of wood pulp produced at Al Pac each day is a function of the number of hours, t, the assembly line is in operation that day and is given by $n(t) = 550t - 2t^2$. The cost, C, of producing the wood pulp is a function of the number of tonnes produced and is given by $C(n) = 7.5n + 1195$.

a) Write the equation of the function $(C \circ n)(t)$ that gives the cost of producing wood pulp in terms of the number of hours, t, the assembly line is in operation on a given day.

b) What was the cost of producing wood pulp on a day when the assembly line was in operation for 18 h?

c) How many hours was the plant in operation on a day when the total cost of production was $91 555?

Chapter 10 Skills Organizer

Complete each Frayer model template for combining functions.

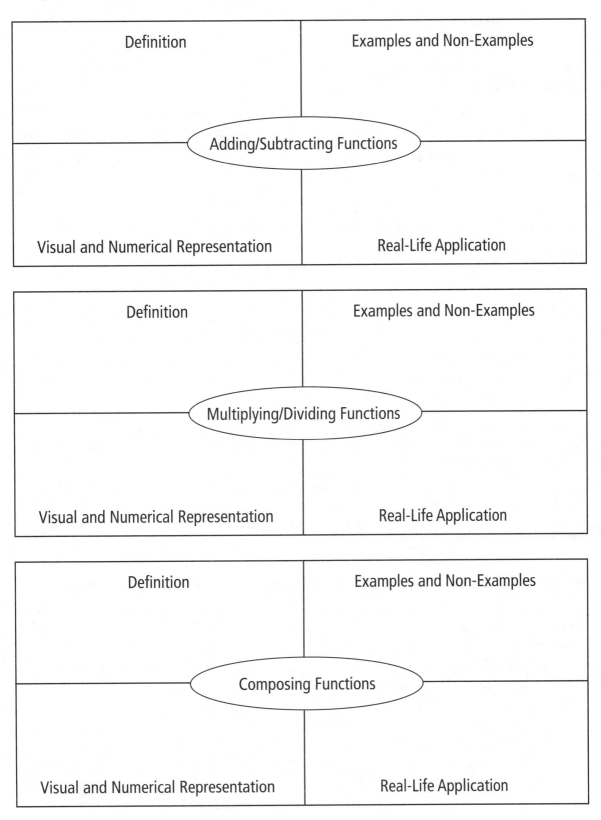

Chapter 11 Permutations, Combinations, and the Binomial Theorem

11.1 Permutations

⟪ KEY IDEAS ⟫

- The fundamental counting principle states that if one task can be performed in a ways and a second task can be performed in b ways, then the two tasks can be performed in $a \times b$ ways.

- For any positive integer n, n factorial or $n!$ represents the product of all of the positive integers up to and including n.

  $n! = n \times (n-1) \times (n-2) \times \cdots \times 3 \times 2 \times 1$. $0!$ is defined as 1.

- Linear permutation is the arrangement of objects or people in a line. The order of the objects is important. When the objects are distinguishable from one another, a new order of objects creates a new permutation.

- The notation $_nP_r$ is used to represent the number of permutations, or arrangements in a definite order, of r items taken from a set of n distinct items. A formula for permutations is

$$_nP_r = \frac{n!}{(n-r)!}, n \in \mathbb{N}$$

- For permutations with repeating objects, a set of n objects with a of one kind that are identical, b of a second kind that are identical, and c of a third kind that are identical, and so on, can be arranged in $\dfrac{n!}{a!b!c!\ldots}$ ways.

- To solve some problems, you must count the different arrangements in all the cases that together cover all the possibilities. Calculate the number of arrangements for each case and then add the values for all cases to obtain the total number of arrangements.

- Whenever you encounter a situation with constraints or restrictions, always address the choices for the restricted positions first.

Working Example 1: Arrangements With or Without Restrictions

a) A school cafeteria offers sandwiches made with fillings of ham, salami, cheese, or egg on white, whole wheat, or rye bread. How many different sandwiches can be made using only one filling?

b) In how many ways can five black cars and four red cars be parked next to each other in a parking garage if a black car has to be first and a red car has to be last?

Solution

a) Method 1: List Outcomes and Count the Total

Use a tree diagram and count the outcomes, or list all of the sandwich choices in a table.

For the fillings, H represents _____, S represents _____, C represents _____, and

E represents _____.

For the bread, W represents _____, WW represents _____, and R represents _____.

Tree Diagram

List

Filling	Bread
S	W

_____ possibilites

Total pathways = _____

There are _____ different sandwiches that can be made.

Method 2: Use the Fundamental Counting Principle

$$\underline{} \times \underline{}$$
(number of choices for sandwich fillings)   (number of choices for bread)

According to the fundamental counting principle there are

(_____)(_____) = _____ different sandwiches that can be made.

b) Use nine blanks to represent the nine cars parked in a row.

There are restrictions. A black car must be in the first position and a red car must be in the last position. Fill these positions first.

_____ _____ _____ _____ _____ _____ _____ _____ _____

There are _____ black cars for the first position.

There are _____ red cars for the last position.

After filling the end positions, there are _____ positions to fill with _____ cars remaining.

Use the numbers you have determined to fill in the blanks that represent the nine cars parked in a row.

By the fundamental counting principle, there are

(_____)(_____)(_____)(_____)(_____)(_____)(_____)(_____)(_____)

= _____ ways to park the cars in a row.

> 📖 For a similar example, see Example 1b) on page 518 of *Pre-Calculus 12*.

Working Example 2: Using Factorial Notation

a) Evaluate $_{10}P_6$.

b) Show that $20! - 19! + 18! = (362)18!$

c) Solve for n if $_nP_2 = 110$.

Solution

a) $_{10}P_6 = \dfrac{\boxed{}!}{\left(\boxed{} - \boxed{}\right)!}$

$= \dfrac{\boxed{}!}{\boxed{}!}$

$= \dfrac{(10)(9)(8)(7)(6)(5)4!}{4!}$

$= \underline{}$

b) $20! - 19! + 18!$

> Determine a common factor among the terms.

$= \underline{} \times \underline{} \times 18! - \underline{} \times \underline{}! + 18!$

$= 18!(\underline{} \times \underline{} - \underline{} + \underline{})$

$= 18!(\underline{})$

c) $_nP_2 = 110$

$$\frac{n!}{(n-2)!} = 110$$

$$\frac{\boxed{}\left(\boxed{} - \boxed{}\right)\left(\boxed{} - \boxed{}\right)!}{(n-2)!} = 110$$

$$\underline{}\left(\underline{} - \underline{}\right) = 110$$

$$n^2 - n - 110 = 0$$

$$n = \underline{}$$

The solution to $_nP_2 = 110$ is $n = \underline{}$.

📖 To see how algebra or graphing can be used to solve part c), refer to Example 2c) on page 520 of *Pre-Calculus 12*.

Working Example 3: Permutations With Repeating Objects

How many different ten-letter arrangements can you make using the letters of BASKETBALL?

Solution

There are _____ letters in BASKETBALL. There are _____ ways to arrange all the letters.

There are _____ letters _____ that can be arranged in _____ ways.

There are _____ letters _____ that can be arranged in _____ ways.

There are _____ letters _____ that can be arranged in _____ ways.

The number of different ten-letter arrangements is $\dfrac{\boxed{}!}{\boxed{}!\;\boxed{}!}$

$$= \underline{}$$

📖 To see a similar problem, refer to Example 3 on page 521 of *Pre-Calculus 12*.

Working Example 4: Using Cases to Determine Permutations

In how many ways can eight basketball players sit on a bench if either the one centre or both of the two forwards must sit at the end where the coach always sits?

Solution

There are two different cases to be considered.

Case 1: The _____ sits beside the coach.

Case 2: _____ sit at the end beside the coach.

Case 1: Centre Sits Beside the Coach

Use a diagram to show the number of choices for the seating arrangement:

Coach _____ _____ _____ _____ _____ _____ _____ _____

Calculate the total number of seating arrangements for this case.

Case 2: Two Forwards Sit Beside the Coach

Use a diagram to show the number of choices for the seating arrangement:

Coach _____ _____ _____ _____ _____ _____ _____

> Consider the two forwards as one object.

Calculate the total number of seating arrangements for this case.

To find the total number of seating arrangements, _____ the possibilities from the two cases.

Therefore, there are _____ possible seating arrangements.

> To see an example similar to the above, refer to Example 5 on page 523 of *Pre-Calculus 12*.

Check Your Understanding

Practise

1. Use a tree diagram to identify the possible arrangements.
   a) Brett is purchasing a new car. He is given a choice of two upholstery materials (cloth or leather) and four colours (black, red, silver, or taupe).

b) Jireesha wears a uniform to work. She has the option of a blue, pink, or white T-shirt with pants that are black, grey, brown, or beige.

2. Use an organized list or table to identify the possible arrangements.

   a) the ways that you can arrange the digits 3, 4, 6, 7, and 8 to form two-digit numbers

   b) the ways you can travel from Toronto to Vancouver via Calgary, if you can go from Toronto to Calgary by either plane or train, and you can go from Calgary to Vancouver by bus, plane, train, or car.

3. Evaluate each expression.

a) $_7P_2$

b) $_6P_1$

c) $_{12}P_9$

d) $_8P_4$

4. a) Show that $5! - 3! \neq (5 - 3)!$

Left Side	Right Side
$5! - 3!$	$(5 - 3)!$
$=$	$=$

b) Show that $6! - 4! = 29(4!)$

5. What is the value of each expression?

a) $\dfrac{50!}{3!47!}$

b) $7! - 6!$

c) $\dfrac{14!}{12!2!}$

d) $10!$

6. In how many ways can you arrange all the letters of each word?

a) schools

b) curriculum

c) winter

d) arrangement

7. Seven students are running in an election for student council president. In how many ways can the seven names be listed on a ballot?

8. Solve for the variable.

    a) $_nP_4 = 840$ **b)** $_5P_r = 20$

    c) $_nP_3 = 720$ **d)** $_9P_r = 3024$

Apply

9. Describe the cases you could use to solve each problem, and then solve.

    a) How many three-digit odd numbers greater than 300 can you make using the digits 1, 2, 3, 4, 5, and 6? No digits are repeated.

        Case 1: Numbers that begin with 3 and end with _____ or _____

Number of choices for first digit	Number of choices for second digit	Number of choices for third digit
_____	_____	_____

        Number of possibilities for case 1 = _____.

        Case 2: Numbers that begin with 4 and end with _____, _____, or _____

Number of choices for first digit	Number of choices for second digit	Number of choices for third digit
_____	_____	_____

        Number of possibilities for case 2 = _____.

        Case 3: Numbers that begin with _____ and end with _____ or _____

Number of choices for first digit	Number of choices for second digit	Number of choices for third digit
_____	_____	_____

        Number of possibilities for case 3 = _____.

        Case 4: Numbers that begin with _____ and end with _____, _____, or _____

Number of choices for first digit	Number of choices for second digit	Number of choices for third digit
_____	_____	_____

        Number of possibilities for case 4 = _____.

        Total number of possibilities = _____ + _____ + _____ + _____

                                           = _____

b) How many four-letter arrangements beginning with A or B and ending with a vowel can you make using the letters A, B, D, E, I, and U?

Case 1: Four-letter arrangements starting with _____

Number of choices for first letter	Number of choices for second letter	Number of choices for third letter	Number of choices for fourth letter
_____	_____	_____	_____

Number of possibilities for case 1 = _____.

Case 2: Four-letter arrangements starting with _____

Number of choices for first letter	Number of choices for second letter	Number of choices for third letter	Number of choices for fourth letter
_____	_____	_____	_____

Number of possibilities for case 2 = _____.

Total number of possibilities = _____ + _____

= _____

10. In how many ways can four girls and three boys be arranged in a row each situation?

a) A boy must be at each end of the row.

b) The boys must be together.

c) The girls must be together.

d) The ends of the row must be either both boys or both girls.

11. a) How many seven-letter arrangements can you make using all of the letters L, M, N, O, P, I, and U?

b) Of these, how many begin and end with a vowel?

c) Of these, how many begin with a consonant and end with a vowel?

12. A fitness club plans to issue each member their own five-character ID code. The first character and the third character can be different letters chosen from A through M, inclusive. The other three characters must be different digits from 1 to 9, inclusive. What is the maximum number of members that the club can have?

13. a) How many arrangements using all of the letters of the word PARALLELOGRAM are possible?

b) How many of these arrangements have all of the Ls together?

c) How many of these arrangements have all of the As together?

d) How many of these arrangements have all of the Rs together?

e) How many of these arrangements have all of the Ls, all of the As, and all of the Rs together?

Connect

14. Postal codes in Canada have six characters, with the first, third, and fifth characters being letters, and the other characters being digits.

a) What is the maximum number of unique postal codes in Canada if the letters D, F, I, O, Q, and U are not used and neither W nor Z appears as a first character?

b) How many of the postal codes described in part a) have the same letter repeated three times?

c) How many have the same digit repeated three times?

≪	**KEY IDEAS**	≫

- A combination is a selection of objects without regard to order.

- The notation $_nC_r$ represents the number of combinations of n objects taken r at a time, where $n \geq r$ and $r \geq 0$.

- A formula for combinations is $_nC_r = \dfrac{n!}{(n-r)!r!}$, $n \in \mathbb{N}$.

- The number of combinations of n items taken r at a time is equivalent to the number of combinations of n items taken $n - r$ at a time; that is, $_nC_r = {_nC_{n-r}}$.

- To solve some problems, count the different combinations in cases that together cover all the possibilities. Calculate the number of combinations for each case and then add the values for all cases to obtain the total number of combinations.

Working Example 1: Combinations and the Fundamental Counting Principle

Eight female students and nine male students are running for six offices on the student council executive team.

a) How many selections are possible?

b) How many selections are possible if the executive team must have three females and three males?

c) One of the male students is named David. How many six-member selections consisting of David, one other male, and four females are possible?

Solution

a) This is a combination problem because it involves choosing _____ students out of

_____ and the _____ is not important.

Substitute $n =$ _____ and $r =$ _____ into $_nC_r = \dfrac{n!}{(n-r)!r!}$:

$$\square C_\square = \frac{\boxed{}!}{\left(\boxed{} - \boxed{}\right)!\,\boxed{}!}$$

$$= \frac{\boxed{}!}{\boxed{}!\,\boxed{}!}$$

$$= \text{_____}$$

There are _____ possible ways of selecting the executive team.

b) There are $\square C \square$ ways of selecting three female students and $\square C \square$ ways of selecting three male students. Using the fundamental counting principle, the number of ways of selecting three females and three males is

$$\square C \square \times \square C \square$$

$$= \frac{\square !}{(\square - \square)!\,\square !} \times \frac{\square !}{(\square - \square)!\,\square !}$$

$$= \underline{\hspace{1.5cm}} \times \underline{\hspace{1.5cm}}$$

$$= \underline{\hspace{1.5cm}}$$

There are \underline{\hspace{2cm}} ways to select an executive team consisting of three females and three males.

c) There is \underline{\hspace{2cm}} way to select David. There are \underline{\hspace{2cm}} males remaining, so there are

$\square C \square$ or \underline{\hspace{2cm}} choices for the second male.

There are $\square C \square$ ways to select four females.

$$\square C \square = \frac{\square !}{(\square - \square)!\,\square !}$$

$$= \frac{\square !}{\square !\,\square !}$$

$$= \underline{\hspace{1.5cm}}$$

There are \underline{\hspace{1.5cm}} $\times$ \underline{\hspace{1.5cm}} $\times$ \underline{\hspace{1.5cm}} $=$ \underline{\hspace{1.5cm}} ways to select the six-member team that includes David, one other male, and four females.

> 📖 To see a similar problem, refer to Example 1 on pages 530 and 531 of *Pre-Calculus 12*.

Working Example 2: Combinations With Cases

An emergency response team of four people is selected from a group of expert volunteers consisting of two doctors, three surgeons, three firefighters, and four nurses. In how many ways can the team be chosen if it must contain

a) one of each type of volunteer?

b) at least three nurses?

Solution

a) There must be one of each: doctor, surgeon, fireman, and nurse.

There are $_2C_1$ ways of selecting a doctor.

$$_2C_1 = \frac{2!}{(2-1)!1!}$$

$$= \frac{2!}{1!1!}$$

$$= \underline{\hspace{2cm}}$$

There are $\square C \square$ ways of selecting a surgeon.

$$\square C \square = \frac{\boxed{}!}{\left(\boxed{} - \boxed{}\right)!\boxed{}!}$$

$$= \frac{\boxed{}!}{\boxed{}!\boxed{}!}$$

$$= \underline{\hspace{2cm}}$$

There are $\square C \square$ ways of selecting a firefighter.

$$\square C \square = \frac{\boxed{}!}{\left(\boxed{} - \boxed{}\right)!\boxed{}!}$$

$$= \frac{\boxed{}!}{\boxed{}!\boxed{}!}$$

$$= \underline{\hspace{2cm}}$$

There are $\square C \square$ ways of selecting a nurse.

$$\square C \square = \frac{\boxed{}!}{\left(\boxed{} - \boxed{}\right)!\boxed{}!}$$

$$= \frac{\boxed{}!}{\boxed{}!\boxed{}!}$$

$$= \underline{\hspace{2cm}}$$

The total possible ways of selecting the team so there is one doctor, one surgeon, one firefighter, and one nurse is $\underline{\hspace{1.5cm}} \times \underline{\hspace{1.5cm}} \times \underline{\hspace{1.5cm}} \times \underline{\hspace{1.5cm}} = \underline{\hspace{1.5cm}}$.

b) There must be at least three nurses. *At least three* means there could be _____

or _____ nurses.

Case 1: _____ nurses and _____ other member

There are $\square C \square$ ways of selecting three nurse and $\square C \square$ ways of selecting _____

other member.

$$\square C \square \times \square C \square = \frac{\square!}{(\square - \square)!\,\square!} \times \frac{\square!}{(\square - \square)!\,\square!}$$

$$= \frac{\square!}{\square!\,\square!} \times \frac{\square!}{\square!\,\square!}$$

$$= \underline{\hspace{3cm}}$$

There are _____ ways of selecting a team with _____ nurses.

Case 2: _____ nurses and _____ other members

There are $\square C \square$ ways of selecting _____ nurses and $\square C \square$ ways of selecting _____

other members.

$$\square C \square \times \square C \square = \frac{\square!}{(\square - \square)!\,\square!} \times \frac{\square!}{(\square - \square)!\,\square!}$$

$$= \frac{\square!}{\square!\,\square!} \times \frac{\square!}{\square!\,\square!}$$

$$= \underline{\hspace{3cm}}$$

> Recall that 0! is defined as 1.

There is _____ way of selecting a team with _____ nurses.

The total number of ways of selecting the team so that there are at least three nurses is

_____ + _____ = _____.

📖 To see a similar problem, refer to Example 2 on page 532 of *Pre-Calculus 12*.

Working Example 3: Simplifying Expressions and Solving Equations With Combinations

a) Express as factorials and simplify $\dfrac{_nC_7}{_{n-1}C_5}$.

b) Solve for n if $3(_nC_3) = {_{n+1}C_4}$.

Solution

a) $\dfrac{_nC_7}{_{n-1}C_5} = \dfrac{\boxed{}!}{\left(\boxed{}-\boxed{}\right)!\,\boxed{}!} \div \dfrac{(n-1)!}{\left(n-1-\boxed{}\right)!\,\boxed{}!}$

$= \left(\dfrac{\boxed{}!}{\left(\boxed{}-\boxed{}\right)!\,\boxed{}!}\right)\left(\dfrac{\left(\boxed{}-\boxed{}\right)!\,\boxed{}!}{(n-1)!}\right)$

$= \dfrac{n\left(n-\boxed{}\right)!}{(n-7)!(7)(6)\left(\boxed{}!\right)} \times \dfrac{\left(n-\boxed{}\right)(n-7)!\left(\boxed{}!\right)}{(n-1)!}$

$= \underline{} \times \underline{}$

$= \underline{}$

b) $\qquad 3(_nC_3) = {_{n+1}C_4}$

$3\left(\dfrac{\boxed{}!}{\left(\boxed{}-\boxed{}\right)!\,\boxed{}!}\right) = \dfrac{(n+1)!}{\left(n+1-\boxed{}\right)!\,\boxed{}!}$

$3\left(\dfrac{\boxed{}!}{(n-3)!\,\boxed{}!}\right) = \dfrac{(n+1)!}{(n-3)!\,\boxed{}!}$

$\dfrac{\boxed{}!}{2!} = \dfrac{(n+1)!}{4!}$

$\dfrac{\boxed{}!}{2} = \dfrac{\left(\boxed{}\right)n!}{24}$

$12 = \underline{}$

$\underline{} = n$

📖 To see a similar problem, refer to Example 3 on page 533 of *Pre-Calculus 12*.

Check Your Understanding

Practise

1. Decide whether each of the following is a combination or a permutation problem. Briefly describe why. You do not need to solve the problem.

   a) A coin is tossed nine times. In how many ways could the result be six heads followed by three tails?

   b) In how many ways can three coins be selected from nine?

   c) A ski team has 12 members. In how many ways can 5 be selected to compete in the finals?

   d) How many numbers less than 400 can be made using the digits 2, 3, 4, 5, and 6?

2. Describe the difference between $_8P_5$ and $_8C_5$, and then evaluate each one.

3. Evaluate.

   a) $_7C_2$

   b) $_7P_2$

   c) $_9C_3$

   d) $_{10}C_4$

4. From 12 employees, in how many ways can you

   a) select a group of eight?

   b) assign six different jobs?

5. a) How many combinations are there of the letters A, B, C, D, and E taken three at a time?

b) List all the combinations of A, B, C, D, and E taken three at a time.

c) How many three-letter permutations are there of the letters A, B, C, D, and E?

d) How is the number of combinations related to the number of permutations?

6. Solve for n.

a) $_nC_2 = 15$

b) $_{n-1}C_2 = 6$

c) $_{n+1}C_{n-1} = 15$

d) $_{n+2}C_n = 10$

7. Identify the cases you would use to solve each problem. Do not solve.

a) How many numbers less than 800 can you make using any number of the digits 2, 3, 4, 7, 8, and 9?

b) In how many ways can a six-person team be selected from four grade 11 students and six grade 12 students if the six-person team must have four members from either grade?

8. Show that each statement is true.

a) $_{10}C_3 = {}_{10}C_7$

b) $_{12}C_4 = {}_{11}C_4 + {}_{11}C_3$

Apply

9. In how many ways can the coach of the debating club select a team from seven grade 11 students and eight grade 12 students if the team has

a) four members?

b) four members, only one of whom is in grade 11?

c) four members, at least two of whom are in grade 12?

10. A bag contains nine white marbles and seven green marbles. In how many ways can you draw groups of six marbles if

a) exactly four must be green?

b) at least four must be green?

11. Show that $5(_nC_5) = n(_{n-1}C_4)$.

12. Solve for n.

a) $_{n+2}C_3 = _{n+1}C_2$

b) $_{n+1}C_5 = _nC_4$

13. Three rooms in a university residence contain three beds, two beds, and five beds, respectively. In how many ways can ten students be assigned to these rooms?

14. The roster of a hockey team consists of ten forwards, five defenders, and two goalies. How many different teams can a coach select if the coach must select three forwards, two defenders, and one goalie?

Connect

15. Twenty people on a sightseeing tour are to travel on a double-decker bus that can hold 12 passengers on the main level and 8 on the upper level. If four of the passengers refuse to sit on the upper level and five want to sit only on the upper level, in how many ways can the passengers be seated if arrangements are not considered?

11.3 The Binomial Theorem

KEY IDEAS

• Pascal's triangle is a triangular array of numbers with 1 in the first row, and 1 and 1 in the second row. Each row begins and ends with 1. Each number in the interior of any row is the sum of the two numbers above it in the preceding row.

$$
\begin{array}{ccccccccc}
 & & & & 1 & & & & \\
 & & & 1 & & 1 & & & \\
 & & 1 & & 2 & & 1 & & \\
 & 1 & & 3 & & 3 & & 1 & \\
1 & & 4 & & 6 & & 4 & & 1
\end{array}
$$

• In the expansion of the binomial $(x + y)^n$, where $n \in N$, the coefficients of the terms are identical to the numbers in the $(n + 1)$th row of Pascal's triangle.

Binomial	Pascal's Triangle in Binomial Expansion	Row
$(x + y)^0$	1	1
$(x + y)^1$	$1x \quad + \quad 1y$	2
$(x + y)^2$	$1x^2 \quad + \quad 2xy \quad + \quad 1y^2$	3
$(x + y)^3$	$1x^3 \quad + \quad 3x^2y \quad + \quad 3xy^2 \quad + \quad 1y^3$	4
$(x + y)^4$	$1x^4 \quad + \quad 4x^3y \quad + \quad 6x^2y^2 \quad + \quad 4xy^3 \quad + \quad 1y^4$	5

• You can also determine the coefficients represented in Pascal's triangle using combinations.

Pascal's Triangle	Combinations
$\begin{array}{ccccccccccc} & & & & & 1 & & & & & \\ & & & & 1 & & 1 & & & & \\ & & & 1 & & 2 & & 1 & & & \\ & & 1 & & 3 & & 3 & & 1 & & \\ & 1 & & 4 & & 6 & & 4 & & 1 & \\ 1 & & 5 & & 10 & & 10 & & 5 & & 1 \end{array}$	$\begin{array}{ccccccccccc} & & & & & _0C_0 & & & & & \\ & & & & _1C_0 & & _1C_1 & & & & \\ & & & _2C_0 & & _2C_1 & & _2C_2 & & & \\ & & _3C_0 & & _3C_1 & & _3C_2 & & _3C_3 & & \\ & _4C_0 & & _4C_1 & & _4C_2 & & _4C_3 & & _4C_4 & \\ _5C_0 & & _5C_1 & & _5C_2 & & _5C_3 & & _5C_4 & & _5C_5 \end{array}$

• Use the binomial theorem to expand any power of a binomial, $(x + y)^n$, where $n \in N$. Each term in the binomial expansion has the form $_nC_k(x)^{n-k}(y)^k$, where $k + 1$ is the term number. Thus, the general term of a binomial expansion is $t_{k+1} = {_nC_k}(x)^{n-k}(y)^k$.

• Important properties of the binomial expansion $(x + y)^n$ include the following:

  – Write binomial expansions in descending order of the exponent of the first term in the binomial.

  – The expansion contains $n + 1$ terms.

  – The number of objects, k, selected in the combination $_nC_k$ can be taken to match the number of factors of the second variable. That is, it is the same as the exponent on the second variable.

  – The sum of the exponents in any term of the expansion is n.

Working Example 1: Expand Binomials

a) Use Pascal's triangle to expand $(a + b)^7$.

b) Identify patterns in the expansion of $(a + b)^7$.

Solution

a) The coefficients for the terms of the expansion $(a + b)^7$ occur in the _____ row of Pascal's triangle.

The _____ row of Pascal's triangle is 1 7 21 35 35 21 7 1.

$(a + b)^7 =$

b) Some patterns are as follows:

i) There are _____ terms in the expansion of $(a + b)^7$.

ii) The powers of a _____ from _____ to _____ in successive terms of the expansion. *(increase or decrease)*

iii) The powers of b _____ from _____ to _____. *(increase or decrease)*

iv) Each term is of degree _____ (the _____ of the exponents for a and b is _____ for each term).

v) The coefficients are _____, and they begin with _____ and end with

_____.

> To see a similar example, refer to Example 1 on page 539 of *Pre-Calculus 12*.

Working Example 2: Use the Binomial Theorem

a) Use the binomial theorem to expand $(3a - 4b)^5$.

b) What is the third term in the expansion of $(5a^2 + 2)^6$?

c) In the expansion of $\left(a^3 - \dfrac{2}{a}\right)^7$, which term, in simplified form, contains a^5?

Solution

a) Since $n = 5$, write the binomial theorem for $(x + y)^5$.

$(x + y)^5 = {}_5C_0(x)^5(y)^0 +$ _____ $+$ _____ $+$ _____ $+$ _____ $+$ _____

Since it is necessary to expand $(3a - 4b)^5$, substitute $x =$ _____

and $y =$ _____ into the expression.

| What is the sign of y? |

$(3a - 4b)^5 = {}_5C_0($_____$)^5($_____$)^0 +$ _____ $+$ _____ $+$ _____

$+$ _____ $+$ _____

Now, simplify to get the final expansion.

b) The coefficients in the expansion of $(5a^2 + 2)^6$ involve the pattern

${}_6C_0,$ _____ , _____ , _____ , $\ldots$

The coefficient of the third term involves ${}_6C_2$.

In the general term, $t_{k+1} = {}_nC_k(x)^{n-k}(y)^k$, substitute

$x =$ _____ , $y =$ _____ , $n =$ _____ , and $k =$ _____ .

$t_{\square} =$

The third term in the expansion of $(5a^2 + 2)^6$ is _____ .

c) Determine the first three terms of the expanded binomial. Simplify the variable part of each term to find the pattern.

In the binomial expansion, substitute $x =$_____ , $y =$ _____ , and $n =$ _____ .

$\left(a^3 - \dfrac{2}{a}\right)^7 =$

The pattern shows that the exponents for a are decreasing by _____ in each successive

term. The next term contains _____ , the term following that contains _____ , and so

on. Therefore, the _____ term contains a^5.

> Refer to Example 2 on pages 540 and 541 of *Pre-Calculus 12* for a similar problem.

Check Your Understanding

Practise

1. Some rows from Pascal's triangle are shown. What is the next row in each case?

   a) 1   4   6   4   1

   b) 1   6   15   20   15   6   1

   c) 1   9   36   84   126   126   84   36   9   1

2. Express each row of Pascal's triangle using combinations. Leave each term in the form $_nC_r$.

   a) 1   3   3   1

   b) 1   5   10   10   5   1

   c) 1   6   15   20   15   6   1

3. Express each indicated term in the given row of Pascal's triangle as a combination. Leave your answers in factorial form.

   a) 1   4   6   **4**   1

   b) 1   7   21   **35**   35   21   7   1

   c) 1   9   36   84   126   126   **84**   36   9   1

4. How many terms are in the expansion of each expression?

   a) $(m - n)^7$ **b)** $(2x + 1)^6$

   c) $\left(\dfrac{y}{2} - y^2\right)^4$ **d)** $(a^3 + 2)^5$

5. Use Pascal's triangle to expand these binomials from #4.

   a) $(m - n)^7$

   b) $(2x + 1)^6$

   c) $(a^3 + 2)^5$

6. Use the binomial theorem to expand each of the following.

   a) $(x - 2)^6$

   b) $(a - 2b)^4$

   c) $(1 + x^2)^6$

Apply

7. Determine the simplified value of the specified term.

 a) the sixth term of $(a + b)^{10}$

 b) the tenth term of $(1 + x)^{13}$

 c) the fifth term of $\left(x^2 - \dfrac{1}{x}\right)^{10}$

 d) the third term of $\left(x^2 + \dfrac{x}{2}\right)^7$

 e) the middle term of $(2x - y)^8$

8. Expand and simplify.

 a) $\left(a - \dfrac{1}{a}\right)^5$

 b) $\left(x - \dfrac{2}{x^2}\right)^5$

9. Use the binomial theorem to determine the first four terms of each.

 a) $\left(2a - \dfrac{1}{a}\right)^9$

 b) $\left(2x - \dfrac{3}{x}\right)^8$

10. Express each expansion in the form $(a + b)^n$, where $n \in N$.

What do the patterns of the signs of the terms tell you about the sign of b?

a) $_5C_0x^5 - _5C_1x^4y + _5C_2x^3y^2 - _5C_3x^2y^3 + _5C_4xy^4 - _5C_5y^5$

$a =$ _____ , $b =$ _____ , and $n =$ _____ . Substitute into $(a + b)^n$:

b) $_6C_0x^6 - _6C_1(2x^5) + _6C_2(4x^4) - _6C_3(8x^3) + _6C_4(16x^2) - _6C_5(32x) + _6C_6(64)$

$a =$ _____ , $b =$ _____ , and $n =$ _____ . Substitute into $(a + b)^n$:

11. Determine the general term, in simplified form, in the expansion of $(a^2 + 1)^7$.

12. In the expansion of $\left(x - \frac{1}{x}\right)^6$, determine the term containing x^4.

13. Expand $(x^2 + 1)\left(x + \frac{1}{x}\right)^5$ and simplify. Use the binomial theorem.

Connect

14. Use the binomial theorem to determine the value of $(1.02)^9$, to four decimal places.

11.1 Permutations, pages 364–373

1. Evaluate each expression.

   a) $_{10}P_7$ **b)** $_7P_4$

2. In how many ways can you arrange all the letters of each word?

   a) province   **b)** Canada

3. Solve for the variable.

   a) $_nP_3 = 60$ **b)** $_7P_r = 42$

4. The number of different permutations using all of the letters of a word is given by $\frac{9!}{2!3!}$. What word could have this number of arrangements of its letters?

5. In how many ways can five girls and three boys be arranged in a row if

   a) a boy must be at each end of the row?

   b) the boys must be together?

   c) the girls must be together?

11.2 Combinations, pages 374–382

6. Decide whether each of the following is a combination or a permutation problem. Briefly explain why. You do not need to solve the problem.

   a) A *Reach for the Top* team has eight members. In how many ways can they be seated in a row?

   b) A *Reach for the Top* team has eight members. In how many ways can four be selected for a competition?

7. Describe the difference between $_9P_6$ and $_9C_6$.

8. Solve for n.

   a) $_nC_2 = 10$

   b) $_{n+1}C_{n-1} = 28$

9. From a deck of 52 cards, how many different four-card hands could be dealt that include a card from each suit?

10. A committee of students and teachers is being formed to study the issue of student parking. Fifteen staff members and 18 students have expressed an interest in serving on the committee. In how many ways can a five-person committee be formed if

    a) it must include two teachers?

    b) it must include at least two students and one teacher?

11.3 The Binomial Theorem, pages 383–389

11. Two rows from Pascal's triangle are shown. What is the next row in each case?

a) 1 1

b) 1 5 10 10 5 1

12. Express each row of Pascal's triangle using combinations. Leave each term in the form $_nC_r$.

a) 1 4 6 4 1

b) 1 8 28 56 70 56 28 8 1

13. State the number of terms in the expansion of each expression. Then, expand using Pascal's triangle.

a) $(2x + 3y)^4$

b) $(a^2 - 4)^5$

14. Use the binomial theorem to expand each of the following.

a) $\left(x + \dfrac{1}{x}\right)^4$

b) $\left(2x - \dfrac{1}{x}\right)^6$

15. Determine the simplified value of the specified term.

a) the fourth term of $(4 - 2a)^7$

b) the fifth term of $(a + b)^{25}$

Chapter 11 Skills Organizer

Complete the chart to summarize the concepts from this chapter.

	Permutations	Combinations	Binomial Theorem	Pascal's Triangle
Used For				
Related Definitions and Vocabulary				
Related Formulas				
Special Situations				
Examples				

Answers

Chapter 1

1.1 Horizontal and Vertical Translations, pages 1–8

1. a) $h = 10, k = 0$ b) $h = -2, k = 3$
   c) $h = 17, k = 13$ d) $h = -1, k = -7$
   e) $h = 0, k = 4$

2. a) $y + 5 = (x - 2)^2$ b) $y + 5 = |x - 2|$
   c) $y + 5 = \dfrac{1}{x - 2}, x \neq 2$

3. a) $(x, y) \rightarrow (x + 25, y)$; horizontal translation 25 units to the right
   b) $(x, y) \rightarrow (x, y - 50)$; vertical translation 50 units down
   c) $(x, y) \rightarrow (x - 20, y + 10)$; horizontal translation 20 units to the left and vertical translation 10 units up

4. a) $(x, y) \rightarrow (x - 2, y - 7)$

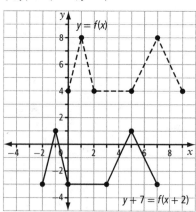

   b) $(x, y) \rightarrow (x + 5, y - 2)$

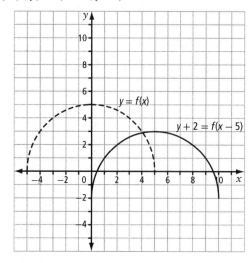

5. a) $h = 6, k = -4$ b) $(x, y) \rightarrow (x + 6, y - 4)$
   c) $y = (x - 6)^2 - 4$
   d)

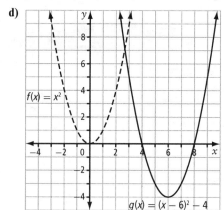

   e) $(0, 0), (6, -4)$; vertex has coordinates (h, k)
   f) domain of each function: $\{x \mid x \in \mathbb{R}\}$; range of $f(x)$: $\{y \mid y \geq 0, y \in \mathbb{R}\}$, range of $g(x)$: $\{y \mid y \geq -4, y \in \mathbb{R}\}$; in general, the range is $\{y \mid y \geq k, y \in \mathbb{R}\}$

6. a) $h = -5, k = 2$ b) $(x, y) \rightarrow (x - 5, y + 2)$
   c) $y = \dfrac{1}{x + 5} + 2$
   d)

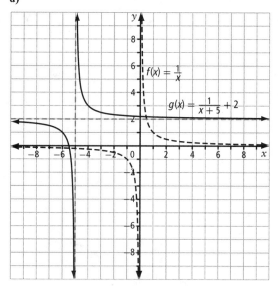

   e) For $f(x)$: domain $\{x \mid x \neq 0, x \in \mathbb{R}\}$, range $\{y \mid y \neq 0, y \in \mathbb{R}\}$, asymptotes $y = 0, x = 0$; For $g(x)$: domain $\{x \mid x \neq -5, x \in \mathbb{R}\}$, range $\{y \mid y \neq 2, y \in \mathbb{R}\}$, asymptotes $y = 2, x = -5$; restriction on the domain of $g(x)$ is $x \neq h$, restriction on the range of $g(x)$ is $y \neq k$, asymptotes are at $x = h$ and $y = k$

7.

Function	Horizontal Translation		Vertical Translation	
	to the right 1 unit	to the left 3 units	up 2 units	down 4 units
Quadratic $y = x^2$	$y = (x - 1)^2$ $(x, y) \rightarrow (x + 1, y)$ vertex at $(1, 0)$	$y = (x + 3)^2$ $(x, y) \rightarrow (x - 3, y)$ vertex at $(-3, 0)$	$y - 2 = x^2$ $(x, y) \rightarrow (x, y + 2)$ vertex at $(0, 2)$	$y + 4 = x^2$ $(x, y) \rightarrow (x, y - 4)$ vertex at $(0, -4)$
Absolute value $y = |x|$	$y = |x - 1|$ $(x, y) \rightarrow (x + 1, y)$ vertex at $(1, 0)$	$y = |x + 3|$ $(x, y) \rightarrow (x - 3, y)$ vertex at $(-3, 0)$	$y - 2 = |x|$ $(x, y) \rightarrow (x, y + 2)$ vertex at $(0, 2)$	$y + 4 = |x|$ $(x, y) \rightarrow (x, y - 4)$ vertex at $(0, -4)$
Reciprocal $y = \frac{1}{x}$	$y = \frac{1}{x - 1}$ $(x, y) \rightarrow (x + 1, y)$ vertical asymptote; $x = 1$; horizontal asymptote: $y = 0$	$y = \frac{1}{x + 3}$ $(x, y) \rightarrow (x - 3, y)$ vertical asymptote; $x = -3$; horizontal asymptote: $y = 0$	$y - 2 = \frac{1}{x}$ $(x, y) \rightarrow (x, y + 2)$ vertical asymptote; $x = 0$; horizontal asymptote: $y = 2$	$y + 4 = \frac{1}{x}$ $(x, y) \rightarrow (x, y - 4)$ vertical asymptote; $x = 0$; horizontal asymptote: $y = -4$
Any function $y = f(x)$	$y = f(x - 1)$ $(x, y) \rightarrow (x + 1, y)$	$y = f(x + 3)$ $(x, y) \rightarrow (x - 3, y)$	$y - 2 = f(x)$ $(x, y) \rightarrow (x, y + 2)$	$y + 4 = f(x)$ $(x, y) \rightarrow (x, y - 4)$

1.2 Reflections and Stretches, pages 9–17

1. a)

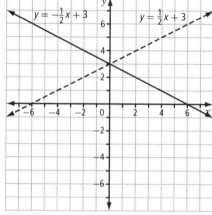

$y = -\frac{1}{2}x + 3$; same y-intercept, different x-intercepts, opposite slopes, same domain and range

b)

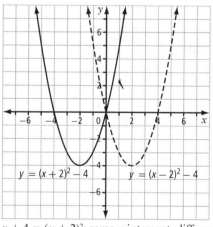

$y + 4 = (x + 2)^2$; same y-intercept, different x-intercepts, same domain and range, same shape, same orientation, vertex has opposite x-coordinate (h) but same y-coordinate (k)

c)

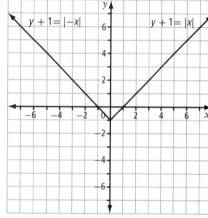

$y + 1 = |-x|$; reflection maps to the original graph

2. a)

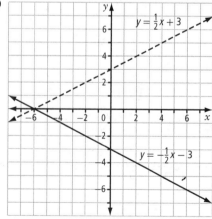

$y = -\frac{1}{2}x - 3$; same x-intercept, different y-intercepts, opposite slopes, same domain and range

b)

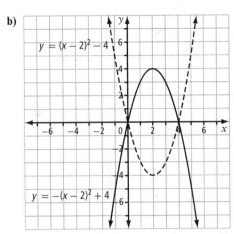

$y = (x-2)^2 - 4$

$y = -(x-2)^2 + 4$

$y - 4 = -(x-2)^2$; same y-intercept, same x-intercepts (zeros), different orientation, one has a maximum value and one has a minimum value, same shape, vertex has same x-coordinate (h) and opposite y-coordinate (k)

c)

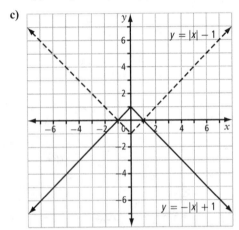

$y = |x| - 1$

$y = -|x| + 1$

$y - 1 = -|x|$; same x-intercepts (zeros), different y-intercepts, different orientation, one has a maximum value and one has a minimum value, same shape, vertex has same x-coordinate (h) and opposite y-coordinate (k)

3. a) $(x, y) \rightarrow \left(x, \frac{1}{4}y\right)$; $f(x) = \frac{1}{4}x^2$

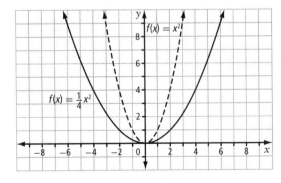

$f(x) = x^2$

$f(x) = \frac{1}{4}x^2$

b) $(x, y) \rightarrow (2x, y)$; $f(x) = \left(\frac{1}{2}x\right)^2$

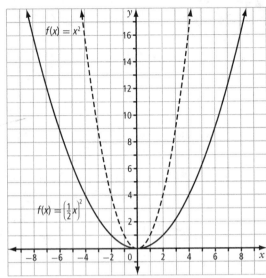

$f(x) = x^2$

$f(x) = \left(\frac{1}{2}x\right)^2$

4. a) $\left(\frac{1}{2}x\right)^2 = \left(\frac{1}{2}\right)^2 (x)^2 = \frac{1}{4}x^2$

b) Example: Given $f(x) = x^2$, any horizontal stretch by a factor of p is equivalent to a vertical stretch by a factor of $\frac{1}{p^2}$.

5. a) $y = 2f(x)$ **b)** $y = -f\left(\frac{1}{2}x\right)$ **c)** $y = f(-2x)$

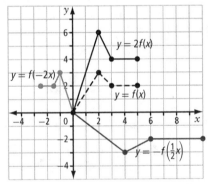

$y = 2f(x)$

$y = f(-2x)$

$y = f(x)$

$y = -f\left(\frac{1}{2}x\right)$

6. Answers may vary.

1.3 Combining Transformations, pages 18–25

1. Steps i) and ii) may be reversed and the answer will still be correct.

a) i) reflection in the y-axis, ii) vertical stretch by a factor of 4, iii) translation 5 units down

b) i) horizontal stretch by a factor of $\frac{1}{2}$, ii) reflection in the x-axis, iii) translation 7 units to the left

c) i) horizontal stretch by a factor of 4, ii) vertical stretch by a factor of 1.75, iii) translation 1.5 units to the right

d) i) horizontal stretch by a factor of $\frac{1}{3}$ and reflection in the y-axis, ii) vertical stretch by a factor of $\frac{1}{2}$ and reflection in the x-axis, iii) translation 3 units up and 1 unit to the left

2. a) $y + 7 = -f\left(\frac{1}{6}x\right)$

   b) $y = \frac{1}{2}|-(x - 3)|$

   c) $y + 4 = -\frac{1}{9}(x - 10)^2$ or $y + 4 = -\left[\frac{1}{3}(x - 10)\right]^2$

3. a) $(6, 6)$

   b) $(-11, -10)$

   c) $(18, 30)$

4. $(3, -12)$, $(-14, 8)$, and $(24, -24)$

5. a) i) horizontal stretch by a factor of $\frac{1}{2}$, ii) reflection in the x-axis, iii) translation 2 units down

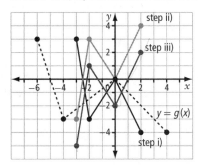

   b) i) horizontal stretch by a factor of $\frac{1}{4}$, ii) reflection in the y-axis, iii) translation 3 units to the right

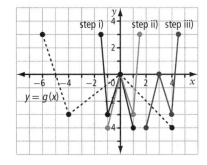

6. a) $y = -2|x + 6| - 3$

   b)

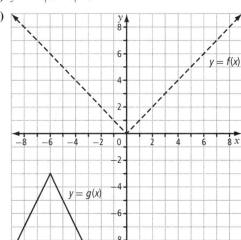

7. a) $y = -\dfrac{1}{\frac{1}{4}(x - 4)} - 1$ or $y = -\dfrac{4}{x - 4} - 1$

   b)

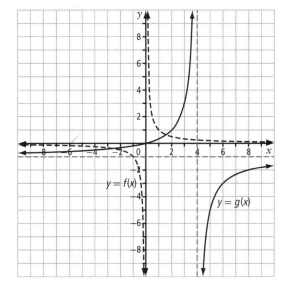

8. $y - 7 = -2f(x + 5)$

9. $y = 2f\left(-\frac{1}{2}x\right)$

10. $y = f(-2x) + 3$

11. Answers may vary.

1.4 Inverse of a Relation, pages 26–34

1. a)

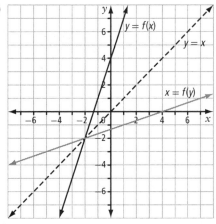

The inverse of $f(x)$ is a function; invariant point at $(-2, -2)$.

b)

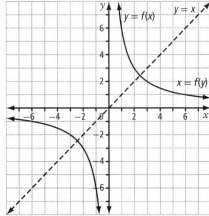

The inverse of $f(x)$ is not a function.

c)

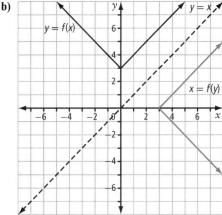

The inverse of $f(x)$ is a function; invariant points at approximately $(2.5, 2.5)$ and $(-2.5, -2.5)$.

d)

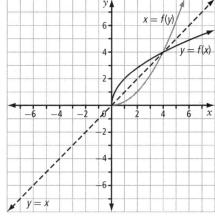

The inverse of $f(x)$ is a function; invariant points at $(0, 0)$ and $(4, 4)$.

e)

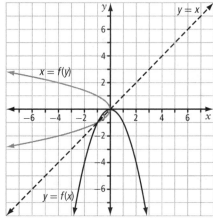

The inverse of $f(x)$ is not a function; invariant points at $(-1, -1)$ and $(0, 0)$.

f)

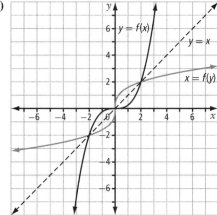

The inverse of $f(x)$ is a function; invariant points at $(-2, -2)$, $(0, 0)$, and $(2, 2)$.

2. a) $f^{-1}(x) = x + 4$ **b)** $f^{-1}(x) = -\frac{1}{6}x - \frac{1}{3}$

c) $f^{-1}(x) = \frac{5}{3}x + 5$ **d)** $f^{-1}(x) = 2x - 6$

3. Examples: **a)** $\{x \mid x \geq 2, x \in R\}$ or $\{x \mid x \leq 2, x \in R\}$

b) $\{x \mid x \geq -4, x \in R\}$ or $\{x \mid x \leq -4, x \in R\}$

4. a) For $f(x) = -x^2 + 6$, $x \geq 0$, the inverse is
$f^{-1}(x) = \sqrt{-(x - 6)}$. For $f(x) = -x^2 + 6$, $x \leq 0$,
the inverse is $f^{-1}(x) = -\sqrt{-(x - 6)}$.

b) For $f(x) = \frac{1}{2}x^2 + 4$, $x \geq 0$, the inverse is
$f^{-1}(x) = \sqrt{2(x - 4)}$. For $f(x) = \frac{1}{2}x^2 + 4$, $x \leq 0$, the
inverse is $f^{-1}(x) = -\sqrt{2(x - 4)}$.

5. $y = \pm\sqrt{x + 2} - 3$

6. a) $42 < x < 105$

b) $f^{-1}(x) = \sqrt{\dfrac{x}{0.01634}} + 26.643$, where $x = $ CRL,
in millimetres

c) 14.3 weeks

7. Answers may vary.

Chapter 1 Review, pages 35–37

1. a) $y + 3 = |x - 5|$ **b)** $y - 1 = |x + 4|$

2. a)

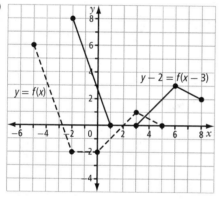

b)

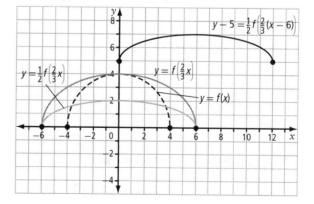

3. a) $(12, 5)$ **b)** $(-3, -5)$ **c)** $(36, -10)$

4. a) reflection in the y-axis and reflection in the x-axis

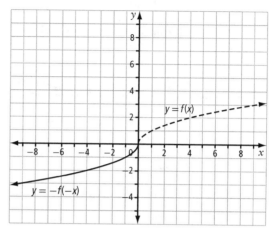

b) horizontal stretch by a factor of $\frac{1}{2}$, vertical
stretch by a factor of 3

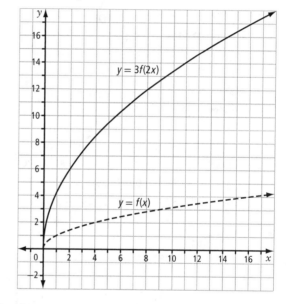

5. a)

b)

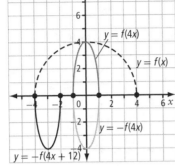

6. a) $f^{-1}(x) = -2x + 10$

   b) Example: restricted domain of $f(x)$:
$$\{x \mid x \geq 1, x \in \mathrm{R}\}, f^{-1}(x) = \sqrt{\frac{1}{2}x} + 1$$

Chapter 2

2.1 Radical Functions and Transformations, pages 39–46

1. a) vertical stretch by a factor of 3, reflection in the y-axis, translation 4 units left and 2 units down; domain: $\{x \mid x \leq -4, x \in \mathrm{R}\}$; range: $\{y \mid y \geq -2, y \in \mathrm{R}\}$

   b) vertical stretch by a factor of 2, reflection in the x-axis, horizontal stretch by a factor of $\frac{1}{4}$, translation of 3 units right and 5 units up; domain: $\{x \mid x \geq 3, x \in \mathrm{R}\}$; range: $\{y \mid y \leq 5, y \in \mathrm{R}\}$

   c) vertical stretch by a factor of 4, horizontal stretch by a factor of $\frac{1}{5}$, translation of 1 unit left and 4 units down; domain: $\{x \mid x \geq -1, x \in \mathrm{R}\}$; range: $\{y \mid y \geq -4, y \in \mathrm{R}\}$

   d) horizontal stretch by a factor of $\frac{1}{3}$, reflection in the x-axis and y-axis, translation 2 units left; domain: $\{x \mid x \leq -2, x \in \mathrm{R}\}$; range: $\{y \mid y \leq 0, y \in \mathrm{R}\}$

2. a) $y = -3\sqrt{x-4} - 2$

   b) $y = \sqrt{-4(x+5)} + 3$

   c) $y = 2\sqrt{\frac{1}{3}(x+4)} + 1$

   d) $y = -3\sqrt{-2(x+6)}$

3. a) B   **b)** C   **c)** D   **d)** A

4. a)

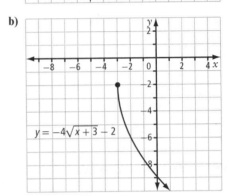

b)

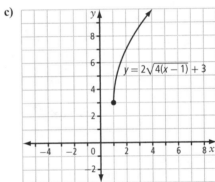

c)

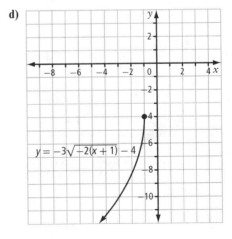

d)

5. a) $y = 3\sqrt{(x-4)} + 1$ or $y = \sqrt{9(x-4)} + 1$

b) $y = 2\sqrt{(x+3)} - 2$ or $y = \sqrt{4(x+3)} - 2$

c) $y = -4\sqrt{x-2} + 3$ or $y = -\sqrt{16(x-2)} + 3$

d) $y = -2\sqrt{x+3} - 4$ or $y = -\sqrt{4(x+3)} - 4$

6. a) vertical stretch by a factor of $\frac{1}{2}$ and horizontal stretch by a factor of $\frac{1}{6}$

b) $y = \frac{\sqrt{6}}{2}\sqrt{x}$; vertical stretch by a factor of $\frac{\sqrt{6}}{2}$

c) $y = \sqrt{\frac{3}{2}x}$; horizontal stretch by a factor of $\frac{2}{3}$

7. Yes. You only need to find the translations, h and k, and either the vertical or the horizontal stretch. Example: $y = 3\sqrt{(x-2)} - 3$ and $y = \sqrt{9(x-2)} - 3$ are the same function, one with a vertical stretch and the other with a horizontal stretch.

2.2 Square Root of a Function, pages 47–54

1. a) $(3, 0)$ **b)** $(-5, 5)$ **c)** $(9, 3.9)$

d) This is not possible because you cannot take the square root of a negative number.

2. a)

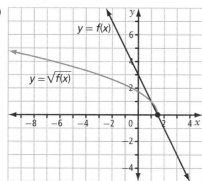

b)

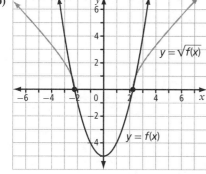

3. a) C   **b)** A   **c)** D   **d)** B

4. a) $f(x)$: domain: $\{x \mid x \in \mathbb{R}\}$; range: $\{y \mid y \in \mathbb{R}\}$
$\sqrt{f(x)}$: domain: $\{x \mid x \geq 2, x \in \mathbb{R}\}$;
range: $\{y \mid y \geq 0, y \in \mathbb{R}\}$

b) $f(x)$: domain: $\{x \mid x \in \mathbb{R}\}$;
range: $\{y \mid y \geq 2, y \in \mathbb{R}\}$
$\sqrt{f(x)}$: domain: $\{x \mid x \in \mathbb{R}\}$;
range: $\{y \mid y \geq \sqrt{2}, y \in \mathbb{R}\}$

c) $f(x)$: domain: $\{x \mid x \in \mathbb{R}\}$;
range: $\{y \mid y \geq -4, y \in \mathbb{R}\}$
$\sqrt{f(x)}$: domain: $\{x \mid x \leq -2 \text{ and } x \geq 2, x \in \mathbb{R}\}$;
range: $\{y \mid y \geq 0, y \in \mathbb{R}\}$

d) $f(x)$: domain: $\{x \mid x \in \mathbb{R}\}$;
range: $\{y \mid y \leq 3, y \in \mathbb{R}\}$
$\sqrt{f(x)}$: domain: $\{x \mid -\sqrt{3} \leq x \leq \sqrt{3}, x \in \mathbb{R}\}$;
range: $\{y \mid 0 \leq y \leq \sqrt{3}, y \in \mathbb{R}\}$

5. a)

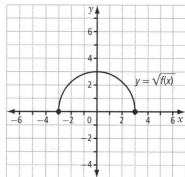

b)

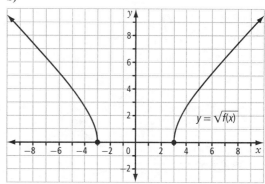

6. The values of 0 and 1 are unchanged when the square root is taken. That is, $1 = \sqrt{1}$ and $0 = \sqrt{0}$.

7. a) When you graph the square root of a function, the graph of $y = \sqrt{f(x)}$ is always above the graph of $y = f(x)$ between the invariant points when $f(x) = 0$ and $f(x) = 1$. This means that the value of $y = \sqrt{f(x)}$ is greater than $y = f(x)$ for the corresponding x-values.

b) Example: He could change the window settings so that the focus is more on the x-values between the invariant points. He could also use the table function on his calculator to create a table of values.

c)
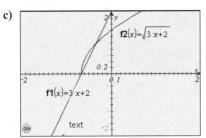

2.3 Solving Radical Equations Graphically, pages 55–62

1. a) $x = 22$ **b)** $x = 43$

     c) $x = 20$ **d)** $x = 3$

2. a) $x = 3$

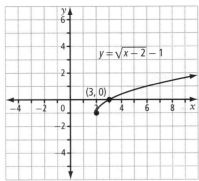

b) $x = 1$

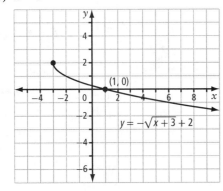

c) $x = -1$

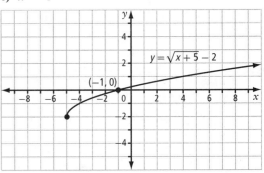

d) no solution

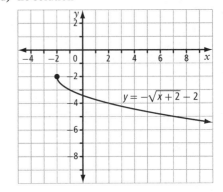

3. a) $x \geq 2$; $x = 2$

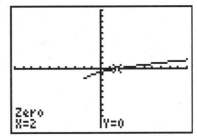

b) $x \geq 5$; $x = 14$

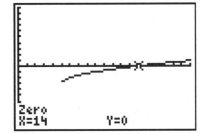

c) $x \le 1; x = -15$

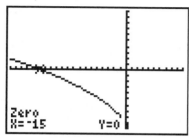

d) $x \le 0.25; x = -2$

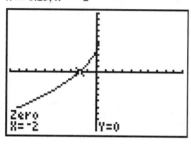

4. a) $x \ge -10; x = 6$ **b)** $x \le -2; x = -2$

    c) $x \le 4; x = 4$ **d)** $x \le 5.2; x = 5$

5. a) In solving the equation algebraically you obtain
$x = 7$, but when you substitute $x = 7$ into the
original equation it does not satisfy the equation.

    b) If you graph a single function, $y = \sqrt{2x - 5} + 3$,
there is no x-intercept. If you graph two functions,
$y = \sqrt{2x - 5} + 4$ and $y = 1$, there is no point of
intersection.

6. a) The graph of $y = \sqrt{x}$ is translated 4 units right.

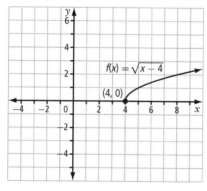

$x = 4$

b) The graph of $y = \sqrt{x}$ is translated 3 units down.

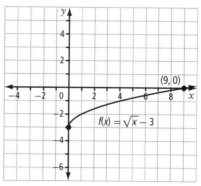

$x = 9$

c) The graph of $y = \sqrt{x}$ is reflected in the x-axis,
and translated 1 unit up.

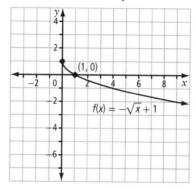

$x = 1$

d) The graph of $y = \sqrt{x}$ is reflected in the y-axis, and
then translated 3 units left.

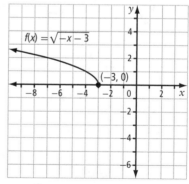

$x = -3$

7. $f(x) = \sqrt{2x} - 4$

8. Her error is that she squared each term. The correct solution is

$$\sqrt{3x-1} - 4 = 1$$
$$\sqrt{3x-1} = 5$$
$$(\sqrt{3x-1})^2 = 5^2$$
$$3x - 1 = 25$$
$$3x = 26$$
$$x = 8\tfrac{2}{3}$$

9. a) It has no solution because $\sqrt{2x+7} \neq -2$.

   b) Example: $\sqrt{4x+10} + 6 = 2$.

Chapter 2 Review, pages 63–64

1. a) vertical stretch by a factor of 4, reflection in the y-axis, and a translation of 5 units right and 1 unit up

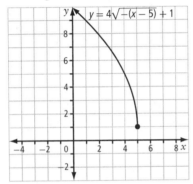

   b) vertical stretch by a factor of 3, reflection in the x-axis, horizontal stretch by a factor of 0.5, and a translation of 1 unit left and 3 units down

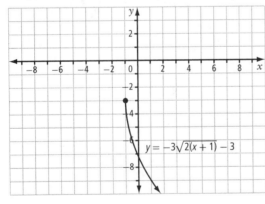

2. a) $y = -4\sqrt{x+5} + 3$; domain: $\{x \mid x \geq -5, x \in R\}$; range: $\{y \mid y \leq 3, y \in R\}$

   b) $y = 3\sqrt{x-2} - 5$; domain: $\{x \mid x \geq 2, x \in R\}$; range: $\{y \mid y \geq -5, y \in R\}$

3. a) domain: $\{x \mid x \geq 0.25, x \in R\}$; range: $\{y \mid y \geq 0, y \in R\}$

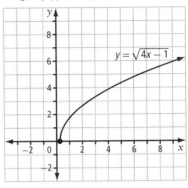

   b) domain: $\{x \mid x \leq -3 \text{ and } x \geq 3, x \in R\}$; range: $\{y \mid y \geq 0, y \in R\}$

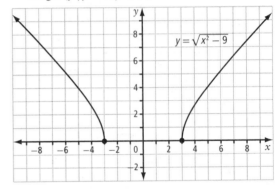

4. a) $x = 11$ **b)** $x = 6$

5. a) $x \geq 1$; $x = 10$

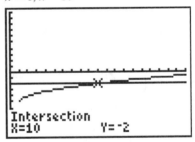

   b) $x \geq -3$; no solution

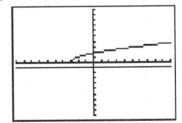

Chapter 3

3.1 Characteristics of Polynomial Functions, pages 66–77

1. a) Yes; polynomial function of degree 4

b) No; exponential function

c) Yes; polynomial function of degree 0

d) No; function has a variable with a negative exponent

2.

Polynomial Function	Degree	Type	Leading Coefficient	Constant Term
a) $f(x) = 6x^3 - 5x^2 + 2x - 8$	3	Cubic	6	−8
b) $y = -2x^5 + 5x^3 + x^2 + 1$	5	Quintic	−2	1
c) $g(x) = x^3 - 7x^4$	4	Quartic	−7	0
d) $p(x) = 10x - 9$	1	Linear	10	−9
e) $y = -0.5x^2 + 4x + 3$	2	Quadratic	−0.5	3
f) $h(x) = 3x^4 - 8x^3 + x^2 + 2$	4	Quartic	3	2
g) $y = -5$	0	Constant	0	−5

3. a) odd degree; negative leading coefficient; 2 x-intercepts; domain: $\{x \mid x \in \mathbb{R}\}$; range: $\{y \mid y \in \mathbb{R}\}$

b) even degree; positive leading coefficient; 2 x-intercepts; domain: $\{x \mid x \in \mathbb{R}\}$; range: $\{y \mid y \geq -5, y \in \mathbb{R}\}$

c) odd degree; positive leading coefficient; 5 x-intercepts; domain: $\{x \mid x \in \mathbb{R}\}$; range: $\{y \mid y \in \mathbb{R}\}$

4. a) degree 5; positive leading coefficient; extends from quadrant III to I; maximum of 5 x-intercepts; y-intercept of 2

b) degree 5; negative leading coefficient; extends from quadrant II to IV; maximum of 5 x-intercepts; y-intercept of 0

c) degree 3; negative leading coefficient; extends from quadrant II to IV; maximum of 3 x-intercepts; y-intercept of −6

d) degree 5; positive leading coefficient; extends from quadrant III to I; maximum of 5 x-intercepts; y-intercept of 3

e) degree 4; positive leading coefficient; opens upward; maximum of 4 x-intercepts; y-intercept of −1

5. No. Example: $y = 5x^3 + x + 1$ extends from quadrant III to I

6. a) degree 4

b) leading coefficient: 1.25; constant: −3200; The constant represents the initial cost.

c) degree 4; positive leading coefficient; opens upward

d) domain: $\{x \mid x \geq 0, x \in \mathbb{R}\}$; it is impossible to have negative skateboard sales

e) The positive x-intercept represents the break-even point.

f) $P(12) = 34\ 720$. The profit from the sale of 1200 skateboards is $34 720.

7. a) 3

b) leading coefficient: 1; constant: 5; The constant represents the initial distance from the tree.

c) degree 3; positive leading coefficient; extends from quadrant III to quadrant I

d) domain: $\{t \mid t \geq 0, t \in \mathbb{R}\}$; time cannot be negative

e) $D(7) = 12$; 12 m

f)

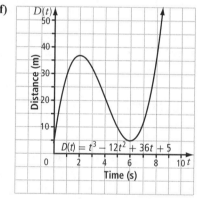

8. a) degree 4; positive leading coefficient; opens upward; extends from quadrant II to I; domain: $\{x \mid x \in \mathbb{R}\}$; range: $\{y \mid y \geq 11\ 738, y \in \mathbb{R}\}$; The range for the time period $\{x \mid 0 \leq x \leq 15, x \in \mathbb{R}\}$ that the population model can be used is $\{y \mid 12\ 000 \leq y \leq 298\ 500, y \in \mathbb{R}\}$; no x-intercepts, y-intercept: 12 000

b) 12 000

c) 68 000

d) approximately 13 years from now

9. Examples:

a)

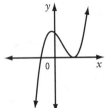

b)

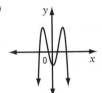

c)

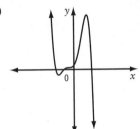

d)

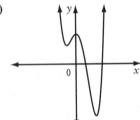

3.2 The Remainder Theorem, pages 78–83

1. a) $\dfrac{x^3 + 3x^2 - 2x + 5}{x + 1} = x^2 + 2x - 4 + \dfrac{9}{x + 1}$

b) $x \neq -1$

c) $(x + 1)(x^2 + 2x - 4) + 9 = x^3 + 3x^2 - 2x + 5$

2. a) $Q(x) = 2x - 7$, $R = 26$

b) $Q(x) = x^2 - 4x + 15$, $R = -70$

c) $Q(x) = 3x^3 + 2x^2 - 6$, $R = 1$

d) $Q(x) = -4x^3 - 12x^2 - 36x - 97$, $R = -298$

3. a) $\dfrac{2x^2 - x + 5}{x + 3} = 2x - 7 + \dfrac{26}{x + 3}$, $x \neq -3$

b) $\dfrac{x^3 - x - 10}{x + 4} = x^2 - 4x + 15 - \dfrac{70}{x + 4}$, $x \neq -4$

c) $\dfrac{3x^4 + 2x^3 - 6x + 1}{x} = 3x^3 + 2x - 6 + \dfrac{1}{x}$, $x \neq 0$

d) $\dfrac{-4x^4 + 11x - 7}{x - 3} = -4x^3 - 12x^2 - 36x - 97 - \dfrac{298}{x - 3}$, $x \neq 3$

4. a) -36 **b)** 8

5. a) 22 **b)** -9 **c)** -2 **d)** -4

6. a) $k = 1$ **b)** $k = -1$ **c)** $k = -2$ **d)** $k = 2$

7. $m = 3$

8. $x - 2$, $3x + 1$

9. a) $(x - a)$ is a factor of $bx^3 + cx^2 + dx + e$.

b) $e + ad + a^2c + a^3b$

3.3 The Factor Theorem, pages 84–90

1. a) $x - 2$ **b)** $x + 4$ **c)** $x - b$ **d)** $x + d$

2. a) Yes **b)** Yes **c)** No **d)** Yes

3. a) No **b)** Yes **c)** Yes **d)** Yes

4. a) $\pm 1, \pm 2, \pm 4, \pm 8, \pm 16$

b) $\pm 1, \pm 2, \pm 3, \pm 4, \pm 6, \pm 12$

c) $\pm 1, \pm 2, \pm 4, \pm 8, \pm 16, \pm 32$

d) $\pm 1, \pm 2, \pm 3, \pm 6, \pm 9, \pm 18$

5. a) $(x - 2)(x + 2)(x - 1)$

b) $(x - 2)^2(x + 2)$

c) $(x + 1)^3$

d) $(x - 1)(x + 2)(x^2 + x + 1)$

6. a) $(x + 2)(x - 3)(x + 3)$

b) $(2x + 1)(x - 1)(2x - 3)$

c) $(x - 2)(2x + 5)(3x - 1)$

d) $(x + 1)^2(x + 3)(x - 4)$

7. a) $k = 9$ **b)** $k = 3$

8. $x - 1$, $x + 3$, and $x + 5$

9. $V(x) = (x - 1)(x + 2)(3x - 1)$

10. Example: Start by using the integral zero theorem to check for a first possible integer value. Apply the factor theorem using the value found from the integral zero theorem. Use division to determine the remaining factor. Repeat the process until all factors are found.

3.4 Equations and Graphs of Polynomials Functions, pages 91–102

1. **a)** $x = 0, -2, \frac{1}{2}$

   b) $x = -1, 3, 5$

   c) $x = 2$

2. **a)** $f(x) = -2(x-1)(x+1)(x-3); -1, 1, 3$

   b) $f(x) = 0.5(x-2)^2(x+1)(x+3); -1, -3, 2$

   c) $f(x) = -0.2(x-2)^3(x+4)^2; -4, 2$

3. **a)** −4 and 5; positive for $-4 < x < 5$; negative for $x < -4$ and $x > 5$; −4 (multiplicity 1) and 5 (multiplicity 3); the function changes sign at both, but is flatter at $x = 5$

   b) −6 and 3; positive for $-6 < x < 3$ and $x > 3$; negative for $x < -6$; −6 (multiplicity 3) and 3 (multiplicity 2); the function changes sign at $x = -6$, but not at $x = 3$

   c) −4, −1, and 3; positive for $x < -4$, $-4 < x < -1$, and $x > 3$; negative for $-1 < x < 3$; −4 (multiplicity 2), −1 (multiplicity 1), and 3 (multiplicity 1); the function changes sign at $x = -1$ and at $x = 3$, but not at $x = -4$

4. **a)** x-intercepts: −2, 0.5, 3 (all of multiplicity 1); y-intercept: −6

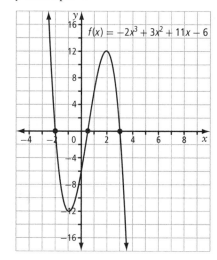

b) x-intercepts: −2 (multiplicity 3) and 1 (multiplicity 1); y-intercept: −8

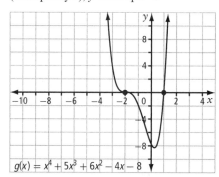

$g(x) = x^4 + 5x^3 + 6x^2 - 4x - 8$

5. **a)** $f(x) = (x+4)(x-1)(x+2)$

   b) $f(x) = -(2x+1)(x-3)(x+2)$

   c) $f(x) = -0.25(x+2)^2(x-3)^3$

6. **a)** $a = \frac{1}{2}$; vertical stretch by a factor of $\frac{1}{2}$

   $b = 3$; horizontal stretch by a factor of $\frac{1}{3}$

   $h = -4$; translation of 4 units left

   $k = -5$; translation of 5 units down

   b) domain: $\{x \mid x \in \mathbb{R}\}$; range: $\{y \mid y \in \mathbb{R}\}$

7. **a)** $y = -\frac{3}{4}(x-2)^3(x+5)$

   b) $y = (x+1)^2(x-3)(x+2)^2$

8. 26 ft by 46 ft

9. h and k; these parameters represent the horizontal translation and the vertical translation, respectively, of the graph and do not change its shape or orientation.

Chapter 3 Review, pages 103–107

1.

Polynomial Function	Degree	Type	Leading Coefficient	Constant Term
a) $f(x) = -2x^4$ $-x^3 + 3x - 7$	4	Quartic	−2	−7
b) $y = 3x^5 + 2x^4$ $-x^3 + 3$	5	Quintic	3	3
c) $g(x) = 0.5x^3 - 8x^2$	3	Cubic	0.5	0
d) $p(x) = 10$	0	Constant	0	10

2. **a)** even degree; negative leading coefficient; 2 x-intercepts; domain: $\{x \mid x \in \mathbb{R}\}$; range: $\{y \mid y \le 19, y \in \mathbb{R}\}$

   b) odd degree; positive leading coefficient; 3 x-intercepts; domain: $\{x \mid x \in \mathbb{R}\}$; range: $\{y \mid y \in \mathbb{R}\}$

3. a) degree 3

b) leading coefficient: 0.002; constant: 0; The constant represents the distance that the boat is from the shore at time 0 s (the initial position of the boat).

c) degree: 3; positive leading coefficient; extends from quadrant III to I

d) domain: $\{t \mid t \geq 0, t \in \mathbb{R}\}$; it is impossible to have negative time

e) When $t = 15$, $d(15) = 22.5$. After 15 s, the boat is 22.5 m from the shore.

f)

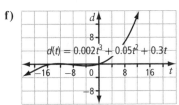

$d(t) = 0.002t^3 + 0.05t^2 + 0.3t$

4. a) $\dfrac{5x^3 - 7x^2 - x + 6}{x - 1} = 5x^2 - 2x - 3 + \dfrac{3}{x - 1}$

b) $x \neq 1$

c) $(x - 1)(5x^2 - 2x - 3) + 3 = 5x^3 - 7x^2 - x + 6$

5. a) $R = 9$ **b)** $R = 15$

c) $R = 41$ **d)** $R = 595$

6. a) $m = 4$ **b)** 28

7. $P(x) = x^3 + 2x^2 - 15x + 10$

8. a) $x - 7$ **b)** $x + 6$ **c)** $x - c$

9. a) Yes   **b)** No

10. a) $\pm 1, \pm 3, \pm 9, \pm 27$

b) $\pm 1, \pm 2, \pm 3, \pm 4, \pm 6, \pm 9, \pm 12, \pm 18, \pm 36$

11. a) $(x - 3)(x - 2)(x + 1)$

b) $(x - 4)(x + 2)(3x + 1)$

c) $(x - 3)(x - 1)(x + 6)(5x + 2)$

d) $x(x - 2)(x + 2)(2x + 5)$

12. $x - 1$, $x + 2$, and $5x + 2$

13. a) degree 5; negative leading coefficient; -3 (multiplicity 2) and 1 (multiplicity 3); the function changes sign at $x = 1$, but not at $x = -3$; positive for $x < -3$ and $-3 < x < 1$; negative for $x > 1$; $f(x) = -0.25(x + 3)^2(x - 1)^3$

b) degree 4; positive leading coefficient; -2 (multiplicity 1), -0.5 (multiplicity 1), and 2 (multiplicity 2); the function changes sign at $x = -2$ and at $x = -0.5$, but not at $x = 2$; positive for $x < -2$, $-0.5 < x < 2$, and $x > 2$; negative for $-2 < x < -0.5$; $f(x) = 0.5(x + 2)(2x + 1)(x - 2)^2$

14. a) $a = -2$; vertical stretch by a factor of 2 and reflection in the x-axis

$b = \dfrac{1}{3}$; horizontal stretch by a factor of 3

$h = 1$; translation of 1 unit to the right

$k = 4$; translation of 4 units up

b) domain: $\{x \mid x \in \mathbb{R}\}$; range: $\{y \mid y \in \mathbb{R}\}$

15. $y = -3(x + 2)^2(x - 3)$

Chapter 4

4.1 Angles and Angle Measure, pages 109–119

1. a) $\dfrac{\pi}{3}$

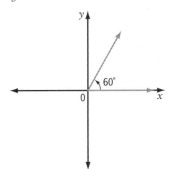

b) $\dfrac{7\pi}{4}$

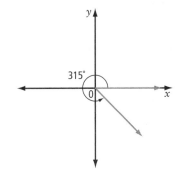

c) $-\dfrac{7\pi}{6}$

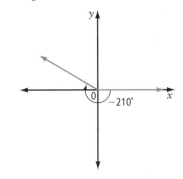

d) $\dfrac{10\pi}{3}$

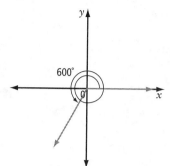

b) 240°

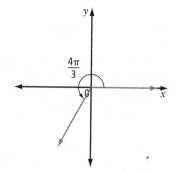

2. a) 1.76

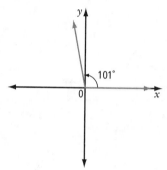

c) −40°

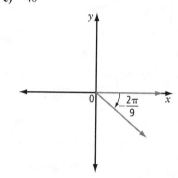

b) 1.00

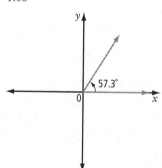

d) 114.59°

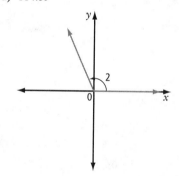

3. a) 90°

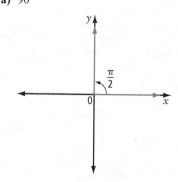

4. Examples: **a)** −11°, 709° **b)** −127°, 233°

c) $\dfrac{8\pi}{3}, -\dfrac{4\pi}{3}$ **d)** $\dfrac{\pi}{4}, -\dfrac{7\pi}{4}$

5. a) −465°, −105°, 615°; 255° ± 360°n, $n \in \mathrm{N}$

b) −3π, −π, 3π; π ± 2πn, $n \in \mathrm{N}$

c) $-\dfrac{7\pi}{6}, \dfrac{17\pi}{6}, \dfrac{29\pi}{6}; \dfrac{5\pi}{6} \pm 2\pi n$, $n \in \mathrm{N}$

6. a) 41.89 cm **b)** 51.05 mm

7. a) Example: Arc length, $a = \theta r$, is dependent on the radius of the circle. For a given central angle, θ, as the radius increases or decreases, the arc length also increases or decreases. Angular velocity, $\omega = \frac{\theta}{t}$, is independent of the radius of the circle. The angular velocity does not change as the radius of the circle increases or decreases.

b) $\frac{\pi}{10}$ or 0.31 radians/min; $\frac{33\pi}{200}$ or 0.52 m/s

c) 39π or 122.5 m

d) approximately 3706 km/h

8. Angles in first rotation:

0°, 0 radians; 30°, $\frac{\pi}{6}$ radians; 45°, $\frac{\pi}{4}$ radians; 60°, $\frac{\pi}{3}$ radians; 90°, $\frac{\pi}{2}$ radians; 120°, $\frac{2\pi}{3}$ radians; 135°, $\frac{3\pi}{4}$ radians; 150°, $\frac{5\pi}{6}$ radians; 180°, π radians; 210°, $\frac{7\pi}{6}$ radians; 225°, $\frac{5\pi}{4}$ radians; 240°, $\frac{4\pi}{3}$ radians; 270°, $\frac{3\pi}{2}$ radians; 300°, $\frac{5\pi}{3}$ radians; 315°, $\frac{7\pi}{4}$ radians; 330°, $\frac{11\pi}{6}$ radians

Angles in second rotation:

360°, 2π radians; 390°, $\frac{13\pi}{6}$ radians; 405°, $\frac{9\pi}{4}$ radians; 420°, $\frac{7\pi}{3}$ radians; 450°, $\frac{5\pi}{2}$ radians; 480°, $\frac{8\pi}{3}$ radians; 495°, $\frac{11\pi}{4}$ radians; 510°, $\frac{17\pi}{6}$ radians; 540°, 3π radians; 570°, $\frac{19\pi}{6}$ radians; 585°, $\frac{13\pi}{4}$ radians; 600°, $\frac{10\pi}{3}$ radians; 630°, $\frac{7\pi}{2}$ radians; 660°, $\frac{11\pi}{3}$ radians; 675°, $\frac{15\pi}{4}$ radians; 690°, $\frac{23\pi}{6}$ radians

4.2 The Unit Circle, pages 120–128

1. a) $x^2 + y^2 = 625$ **b)** $x^2 + y^2 = 1.21$

2. a) Yes **b)** Yes **c)** No

3. a) $-\frac{12}{13}$

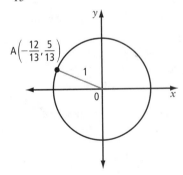

b) $-\frac{\sqrt{35}}{6}$

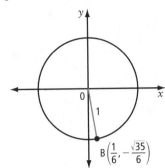

c) $-\frac{\sqrt{3}}{2}$

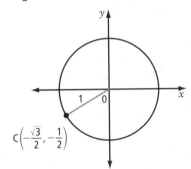

4. a) $(0, 1)$ **b)** $(1, 0)$

c) $\left(-\frac{1}{2}, \frac{\sqrt{3}}{2}\right)$ **d)** $\left(-\frac{1}{\sqrt{2}}, -\frac{1}{\sqrt{2}}\right)$

e) $\left(\frac{1}{\sqrt{2}}, -\frac{1}{\sqrt{2}}\right)$ **f)** $\left(\frac{\sqrt{3}}{2}, -\frac{1}{2}\right)$

5. a) π **b)** $\frac{\pi}{6}$

c) $\frac{3\pi}{4}$ **d)** $\frac{4\pi}{3}$

6. a) $\frac{\pi}{2}$ **b)** $\frac{5\pi}{6}$

7. a) $x^2 + y^2 = 2.25 \times 10^{16}$

b) $x^2 + y^2 = 1$

c) Mars has a larger circle with radius 1.38.

d) 2.76π or 8.67 radians; 503.7 days

8. $P(0) = (1, 0)$; $P\left(\frac{\pi}{6}\right) = \left(\frac{\sqrt{3}}{2}, \frac{1}{2}\right)$; $P\left(\frac{\pi}{4}\right) = \left(\frac{1}{\sqrt{2}}, \frac{1}{\sqrt{2}}\right)$;

$P\left(\frac{\pi}{3}\right) = \left(\frac{1}{2}, \frac{\sqrt{3}}{2}\right)$; $P\left(\frac{\pi}{2}\right) = (0, 1)$;

$P\left(\frac{2\pi}{3}\right) = \left(-\frac{1}{2}, \frac{\sqrt{3}}{2}\right)$; $P\left(\frac{3\pi}{4}\right) = \left(-\frac{1}{\sqrt{2}}, \frac{1}{\sqrt{2}}\right)$;

$P\left(\frac{5\pi}{6}\right) = \left(-\frac{\sqrt{3}}{2}, \frac{1}{2}\right)$; $P(\pi) = (-1, 0)$;

$P\left(\frac{7\pi}{6}\right) = \left(-\frac{\sqrt{3}}{2}, -\frac{1}{2}\right)$; $P\left(\frac{5\pi}{4}\right) = \left(-\frac{1}{\sqrt{2}}, -\frac{1}{\sqrt{2}}\right)$;

$P\left(\frac{4\pi}{3}\right) = \left(-\frac{1}{2}, -\frac{\sqrt{3}}{2}\right)$; $P\left(\frac{3\pi}{2}\right) = (0, -1)$;

$P\left(\frac{5\pi}{3}\right) = \left(\frac{1}{2}, -\frac{\sqrt{3}}{2}\right)$; $P\left(\frac{7\pi}{4}\right) = \left(\frac{1}{\sqrt{2}}, -\frac{1}{\sqrt{2}}\right)$;

$P\left(\frac{11\pi}{6}\right) = \left(\frac{\sqrt{3}}{2}, -\frac{1}{2}\right)$; $P(2\pi) = (1, 0)$

4.3 Trigonometric Ratios, pages 129–137

1. $\sin\theta = -\frac{24}{25}$, $\cos\theta = \frac{7}{25}$, $\tan\theta = -\frac{24}{7}$,

$\csc\theta = -\frac{25}{24}$, $\sec\theta = \frac{25}{7}$, $\cot\theta = -\frac{7}{24}$

2. a) $-$ **b)** $+$

    c) $+$ **d)** $-$

3. a) I, III   **b)** III

    c) I, II   **d)** II

4. a) $\frac{1}{2}$ **b)** $\frac{1}{\sqrt{2}}$ **c)** 0

    d) $\frac{1}{\sqrt{3}}$ **e)** $-\frac{2}{\sqrt{3}}$ **f)** $-\sqrt{2}$

5. a) 3.628   **b)** -0.249

    c) 2.985   **d)** -1.701

6. a) 108°, 288°, 468°, 648°

    b) $-197°, -163°, 163°, 197°$

7. a) $\frac{4\pi}{3}, \frac{5\pi}{3}, \frac{10\pi}{3}, \frac{11\pi}{3}$

    b) $-\frac{11\pi}{6}, -\frac{7\pi}{6}, \frac{\pi}{6}, \frac{5\pi}{6}$

8. $\sin\theta = \frac{3}{5}$, $\cos\theta = -\frac{4}{5}$, $\tan\theta = -\frac{3}{4}$,

$\sec\theta = -\frac{5}{4}$, $\cot\theta = -\frac{4}{3}$

9. Example:

4.4 Introduction to Trigonometric Equations, pages 138–144

1. a) 30°, 150°   **b)** $\frac{3\pi}{4}, \frac{7\pi}{4}, \frac{11\pi}{4}, \frac{15\pi}{4}$

2. a) 42.8°, 317.2°   **b)** 224.9°, 315.1°

3. a) $\frac{\pi}{6}, \frac{5\pi}{6}, \frac{7\pi}{6}, \frac{11\pi}{6}$ **b)** 11.54°, 168.46°, 210°, 330°

4. a) $\frac{\pi}{6} + 2\pi n, n \in I$ **b)** $\frac{11\pi}{6} + 2\pi n, n \in I$

5. a) $\frac{\pi}{4}, \frac{5\pi}{4}, \frac{9\pi}{4}, \frac{13\pi}{4}$ **b)** $\frac{\pi}{4} + \pi n, n \in I$

6. It is not permissible to divide by tan θ since tan θ can equal 0. To solve, it is necessary to factor the expression to obtain (tan θ)(tan θ − 3) = 0. Setting the factor (tan θ) equal to 0 gives two of the solutions. Setting the factor (tan θ − 3) equal to 0 gives the other two solutions.

Correct solution: 0, 1.25, 3.14, 4.39

7. a) $0, \frac{\pi}{2}, \frac{3\pi}{2}$

    b) $2\pi n, n \in I$; $\frac{\pi}{2} + 2\pi n, n \in I$;

$\frac{3\pi}{2} + 2\pi n, n \in I$; The three expressions cannot be combined in a single expression, because the intervals between solutions in one revolution are not consistent.

8. No. Example: $n = 1$ does not work.

9. If sin θ < 0, the solutions will be in quadrants III and IV. If csc θ < 0, the solutions will be in quadrants III and IV. If sin θ > 0, the solutions will be in quadrants I and II. If csc θ > 0, the solutions will be in quadrants I and II.

If cos θ < 0, the solutions will be in quadrants II and III. If sec θ < 0, the solutions will be in quadrants II and III. If cos θ > 0, the solutions will be in quadrants I and IV. If sec θ > 0, the solutions will be in quadrants I and IV.

If tan θ < 0, the solutions will be in quadrants II and IV. If cot θ < 0, the solutions will be in quadrants II and IV. If tan θ > 0, the solutions will be in quadrants I and III. If cot θ > 0, the solutions will be in quadrants I and III.

$\theta_R = \frac{\pi}{4}$	Quadrant I	Quadrant II	Quadrant III	Quadrant IV
	$\sin\frac{\pi}{4} = \frac{1}{\sqrt{2}}$	$\sin\frac{3\pi}{4} = \frac{1}{\sqrt{2}}$	$\sin\frac{5\pi}{4} = -\frac{1}{\sqrt{2}}$	$\sin\frac{7\pi}{4} = -\frac{1}{\sqrt{2}}$
	$\csc\frac{\pi}{4} = \sqrt{2}$	$\csc\frac{3\pi}{4} = \sqrt{2}$	$\csc\frac{5\pi}{4} = -\sqrt{2}$	$\csc\frac{7\pi}{4} = -\sqrt{2}$
	$\cos\frac{\pi}{4} = \frac{1}{\sqrt{2}}$	$\cos\frac{3\pi}{4} = -\frac{1}{\sqrt{2}}$	$\cos\frac{5\pi}{4} = -\frac{1}{\sqrt{2}}$	$\cos\frac{7\pi}{4} = \frac{1}{\sqrt{2}}$
	$\sec\frac{\pi}{4} = \sqrt{2}$	$\sec\frac{3\pi}{4} = -\sqrt{2}$	$\sec\frac{5\pi}{4} = -\sqrt{2}$	$\sec\frac{7\pi}{4} = \sqrt{2}$
	$\tan\frac{\pi}{4} = 1$	$\tan\frac{3\pi}{4} = -1$	$\tan\frac{5\pi}{4} = 1$	$\tan\frac{7\pi}{4} = -1$
	$\cot\frac{\pi}{4} = 1$	$\cot\frac{3\pi}{4} = -1$	$\cot\frac{5\pi}{4} = 1$	$\cot\frac{7\pi}{4} = -1$

Chapter 4 Review, pages 145–147

1. a) $\frac{3\pi}{2}$ b) $300°$
   c) $\frac{5\pi}{3}$ d) $\frac{-720°}{\pi}$
   e) $\frac{11\pi}{4}$ f) $585°$

2. Examples:
   a) $\frac{23\pi}{6}$, $-\frac{\pi}{6}$,
      general form: $\frac{11\pi}{6} \pm 2\pi n, n \in N$
   b) $345°$, $-735°$,
      general form: $-375° \pm (360°)n, n \in N$

3. a) 6.3 b) $28.6°$

4. $-\frac{\sqrt{5}}{3}$

5. a) $\frac{\pi}{3}$ b) $\frac{7\pi}{4}$

6. $56°$, $304°$, $416°$, $664°$

7. a) $-\sqrt{3}$ b) $-\frac{2}{\sqrt{3}}$

8. $\theta_1 \approx 128.7° + 360°n, n \in I$;
   $\theta_2 \approx 231.3° + 360°n, n \in I$

9. $\frac{\pi}{6}, \frac{5\pi}{6}, \frac{3\pi}{2}$

Chapter 5

5.1 Graphing Sine and Cosine Functions, pages 149–157

1. a) 2 b) $\frac{1}{4}$
   c) 5 d) 3

2. a) $360°, 2\pi$ b) $180°, \pi$
   c) $1440°, 8\pi$ d) $240°, \frac{4\pi}{3}$

3. a) $2\pi; \frac{1}{2}$ b) $\frac{2\pi}{3}; 1$
   c) $\frac{\pi}{2}; 2$ d) $6\pi; 1.5$

4. a) For $y = \sin \theta$:
   amplitude: 1; maximum value: 1; minimum value: −1; period: 2π; θ-intercepts: $\pi n, n \in I$; y-intercept: 0

   For $y = \sin\left(\frac{1}{3}\theta\right)$:
   amplitude: 1; maximum value: 1; minimum value: −1; period: 6π; θ-intercepts: $3\pi n$, $n \in I$; y-intercept: 0

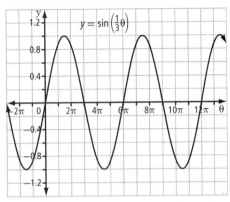

   b) For $y = \sin \theta$:
   amplitude: 1; maximum value: 1; minimum value: −1; period: 2π; θ-intercepts: $\pi n, n \in I$; y-intercept: 0

   For $y = 1.5 \sin (2\theta)$:
   amplitude: 1.5; maximum value: 1.5; minimum value: −1.5; period: π; θ-intercepts: $\frac{\pi}{2}n, n \in I$; y-intercept: 0

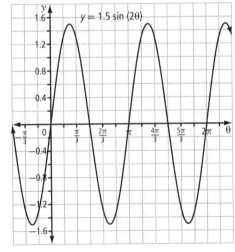

c) For $y = \sin \theta$:
amplitude: 1; maximum value: 1; minimum value: -1; period: 2π; θ-intercepts: πn, $n \in I$; y-intercept: 0

For $y = y = -2 \sin (4\theta)$:
amplitude: 2; reflected in x-axis; maximum value: 2; minimum value: -2; period: $\frac{\pi}{2}$; θ-intercepts: $\frac{\pi}{4}n$, $n \in I$; y-intercept: 0

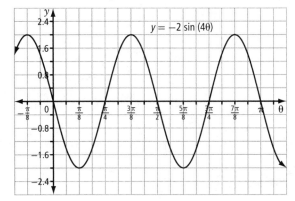

5. a) amplitude: 2; maximum value: 2; minimum value: -2; period: 4π; θ-intercepts: $\pi + 2\pi n$, $n \in I$; y-intercept: 2

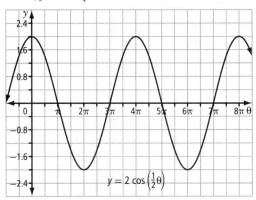

b) amplitude: 1; reflected in the x-axis; maximum value: 1; minimum value: -1; period: π; θ-intercepts: $\frac{\pi}{4} + \frac{\pi}{2} n$, $n \in I$; y-intercept: -1

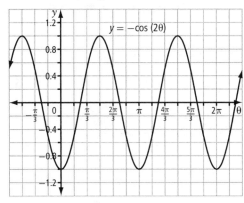

6. $y = \sin x$:

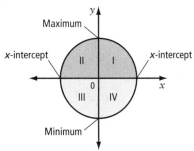

maximum values: $\frac{\pi}{2}, \frac{5\pi}{2}$

minimum values: $-\frac{\pi}{2}, \frac{3\pi}{2}, \frac{7\pi}{2}$

x-intercepts: $-\pi, 0, \pi, 2\pi, 3\pi, 4\pi$

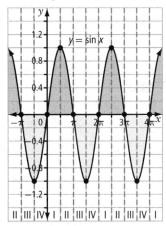

$y = \cos x$:

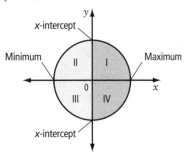

maximum values: 0, 2π, 4π

minimum values: $-\pi$, π, 3π

x-intercepts: $-\dfrac{\pi}{2}$, $\dfrac{\pi}{2}$, $\dfrac{3\pi}{2}$, $\dfrac{5\pi}{2}$, $\dfrac{7\pi}{2}$

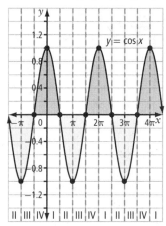

5.2 Transformations of Sinusoidal Functions, pages 158–166

1. a) $\dfrac{\pi}{3}$ units to the right; 1 unit down

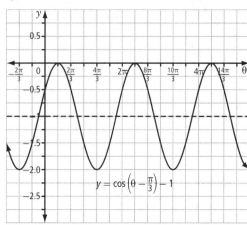

b) $\dfrac{\pi}{4}$ units to the left; 2 units up

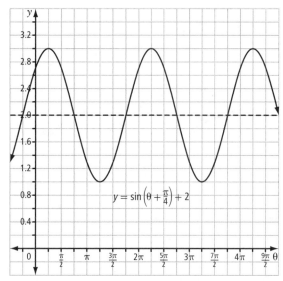

2. a) amplitude: 5; period: 720°; phase shift: 90° to the right; vertical displacement: 15 units up; domain: $\{x \mid x \in R\}$; range: $\{y \mid 10 \leq y \leq 20, y \in R\}$

b) amplitude: 0.1; period: 180°; phase shift: 45° to the left; vertical displacement: 1 unit down; domain: $\{x \mid x \in R\}$; range: $\{y \mid -1.1 \leq y \leq -0.9, y \in R\}$

c) amplitude: 1; period: π; phase shift: $\dfrac{\pi}{12}$ units to the right; vertical displacement: 0.5 units up; domain: $\{x \mid x \in R\}$; range: $\{y \mid -0.5 \leq y \leq 1.5, y \in R\}$

d) amplitude: 1.5; period: 4π; phase shift: $\dfrac{\pi}{2}$ units to the left; vertical displacement: 1 unit down; domain: $\{x \mid x \in R\}$; range: $\{y \mid -2.5 \leq y \leq 0.5, y \in R\}$

3. a) $y = 2 \sin 2\left(x + \dfrac{\pi}{3}\right) - 1$

b) $y = \dfrac{1}{4} \sin \dfrac{1}{3}(x + \pi) + 2$

c) $y = 4 \sin \dfrac{2}{3}(x - 60°)$

4. a)

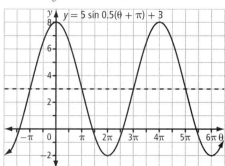

b)

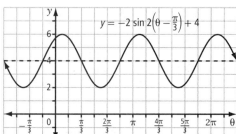

c)

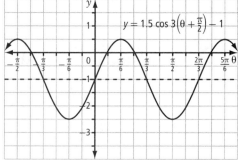

d)

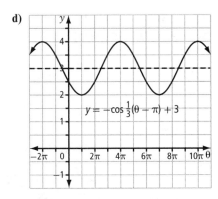

$$y = -\cos\tfrac{1}{3}(\theta - \pi) + 3$$

5. Example: $y = -4\sin(0.5\theta) + 1$;
$y = 4\sin(0.5\theta - 2\pi) + 1$

6. Example: $y = 2.2\cos\left(2\left(\theta - \tfrac{\pi}{6}\right)\right) - 1.8$;

$y = 2.2\cos\left(2\left(\theta + \tfrac{7\pi}{6}\right)\right) - 1.8$

7. Example: $y = 3\sin\left(3\left(\theta - \tfrac{\pi}{6}\right)\right) + 2$;
$y = -3\cos(3\theta) + 2$

8. Examples:

a) $a = 3, b = 2, c = \tfrac{\pi}{2}, d = 2$

b) $a = -3, b = 2, c = 0, d = 2$

c) $a = 3, b = 2, c = -\tfrac{\pi}{4}, d = 2$

5.3 The Tangent Function, pages 167–174

1. a) 0   **b)** undefined   **c)** 1   **d)** −1

2. a) 0   **b)** 0   **c)** 0

3. a) 1   **b)** 1   **c)** 1

4. a) $n\pi,\ n \in I$ **b)** $\tfrac{\pi}{4} + n\pi,\ n \in 1$

5. a) 0.70   **b)** 0.70   **c)** −0.70

6. a) $d = 640\tan\theta$

b) Example:
domain: $\{\theta \mid -90° < \theta < 90°, \theta \in R\}$;
range: $\{d \mid -8000 \le d \le 8000, d \in R\}$

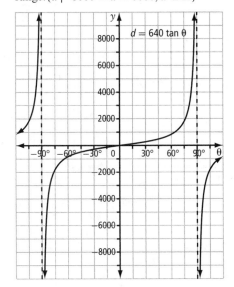

7. a) $s = 10\tan\theta,\ -75° \le \theta \le 75°$

b) Example: the sun passes directly overhead with
no tilt; it is a sunny day

c) 10 cm   **d)** 17.3 cm

8. a) A

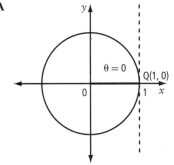

B

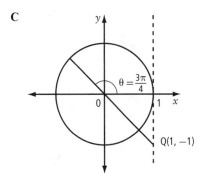

C

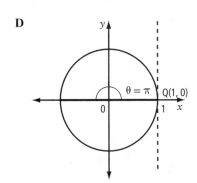

D

E

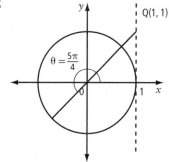

F

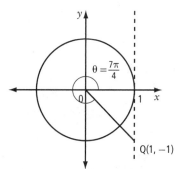

G

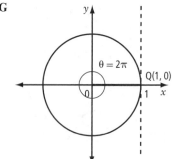

b) i)

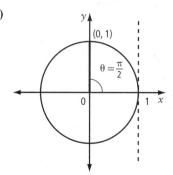

ii)

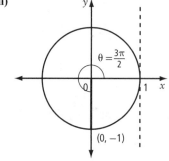

5.4 Equations and Graphs of Trigonometric Functions, pages 175–182

1. **a)** $x = \frac{\pi}{12}, \frac{5\pi}{12}, \frac{7\pi}{12}, \frac{11\pi}{12}$ **b)** $x = \frac{\pi}{4} + \frac{\pi}{2} n, n \in I$

2. Examples:
   a) $t \approx 0.0008, 0.0075, 0.0175, 0.0242$
   b) $t \approx 0.0104, 0.0146, 0.0269$
   c) $t = \frac{n}{120}, n \in I$

3. **a)** $\frac{1}{440}$ s **b)** $y = \sin(880\pi x)$
   c) $y = \sin(523.26\pi x)$ or $y \approx \sin(1643.87x)$

4. **a)** $y = 168 \sin(120\pi x)$
   b) $y = 308 \sin(100\pi x)$

5. **a)**

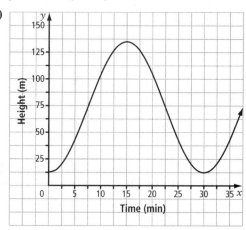

Example: I assume that the ride does not stop to let on passengers, and that the wheel is vertical (perpendicular to the ground).

   b) $y = -61 \cos\left(\frac{\pi}{15} x\right) + 74$;
   domain: $\{x \mid 0 \le x \le 30, x \in R\}$ unless the passenger goes around more than once

6. **a)**

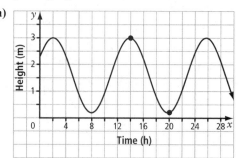

Example: assume that the amplitude of the tide is equal each occurrence, and that the tide comes in every 12 h exactly.

   b) $y = 1.4 \sin\left(\frac{\pi}{6}(x + 1)\right) + 1.6$; The domain should be restricted to some reasonable amount of time such that the assumptions made in part a) are roughly correct.

7. $y = -18.6 \cos\left(\frac{\pi}{6}(x - 1)\right) + 0.3$

8. Examples: precipitation, ocean tides, temperatures, hours of daylight

Chapter 5 Review, pages 183–186

1. amplitude: 3; period: 720°

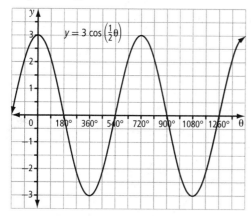

2. amplitude: 0.5; period: π

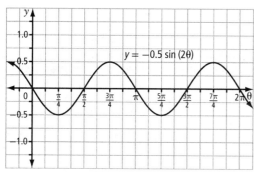

3. **a)** amplitude: 2; period: 120° or $\frac{2\pi}{3}$

  b) amplitude: $\frac{1}{3}$; period: 360° or 2π

  c) amplitude: $\frac{3}{4}$; period: 180° or π

  d) amplitude: 4; period: 540° or 3π

4. **a)** amplitude: 5; period: 8π; phase shift: $\frac{\pi}{3}$ units to the left; vertical displacement: 1 unit down

  b) amplitude: $\frac{1}{2}$; period: π; phase shift: π units to the right; vertical displacement: 3 units down

  c) amplitude: 3; period: 90°; phase shift: 50° to the left; vertical displacement: 6 units up

5.

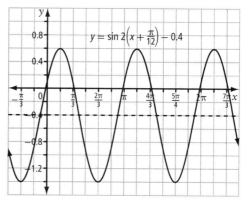

6. Examples: $y = 10 \cos 4\left(\theta - \frac{\pi}{4}\right) - 3$,

  $y = 10 \cos 4\left(\theta + \frac{\pi}{4}\right) - 3$

7.

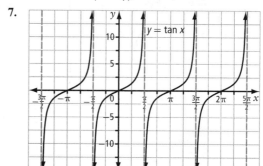

8. **a)** $\tan\theta = 0.58$; $\theta \approx 30.1°$

  b) $\tan\theta = -0.8$; $\theta \approx 141.3°$

9. $y = -7.7 \cos \frac{\pi}{6}(x - 1) + 9.6$

10. **a)** $0, \frac{\pi}{2}, \pi, \frac{3\pi}{2}, 2\pi$ **b)** $\frac{\pi}{2}$

  c) $15° + 180°n$ and $135° + 180°n, n \in I$

Chapter 6

6.1 Reciprocal, Quotient, and Pythagorean Identities, pages 188–196

1. **a)** $x \neq \frac{\pi}{2} + \pi n$, where $n \in I$

  b) $x \neq \frac{\pi}{2}n$, where $n \in I$

  c) $x \neq \pi n$ and $x \neq \frac{3\pi}{2} + 2\pi n$, where $n \in I$

  d) $x \neq \frac{\pi}{2} + \pi n$ and $x \neq 2\pi n$, where $n \in I$

2. a) $\cos x$ **b)** $\tan x$ **c)** $\sin x$

3. a) $\cot x$ **b)** $\sec x$ **c)** $\csc x$

4. a) When substituted, both values satisfy the equation.

b) $x \neq 0°, 90°, 180°,$ and $270°$

5. a) $x \neq \frac{\pi}{2}n$, where $n \in I$

b) The graph of both functions, $f(x) = \tan x + \frac{1}{\tan x}$ and $g(x) = \frac{1}{\cos x \sin x}$, look the same, so this may be an identity.

c) The equation is verified for $x = \frac{\pi}{4}$.

6. a) $\sin^2 \theta$ **b)** $\frac{3}{4}$ **c)** 25%

7. a) $\cos x = \sqrt{1 - \sin^2 x}$ is true only for $x = \frac{\pi}{6}$.

b)

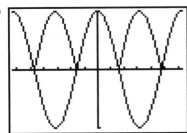

c) Example: Both the graph and the value substitution methods suggest that $\cos x = \sqrt{1 - \sin^2 x}$ is not an identity. In fact, the equation is *not* an identity because $y = \sqrt{1 - \sin^2 x}$ takes the square and then the square root, which removes the negative sign. Cos x is negative from $\frac{\pi}{2}$ to $\frac{3\pi}{2}$.

8. $\csc x, x \neq 0, \frac{\pi}{2}, \pi, \frac{3\pi}{2}$

9. a) graph appears to be equivalent to $\sin x$;
$\sin x = \csc x - \frac{\cot x}{\sec x}$

b) $x \neq \frac{\pi}{2}n$, where $n \in I$

c) $\csc x - \frac{\cot x}{\sec x} = \frac{1}{\sin x} - \frac{1}{\sec x}\left(\frac{\cos x}{\sin x}\right)$

$= \frac{1}{\sin x} - \cos x\left(\frac{\cos x}{\sin x}\right)$

$= \frac{1 - \cos^2 x}{\sin x}$

$= \frac{\sin^2 x}{\sin x}$

$= \sin x$

10. 0

11. a)

Trigonometric Ratio	Non-Permissible Values (degrees)	Non-Permissible Values (radians)
$\tan x$	$x \neq 90° + 180°n$, where $n \in I$	$x \neq \frac{\pi}{2} + \pi n$, where $n \in I$
$\csc x$	$x \neq 180°n$, where $n \in I$	$x \neq \pi n$, where $n \in I$
$\sec x$	$x \neq 90° + 180°n$, where $n \in I$	$x \neq \frac{\pi}{2} + \pi n$, where $n \in I$
$\cot x$	$x \neq 180°n$, where $n \in I$	$x \neq \pi n$, where $n \in I$

b) Example: Both $\sin x$ and $\cos x$ are defined for all values of x and there are no non-permissible values.

c) Example: While both $\sin x$ and $\cos x$ are defined for all values of x, there are values for x where these trigonometric functions are equal to zero. So, if one of these functions is the sole term in the denominator, the fraction will be undefined for these values of x.

12. a)

Trigonometric Ratio	Zero Values (degrees)	Zero Values (radians)
$\sin x$	$x = 180°n$, where $n \in I$	$x = \pi n$, where $n \in I$
$\cos x$	$x = 90° + 180°n$, where $n \in I$	$x = \frac{\pi}{2} + \pi n$, where $n \in I$
$\tan x$	$x = 180°n$, where $n \in I$	$x = \pi n$, where $n \in I$
$\cot x$	$x = 90° + 180°n$, where $n \in I$	$x = \frac{\pi}{2} + \pi n$, where $n \in I$

b) Example: The zeros are non-permissible if they occur in the denominator, in which case the expression is undefined.

c) Example: A zero only exists if there are values of x for which the numerator of the ratio is 0. For both $\csc x$ and $\sec x$, the numerator is 1.

13. No. Non-permissible values occur for values where a trigonometric ratio is undefined and/or values where the denominator of a trigonometric identity has values of zero.

6.2 Sum, Difference, and Double-Angle Identities, pages 197–204

1. a) $\cos 65°$ **b)** $\sin 26°$ **c)** $\tan 61°$

    d) $3 \sin \frac{\pi}{5}$ **e)** $\cos \frac{\pi}{4}$ **f)** $\tan \frac{2\pi}{3}$

2. a) $\sin \frac{\pi}{2} = 1$ **b)** $\cos \frac{\pi}{4} = \frac{\sqrt{2}}{2}$

    c) $\tan 120° = -\sqrt{3}$ **d)** $\cos \pi = -1$

3. a) $\sin 40°$ **b)** $\cos \frac{3\pi}{4}$ **c)** $\tan \frac{7\pi}{12}$

4. a) $-\tan x$ **b)** $\cos \frac{\theta}{2}$ **c)** $\frac{1}{4}\sin\theta$ **d)** $-4\cos 4\theta$

5. a) $x \neq \pi n, n \in I$

    b) $\dfrac{1 - \cos 2x}{\sin x}$

$$= \frac{1 - (1 - 2\sin^2 x)}{\sin x}$$

$$= \frac{2 \sin^2 x}{\sin x}$$

$$= 2 \sin x$$

6. a) $\dfrac{\sqrt{6} + \sqrt{2}}{4}$ **b)** $\dfrac{\sqrt{6} - \sqrt{2}}{4}$ **c)** $\dfrac{1 - \sqrt{3}}{1 + \sqrt{3}}$ **d)** $\dfrac{4}{\sqrt{6} + \sqrt{2}}$

7. $2 \sin x \cos y$

8. a) $\dfrac{336}{625}$ **b)** $\dfrac{527}{625}$ **c)** $\dfrac{336}{527}$

9. a) $-\dfrac{16}{25}$ **b)** $-\dfrac{33}{65}$ **c)** $\dfrac{56}{33}$

10. a) $\dfrac{\sin 2x}{1 - \cos 2x} = \dfrac{2 \sin x \cos x}{1 - (1 - 2\sin^2 x)}$

$$= \frac{2 \sin x \cos x}{2 \sin^2 x}$$

$$= \frac{\cos x}{\sin x}$$

$$= \cot x$$

    b) $\sin(x + y)\sin(x - y)$

$= (\sin x \cos y + \cos x \sin y)(\sin x \cos y - \cos x \sin y)$

$= \sin^2 x \cos^2 y - \sin x \cos y \cos x \sin y$
$\quad + \cos x \sin y \sin x \cos y - \cos^2 x \sin^2 y$

$= \sin^2 x \cos^2 y - \cos^2 x \sin^2 y$

$= \sin^2 x(1 - \sin^2 y) - (1 - \sin^2 x)\sin^2 y$

$= \sin^2 x - \sin^2 x \sin^2 y - \sin^2 y + \sin^2 x \sin^2 y$

$= \sin^2 x - \sin^2 y$

11. a) $-\sqrt{2}\sin x$ **b)** $2 \sin x$

12. a) The double-angle identities are developed by using equal angles in the sum identities, rather than two different angles.

    b) There are three forms of the double-angle identity for cosine because once the sum identity is used to obtain the first cosine identity, the Pythagorean identity can be used to convert to the other two forms.

6.3 Proving Identities, pages 205–214

1. a) $\cos x$ **b)** $\dfrac{\cos x - 5}{4}$ **c)** $\dfrac{3 \sec x}{2 \sin x - 1}$

2. a) $\dfrac{\sin x + \sin^2 x}{\cos x + \sin x \cos x} = \dfrac{\sin x(1 + \sin x)}{(1 + \sin x)\cos x}$

$$= \frac{\sin x}{\cos x}$$

$$= \tan x$$

    b)

$$\frac{\cos^2 x - \sin^2 x}{\cos^2 x + \sin x \cos x} = \frac{(\cos x - \sin x)(\cos x + \sin x)}{\cos x(\cos x + \sin x)}$$

$$= \frac{\cos x - \sin x}{\cos x}$$

$$= 1 - \frac{\sin x}{\cos x}$$

$$= 1 - \tan x$$

    c)

$$\frac{3 \cos^2 x + 5 \cos x - 2}{9 \cos^2 x - 1} = \frac{(3\cos x - 1)(\cos x + 2)}{(3\cos x - 1)(3\cos x + 1)}$$

$$= \frac{\cos x + 2}{3 \cos x + 1}$$

3. a) $\dfrac{\cos^2 x + \sin x}{\sin x \cos x}$ **b)** $2 \cot x \csc x$ **c)** $\sec x$

4. a) Left Side $= \dfrac{1 - \sin^2 x}{\cos x}$

$$= \frac{\cos^2 x}{\cos x}$$

$$= \cos x$$

      Right Side $= \dfrac{\sin 2x}{2 \sin x}$

$$= \frac{2 \sin x \cos x}{2 \sin x}$$

$$= \cos x$$

      Left Side = Right Side

    b) Left Side $= \dfrac{\csc^2 x - 1}{\csc^2 x}$

$$= \frac{\csc^2 x}{\csc^2 x} - \frac{1}{\csc^2 x}$$

$$= 1 - \sin^2 x$$

$$= \cos^2 x$$

$$= \text{Right Side}$$

    c) Left Side $= (\cos x - \sin x)^2$

$$= \cos^2 x - 2 \cos x \sin x + \sin^2 x$$

$$= \cos^2 x + \sin^2 x - 2 \cos x \sin x$$

$$= 1 - 2 \cos x \sin x$$

$$= 1 - \sin 2x$$

$$= \text{Right Side}$$

5. a) C; $\cot x = \dfrac{\cos x}{\sin x}$, so $\sin x\left(\dfrac{\cos x}{\sin x}\right) = \cos x$

b) D; Both are forms of the double-angle identity for cos.

c) B; The quadratic expands to $\sin^2 x + \cos^2 x + 2\sin x \cos x$. Applying the Pythagorean identity, $1 + 2\sin x \cos x$.

d) A;

$$\sin^2 x + \cos^2 x + \tan^2 x = 1 + \tan^2 x$$
$$= \dfrac{\cos^2 x}{\cos^2 x} + \dfrac{\sin^2 x}{\cos^2 x}$$
$$= \dfrac{1}{\cos^2 x}$$
$$= \sec^2 x$$

6. a) The graphs look the same, so this might be an identity.

b) Right Side $= \dfrac{\sin x + \sin 2x}{\cos 2x + 1 + \cos x}$

$$= \dfrac{\sin x + 2\sin x \cos x}{2\cos^2 x - 1 + 1 + \cos x}$$
$$= \dfrac{\sin x(1 + 2\cos x)}{2\cos^2 x + \cos x}$$
$$= \dfrac{\sin x(1 + 2\cos x)}{\cos x(2\cos x + 1)}$$
$$= \dfrac{\sin x}{\cos x}$$
$$= \tan x$$
$$= \text{Left Side}$$

c) $x \neq \dfrac{\pi}{2} + \pi n, \dfrac{2\pi}{3} + 2\pi n,$ and $\dfrac{4\pi}{3} + 2\pi n, n \in I$

7. a)

Right Side $= \dfrac{2(\cos x \sin 2x - \sin x \cos 2x)}{\sin 2x}$

$$= \dfrac{2(\cos x(2\sin x \cos x) - \sin x(2\cos^2 x - 1))}{2\sin x \cos x}$$
$$= \dfrac{2\cos^2 x \sin x - 2\sin x \cos^2 x + \sin x}{\sin x \cos x}$$
$$= \dfrac{\sin x}{\sin x \cos x}$$
$$= \dfrac{1}{\cos x}$$
$$= \sec x$$
$$= \text{Left Side}$$

b) Right Side $= \dfrac{2\csc 2x \tan x}{\sec x}$

$$= 2\csc 2x \tan x\left(\dfrac{1}{\sec x}\right)$$
$$= 2\left(\dfrac{1}{\sin 2x}\right)\left(\dfrac{\sin x}{\cos x}\right)\cos x$$
$$= 2\left(\dfrac{1}{2\sin x \cos x}\right)\sin x$$
$$= \dfrac{1}{\cos x}$$
$$= \sec x$$
$$= \text{Left Side}$$

c) Left Side $= \tan 2x - \sin 2x$

$$= \dfrac{\sin 2x}{\cos 2x} - \sin 2x$$
$$= \dfrac{\sin 2x - \cos 2x \sin 2x}{\cos 2x}$$
$$= \dfrac{\sin 2x(1 - \cos 2x)}{\cos 2x}$$
$$= \dfrac{\sin 2x}{\cos 2x}(1 - \cos 2x)$$
$$= \tan 2x(2\sin^2 x)$$
$$= 2\tan 2x \sin^2 x$$
$$= \text{Right Side}$$

d) Left Side $= \dfrac{1 + \tan x}{1 + \cot x}$

$$= \dfrac{1 + \dfrac{\sin x}{\cos x}}{1 + \dfrac{\cos x}{\sin x}}$$
$$= \dfrac{\dfrac{\cos x + \sin x}{\cos x}}{\dfrac{\sin x + \cos x}{\sin x}}$$
$$= \dfrac{\cos x + \sin x}{\cos x}\left(\dfrac{\sin x}{\cos x + \sin x}\right)$$
$$= \dfrac{\sin x}{\cos x}$$
$$= \tan x$$

Right Side $= \dfrac{1 - \tan x}{\cot x - 1}$

$$= \dfrac{1 - \dfrac{\sin x}{\cos x}}{\dfrac{\cos x}{\sin x} - 1}$$
$$= \dfrac{\dfrac{\cos x - \sin x}{\cos x}}{\dfrac{\cos x - \sin x}{\sin x}}$$
$$= \dfrac{\cos x - \sin x}{\cos x}\left(\dfrac{\sin x}{\sin x - \cos x}\right)$$
$$= \dfrac{\sin x}{\cos x}$$
$$= \tan x$$

Left Side $=$ Right Side

8. a) Left Side $= \sin(45° + x) + \sin(45° - x)$

$$= (\sin 45° \cos x + \cos 45° \sin x)$$
$$+ (\sin 45° \cos x - \cos 45° \sin x)$$
$$= 2\sin 45° \cos x$$
$$= 2\left(\dfrac{\sqrt{2}}{2}\right)\cos x$$
$$= \sqrt{2}\cos x$$
$$= \text{Right Side}$$

b) Left Side $= \sin(x + \pi)$

$$= \sin x \cos \pi + \cos x \sin \pi$$

$$= -\sin x$$

Right Side $= -\cos\left(x + \dfrac{3\pi}{2}\right)$

$$= -\left(\cos x \cos \dfrac{3\pi}{2} - \sin x \sin \dfrac{3\pi}{2}\right)$$

$$= -(-\sin x(-1))$$

$$= -\sin x$$

Left Side = Right Side

9. a)

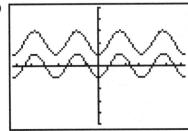

The two graphs are different, so this is not an identity.

b) Evaluating the equation for $x = 0$ is a counterexample.

10. Left Side $= 2(\sin x \cos y + \cos x \sin y)$
$\quad\quad\quad\quad\quad \times (\cos x \cos y - \sin x \sin y)$

$= 2(\sin x \cos x \cos^2 y - \sin^2 x \cos y \sin y$
$\quad + \cos^2 x \sin y \cos y - \cos x \sin x \sin^2 y)$

$= 2(\sin x \cos x(\cos^2 y - \sin^2 y)$
$\quad + \cos y \sin y(\cos^2 x - \sin^2 x))$

$= 2 \sin x \cos x(\cos^2 y - \sin^2 y)$
$\quad + 2 \cos y \sin y(\cos^2 x - \sin^2 x)$

$= \sin 2x \cos 2y + \sin 2y \cos 2x$

$=$ Right Side

11. a) The graphs appear to be the same, so this could be an identity.

b) Left Side $= \sin^4 x + \cos^2 x$

$$= (\sin^2 x)^2 + \cos^2 x$$

$$= (1 - \cos^2 x)^2 + \cos^2 x$$

$$= (1 - 2\cos^2 x + \cos^4 x) + \cos^2 x$$

$$= 1 - 2\cos^2 x + \cos^4 x + \cos^2 x$$

$$= 1 - \cos^2 x + \cos^4 x$$

$$= \sin^2 x + \cos^4 x$$

$$= \text{Right Side}$$

c) Example: In part a), the two graphs look the same, but this is not enough to say with certainty that the equation is an identity. The proof in part b) indicates that the two sides are equal for all permissible values.

6.4 Solving Trigonometric Equations Using Identities, pages 215–223

1. a) $60°, 120°$ **b)** $60°, 300°$

    c) $45°, 225°$ **d)** $135°, 315°$

2. a) $\dfrac{\pi}{6}, \dfrac{5\pi}{6}, \dfrac{7\pi}{6}, \dfrac{11\pi}{6}$ **b)** $\dfrac{\pi}{6}, \dfrac{5\pi}{6}, \dfrac{7\pi}{6}, \dfrac{11\pi}{6}$

    c) $\dfrac{\pi}{3}, \dfrac{2\pi}{3}, \dfrac{4\pi}{3}, \dfrac{5\pi}{3}$ **d)** $\dfrac{\pi}{3}, \dfrac{2\pi}{3}, \dfrac{4\pi}{3}, \dfrac{5\pi}{3}$

3. a) $0, \dfrac{\pi}{2}, \pi$ **b)** $\dfrac{\pi}{2}, \pi, \dfrac{3\pi}{2}$

    c) $0, \dfrac{3\pi}{4}, \pi, \dfrac{7\pi}{4}$ **d)** $\dfrac{\pi}{2}, \dfrac{3\pi}{2}$

4. a) $\dfrac{\pi}{4}, \dfrac{\pi}{2}, \dfrac{5\pi}{4}, \dfrac{3\pi}{2}$ **b)** $0, \dfrac{\pi}{4}, \dfrac{3\pi}{4}, \pi$

    c) $0, \pi$ **d)** $\dfrac{\pi}{6}, \dfrac{5\pi}{6}, \dfrac{7\pi}{6}, \dfrac{11\pi}{6}$

    e) $\dfrac{\pi}{4}, \dfrac{3\pi}{4}, \dfrac{5\pi}{4}, \dfrac{7\pi}{4}$

5. a) $\dfrac{\pi}{3}, \dfrac{2\pi}{3}, \dfrac{4\pi}{3}, \dfrac{5\pi}{3}$ **b)** $\dfrac{\pi}{3}, \dfrac{2\pi}{3}, \dfrac{4\pi}{3}, \dfrac{5\pi}{3}$

    c) $2.30, 3.98, \dfrac{\pi}{3}, \dfrac{5\pi}{3}$ **d)** $0.41, 2.73, \dfrac{7\pi}{6}, \dfrac{11\pi}{6}$

6. a) $0.25, 2.89, \dfrac{\pi}{6}, \dfrac{5\pi}{6}$ **b)** $\dfrac{\pi}{3}, \pi, \dfrac{5\pi}{3}$

    c) $0, \dfrac{\pi}{3}, \dfrac{5\pi}{3}$ **d)** $\dfrac{\pi}{2}$

    e) $0.46, 3.61, \dfrac{\pi}{4}, \dfrac{5\pi}{4}$ **f)** $\dfrac{\pi}{2}, \dfrac{7\pi}{6}, \dfrac{11\pi}{6}$

7. a) i) $\dfrac{2\pi}{3}, \dfrac{4\pi}{3}$ **ii)** $-\dfrac{4\pi}{3}, -\dfrac{2\pi}{3}, \dfrac{2\pi}{3}, \dfrac{4\pi}{3}$ **iii)** $-\dfrac{2\pi}{3}, \dfrac{2\pi}{3}$

    b) The greater the domain, the greater the number of solutions.

    c) The general solution is $x = \dfrac{2\pi}{3} + 2\pi n$ and $x = \dfrac{4\pi}{3} + 2\pi n$, where $n \in I$.

8. a) $\dfrac{\pi}{6}, \dfrac{5\pi}{6}, \dfrac{3\pi}{2}$ **b)** π

    c) $\dfrac{\pi}{6}, \dfrac{5\pi}{6}$ **d)** $1.91, 4.37, \dfrac{2\pi}{3}, \dfrac{4\pi}{3}$

9. $B = 5, C = -2$

10. $x = \dfrac{\pi}{2}n$, where $n \in I$

11. The general solution is $x = \dfrac{\pi}{2} + \pi n$, $x = \dfrac{5\pi}{4} + 2\pi n$, and $x = \dfrac{7\pi}{4} + 2\pi n$, where $n \in I$.

12. The given equation is not factorable since there are no two integers whose product is 3 and whose sum is -5.

13. The step that is wrong in the solution is the line $\cos x \,(\cos x + 1) = 0$. Brooke mistakenly thought that $\cos 2x$ meant $\cos^2 x$. The correct solution is:

$$\cos 2x + \cos x = 0$$
$$2\cos^2 x - 1 + \cos x = 0$$
$$2\cos^2 x + \cos x - 1 = 0$$
$$(2\cos x - 1)(\cos x + 1) = 0$$
$$\cos x = \frac{1}{2} \text{ or } \cos x = -1$$

For $\cos x = \frac{1}{2}$: $x = 60° + 360°n$ or $x = 300° + 360°n$, where $n \in I$

For $\cos x = -1$: $x = 180° + 360°n$, where $n \in I$

Chapter 6 Review, pages 224–227

1. a) $x \neq \frac{\pi}{2}n$, where $n \in I$

b) $x \neq \pi n$, where $n \in I$

c) $x \neq \frac{\pi}{2} + \pi n$, where $n \in I$

2. a) $\cos x$　　　**b)** $\sin x$

3. a) $\csc x$　　　**b)** $\sec x$

4. a) When substituted, both values satisfy the equation.

b) $x \neq 90°, 270°$

5. a) $\cos 30° = \frac{\sqrt{3}}{2}$

b) $\sin 135° = \frac{\sqrt{2}}{2}$

c) $\cos 150° = -\frac{\sqrt{3}}{2}$

6. a) $\frac{\sqrt{2} + \sqrt{6}}{4}$　　**b)** $\frac{\sqrt{6} + \sqrt{2}}{4}$

c) $\frac{\sqrt{2} - \sqrt{6}}{4}$　　**d)** $\frac{-\sqrt{6} + \sqrt{2}}{4}$

7. a) $-\frac{336}{625}$　　**b)** $\frac{527}{625}$

c) $-\frac{336}{527}$

8. Left Side $= \sin(\pi - x) - \tan(\pi + x)$

$\phantom{\text{Left Side }}= \sin \pi \cos x - \sin x \cos \pi - \dfrac{\tan \pi + \tan x}{1 - \tan \pi \tan x}$

$\phantom{\text{Left Side }}= \sin x - \tan x$

Right Side $= \dfrac{\sin x (\cos x - 1)}{\cos x}$

$\phantom{\text{Right Side }}= \dfrac{\sin x \cos x - \sin x}{\cos x}$

$\phantom{\text{Right Side }}= \dfrac{\sin x \cos x}{\cos x} - \dfrac{\sin x}{\cos x}$

$\phantom{\text{Right Side }}= \sin x - \tan x$

Left Side = Right Side

9. a)

Yes. The graphs appear to be equal.

b) Left Side $= \sin^2 x + \tan^2 x + \cos^2 x$

$\phantom{\text{Left Side }}= 1 + \tan^2 x$

$\phantom{\text{Left Side }}= \sec^2 x$

$\phantom{\text{Left Side }}=$ Right Side

10. a) Left Side $= \cos x \tan^2 x$

$\phantom{\text{Left Side }}= \cos x \dfrac{\sin^2 x}{\cos^2 x}$

$\phantom{\text{Left Side }}= \dfrac{\sin^2 x}{\cos x}$

$\phantom{\text{Left Side }}= \sin x \dfrac{\sin x}{\cos x}$

$\phantom{\text{Left Side }}= \sin x \tan x$

$\phantom{\text{Left Side }}=$ Right Side

b) Right Side $= \tan x + \tan x \cos 2x$

$\phantom{\text{Right Side }}= \tan x (1 + \cos 2x)$

$\phantom{\text{Right Side }}= \tan x (1 + (2\cos^2 x - 1))$

$\phantom{\text{Right Side }}= \tan x (2\cos^2 x)$

$\phantom{\text{Right Side }}= 2\dfrac{\sin x}{\cos x} \cos^2 x$

$\phantom{\text{Right Side }}= 2 \sin x \cos x$

$\phantom{\text{Right Side }}= \sin 2x$

$\phantom{\text{Right Side }}=$ Left Side

11. a) $\frac{\pi}{2}$　　　　　**b)** 0

c) $\frac{\pi}{3}, \pi, \frac{5\pi}{3}$

12. a) $\frac{2\pi}{3}, \pi, \frac{4\pi}{3}$　　**b)** $\frac{3\pi}{2}$

c) no solution　　　**d)** π

13. The general solution is $x = \frac{7\pi}{6} + 2\pi n$, $x = \frac{11\pi}{6} + 2\pi n$, $x = \frac{\pi}{2} + 2\pi n$, where $n \in I$. These can be combined as $x = \frac{\pi}{2} + \frac{2\pi}{3}n$, where $n \in I$.

Chapter 7

7.1 Characteristics of Exponential Functions, pages 229–237

1. **a)** No, the variable is not the exponent.

   b) Yes, the base is greater than 0 and the variable is the exponent.

   c) Yes, the base is greater than 0 and the variable is the exponent.

   d) No, the variable is not the exponent.

   e) No, the variable is not the exponent.

2. **a)** C   **b)** A   **c)** D   **d)** B

3. **a)** $y = 10^x$ **b)** $y = 5^x$ **c)** $y = \left(\frac{1}{4}\right)^x$

4. **a)**

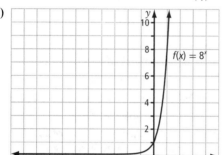

domain: $\{x \mid x \in R\}$; range: $\{y \mid y > 0, y \in R\}$;
y-intercept 1; function increasing; horizontal asymptote $y = 0$

b)

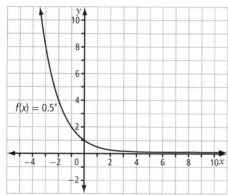

domain: $\{x \mid x \in R\}$; range: $\{y \mid y > 0, y \in R\}$;
y-intercept 1; function decreasing; horizontal asymptote $y = 0$

c)

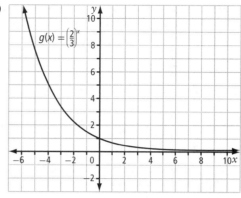

domain: $\{x \mid x \in R\}$; range: $\{y \mid y > 0, y \in R\}$;
y-intercept 1; function decreasing; horizontal asymptote $y = 0$

d)

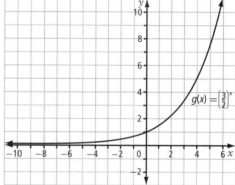

domain: $\{x \mid x \in R\}$; range: $\{y \mid y > 0, y \in R\}$;
y-intercept 1; function increasing; horizontal asymptote $y = 0$

5. **a)**

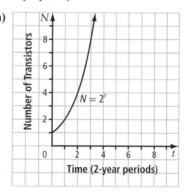

function increasing

   b) domain: $\{t \mid t \geq 0, t \in R\}$;
   range: $\{N \mid N \geq 1, N \in N\}$

   c) 2 transistors; 32 transistors; 1024 transistors

6. a) Example: Since 75% of impurities are removed, 25% remain, or as a decimal, 0.25.

b)

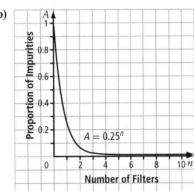

Number of Filters

c) domain: $\{n \mid n \geq 0, n \in W\}$;
range: $\{A \mid 0 < A \leq 1, A \in R\}$

d) 0.0039 of original impurities remain

7. a) $P = \left(\frac{1}{2}\right)^n$

b)

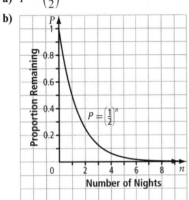

Number of Nights

c) 3.13% after 5 nights;
0.39% after 8 nights

d) No; $y = 0$ is a horizontal asymptote.

8. a) $V = (1.045)^t$

b)

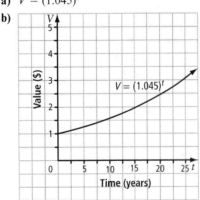

Time (years)

c) $1.94

d) 25 years

9. a) Example: All exponential functions are defined for all real numbers, and all powers of positive bases are positive.

b) Example: All exponential functions have a y-intercept of 1 because $c^0 = 1$ for all $c > 0$.

c) Example: whether the function is increasing or decreasing

7.2 Transformations of Exponential Functions, pages 238–248

1. a) No   **b)** Yes
c) No   **d)** No

2. a) No   **b)** No
c) No   **d)** Yes

3. a) No   **b)** No
c) Yes   **d)** No

4. a) horizontally stretched by a factor of $\frac{1}{2}$, translated 5 units right and 6 units down

b) vertically stretched by a factor of $\frac{2}{3}$, reflected in the y-axis, translated 9 units up

c) vertically stretched by a factor of 2, reflected in the x-axis, horizontally stretched by a factor of 4

d) vertically stretched by a factor of 500, horizontally stretched by a factor of $\frac{1}{2}$, translated 3 units left and 8 units down

5. a)

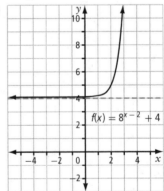

$f(x) = 8^{x-2} + 4$

domain: $\{x \mid x \in R\}$; range: $\{y \mid y > 4, y \in R\}$;

y-intercept $\frac{257}{64}$ or ≈ 4.02; function increasing; horizontal asymptote $y = 4$

b)

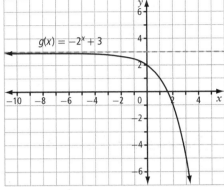

domain: $\{x \mid x \in \mathbb{R}\}$; range: $\{y \mid y < 3, y \in \mathbb{R}\}$;
y-intercept 2; function decreasing; horizontal
asymptote $y = 3$

c)

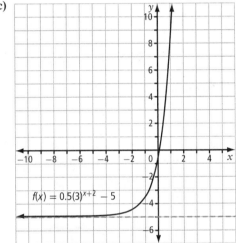

domain: $\{x \mid x \in \mathbb{R}\}$; range $\{y \mid y > -5, y \in \mathbb{R}\}$;
y-intercept $-\frac{1}{2}$; function increasing; horizontal
asymptote $y = -5$

6. a) $M(d) = 250\left(\frac{1}{2}\right)^{\frac{d}{8}}$; vertical stretch by a factor
of 250; horizontal stretch by a factor of 8

b)

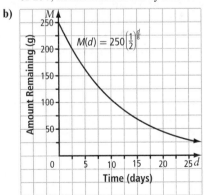

domain: $\{d \mid d \geq 0, d \in \mathbb{R}\}$;
range: $\{M \mid 0 < M \leq 250, M \in \mathbb{R}\}$; $M = 0$;
M-intercept 250

c) approximately 192.8 g; Example: substitute $x = 3$
and check against the graph

7. a) $V = 12\ 500(3)^{\frac{t}{15}}$; vertically stretched by a factor
of 12 500; horizontally stretched by a factor
of 15

b)

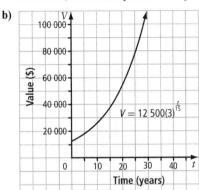

domain: $\{t \mid t \geq 0, t \in \mathbb{R}\}$;
range: $\{V \mid V \geq 12\ 500, V \in \mathbb{R}\}$

c) \$234 009.43; assumes that the growth rate does
not change

d) approximately 19 years

8. a) $P = 11\ 568(0.98)^t$

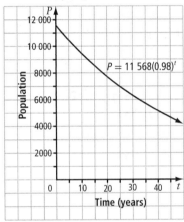

b) vertically stretched by a factor of 11 568

c) approximately 10 456

d) approximately 7722

e) Example: According to the equation, no, but
since fractions of people are not possible, the
population may reach zero in the future.

9. a) vertically stretched by a factor of 500, horizontally stretched by a factor of $\frac{1}{2}$

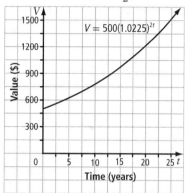

b) $500; This is the initial investment.

c) $974.70

d) approximately 16 years

10. a) Example: They are both correct. David is correct because the y-intercepts of the graphs are 1 and 2, which suggests a vertical stretch of 1. But Jodi is also correct because the points on the transformed graph are 1 unit left of the same points on the base function, suggesting a horizontal translation by 1 unit left.

b) Example: The laws of exponents mean that $2(2)^x = 2^1 \times 2^x = 2^{x+1}$.

c) Example: $y = 3^{-x}$ and $y = \left(\frac{1}{3}\right)^x$

7.3 Solving Exponential Equations, pages 249–255

1. a) 3^4 **b)** 3^{15}

   c) $3^{\frac{3}{2}}$ **d)** $3^{\frac{5}{3}}$

   e) $3^{\frac{14}{3}}$ **f)** 3^{-6}

   g) $3^{\frac{21}{2}}$

2. a) $2^3, 2^6$ **b)** $3^2, 3^6$

   c) $5^{x+6}, 5^3$ **d)** $2^{3x}, 2^{6x+12}$

   e) $3^{15x+12}, 3^{-2x-6}$ **f)** $2^{-2x-14}, 2^{-9x}$

3. a) $x \approx 3.2$ **b)** $x \approx 3.4$

4. a) 3   **b)** 4

   c) −6   **d)** −2

5. a) 1   **b)** $\frac{13}{4}$

   c) −2   **d)** $-\frac{12}{5}$

   e) 3

6. a) Example: Graph $y = 5^x$ and $y = 32$, and calculate the point of intersection.

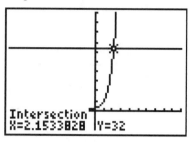

$x \approx 2.15$

b) Example: Graph $y = 10^{2x} - 439$ and calculate the x-intercept.

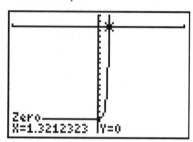

$x \approx 1.32$

c) Example: Graph $y = 25\left(\frac{1}{2}\right)^{4x}$ and $y = 5$ and calculate the point of intersection.

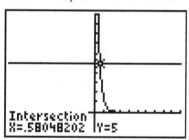

$x \approx 0.58$

d) Example: Graph $y = 200(1.05)^{12x} - 1250$ and calculate the x-intercept.

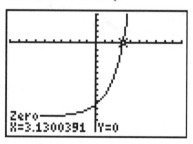

$x \approx 3.13$

7. a) $N = 4(2)^t$, where N is the number of bacteria, and t is the time, in hours.

b) 10 h

8. a) $V = 1000(2)^{\frac{t}{8}}$, where V is the value of the painting and t is the time, in years.

b) approximately 13.5 years

9. a) $M = 350(1.03)^t$, where M is the number of members and t is the time, in years.

b) 16 years

10. a) $V = 1000(1.0375)^t$, where V is the value of the investment and t is the time, in years.

b) systematic trial or use technology to graph either one or two functions

c)

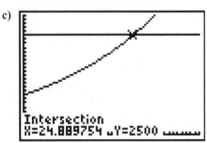

approximately 25 years

d) Example: There is no common base, so once I reach the point in the equation $1.0375^t = 2.5$, I do not have an algebraic method to calculate t other than systematic trial.

Chapter 7 Review, pages 256–258

1. a) domain: $\{x \mid x \in R\}$; range: $\{y \mid y > 0, y \in R\}$; y-intercept 1; horizontal asymptote $y = 0$; function increasing

b) domain: $\{x \mid x \in R\}$; range: $\{y \mid y > 0, y \in R\}$; y-intercept 1; horizontal asymptote $y = 0$; function decreasing

2. a) $y = 5^x$ **b)** $y = \left(\frac{1}{3}\right)^x$

3. a) $P = 0.85^n$

b)

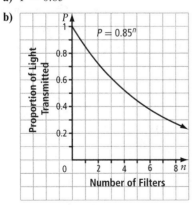

approximately 4 filters

4. a) vertically stretched by a factor of 2, translated 3 units down

b) translated 3 units left

c) horizontally stretched by a factor of $\frac{1}{2}$, translated 4 units right and 1 unit up

d) vertically stretched by a factor of 5, horizontally stretched by a factor of $\frac{1}{6}$, translated 2 units left

5. a) $y = \frac{1}{2}(4)^{x+2} - 6$; domain: $\{x \mid x \in R\}$; range: $\{y \mid y > -6, y \in R\}$

b) $y = 5(4)^{3x}$; domain: $\{x \mid x \in R\}$; range: $\{y \mid y > 0, y \in R\}$

c) $y = (4)^{\frac{1}{2}(x-3)} - 1$; domain: $\{x \mid x \in R\}$; range: $\{y \mid y > -1, y \in R\}$

6. a) 3   **b)** −2

c) $\frac{15}{8}$ **d)** $-\frac{20}{7}$

7. a) $P = \left(\frac{1}{2}\right)^{\frac{t}{4}}$ **b)** 8 days

c)

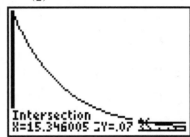

15.3 days

8. a) $N = 64(2)^{\frac{t}{10}}$

b) 337 colonies

c) 40 h

d)

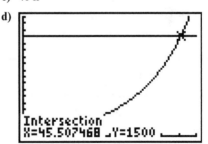

46 h

Chapter 8

8.1 Understanding Logarithms, pages 260–266

1. a)

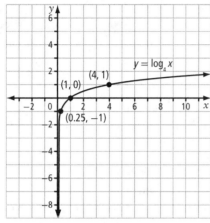

domain: $\{x \mid x > 0, x \in R\}$;
range: $\{y \mid y \in R\}$; x-intercept 1;
vertical asymptote $x = 0$; $y = \log_4 x$

b)

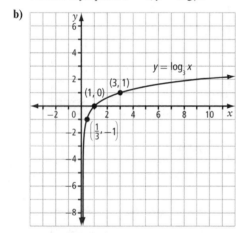

domain: $\{x \mid x > 0, x \in R\}$;
range: $\{y \mid y \in R\}$; x-intercept 1;
vertical asymptote $x = 0$; $y = \log_3 x$

2. a) $\log_3 243 = 5$ **b)** $\log 10\,000 = 4$
c) $\log_{16} 4 = \frac{1}{2}$ **d)** $\log_8 \frac{1}{64} = -2$
e) $\log 0.01 = -2$ **f)** $\log_{27} 9 = \frac{2}{3}$
g) $\log_{12} 2y = x$ **h)** $\log_2 (y - 1) = 2x - 5$

3. a) $2^5 = 32$ **b)** $8^3 = 512$
c) $5^4 = 625$ **d)** $10^3 = 1000$
e) $10^{-4} = 0.0001$ **f)** $\left(\frac{1}{2}\right)^{-3} = 8$
g) $3^y = x + 1$ **h)** $4^{(y + 1)} = 2x$

4. a) 2   **b)** 6   **c)** 2
d) −2   **e)** −3   **f)** 1
g) 4   **h)** $\frac{11}{2}$ **i)** 0
j) $\frac{1}{2}$

5. $\log_{10} 300$, $\log_6 400$, $\log_2 100$

6. a) 3   **b)** 3   **c)** 16
d) $\frac{1}{25}$ **e)** 4   **f)** $\frac{1}{2}$
g) 3   **h)** 36   **i)** 5
j) 4

7. a) 216   **b)** 4   **c)** 12
d) 7   **e)** −8   **f)** 10

8. a) 13 dB   **b)** 1000 times

9. Examples:

a) The graph will increase more slowly.

b) The graph of $y = 5^x$ increases more quickly.

c) Because the graph of $y = 5^x$ increases more quickly, the graph of $y = \log_5 x$ will increase more slowly.

d) A larger base leads to a logarithmic graph that increases more slowly.

10. Examples:

a) If $c < 0$, the function is discontinuous and is not defined for many real numbers.

b) Since $1^x = 1$ for all values of x, the only domain of $y = \log_1 x$ is 1.

8.2 Transformations of Logarithmic Functions, pages 267–274

1. a) translated 1 unit left and 8 units down

b) vertically stretched by a factor of 2 and horizontally stretched by a factor of $\frac{1}{4}$

c) reflected in the x-axis and horizontally stretched by a factor of $\frac{1}{3}$

d) vertically stretched by a factor of 5, horizontally stretched by a factor of $\frac{1}{2}$, reflected in the y-axis, translated 4 units left

2. a) $y = 3 \log_5 (x - 2)$

b) $y = -\log_5 (x + 4) - 1$

c) $y = \frac{1}{2} \log_5 (2x)$

d) $y = 4 \log_5 (-x) - 2.5$

3. a)

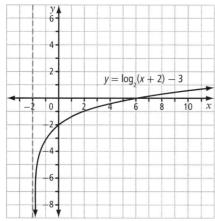

$y = \log_2(x + 2) - 3$

b)

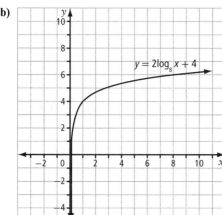

$y = 2\log_8 x + 4$

c)

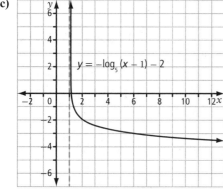

$y = -\log_5(x - 1) - 2$

d)

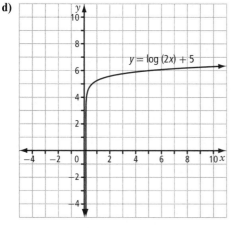

$y = \log(2x) + 5$

4. a) horizontally stretched by a factor of $\frac{1}{2}$, translated 3 units to the left

b) horizontally stretched by a factor of $\frac{1}{3}$, translated 4 units to the right

c) horizontally stretched by a factor of 2, translated 6 units to the right

d) horizontally stretched by a factor of 3, translated 18 units to the left

5. a) vertically stretched by a factor of B and translated 1 unit left

b) 50 000 bits per second

6. a) domain: $\{x \mid x > 8, x \in \mathbb{R}\}$; range: $\{y \mid y \in \mathbb{R}\}$; x-intercept: 244 140 633; no y-intercept; vertical asymptote $x = 8$

b) domain: $\{x \mid x > 1, x \in \mathbb{R}\}$; range: $\{y \mid y \in \mathbb{R}\}$; x-intercept: 2.1; no y-intercept; vertical asymptote $x = 1$

c) domain: $\{x \mid x > 0, x \in \mathbb{R}\}$; range: $\{y \mid y \in \mathbb{R}\}$; x-intercept: 71 663 616; no y-intercept; vertical asymptote $x = 0$

d) domain: $\{x \mid x > -3, x \in \mathbb{R}\}$; range: $\{y \mid y \in \mathbb{R}\}$; x-intercept 125; y-intercept −5.4; vertical asymptote $x = -3$

7. a) translated 2 units right and 5 units down

b) translated 1 unit left and 2 units down

8. a) vertically stretched by a factor of 3

b) vertically stretched by a factor of $\frac{1}{2}$

9. a)

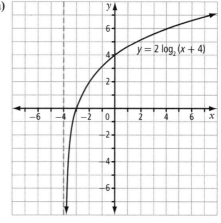

$y = 2\log_2(x + 4)$

b)

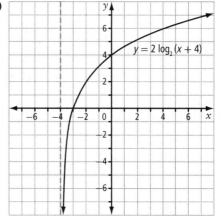

$y = 2\log_2(x + 4)$

c) The graphs are identical. The order of the transformations does not matter when performing a vertical stretch and a horizontal translation.

d) Example: a horizontal stretch by a factor of 2 and a translation 3 units up; a vertical stretch by a factor of 3 and a translation 1 unit right

e) Example: when a stretch and a translation are in the same direction

8.3 Laws of Logarithms, pages 275–281

1. a) 2 **b)** 3 **c)** 5 **d)** 2 **e)** 2
f) 3 **g)** 5 **h)** 11 **i)** 16 **j)** 1000

2. a) $4 \log_7 x + \frac{3}{2} \log_7 y$

b) $3 \log_{12} x + 6 \log_{12} y + 15 \log_{12} z$

c) $3 \log_8 x - \frac{1}{2} \log_8 y - \frac{5}{2} \log_8 z$

d) $\frac{1}{2} \log x - \frac{3}{2} \log y$

3. a) $2 + \frac{5}{3} \log_7 x$ **b)** $2 - 2 \log x - 2 \log y$

c) $\frac{7}{3} \log_5 y - 3 - \log_5 x$ **d)** $6 \log_2 x - 5 - 2 \log_2 y$

4. a) $\log_6 54x^4$ **b)** $\log_2 \frac{y^8}{2x}$ **c)** $\log_4 x^{16} y^{20}$

d) $\log_3 (xy)^{\frac{11}{3}}$ **e)** $\log \frac{2}{25 x^{\frac{3}{2}} y^{\frac{1}{4}}}$ **f)** $\log_7 \frac{x^{\frac{9}{2}}}{\sqrt[6]{5}}$

g) $\log \frac{2x^{\frac{5}{3}}}{3}$ **h)** $\log_9 x^6 y^9$

5. a) $L = \log I^{10} - \log I_0^{10}$ **b)** $I = 10^{0.1L + \log I_0}$

6. a) $[H_3O]^+ = 10^{-pH}$

b) $pH = \log ([H_3O]^+)^{-1} = \log \frac{1}{[H_3O^+]}$

7. a) False; it must be a multiplication inside the logarithm.

b) False; the division must take place inside the logarithm.

c) True **d)** True

e) False; the exponent must apply to the entire argument of the logarithm.

8. a) $\frac{1}{6}$ **b)** 3 **c)** 8

9. a) $7P$ **b)** $P + 1$ **c)** $2P$

d) $P - 1$ **e)** $-P$ **f)** $\frac{P}{2}$

10. a) The function $y = \log_2 x^2$ can be written as $y = 2 \log_2 x$, which is a vertical stretch by a factor of 2 of $y = \log_2 x$.

b) The function $y = \log_2 3x$ is of the form $y = \log_2 bx$. This is a horizontal stretch by a factor of $\frac{1}{3}$ of the function $y = \log_2 x$.

c) The function $y = \log_2 3x$ can be written as $y = \log_2 x + \log_2 3$, which is a translation of $\log_2 3$ units up.

d) No. Example: $y = \log_2 \frac{1}{x}$ can be written as $y = -\log_2 x$, which is a reflection in the x-axis, not the reciprocal transformation.

8.4 Logarithmic and Exponential Equations, pages 282–291

1. a) 1024 **b)** 25 **c)** 32
d) 213 **e)** 5 **f)** 1005

2. a) 0.93 **b)** 1.13 **c)** −3.64 **d)** 8.00

3. a) $\frac{\log 205}{\log 5}$ **b)** $\frac{\log 311}{\log 4} + 3$

c) $\frac{\log 7539 - 1}{2}$ **d)** $\frac{\log 40}{\log 4} - 2$

e) $\frac{2 \log 85}{\log 6}$

4. a) 6 **b)** 10 or −10
c) 16 **d)** 9

5. a) $x > 0$ **b)** $x > 2$
c) undefined for all x

6. a) $\frac{3 \log 5}{\log 5 - 1} \approx -6.97$

b) $\frac{-3 \log 8}{2 \log \frac{2}{3}} \approx 7.69$

c) $\frac{2 \log 6 + 5 \log 2}{2 \log 2 - \log 6} \approx -17.39$

d) $\frac{3 \log 3 + 2 \log 6 + \log 2}{2 \log 3 - \log 6} \approx 18.68$

7. a) $\frac{5}{2}$ **b)** $\frac{17}{4}$ **c)** 2 **d)** no soluion

8. a) 2 **b)** 6 **c)** 6 **d)** 3

9. a) $m = 65\left(\frac{1}{2}\right)^{\frac{t}{88}}$ **b)** 43.84 g **c)** 149.6 years

10. a) $p = 974(1.015)^t$ **b)** 1049 **c)** 14 years

11. a) $\frac{3}{2}$ or 1 **b)** −3 or $\frac{3}{2}$

Chapter 8 Review, pages 292–295

1. a)

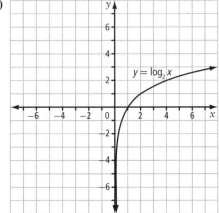

domain: $\{x \mid x > 0, x \in R\}$;
range: $\{y \mid y \in R\}$; x-intercept 1;
vertical asymptote $x = 0$

b)

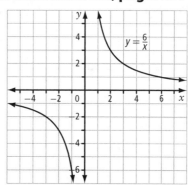

domain: $\{x \mid x > 0, x \in \mathbb{R}\}$;
range: $\{y \mid y \in \mathbb{R}\}$; x-intercept 1;
vertical asymptote $x = 0$

2. a) $\log_6 216 = 3$ **b)** $\log_2 1024 = 10$

    c) $\log 0.001 = -3$ **d)** $\log_5 125 = x$

3. a) $3^4 = 81$ **b)** $25^{\frac{1}{2}} = 5$

    c) $10^0 = 1$ **d)** $2^9 = 3x - 4$

4. a) vertically stretched by a factor of 2, translated
1 unit left; domain: $\{x \mid x > -1, x \in \mathbb{R}\}$;
range: $\{y \mid y \in \mathbb{R}\}$; x-intercept: 0; y-intercept: 0

    b) translated 3 units right and 5 units up; domain:
$\{x \mid x > 3, x \in \mathbb{R}\}$; range: $\{y \mid y \in \mathbb{R}\}$;
x-intercept: 3.0; no y-intercept

5. a) $y = \log(x - 5) - 4$; domain: $\{x \mid x > 5, x \in \mathbb{R}\}$;
range: $\{y \mid y \in \mathbb{R}\}$

    b) $y = 3\log(x + 2) - 6$; domain: $\{x \mid x > -2, x \in \mathbb{R}\}$;
range: $\{y \mid y \in \mathbb{R}\}$

    c) $y = \log(3x) + 1$; domain: $\{x \mid x > 0, x \in \mathbb{R}\}$;
range: $\{y \mid y \in \mathbb{R}\}$

6. a) 2   **b)** 3   **c)** 2   **d)** 0

7. a) $2 + 4\log_5 x + \frac{3}{4}\log_5 y$

    b) $5\log y - 2 - \frac{1}{2}\log x$

8. a) $3\log_4 xy$ **b)** $\log \dfrac{x^5}{\sqrt[5]{y^5}}$

9. a) $\dfrac{2}{\log 3} \approx 4.19$ **b)** $\dfrac{\log 517}{\log 7} + 3 \approx 6.21$

    c) $\dfrac{\log 5500 - 1}{2} \approx 1.37$ **d)** $\dfrac{4\log 2}{\log 2 - \log 5} \approx -3.03$

10. a) 128   **b)** $\dfrac{117}{2}$ **c)** no solution   **d)** 5

11. Example: $10^{9.3 - 9.0} \approx 2$

12. a) $N = 40(2)^{\frac{t}{4}}$ **b)** 18.58 h

    c) 6.34 h; does not depend on the number of
bacteria present at the beginning

13. a) $P = 100(0.6)^n$ **b)** 21.6%

    c) 9 filters

Chapter 9

9.1 Exploring Rational Functions Using Transformations, pages 297–304

1. a)

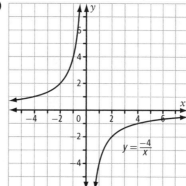

vertical asymptote: $x = 0$
horizontal asymptote: $y = 0$

b)

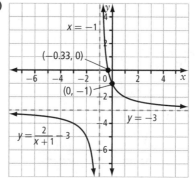

vertical asymptote: $x = 0$
horizontal asymptote: $y = 0$

2. a)

b)

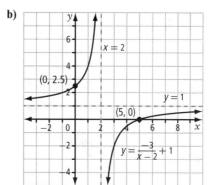

3. a)

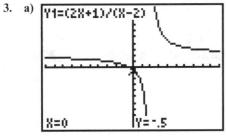

vertical asymptote: $x = 2$; horizontal asymptote
$y = 2$; x-intercept -0.5; y-intercept -0.5

b)

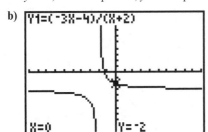

vertical asymptote: $x = -2$; horizontal asymptote
$y = -3$; x-intercept $-\dfrac{4}{3}$; y-intercept -2

4. a) C   **b)** A

    c) D   **d)** B

5. a) $y = \dfrac{1}{x - 2} + 3$

    b) $y = \dfrac{2}{x - 1} + 3$

    c) $y = \dfrac{3}{x + 2} - 4$

6. a) $y = \dfrac{5}{x - 4} + 7$

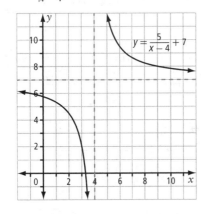

b) $y = \dfrac{9}{x + 2} - 5$

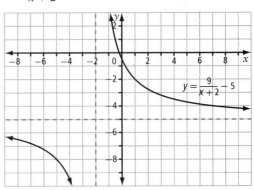

7. a) Example: $y = \dfrac{5}{x + 3} - 4$; The non-permissible
value is the vertical asymptote and the horizontal
asymptote is equal to parameter k, or -4.

b) Example:

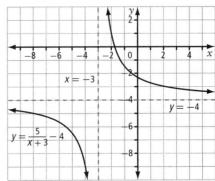

c) domain: $\{x \mid x \neq -3, x \in \mathrm{R}\}$,
range: $\{y \mid y \neq -4, y \in \mathrm{R}\}$

d) Yes, there are many functions with different
a values for which the asymptotes are the same.

8. Example: Similarity: The graphs are all transformed
by a vertical stretch by a factor of 2 and a
translation of 4 units right and 3 units down.
Difference: Their base functions are all different.
The base functions are $y = \dfrac{1}{x}$, $y = x^2$, and $y = \sqrt{x}$.

9.2 Analysing Rational Functions, pages 305–313

1. a) vertical asymptote; the numerator and
denominator have no common factors

    b) point of discontinuity; the numerator and
denominator have a common factor and simplify
to become a linear function

c) both; the numerator and denominator have a common factor and simplify to become a rational function

d) vertical asymptote; the numerator and denominator have no common factors

2. a) vertical asymptote: $x = 4$; x-intercept: -1; y-intercept: -0.25

b) point of discontinuity: $(-3, 1)$; no vertical asymptotes; x-intercept: -4; y-intercept: 4

c) point of discontinuity: $(5, 0.5)$; vertical asymptote: $x = -1$; x-intercept: 2; y-intercept: -2

d) no points of discontinuity; vertical asymptotes: $x = 6$, $x = -1$; x-intercepts: $-2, -4$; y-intercept: $-\dfrac{4}{3}$

3. a) C   **b)** B   **c)** D   **d)** A

4. a) vertical asymptote: $x = 2$; horizontal asymptote: $y = 1$; x-intercept: -3; y-intercept: $-\dfrac{3}{2}$

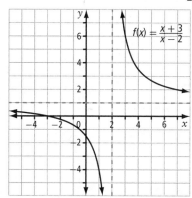

b) point of discontinuity: $(2, -1)$; x-intercept: 3; y-intercept: -3

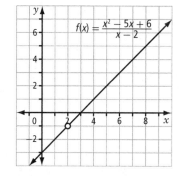

c) vertical asymptote: $x = 2$; horizontal asymptote: $y = 1$; x-intercept: 1; y-intercept: $\dfrac{1}{2}$; point of discontinuity: $\left(-4, \dfrac{5}{6}\right)$

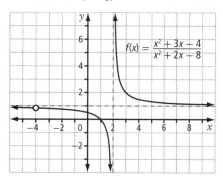

5. a) $f(x) = \dfrac{x + 2}{x - 4}$ or $f(x) = \dfrac{6}{x - 4} + 1$

b) $f(x) = \dfrac{x^2 - 5x - 6}{x + 1}$ or $f(x) = \dfrac{(x - 6)(x + 1)}{x + 1}$

c) $f(x) = \dfrac{x^2 - 2x - 3}{x^2 - 4x + 3}$ or $f(x) = \dfrac{(x + 1)(x - 3)}{(x - 1)(x - 3)}$

6. a) Example: $f(x) = \dfrac{(x - 2)(x + 4)}{(x + 4)}$

b) Example: $f(x) = \dfrac{(x + 1)(x - 3)}{(x - 1)(x - 3)}$

c) Example: $f(x) = \dfrac{x}{(x - 4)(x + 3)}$

d) Example: $f(x) = \dfrac{(x + 1)(x + 3)}{x - 7}$

7. a) $\left(\dfrac{3}{2}, \dfrac{1}{2}\right)$

b) There is a "hole" or gap in the graph at this point. This means that the value at this point is indeterminate because value of the function at this point is $\dfrac{0}{0}$.

8. a) Example: Factor the numerator and denominator. The factor common to both the numerator and the denominator corresponds to a point of discontinuity.

b) Example: Factor the numerator and denominator. The factor of only the denominator corresponds to a vertical asymptote.

c) Example: Factor the numerator and denominator. The factor common to both the numerator and the denominator corresponds to a point of discontinuity, while the factor of only the denominator corresponds to a vertical asymptote.

9. Example: Yes. If the polynomial in the denominator is a constant, there will be neither a point of discontinuity nor a vertical asymptote.

9.3 Connecting Graphs and Rational Equations, pages 314–320

1. a) $x = -2, x = 7$ **b)** $x = -3, x = -8$

   c) $x = -2$ **d)** $x = \dfrac{5}{2}, x = -1$

2. a) $x = -2$

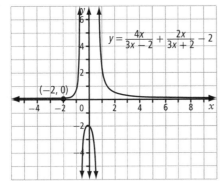

$$y = \frac{4x}{3x - 2} + \frac{2x}{3x + 2} - 2$$

$(-2, 0)$

   b) $x = 5$

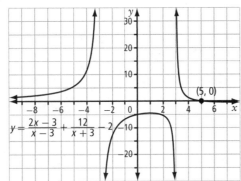

$$y = \frac{2x - 3}{x - 3} + \frac{12}{x + 3} - 2$$

$(5, 0)$

   c) $x = -0.5$

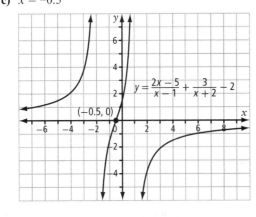

$$y = \frac{2x - 5}{x - 1} + \frac{3}{x + 2} - 2$$

$(-0.5, 0)$

d) $x = 0.5$

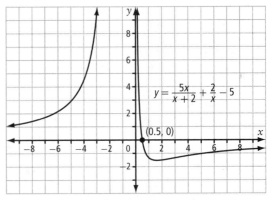

$$y = \frac{5x}{x + 2} + \frac{2}{x} - 5$$

$(0.5, 0)$

3. a) $x = -1.5$

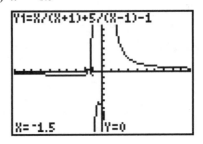

Y1=X/(X+1)+5/(X-1)-1

X=-1.5   Y=0

   b) $x = \dfrac{1 \pm \sqrt{17}}{2}$ or $x \approx -1.56, x \approx 2.56$

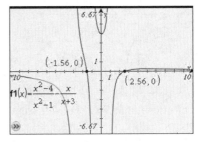

$(-1.56, 0)$ $(2.56, 0)$

$$f1(x) = \frac{x^2 - 4}{x^2 - 1} \cdot \frac{x}{x + 3}$$

4. a) $x = -5$; no extraneous root

   b) $x = -3$; extraneous root: $x = 1$

   c) $x = -7$; extraneous root: $x = 2$

   d) $x = 2$; extraneous root: $x = -2$

5. a) Amber: $\dfrac{400}{x}$, Matteo: $\dfrac{400}{(x - 1)}$

   b) $\dfrac{400}{(x - 1)} - \dfrac{400}{x} = 20$; Amber: 80 km/h, Matteo: 100 km/h

6. Example: Solving an equation algebraically gives an exact solution because you can answer as a fraction or a radical, if necessary. Solving graphically gives a whole number value or a decimal approximation.

7. Example: Solving algebraically, extraneous solutions are determined by comparing the answer to the restrictions. Solving graphically only solves equations in their simplest form.

Chapter 9 Review, pages 321–323

1. a)

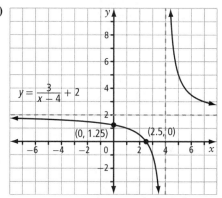

$$y = \frac{3}{x-4} + 2$$

(0, 1.25)   (2.5, 0)

b)

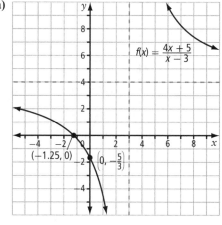

(0, 5)

$$y = \frac{7}{x-1} - 2$$

(2.5, 0)

2. a)

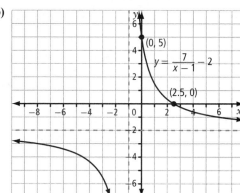

$$f(x) = \frac{4x+5}{x-3}$$

(−1.25, 0) $\left(0, -\frac{5}{3}\right)$

b)

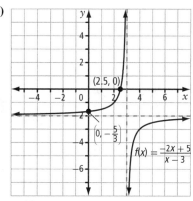

(2.5, 0)

$\left(0, -\frac{5}{3}\right)$

$$f(x) = \frac{-2x+5}{x-3}$$

3. a) vertical asymptotes at $x = -3$ and $x = 2$, no points of discontinuity, x-intercept of 0; D

b) vertical asymptote at $x = 6$, point of discontinuity $(-4, 0.7)$, x-intercept of 3; A

c) point of discontinuity at $(3, 1)$, no vertical asymptotes, x-intercept of 2; C

d) vertical asymptotes at $x = 1$ and $x = 2$, no points of discontinuity, x-intercepts of -3 and 4; B

4. a) no points of discontinuity; vertical asymptote: $x = -5$; x-intercept: $-\frac{1}{2}$; y-intercept: $\frac{1}{5}$

b) point of discontinuity: $(2, -4)$; no vertical asymptotes; x-intercept: 6; y-intercept: -6

5. a) $x = -4, x = -6$ **b)** $x = 2, x = 6$

c) $x = -7$ **d)** $x = -2, x = 5$

6. a) $x \approx -0.6, x \approx 13.6$

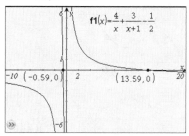

b) $x \approx -2.1, x \approx 5.3$

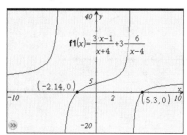

Chapter 10

10.1 Sums and Differences of Functions, pages 325–334

1.

x	$f(x)$	$g(x)$	$(f + g)(x)$	$(f - g)(x)$
–6	2	4	6	–2
–4	4	2	6	2
–2	6	0	6	6
0	8	–2	6	10
2	10	–4	6	14
4	12	–6	6	18
6	14	–8	6	22

2. **a)** $(f + g)(x) = \{(-6, 7), (-4, 8), (-2, 9), (0, 10)\}$
   b) $(f - g)(x) = \{(-6, 1), (-4, -4), (-2, -9), (0, -14)\}$

3. **a)** $(f + g)(x) = 5x - 1$
   b) $(f - g)(x) = x - 3$
   c) $(g - f)(x) = -x + 3$

4. **a)** 36 **b)** 6 **c)** 4

5. **a)** $y = 5x^2 + \sqrt{x^2 - 4}$; $\{x \mid x \le -2 \text{ and } x \ge 2, x \in \mathbb{R}\}$
   b) $y = 5x^2 - \sqrt{x^2 - 4}$; $\{x \mid x \le -2 \text{ and } x \ge 2, x \in \mathbb{R}\}$
   c) $y = \sqrt{x^2 - 4} - 5x^2$; $\{x \mid x \le -2 \text{ and } x \ge 2, x \in \mathbb{R}\}$

6. **a)**
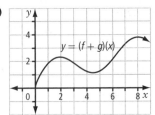
domain: $\{x \mid x \ge 0, x \in \mathbb{R}\}$;
range: $\{y \mid y \ge 0, y \in \mathbb{R}\}$

   b)
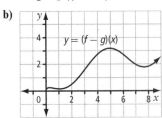
domain: $\{x \mid x \ge 0, x \in \mathbb{R}\}$;
range: $\{y \mid y \ge 0, y \in \mathbb{R}\}$

7. **a)** 9 **b)** –1 **c)** 3 **d)** 3
   e) The domain of $f(x)$ does not include the value 5.

8. **a)**
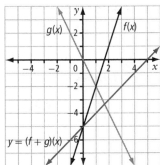

   b)
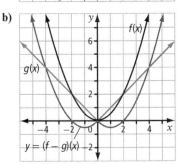

9. **a)** $y = -x^2 + x + 8$ **b)** $y = x^2 + 3x - 2$
   c) $y = x^2 + x - 2$

10. **a)** $g(x) = x^2 - 6x + 7$ **b)** $g(x) = -5x + 11$
    c) $g(x) = -2x^2 - 3x + 8$

11. **a)** $C(n) = 25n + 45\,000$ **b)** $R(n) = 100n$
    c) $P(n) = 75n - 45\,000$ **d)** $(600, 0)$

12. **a)**
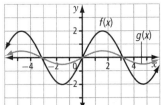

    b)
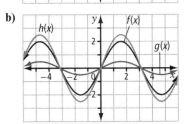

    c) 2.5 units

13. Example: $f(x) = \sqrt{x - 1}$ and $g(x) = \sqrt{-x}$
    The domain of $f(x)$ is $\{x \mid x \ge 1, x \in \mathbb{R}\}$ and the domain of $g(x)$ is $\{x \mid x \le 0, x \in \mathbb{R}\}$. Since there are no values of x common to the two domains, there are no possible values for the range.

14. Example: No, it is not possible. Subtraction is not commutative.

10.2 Products and Quotients of Functions, pages 335–344

1. a) $h(x) = 4x^2 - 8x + 3$; $k(x) = \dfrac{2x-1}{2x-3}$, $x \neq \dfrac{3}{2}$

  b) $h(x) = -3x^3 - 12x$; $k(x) = \dfrac{3x}{-x^2-4}$

  c) $h(x) = (5x-1)(\sqrt{4-x})$; $k(x) = \dfrac{\sqrt{4-x}}{5x-1}$, $x \neq \dfrac{1}{5}$

2. a) -20 **b)** $-\dfrac{2}{3}$ **c)** 0 **d)** -24

3. a)

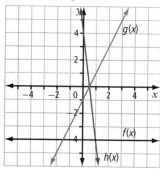

  b)

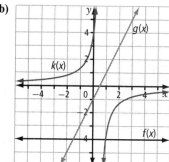

4. a) $h(x) = 2x^3 + 3x^2 - 1$

  b) $k(x) = \dfrac{2x-1}{x^2 + 2x + 1}$, $x \neq -1$

  c)

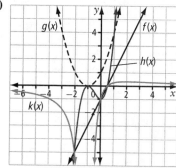

  d) $h(x)$: domain: $\{x \mid x \in \mathbb{R}\}$, range: $\{y \mid y \in \mathbb{R}\}$;
  $k(x)$: domain: $\{x \mid x \neq -1, x \in \mathbb{R}\}$,
  range $\{y \mid y \leq 0.33, y \in \mathbb{R}\}$

5. a) -260 **b)** $\dfrac{5}{4}$ **c)** $-\dfrac{4}{5}$

6. a) $y = (4x^3 - 5x^2)(\sqrt{x-1})$, $x \geq 1$

  b) $y = \dfrac{(4x-5)(\sqrt{x-1})}{x^2}$, $x \geq 1$

7. a) $g(x) = -x$ **b)** $g(x) = \dfrac{\sqrt{x^2-4}}{2-x}$, $x \leq -2$ and $x > 2$

8. a) $f(x) = -2x^3 - 12x^2$, $x \neq 0$

  b) $f(x) = 2x^2 + 6x$, $x \neq 0$

9. a) $h(x) = \dfrac{f(x)}{g(x)} = \dfrac{1}{\sin x}$

  b)

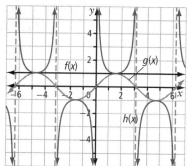

  restrictions on $h(x)$: $x \neq \pi n$, $n \in I$

10. a)

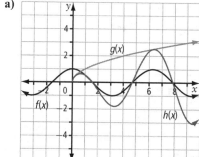

  b) domain: $\{x \mid x \geq 0, x \in \mathbb{R}\}$; range: $\{y \mid y \in \mathbb{R}\}$

11. a) $T(w) = 300 - 8w - 0.8w^2$

  b) 223.2 h

  c) week 15; Example: I graphed the function
  $T(w) = 300 - 8w - 0.8w^2$ using graphing
  technology and determined the w-intercept in
  quadrant I. In other words, I determined the
  value of w when $T(w) = 0$.

  d) domain: $\{w \mid 0 \leq w \leq 15, w \in W\}$;
  range: $\{T \mid 0 \leq T \leq 300, T \in \mathbb{R}\}$

12. a) $R(a) = \dfrac{a^2 + 0.25a}{12 + 1.41a}$

  b) 33.15 tonnes; 228.75 tonnes

  c)

  domain: $\{a \mid a > 0, a \in \mathbb{R}\}$;
  range: $\{R \mid R > 0, R \in \mathbb{R}\}$

13. a) $A(x) = 6.25\pi x^2$

b)
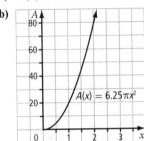
domain: $\{x \mid x \geq 0, x \in R\}$;
range: $\{A \mid A \geq 0, A \in R\}$

c) $H(x) = 4x - 2$

d)
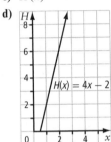
domain: $\{x \mid x \geq 0.5, x \in R\}$;
range: $\{H \mid H \geq 0, H \in R\}$

10.3 Composite Functions, pages 345–355

1. a) 0   **b)** 2   **c)** 6   **d)** 5

2. a) 23   **b)** −13   **c)** 62   **d)** 11

3. a) $(f \circ g)(x) = \sqrt{x^2 + 4}$; $(g \circ f)(x) = x + 4$

b) $(f \circ g)(x) = |-1 - x|$; $(g \circ f)(x) = 3 - |x - 4|$

c) $(f \circ g)(x) = \dfrac{1}{x + 3}$; $(g \circ f)(x) = \dfrac{1}{x} + 3$

4. a)
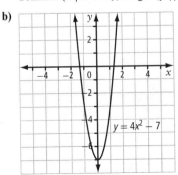
domain: $\{x \mid x \in R\}$; range: $\{y \mid y \geq -2, y \in R\}$

b)
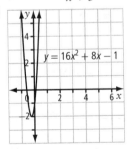
domain: $\{x \mid x \in R\}$; range: $\{y \mid y \geq -7, y \in R\}$

5. a) $g(x) = x - 2$ **b)** $g(x) = x^2 - 2$ **c)** $g(x) = x - 5$

6. a) $(f \circ g)(x) = \sqrt{3x - 3}$; domain: $\{x \mid x \geq 1, x \in R\}$

b) $(g \circ f)(x) = 3\sqrt{x - 4} + 1$; domain: $\{x \mid x \geq 4, x \in R\}$

7. a) $f(g(x)) = x + 4$ **b)** $g(f(x)) = x + 4$

c) restriction on domain of $f(g(x))$: $x \neq 1$;
restriction on domain of $g(f(x))$: $x \neq \pm 1$

8. a) $h(k(x)) = k(h(x)) = \dfrac{1}{x^2}$ **b)** $x \neq 0$

9. a) $C(x(t)) = 787.5t + 900$

b) $C(x(t))$ represents the cost of manufacturing engines after t hours of production.

c) $7200   **d)** 42 h

10. a) $R = p - 1200$ **b)** $D = 0.9p$

c) $(R \circ D)(p) = 0.9p - 1200$; The composite function represents the cost of the snowmobile when the dealer discount is computed before the factory rebate.

d) $(D \circ R)(p) = 0.9p - 1080$; The composite function represents the cost of the snowmobile when the factory rebate is subtracted before the dealer discount.

e) $8475; $8595; The lower cost is given by the composite function $(R \circ D)(p)$. Example: The price is lower when the $1200 is subtracted after the dealer discount.

11. The sales representative's bonus is represented by $g(f(x)) = 0.5(x - 50\,000)$. Example: The bonus is computed after the $50 000 is subtracted.

12. a) $f(x) = x^2$; $g(x) = 2x + 1$

b) $f(x) = \sqrt{x}$; $g(x) = 9 - x$

13. a) Example: $f(x) = 2x$, $g(x) = x - 3$, $h(x) = 5x + 1$

b) $((f \circ g) \circ h)(x) = 10x - 4$, $(f \circ (g \circ h))(x) = 10x - 4$; Therefore, the composition of functions does follow the associative property.

14. a) Example: $f(x) = x^2$, $g(x) = 3x - 2$

b) $(f \circ g)(x) = 9x^2 - 12x + 4$, $(g \circ f)(x) = 3x^2 - 2$; Therefore, the composition of functions does not follow the commutative property. There are no restrictions in this case.

Chapter 10 Review, pages 356–362

1. a) 6   **b)** −13

2. a) $h(x) = \sqrt{x + 6} + 4x^2 - 1$

b)
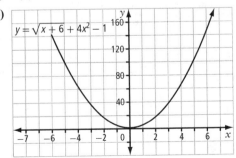

c) domain: $\{x \mid x \geq -6, x \in R\}$;
range: $\{y \mid y \geq 1.4, y \in R\}$

d) $k(x) = \sqrt{x + 6} - 4x^2 + 1$

e)

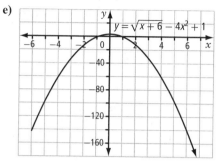

f) domain: $\{x \mid x \geq -6, x \in R\}$;
range: $\{y \mid y \leq 3.5, y \in R\}$

3. a) $g(x) = -4x^2 + 11x - 3$

b) $g(x) = -2x - \sqrt{x} + 12$

4. a)

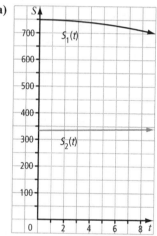

b) $(S_1 + S_2)(t) = 1085 - 0.6t^2 + 0.8t$

c)

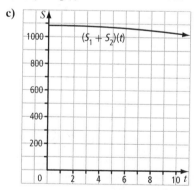

d) The total sales have been decreasing. Example:
The combined sales in 2007 were \$1 061 200. The
combined sales in 2012 were \$1 008 200.

5. a) $h(x) = -2x^3 + x^2 - 6x + 3$

b) $k(x) = \dfrac{x^2 + 3}{1 - 2x}, x \neq \dfrac{1}{2}$

6. a) 1   **b)** 12   **c)** -3 **d)** $\dfrac{5}{9}$

7. a) $h(x) = \dfrac{x}{x - 1}$

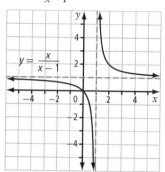

domain: $\{x \mid x \neq 1, x \in R\}$

b) $k(x) = \dfrac{1}{x^2 - x}$

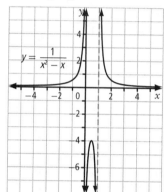

domain: $\{x \mid x \neq 0, 1, x \in R\}$

8. a) $g(x) = x - 1$ **b)** $g(x) = \sin x$

c) $g(x) = -x^2$

9. a)

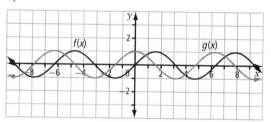

b)

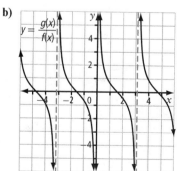

c) domain: $\{x \mid x \neq n\pi, n \in I, x \in R\}$;
range: $\{y \mid y \in R\}$

d) $y = \cot x$

10. a) $(f \circ g)(x) = -x^2 - 2$ **b)** $(g \circ g)(x) = -x^4 + 2x^2$

    c) -11 **d)** -8

11. a)

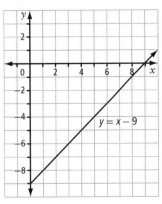

domain: $\{x \mid x \geq 0, x \in R\}$;
range: $\{y \mid y \geq -9, y \in R\}$

b)

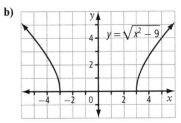

domain: $\{x \mid x \leq -3 \text{ and } x \geq 3, x \in R\}$;
range: $\{y \mid y \geq 0, y \in R\}$

12. a) $g(x) = 9 - x$

    b) $g(x) = 7x - 2$

    c) $g(x) = 2x - 5$

13. a) $d = 2r$ **b)** $V = 8r^3$ **c)** 3375 cm^3

14. a) $(C \circ n)(t) = -15t^2 + 4125t + 1195$

    b) $70\ 585$

    c) 24 h

Chapter 11

11.1 Permutations, pages 364–373

1. a)

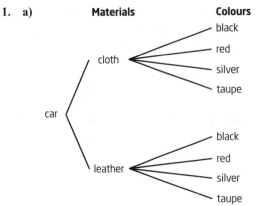

b)

T-Shirt / Pants tree diagram:

- blue → black, grey, brown, beige
- uniform → pink → black, grey, brown, beige
- white → black, grey, brown, beige

2. a)

First	Second Digit
3	4
3	6
3	7
3	8
4	3
4	6
4	7
4	8
6	3
6	4
6	7
6	8
7	3
7	4
7	6
7	8
8	3
8	4
8	6
8	7

b)

Toronto to Calgary	Calgary to Vancouver
Plane	Bus
Plane	Plane
Plane	Train
Plane	Car
Train	Bus
Train	Plane
Train	Train
Train	Car

3. a) 42   **b)** 6   **c)** 79 833 600   **d)** 1680

4. a) Left Side = $5! - 3!$
$$= (5 \times 4 \times 3 \times 2!) - (3 \times 2!)$$
$$= (60)(2!) - (3)(2!)$$
$$= (60 - 3)(2!)$$
$$= 57(2!)$$

Right Side = $(5! - 3!)$
$$= 2!$$

Left Side $\neq$ Right Side

b) Left Side = $6! - 4!$
$$= (6 \times 5 \times 4!) - (4!)$$
$$= (30)(4!) - (4!)$$
$$= (30 - 1)(4!)$$
$$= 29(4!)$$

Right Side = $29(4!)$

Left Side = Right Side

5. a) 19 600   **b)** 4320

c) 91   **d)** 3 628 800

6. a) $\frac{7!}{2!2!} = 1260$ **b)** $\frac{10!}{2!2!3!} = 151\,200$

c) $6! = 720$ **d)** $\frac{11!}{2!2!2!2!} = 2\,494\,800$

7. $7! = 5040$

8. a) $n = 7$ **b)** $r = 2$ **c)** $n = 10$ **d)** $r = 4$

9. a) 40   **b)** 72

10. a) $3(5!)2 = 720$

b) $(5!)(3!) = 720$ (count group of 3 boys as $1 : 1 + 4$ girls = 5)

c) $(4!)(4!) = 576$ (count group of 4 girls as $1 : 1 + 3$ boys = 4)

d) $3(5!)2 + 4(5!)3 = 720 + 1440 = 2160$

11. a) $7! = 5040$

b) $3(5!)2 = 720$

c) $4(5!)3 = 1440$

12. $13(9)(12)(8)(7) = 78\,624$

13. a) $\frac{13!}{3!3!2!} = 86\,486\,400$

b) $\frac{11!}{3!2!} = 3\,326\,400$ **c)** $\frac{11!}{3!2!} = 3\,326\,400$

d) $\frac{12!}{3!3!} = 13\,305\,600$ **e)** $8! = 40\,320$

14. a) 7 200 000   **b)** 18 000   **c)** 72 000

11.2 Combinations, pages 374–382

1. a) permutation; order matters

b) combination; order does not matter

c) combination; order does not matter

d) permutation; order matters

2. $_8P_5$ represents an arrangement of 8 objects taken 5 at a time, and order matters. $_8C_5$ represents a selection of 5 objects taken from 8, and order does not matter. $_8P_5 = 6720$; $_8C_5 = 56$

3. a) 21   **b)** 42   **c)** 84   **d)** 210

4. a) $_{12}C_8 = 495$ **b)** $_{12}P_6 = 665\,280$

5. a) $_5C_3 = 10$

b) ABC, ABD, ABE, ACD, ACE, ADE, BCD, BCE, BDE, CDE

c) $_5P_3 = 60$

d) There are $3! = 6$ times as many permutations as there are combinations.

6. a) $n = 6$ **b)** $n = 5$ **c)** $n = 5$ **d)** $n = 3$

7. a) case 1: single-digit numbers less than 800;
case 2: double-digit numbers less than 800;
case 3: triple-digit numbers less 800

b) case 1: 4 members are from grade 11;
case 2: 4 members are from grade 12

8. a) Left Side = $_{10}C_3$
$$= \frac{10!}{(10 - 3)!3!}$$
$$= \frac{10!}{7!3!}$$

Right Side = $_{10}C_7$
$$= \frac{10!}{(10 - 7)!7!}$$
$$= \frac{10!}{3!7!}$$

Left Side = Right Side

b) Left Side = $_{12}C_4$
$$= \frac{12!}{(12 - 4)!4!}$$
$$= \frac{12 \times 11 \times 10 \times 9 \times 8!}{8!4!}$$
$$= \frac{12 \times 11 \times 10 \times 9}{4!}$$

Right Side = $_{11}C_4 + _{11}C_3$
$$= \frac{11!}{(11 - 4)!4!} + \frac{11!}{(11 - 3)!3!}$$
$$= \frac{11 \times 10 \times 9 \times 8 \times 7!}{7!4!}$$
$$+ \frac{11 \times 10 \times 9 \times 8!}{8!3!}$$
$$= \frac{11 \times 10 \times 9 \times 8}{4!} + \frac{11 \times 10 \times 9}{3!}$$
$$= \frac{(11 \times 10 \times 9 \times 8) + (11 \times 10 \times 9 \times 4)}{4!}$$
$$= \frac{(11 \times 10 \times 9)(8 + 4)}{4!}$$
$$= \frac{12 \times 11 \times 10 \times 9}{4!}$$

Left Side = Right Side

9. a) $_{15}C_4 = 1365$

b) $_7C_1 \times {}_8C_3 = 392$

c) $_8C_2 \times {}_7C_2 + {}_8C_3 \times {}_7C_1 + {}_8C_4$
$= 28 \times 21 + 56 \times 7 + 70$
$= 1050$

10. a) $_7C_4 \times {}_9C_2 = 1260$

b) $_7C_4 \times {}_9C_2 + {}_7C_5 \times {}_9C_1 + {}_7C_6$
$= 35 \times 36 + 21 \times 9 + 7$
$= 1456$

11. Left Side $= 5({}_nC_5)$

$= \dfrac{5(n!)}{(n-5)!5!}$

$= \dfrac{n!}{(n-5)!4!}$

Right Side $= n({}_{n-1}C_4)$

$= \dfrac{n(n-1)!}{(n-5)!4!}$

$= \dfrac{n!}{(n-5)!4!}$

Left Side = Right Side

12. a) $n = 1$ **b)** $n = 4$

13. 2520

14. 2400

15. $_{11}C_8 = 165$

11.3 The Binomial Theorem, pages 383–389

1. a) 1 5 10 10 5 1

b) 1 7 21 35 35 21 7 1

c) 1 10 45 120 210 252 210 120 45 10 1

2. a) $_3C_0$ $_3C_1$ $_3C_2$ $_3C_3$

b) $_5C_0$ $_5C_1$ $_5C_2$ $_5C_3$ $_5C_4$ $_5C_5$

c) $_6C_0$ $_6C_1$ $_6C_2$ $_6C_3$ $_6C_4$ $_6C_5$ $_6C_6$

3. a) $_4C_3 = \dfrac{4!}{1!3!}$

b) $_7C_3 = \dfrac{7!}{4!3!}$

c) $_9C_6 = \dfrac{9!}{3!6!}$

4. a) 8 **b)** 7 **c)** 5 **d)** 6

5. a) $m^7 - 7m^6n + 21m^5n^2 - 35m^4n^3 + 35m^3n^4$
$- 21m^2n^5 + 7mn^6 - n^7$

b) $64x^6 + 192x^5 + 240x^4 + 160x^3 + 60x^2 + 12x + 1$

c) $a^{15} + 10a^{12} + 40a^9 + 80a^6 + 80a^3 + 32$

6. a) $x^6 - 12x^5 + 60x^4 - 160x^3 + 240x^2 - 192x + 64$

b) $a^4 - 8a^3b + 24a^2b^2 - 32ab^3 + 16b^4$

c) $1 + 6x^2 + 15x^4 + 20x^6 + 15x^8 + 6x^{10} + x^{12}$

7. a) $252a^5b^5$ **b)** $715x^9$ **c)** $210x^8$ **d)** $\dfrac{21}{4}x^{12}$

e) $1120x^4y^4$

8. a) $a^5 - 5a^3 + 10a - \dfrac{10}{a} + \dfrac{5}{a^3} - \dfrac{1}{a^5}$

b) $x^5 - 10x^2 + \dfrac{40}{x} - \dfrac{80}{x^4} + \dfrac{80}{x^7} - \dfrac{32}{x^{10}}$

9. a) $512a^9 - 2304a^7 + 4608a^5 - 5376a^3$

b) $256x^8 - 3072x^6 + 16\,128x^4 - 48\,384x^2$

10. a) $(x - y)^5$ **b)** $(x - 2)^6$

11. $t_{k+1} = {}_7C_k a^{14-2k}$

12. $-6x^4$

13. $x^7 + 6x^5 + 15x^3 + 20x + 15x^{-1} + 6x^{-3} + x^{-5}$

14. 1.1951

Chapter 11 Review, pages 390–392

1. a) 604 800 **b)** 840

2. a) $8! = 40\,320$ **b)** $\dfrac{6!}{3!} = 120$

3. a) $n = 5$ **b)** $r = 2$

4. To satisfy the requirements, the word must have a total of nine letters, with three of one kind and two of another kind. Example: excellent

5. a) $3(6!)2 = 4320$

b) $(6!)(3!) = 4320$

c) $(4!)(5!) = 2880$

6. a) permutation; order matters

b) combination; order does not matter

7. $_9P_6$ represents an arrangement of 9 objects taken 6 at a time, and order matters. $_9C_6$ represents a selection of 6 objects taken from 9, and order does not matter.

8. a) $n = 5$ **b)** $n = 7$

9. $_{13}C_1 \times {}_{13}C_1 \times {}_{13}C_1 \times {}_{13}C_1 = 28\,561$

10. a) $_{15}C_2 \times {}_{18}C_3 = 105 \times 816 = 85\,680$

b) $_{15}C_3 \times {}_{18}C_2 + {}_{15}C_2 \times {}_{18}C_3 + {}_{15}C_1 \times {}_{18}C_4$
$= 455 \times 153 + 105 \times 816 + 15 \times 3060$
$= 201\,195$

11. a) 1 2 1 **b)** 1 6 15 20 15 6 1

12. a) $_4C_0$ $_4C_1$ $_4C_2$ $_4C_3$ $_4C_4$

b) $_8C_0$ $_8C_1$ $_8C_2$ $_8C_3$ $_8C_4$ $_8C_5$ $_8C_6$ $_8C_7$ $_8C_8$

13. a) 5 terms; $16x^4 + 96x^3y + 216x^2y^2 + 216xy^3 + 81y^4$

b) 6 terms; $a^{10} - 20a^8 + 160a^6 - 640a^4 + 1280a^2$
$- 1024$

14. a) $x^4 + 4x^2 + 6 + \dfrac{4}{x^2} + \dfrac{1}{x^4}$

b) $64x^6 - 192x^4 + 240x^2 - 160 + 60x^{-2} - 12x^{-4} + x^{-6}$

15. a) $-71\,680a^3$ **b)** $12\,650a^{21}b^4$